Sources for America's History

Volume 1: To 1877

Sources for America's History

Volume 1: To 1877

Tenth Edition

Kevin B. Sheets
State University of New York, College at Cortland

Boston | New York

Vice President: Leasa Burton
Senior Program Director: Michael Rosenberg
Senior Executive Program Manager: William J. Lombardo
Director of Content Development: Jane Knetzger
Senior Development Editor: Heidi Hood
Assistant Editor: Carly Lewis
Director of Media Editorial: Adam Whitehurst
Media Editor: Mollie Chandler
Senior Marketing Manager: Melissa Rodriguez
Senior Director, Content Management Enhancement: Tracey Kuehn
Senior Managing Editor: Michael Granger
Assistant Content Project Manager: Natalie Jones
Senior Workflow Project Manager: Lisa McDowell
Production Supervisor: Robin Besofsky
Director of Design, Content Management: Diana Blume
Interior Design: Lumina Datamatics, Inc.
Cover Design: William Boardman
Text Permissions Editor: Michael McCarty
Text Permissions Researcher: Udayakumar Kannadasan
Photo Permissions Editors: Christine Buese and Jirarut Anderson
Photo Researcher: Bruce Carson
Director of Digital Production: Keri deManigold
Executive Media Project Manager: Michelle Camisa
Copyeditor: Harold Johnson
Composition: Lumina Datamatics, Inc.
Cover Image: The Old Plantation, attributed to John Rose, Beaufort County, South Carolina, c. 1785–1790/The Colonial Williamsburg Foundation, Gift of Abby Aldrich Rockefeller
Printing and Binding: LSC Communications

Library of Congress Control Number: 2020938156

ISBN: 978-1-319-27483-2

Printed in the United States of America.

1 2 3 4 5 6 25 24 23 22 21 20

Acknowledgments
Text acknowledgments and copyrights appear at the back of the book on page 306, which constitute an extension of the copyright page. Art acknowledgments and copyrights appear on the same page as the art selections they cover.

For information, write: Bedford/St. Martin's, 75 Arlington Street, Boston, MA 02116

PREFACE

My goal in compiling the tenth edition of *Sources for America's History* is to help students encounter the past in its most raw and visceral form. Designed to accompany the tenth edition of *America's History, America's History, Concise Edition,* and *America's History, Value Edition,* the sources collected here put students in unmediated contact with those whose experiences shaped our past. Historians are fond of quoting L. P. Hartley's famous line: "The past is a foreign country; they do things differently there." It is a helpful image that emphasizes the distance, remoteness, and inscrutability of the past. Visiting a country whose language you do not speak can be disorienting until you start deciphering the gestures, unlocking the meaning behind facial expressions, and picking apart the cultural practices natives take for granted. For many students, the past is equally disorienting, and to seek safe harbor they ignore differences to emphasize commonalities. "Those people in the past are just like me, except they wear funny clothes." Stripped down, they do resemble us, but more often they encountered their world in radically different ways. Understanding these differences is what makes the study of history so compelling.

Textbook authors present an argument about the past, something historians refer to as a "narrative." Those arguments, of course, are based on historians' interpretation and assessment of primary sources. This document collection makes its own argument based on the specific sources selected for inclusion, but invites debate by encouraging the reader to interpret sources in different ways. *Sources for America's History* is designed to encourage a productive intellectual give-and-take, enabling students of history to offer their own perspective on the past. In this way, students join the ongoing discussion among the community of scholars seeking to understand the long and complex history of what became the United States.

Each chapter in *Sources for America's History* includes a variety of both obscure and well-known voices, whose testimony highlights key themes of the period. The sources in each chapter give competing perspectives on leading events and ideas. This purposeful tension between sources is not intended to frustrate the reader. Instead, the differing viewpoints introduce students to the challenge that historians face in sifting through the evidence left to us. How do we make sense of the large body of primary sources that we have related to America's half millennium of recorded lived experience?

To facilitate this effort, *Sources for America's History* includes a number of key features. Each chapter in the collection includes five or six documents that support the periodization and themes of the corresponding parent text chapter. Every chapter begins with an introduction that situates the documents within their wider historical context. Individual documents follow, each accompanied by its own headnote and a set of Reading and Discussion Questions designed to help students practice historical thinking skills. The variety of readings, ranging from political cartoons and speeches by celebrated historical figures to personal letters and diary entries by ordinary people, offers students the opportunity to compare and contrast different types of documents. Each chapter concludes with Comparative Questions designed to encourage students to recognize connections between documents and relate the sources to larger historical themes. To further support the structure of the parent text, unique Part Document Sets at the end of every part section present five or six sources chosen specifically to illustrate the major themes and developments covered in each of the parent text's nine thematic parts, allowing students to make even broader comparisons and connections across time and place.

New to This Edition

In response to reviewers' comments, we have included even more visual sources than in previous editions and also trimmed the length of some of the primary source texts to focus on key ideas, themes, and arguments. This edition features over thirty new image sources, including more political cartoons from both American and British sources. Several photographs capture moments of political mobilization, including women's rights marches and anti-tax protests. We bring the collection up to the present moment with a photograph of protesters rallying against President Trump's 2017 immigration policies. We also added a collection of immigration-related tweets from President Trump, both to highlight immigration as a national issue and to showcase the power of social media.

We have continued to emphasize the first-person experience. In this edition, we hear from African Americans whose poignant letters written to Abraham Lincoln and former masters in the wake of the Emancipation Proclamation demonstrate the agency and determination of the formerly enslaved as they fought for recognition in a hostile, rebellious South. Several sources invite consideration of the Native American experience. Two new sources give voice to Native American protest against federally imposed land and citizenship policies. This edition also includes more LGBTQ sources, including congressional investigations into homosexuality in the federal workforce, an account of the now-famous Stonewall riot, and a photograph of protestors demanding resources for AIDS research.

Acknowledgments

As with any big undertaking, many hands helped craft the book you are holding. Thanks go to Rebecca Edwards from Vassar College, one of the lead authors of *America's History*, for her confidence in me. Several instructors at the college, community college, and high school levels offered insightful suggestions based on their teaching experiences. They will see here many of the suggestions they recommended, though I could not accommodate all of the excellent ideas they shared. Particular thanks go to Paul Rubinson, Bridgewater State University; Matthew D. McDonough, Coastal Carolina University; Michael H. Kim, Schurr High School; and Colette A. Hyman, Winona State University.

My editor for this edition, Carly Lewis, perfected the art of the gentle reminder, while also giving insightful feedback on sources. The following colleagues at Bedford/St. Martin's helped in innumerable ways, most of which occurred silently and behind the scenes: Bill Lombardo, Heidi Hood, and Michael Rosenberg. Thanks also to Natalie Jones, who managed the production process.

My colleagues in the history department at the State University of New York, College at Cortland, have always provided an intellectually enriching environment in which to work and live. Special thanks go to my wife, Laura Gathagan, a medieval historian, and my two boys, William and Alexander, who excused my many exits from the room, announced with my refrain: "I'm going to work on Bedford." Family: Bedford is done. What should we do?

INTRODUCTION FOR STUDENTS

I was this close to wearing Eisenhower's pajamas. During my junior year in college, I interned at the Smithsonian's National Museum of American History in Washington, D.C. Every now and again, when I had a few minutes of free time, I poked around the collection of artifacts in storage. There was Lincoln's top hat. On a high shelf was the table where Lee surrendered to Grant. A pullout metal rack filled with paintings also housed a disturbing framed collection of hair from the first sixteen presidents. One day I spied a box containing President Dwight D. Eisenhower's pajamas. These were the PJs Ike wore while recovering in Denver from his 1955 heart attack. Oh, the temptation to slip them on, but reason and self-preservation prevailed. Back on the shelf they went.

Those whom the past enchants were often first beguiled by the stuff of history. Touching those objects helps collapse time, putting us in the immediate presence of someone else at some other time. I once held John Brown's gun and while peering down the long barrel wondered who or what he was aiming at. His trigger finger and mine overlapped and briefly spirited me back to 1850s Pottawatomie, Kansas, where Brown waged his own civil war against slavery. The past is contained in those leavings, the letters and diaries, the political cartoons and music, the paintings and the guns and pajamas. Primary sources bring alive the past and help us to understand its significance and meaning.

This collection of primary sources aims to engage you in a conversation with the past. There will be times when you burst out laughing. Some sources will make you so mad you'll want to throw the book across the room. (Please don't. I spent a lot of time writing it, but I share your frustration.) Other times, you'll shake your head in disbelief. (Yes, they really thought that back then!) You are about to enter an amazing world of difference populated with people some of whom you will admire, many of whom you won't like, and others whom you will despair of ever really knowing or understanding. Good. I hope you laugh. I hope you get mad. I even hope you get confused at times and scratch your head wondering what on earth these people were talking about. Out of your responses to these texts comes insight.

My advice? Read these texts with a fist full of questions. Historians do something called "sourcing" when they first encounter a primary text, and it is a good practice for you, too. Start with the author. ***Who wrote or created the source?*** What do you know about this person? Was he rich, poor, or middling? Was she educated? Where was he or she born and to what sort of family?

You might know the answers to some of these questions, but even if you do not, keeping the questions in mind might help you understand where the author is coming from. ***When was this source created?*** While it is important to know the date, it can also be revealing to know when in the person's life he or she created the source. Was she a young girl or an older woman raising children? Was he at the beginning of his career or already famous? ***What was happening when the source was created?*** We call this "context," and it is an important element in making sense of the source you are reading. (You will encounter the word *context* often in the Reading and Discussion Questions and Comparative Questions following the sources and at the end of each chapter.) In addition to author and context, consider audience and purpose. ***Who was this source for, and why was it created?*** Was the source intended for a public or private audience? Was the source created to persuade or to inform? Was the author talking to allies or foes? What did he or she assume about their audience? A final and related point touches upon the format of the source. ***What type of source is it?*** Historians think about and interpret sources differently. You might be more honest in a private letter to your spouse than you would be in a letter to a political opponent, for example. Similarly, a campaign poster for a particular candidate has a different purpose than a portrait of a politician commissioned for a private residence. As these examples show, the format of a source is often linked to audience and purpose.

What a source tells a historian is not always self-evident. Very few of the sources that historians use were created *for* historians. (No one writes letters that begin: "Dear Historian of a hundred years from now, here is what I am thinking about the Obama presidency.") Historians need to "read between the lines" to derive meaning. As you read the documents in this book, you can unearth the meaning in these sources by asking questions, thinking about context, paying attention to vocabulary and cultural references, and comparing them to other sources related to the same topic or event.

This form of active reading takes a bit more time than it would if you were to simply read starting at the first word and running through to the end. To truly think like a historian, be an active reader. Engage the texts. Ask them questions. If this is your own copy of the book, don't be afraid to write in it. Draw circles around important words or phrases. Write "key point" in the margins where you think the author is hitting his mark. Don't be afraid to throw in a few question marks where you get confused. If you have a furrowed brow, chances are someone else in class is confused, too. Bring it up in discussion and you'll be the class superhero. Take advantage of the questions I pose at the end of each source and chapter. I wrote them to inspire you to go back to the texts and think about what you read. The end-of-chapter Comparative Questions encourage you to see connections between and among multiple texts.

Remember, the past is about having a conversation. These texts speak to one another. It is OK to eavesdrop on their discussions. In fact (here's me being bold), I think you have an obligation to listen in on their chatter. Many of the issues these sources address, though sometimes distant to us in time, remain relevant: What is just? What kind of society do we want to live in? How should we treat each other? How do we balance rights and responsibilities? The authors included in this book do not solve these enduring questions. But they all have a perspective that helps to clarify our own responses.

My hope is that you will engage these texts to understand how different people, in different places and different times, constructed the specific world they inhabited. I hope, too, that you find your voice and come to know that you have an opportunity and a responsibility to engage in the conversation. The thrill of history is to know that you are part of a very long conversation about meaning. So, the next time you are wearing Ike's PJs while shouldering John Brown's gun, think about the contribution to that conversation you want others to remember you by. What will you say?

CONTENTS

Sources for America's History

Volume 1: To 1877

1

Colliding Worlds

1491–1600

In the fifteenth and sixteenth centuries, it was common to refer to the Americas as a "new world" or "virgin soil." Such terms captured the wonder and enthusiasm of European explorers, to whom everything on the continent appeared new and untouched. Those terms also reveal the confidence, or even arrogance, animating many of those explorers, who viewed the continent as a blank slate waiting for them to write the next chapter of Europe's great unfolding destiny. Their visions of gold and glory ultimately came into conflict with the many thousands of indigenous inhabitants who had for centuries developed thriving societies and sophisticated cultures in the Americas. Another group of unwilling participants added to the collision of civilizations, when Africans captured and sold into slavery began populating American lands in the sixteenth century. In this chapter, we illuminate how the interaction among these three worlds transformed North America and forged the modern world.

1-1 | An Englishman Describes the Algonquin People

THOMAS HARIOT, *A Briefe and True Report of the New Found Land of Virginia* (1588)

Much of what Europeans would understand about the indigenous peoples of Virginia came from the evocative descriptions Thomas Hariot provided in his firsthand observations. In 1585, Hariot (c. 1560–1621) accompanied Sir Walter Raleigh on his voyage to establish an English colony on Roanoke Island. While there, he learned the Algonquian language and explored the Chesapeake, producing one of the earliest accurate maps of the North Atlantic coast. After his return to England, Hariot published *A Briefe and True Report of the New Found Land of Virginia*, which made the case for English colonization. In the excerpt included here, Hariot provides the English with a description of the Algonquin Indians' religious beliefs.

It resteth I speake a word or two of the naturall inhabitants, their natures and maners, leaving large discourse thereof untill time more convenient hereafter: now onely so farre foorth, as that you may know, how that they in respect of troubling our inhabiting and planting, are not to be feared; but that they shall have cause both to feare and love us, that shall inhabite with them.

They are a people clothed with loose mantles made of Deere skins, and aprons of the same rounde about their middles; all els naked; of such a difference of statures only as wee in England; having no edge tooles or weapons of yron or steele to offend us withall, neither know they how to make any: those weapons they have, are onlie bowes made of Witch hazle, & arrowes of reeds; flat edged truncheons also of wood about a yard long, neither have they any thing to defend themselves but targets made of barks; and some armours made of stickes wickered together with thread.

Their townes are but small, and neere the sea coast but few, some containing but 10. or 12. houses: some 20. the greatest that we have seene have bene but of 30. houses: if they be walled it is only done with barks of trees made fast to stakes, or els with poles onely fixed upright and close one by another.

Their houses are made of small poles made fast at the tops in rounde forme after the maner as is used in many arbories in our gardens of England, in most townes covered with barkes, and in some with artificiall mattes made of long rushes; from the tops of the houses downe to the ground. The length of them is commonly double to the breadth, in some places they are but 12. and 16. yardes long, and in other some wee have seene of foure and twentie.

In some places of the countrey one onely towne belongeth to the government of a Wiróans or chiefe Lorde; in other some two or three, in some sixe, eight, and more; the greatest Wiróans that yet we had dealing with had but eighteene townes in his government, and able to make not above seven or eight hundred fighting men at the most: The language of every government is different from any other, and the farther they are distant the greater is the difference.

Thomas Hariot, *A Briefe and True Report of the New Found Land of Virginia* (London, 1588).

Their maner of warres amongst themselves is either by sudden surprising one an other most commonly about the dawning of the day, or moone light; or els by ambushes, or some suttle devises: Set battels are very rare, except it fall out where there are many trees, where eyther part may have some hope of defence, after the deliverie of every arrow, in leaping behind some or other.

If there fall out any warres between us & them, what their fight is likely to bee, we having advantages against them so many maner of waies, as by our discipline, our strange weapons and devises els; especially by ordinance great and small, it may be easily imagined; by the experience we have had in some places, the turning up of their heeles against us in running away was their best defence.

In respect of us they are a people poore, and for want of skill and judgement in the knowledge and use of our things, doe esteeme our trifles before thinges of greater value: Notwithstanding in their proper manner considering the want of such meanes as we have, they seeme very ingenious; For although they have no such tooles, nor any such craftes, sciences and artes as wee; yet in those thinges they doe, they shewe excellencie of wit. And by howe much they upon due consideration shall finde our manner of knowledges and craftes to exceede theirs in perfection, and speed for doing or execution, by so much the more is it probable that they shoulde desire our friendships and love, and have the greater respect for pleasing and obeying us. Whereby may bee hoped if meanes of good government bee used, that they may in short time be brought to civilitie, and the embracing of true religion.

Some religion they have alreadie, which although it be farre from the truth, yet being as it is, there is hope it may bee the easier and sooner reformed.

They beleeve that there are many Gods which they call Montóac, but of different sortes and degrees; one onely chiefe and great God, which hath bene from all eternitie. Who as they affirme when hee purposed to make the worlde, made first other goddes of a principall order to bee as meanes and instruments to bee used in the creation and government to follow; and after the Sunne, Moone, and Starres, as pettie goddess and the instruments of the other order more principall. First they say were made waters, out of which by the gods was made all diversitie of creatures that are visible or invisible

For mankind they say a woman was made first, which by the woorking of one of the goddes, conceived and brought foorth children: And in such sort they say they had their beginning.

But how manie yeeres or ages have passed since, they say they can make no relation, having no letters nor other such meanes as we to keepe recordes of the particularities of times past, but onelie tradition from father to sonne.

They thinke that all the gods are of humane shape, and therfore they represent them by images in the forms of men, which they call Kewasówok one alone is called Kewás; Them they place in houses appropriate or temples which they call Machicómuck; Where they woorship, praie, sing, and make manie times offerings unto them. In some Machicómuck we have seene but one Kewas, in some two, and in other some three; The common sort thinke them to be also gods.

They beleeve also the immortalitie of the soule, that after this life as soone as the soule is departed from the bodie according to the workes it hath done, it is eyther carried to heaven the habitacle of gods, there to enjoy perpetuall blisse and happinesse, or els to a great pitte or hole, which they thinke to bee in the furthest partes of their part of the worlde towarde the sunne set, there to burne continually: the place they call Popogusso.

For the confirmation of this opinion, they tolde mee two stories of two men that had been lately dead and revived againe, the one happened but few yeres before our comming into the countrey of a wicked man which having beene dead and buried, the next day the earth of the grave beeing seene to move, was taken up againe; Who made declaration where his soule had beene, that is to saie very neere entring into Popogusso, had not one of the gods saved him & gave him leave to returne againe, and teach his friends what they should doe to avoid that terrible place of torment.

The other happened in the same yeere wee were there, but in a towne that was threescore miles from us, and it was tolde mee for straunge newes that one being dead, buried and taken up againe as the first, shewed that although his bodie had lien dead in the grave, yet his soule was alive, and had travailed farre in a long broade waie, on both sides whereof grewe most delicate and pleasaunt trees, bearing more rare and excellent fruites then ever hee had seene before or was able to expresse, and at length came to most brave and faire houses, neere which hee met his father, that had beene dead before, who gave him great charge to goe backe againe and shew his friendes what good they were to doe to enioy the pleasures of that place, which when he had done he should after come againe.

What subtilty soever be in the Wiroances and Priestes, this opinion worketh so much in manie of the common and simple sort of people that it maketh them have great respect to their Governours, and also great care what they do, to avoid torment after death, and to enioy blisse; although notwithstanding there is punishment ordained for malefactours, as stealers, whoremoongers, and other sortes of wicked doers; some punished with death, some with forfeitures, some with beating, according to the greatnes of the factes.

And this is the summe of their religion, which I learned by having special familiarity with some of their priestes. Wherein they were not so sure grounded, nor gave such credite to their traditions and stories but through conversing with us they were brought into great doubts of their owne, and no small admiration of ours, with earnest desire in many, to learne more than we had meanes for want of perfect utterance in their language to expresse.

READING AND DISCUSSION QUESTIONS

1. What attitude does Hariot seem to have toward the religion of the Algonquin Indians he encountered?
2. What effect do you imagine Hariot's account of the Algonquins had on his English readers?

1-2 | Inca Artist Imagines European Encounter

FELIPE GUAMAN POMA DE AYALA, *The First New Chronicle and Good Government* (sixteenth century)

Images such as the one below can help us peek into the complex encounters that defined the relationship between indigenous peoples and the Europeans who arrived in the Americas during the fifteenth and sixteenth centuries. This drawing was done in the early seventeenth century by an Andean chronicler named Felipe Guaman Poma de Ayala. It depicts an event that never happened: the meeting of the Inca emperor Huayna Capac (see below) and Pedro de Candia, a Greek adventurer in the employ of Spain who joined an expedition to Peru in 1526. One chronicler recounted the moment when Candia landed on the beach in northern Peru and fired an arquebus, or a gun that rested on a tripod. The indigenous peoples threw themselves on the ground in awe and the Inca leader of the region called him "thunder in the heavens." In this image, Guaman Poma comments on European desire for gold. While the Inca were good metalsmiths, it appears that they valued fabric and textiles more highly than the gold and silver conquistadors sought. Here the Inca emperor holds a plate of gold nuggets and asks Candia: "Do you eat this gold?" Candia responds: "This is the gold we eat."

Spanish conquistadors' hunger for gold

READING AND DISCUSSION QUESTIONS

1. What does the Inca emperor's question (and Candia's answer as told by the Peruvian artist) tell you about the differing values of the Inca and Europeans?
2. For historians, this illustration is less important for the event it purports to describe than for the evidence it provides of indigenous attitudes and perspective. What do you think the artist wants us to believe about the Spanish and the Indians?

1-3 | Columbus Encounters Native Peoples

CHRISTOPHER COLUMBUS, *Journal of the First Voyage* (1492)

Christopher Columbus (1451–1506), in the pay of the Spanish court, sailed west from Europe crossing the Atlantic in 1492 en route to India and the legendary hoards of gold and spices rumored to be found in the East. As we know, Columbus failed to reach India, but the world he encountered opened Europe to riches of a different sort. In the journal of Columbus's first voyage, he describes the native peoples he encountered, including comments on their appearance, dress, and behavior toward him. While his comments provide a peek into the native culture, they also reveal Columbus's attitudes and worldview.

Friday, 12th of October

What follows is in the actual words of the Admiral[1] in his book of the first navigation and discovery of the Indies. "I," he says, "that we might form great friendship, for I knew that they were a people who could be more easily freed and converted to our holy faith by love than by force, gave to some of them red caps, and glass beads to put round their necks, and many other things of little value, which gave them great pleasure, and made them so much our friends that it was a marvel to see. They afterwards came to the ship's boats where we were, swimming and bringing us parrots, cotton threads in skeins, darts, and many other things; and we exchanged them for other things that we gave them, such as glass beads and small bells. In fine, they took all, and gave what they had with good will. It appeared to me to be a race of people very poor in everything. They go as naked as when their mothers bore them, and so do the women, although I did not see more than one young girl. All I saw were youths, none more than thirty years of age. They are very well made with very handsome bodies, and

---

Christopher Columbus, "Journal of the First Voyage," in *The Voyages of Columbus and of John Cabot,* ed. Edward Gaylord Bourne (New York: Charles Scribner's Sons, 1906), 110–114.

[1]Columbus's journal was lost but not before Bartolome de Las Casas (c. 1484–1566) had summarized the original when preparing his *Historia General de las Indias* (1522). The text we have of Columbus's journal is based on Las Casas's summary. When Las Casas mentions the "Admiral," he is referring to Columbus.

very good countenances. Their hair is short and coarse, almost like the hairs of a horsetail. They wear the hairs brought down to the eyebrows except a few locks behind, which they wear long and never cut. They paint themselves black, and they are the color of the Canarians, neither black nor white. Some paint themselves white, others red, and others of what color they find. Some paint their faces, others the whole body, some only round the eyes, others only on the nose. They neither care nor know anything of arms, for I showed them swords, and they took them by the blade and cut themselves through ignorance. They have no iron, their darts being wands without iron, some of them having a fish's tooth at the end, and others being pointed in various ways. They are all of fair stature and size, with good faces, and well made. I saw some with marks of wounds on their bodies, and I made signs to ask what it was, and they gave me to understand that people from other adjacent islands came with the intention of seeing them, and that they defended themselves. I believed, and still believe, that they come here from the mainland to take them prisoners. They should be good servants and intelligent, for I observed that they quickly took in what was said to them, and I believe that they would easily be made Christians, as it appeared to me that they had no religion. I, our Lord being pleased, will take hence, at the time of my departure, six natives for your Highnesses, that they may learn to speak. I saw no beast of any kind except parrots, on this island." The above is in the words of the Admiral.

Saturday, 13th of October

"As soon as dawn broke many of these people came to the beach, all youths, as I have said, and all of good stature, a very handsome people. Their hair is not curly, but loose and coarse, like horse hair. In all the forehead is broad, more so than in any other people I have hitherto seen. Their eyes are very beautiful and not small, and themselves far from black, but the color of the Canarians. Nor should anything else be expected, as this island is in a line east and west from the island of Hierro in the Canaries. Their legs are very straight, all in one line, and no belly, but very well formed. They came to the ship in small canoes, made out of the trunk of a tree like a long boat, and all of one piece, and wonderfully worked, considering the country. They are large, some of them holding 40 to 45 men, others smaller, and some only large enough to hold one man. They are propelled with a paddle like a baker's shovel, and go at a marvelous rate. If the canoe capsizes, they all promptly begin to swim, and to bale it out with calabashes that they take with them. They brought skeins of cotton thread, parrots, darts, and other small things which it would be tedious to recount, and they give all in exchange for anything that may be given to them. I was attentive, and took trouble to ascertain if there was gold. I saw that some of them had a small piece fastened in a hole they have in the nose, and by signs I was able to make out that to the south, or going from the island to the south, there was a king who had great cups full, and who possessed a great quantity. I tried to get them to go there, but afterwards I saw that they had no inclination. I resolved to wait until to-morrow in the afternoon and then to depart, shaping a course to the S.W., for, according to what many of them told me, there was land to the S., to the S.W., and N.W., and that the natives from the N.W. often came to attack them, and went on to the S.W. in search of gold and precious stones.

"This island is rather large and very flat, with bright green trees, much water, and a very large lake in the centre, without any mountain, and the whole land so green that it is a pleasure to look on it. The people are very docile, and for the longing to possess our things, and not having anything to give in return, they take what they can get, and presently swim away. Still, they give away all they have got, for whatever may be given to them, down to broken bits of crockery and glass. I saw one give 16 skeins of cotton for three *ceotis* of Portugal, equal to one *blanca* of Spain, the skeins being as much as an *arroba* of cotton thread. I shall keep it, and shall allow no one to take it, preserving it all for your Highnesses, for it may be obtained in abundance. It is grown in this island, though the short time did not admit of my ascertaining this for a certainty. Here also is found the gold they wear fastened in their noses. But, in order not to lose time, I intend to go and see if I can find the island of Cipango. Now, as it is night, all the natives have gone on shore with their canoes."

Sunday, 14th of October

"At dawn I ordered the ship's boat and the boats of the caravels to be got ready, and I went along the coast of the island to the N.N.E., to see the other side, which was on the other side to the east, and also to see the villages. Presently I saw two or three, and the people all came to the shore, calling out and giving thanks to God. Some of them brought us water, others came with food, and when they saw that I did not want to land, they got into the sea, and came swimming to us. We understood that they asked us if we had come from heaven. One old man came into the boat, and others cried out, in loud voices, to all the men and women, to come and see the men who had come from heaven, and to bring them to eat and drink. Many came, including women, each bringing something, giving thanks to God, throwing themselves on the ground and shouting to us to come on shore. But I was afraid to land, seeing an extensive reef of rocks which surrounded the island, with deep water between it and the shore forming a port large enough for as many ships as there are in Christendom, but with a very narrow entrance. It is true that within this reef there are some sunken rocks, but the sea has no more motion than the water in a well. In order to see all this I went this morning, that I might be able to give a full account to your Highnesses, and also where a fortress might be established. I saw a piece of land which appeared like an island, although it is not one, and on it there were six houses. It might be converted into an island in two days, though I do not see that it would be necessary, for these people are very simple as regards the use of arms, as your Highnesses will see from the seven that I caused to be taken, to bring home and learn our language and return; unless your Highnesses should order them all to be brought to Castile, or to be kept as captives on the same island; for with fifty men they can all be subjugated and made to do what is required of them. Close to the above peninsula there are gardens of the most beautiful trees I ever saw, and with leaves as green as those of Castile in the month[s] of April and May, and much water. I examined all that port, and afterwards I returned to the ship and made sail. I saw so many islands that I hardly knew how to determine to which I should go first. Those natives I had with me said, by signs, that there were so many that they could not be numbered, and they gave the names of more than a hundred. At last I looked out for the largest, and resolved to shape a course for it, and so I did. It will be distant five leagues from this of San Salvador, and the others some more, some less. All are very flat, and all are inhabited. The natives make war on each other, although these are very simple-minded and handsomely-formed people."

READING AND DISCUSSION QUESTIONS

1. Why do you think Columbus focused on these details about the natives he encountered?
2. Besides riches, what motivation for exploration can you see in Columbus's account of his meeting with the natives?

1-4 | Las Casas Describes European Atrocities

BARTOLOME DE LAS CASAS, *A Brief Account of the Destruction of the Indies* (1552)

Bartolome de Las Casas (c. 1484–1566), born in Seville, migrated to Hispaniola early in the sixteenth century and participated in the colonial economy, owning slaves and waging military attacks against the indigenous population. Unlike other Spanish conquerors, however, Las Casas gradually renounced slavery and its cruelties, and by 1514 he was urging others to do the same. His graphic portrayal of Spanish atrocities, published in 1552 as *A Brief Account of the Destruction of the Indies*, describes the tortures inflicted on the indigenous peoples of the West Indies.

America was discovered and found out *Ann. Dom.* 1492, and the Year insuing inhabited by the Spaniards, and afterward a multitude of them travelled thither from Spain for the space of Nine and Forty Years. Their first attempt was on the Spanish Island, which indeed is a most fertile soil, and at present in great reputation for its Spaciousness and Length, containing in Circumference Six Hundred Miles: Nay it is on all sides surrounded with an almost innumerable number of Islands, which we found so well peopled with Natives and Forreigners, that there is scarce any Region in the Universe fortified with

---

Bartolome de Las Casas, *A Brief Account of the Destruction of the Indies* (London: R. Hewson, 1689).

so many Inhabitants: But the main Land or Continent, distant from this Island Two Hundred and Fifty Miles and upwards, extends it self above Ten Thousand Miles in Length near the sea-shore, which Lands are some of them already discover'd, and more may be found out in process of time: And such a multitude of People inhabits these Countries, that it seems as if the Omnipotent God has Assembled and Convocated the major part of Mankind in this part of the World.

Now this infinite multitude of Men are by the Creation of God innocently simple, altogether void of and averse to all manner of Craft, Subtlety and Malice, and most Obedient and Loyal Subjects to their Native Sovereigns; and behave themselves very patiently, su[b]missively and quietly towards the Spaniards, to whom they are subservient and subject; so that finally they live without the least thirst after revenge, laying aside all litigiousness, Commotion and hatred.

This is a most tender and effeminate people, and [of] so imbecile and unequal-balanced temper, that they are altogether incapable of hard labour, and in few years, by one Distemper or other soon expire, so that the very issue of Lords and Princes, who among us live with great affluence, and fard deliciously, are not more eff[e]minate and tender than the Children of their Husbandmen or Labourers: This Nation is very Necessitous and Indigent, Masters of very slender Possessions, and consequently, neither Haughty, nor Ambitious. They are parsimonious in their Diet, as the Holy Fathers were in their frugal life in the Desert, known by the name of Eremites. They go naked, having no other Covering but what conceals their Pudends from publick sight. An hairy Plad, or loose Coat, about an Ell, or a coarse woven Cloth at most Two Ells long serves them for the warmest Winter Garment. They lye on a coarse Rug or Matt, and those that have the most plentiful Estate or Fortunes, the better sort, use Net-work, knotted at the four corners in lieu of Beds, which the Inhabitants of the Island of Hispaniola, in their own proper Idiom, term *Hammacks.* The Men are pregnant and docible. The natives tractable, and capable of Morality or Goodness, very apt to receive the instill'd principles of Catholick Religion; nor are they averse to Civility and good Manners, being not so much discompos'd by variety of Obstructions, as the rest of Mankind; insomuch, that having suckt in (if I may so express my self) the very first Rudiments of the Christian Faith, they are so transported with Zeal and Furvor in the exercise of Ecclesiastical Sacraments, and Divine Service, that the very Religioso's themselves, stand in need of the greatest and most signal patience to undergo such extream Transports. And to conclude, I my self have heard the Spaniards themselves (who dare not assume the Confidence to deny the good Nature praedominant in them) declare, that there was nothing wanting in them for the acquisition of Eternal Beatitude, but the sole Knowledge and Understanding of the Deity.

The Spaniards first assaulted the innocent Sheep, so qualified by the Almighty, as is premention'd, like most cruel Tygers, Wolves and Lions hunger-starv'd, studying nothing, for the space of Forty Years, after their first landing, but the Massacre of these Wretches, whom they have so inhumanely and barbarously butcher'd and harass'd with several kinds of Torments, never before known, or heard (of which you shall have some account in the following

Discourse) that of Three Millions of Persons, which lived in Hispaniola itself, there is at present but the inconsiderable remnant of scarce Three Hundred. Nay the Isle of Cuba, which extends as far, as Valledolid in Spain is distant from Rome, lies now uncultivated, like a Desert, and intomb'd in its own Ruins. You may also find the Isles of St. John, and Jamaica, both large and fruitful places, unpeopled and desolate. The Lucayan Islands on the North Side, adjacent to Hispaniola and Cuba, which are Sixty in number, or thereabout, together with those, vulgarly known by the name of the Gigantic Isles, and others, the most infertile whereof, exceeds the Royal Garden of Sevil in fruitfulness, a most Healthful and pleasant Climat, is now laid waste and uninhabited; and whereas, when the Spaniards first arriv'd here, about Five Hundred Thousand Men dwelt in it, they are now cut off, some by slaughter, and others ravished away by Force and Violence, to work in the Mines of Hispanioloa [*sic*], which was destitute of Native Inhabitants: For a certain Vessel, sailing to this Isle, to the end, that the Harvest being over (some good Christian, moved with Piety and Pity, undertook this dangerous Voyage, to convert Souls to Christianity) the remaining gleanings might be gathered up, there were only found Eleven Persons, which I saw with my own Eyes. There are other Islands Thirty in number, and upward bordering upon the Isle of St. John, totally unpeopled; all which are above Two Thousand miles in Lenght, and yet remain without Inhabitants, Native, or People.

As to the firm land, we are certainly satisfied, and assur'd, that the Spaniards by their barbarous and execrable Actions have absolutely depopulated Ten Kingdoms, of greater extent than all Spain, together with the Kingdoms of Arragon and Portugal, that is to say, above One Thousand Miles, which now lye wast[e] and desolate, and are absolutely ruined, when as formerly no other Country whatsoever was more populous. Nay we dare boldly affirm, that during the Forty Years space, wherein they exercised their sanguinary and detestable Tyranny in these Regions, above Twelve Millions (computing Men, Women, and Children) have undeservedly perished; nor do I conceive that I should deviate from the Truth by saying that above Fifty Millions in all paid their last Debt to Nature.

Those that arriv'd at these Islands from the remotest parts *of Spain, and* who pride themselves in the Name of Christians, steer'd Two courses principally, in order to the Extirpation, and Exterminating of this People from the face of the Earth. The first whereof was raising an unjust, sanguinolent, cruel War. The other, by putting them to death, who hitherto, thirsted after their Liberty, or design'd (which the most Potent, Strenuous and Magnanimous Spirits intended) to recover their pristin Freedom, and shake off the Shackles of so injurious a Captivity: For they being taken off in War, none but Women and Children were permitted to enjoy the benefit of that Country-Air, in whom they did in succeeding times lay such a heavy Yoak, that the very Brutes were more happy than they: To which Two Species of Tyranny as subalternate things to the Genus, the other innumerable Courses they took to extirpate and make this a desolate People, may be reduced and referr'd.

Now the ultimate end and scope that incited the Spaniards to endeavor the Extirpation and Desolation of this People, was Gold only; that thereby growing opulent in a short time, they might arrive at once at such Degrees and Dignities, as were no wayes consistent with their Persons.

Finally, in one word, their Ambition and Avarice, than which the heart of Man never entertained greater, and the vast Wealth of those Regions; the Humility and Patience of the Inhabitants (which made their approach to these Lands more facil and easie) did much [to] promote the business: Whom they so despicably contemned, that they treated them (I speak of things which I was an Eye Witness of, without the least fallacy) not as Beasts, which I cordially wished they would, but as the most abject dung and filth of the Earth; and so sollicitous they were of their Life and Soul, that the above-mentioned number of People died without understanding the true Faith or Sacraments. And this also is as really true as the praecendent Narration (which the very Tyrants and cruel Murderers cannot deny without the stigma of a lye) that the Spaniards never received any injury from the Indians, but that they rather reverenced them as Persons descended from Heaven, until that they were compelled to take up Arms, provoked thereunto by repeated Injuries, violent Torments, and injust Butcheries.

READING AND DISCUSSION QUESTIONS

1. How does Las Casas characterize the native peoples he writes about? How does his description compare to those provided by Hariot (Document 1-1) and Columbus (Document 1-3)?
2. By the time Las Casas wrote his *Brief Account*, he had been a Dominican friar for nearly thirty years. What role did religion play in shaping his interpretation of Spain's treatment of natives?

1-5 | Huejotzingo Petitions the Spanish King for Relief

COUNCIL OF HUEJOTZINGO, *Letter to the King of Spain* (1560)

Huejotzingo, pronounced "way-HOT-zin-go," located in central Mexico, suffered under Aztec domination in the fifteenth century. When Hernán Cortés, the Spanish conquistador, began his campaign against the Aztecs in 1519, the indigenous people of Huejotzingo allied themselves with him. They sided with the victor, for Cortés crushed the Aztecs by 1521, claiming the empire for Spain. In time, the inhabitants of Huejotzingo came to understand the price of empire. This petition, drafted by the city's council, shows the influence of European culture on indigenous peoples. Here, Huejotzingo's leaders asked King Philip II of Spain for relief from the massive tribute now being demanded of them. Their appeal was ultimately unsuccessful.

"Letter to King of Spain" (1560). *Beyond the Codices,* trans. and eds. Arthur J. O. Anderson, Frances Berdan, and James Lockhart (Berkeley: University of California Press, 1976), 179, 181, 183, 185, 187, 189.

Our lord sovereign, king don Felipe our lord, with our words we appear and stand before you, we of Huejotzingo who guard for you your city—we citizens, I the governor and we the alcaldes and councilmen and we the lords and nobles, your men and your servants. Very humbly we implore you: Oh unfortunate are we, very great and heavy sadness and affliction lie upon us, nowhere do your pity and compassion extend over us and reach us, we do not deserve, we do not attain your rulership. And all the while since your subjects the Spaniards arrived among us, all the while we have been looking toward you, we have been confidently expecting that sometime your pity would reach us, as we also had confidence in and were awaiting the mercy of your very revered dear father the ruler of the world, don Carlos the late emperor. Therefore now, our lord sovereign, we bow humbly before you; may we deserve your pity, may the very greatly compassionate and merciful God enlighten you so that your pity is exercised on us, for we hear, and so it is said to us, that you are very merciful and humane towards all your vassals;. . . May you only in your very great Christianity and very revered high majesty attend well to this our prayer.

Our lord sovereign, before anyone told us of or made us acquainted with your fame and your story, most high and feared universal king who rules all, and before we were told or taught the glory and name of our Lord God, before the faith reached us, and before we were Christians, when your servants the Spaniards reached us and your captain general don Hernando Cortés arrived, although we were not yet acquainted with the omnipotent, very compassionate holy Trinity, our Lord God the ruler of heaven and possessor of earth caused us to deserve that in his mercy he enlightened us so that we took you as our king to belong to you and become your people and your subjects; not a single town surpassed us here in New Spain in that first and earliest we threw ourselves toward you, we gave ourselves to you, and furthermore no one intimidated us, no one forced us into it, but truly God caused us to deserve that voluntarily we adhered to you so that we gladly received the newly arrived Spaniards who reached us here in New Spain,. . . nowhere did we attack them. Truly we fed them and served them; some arrived sick, so that we carried them in our arms and on our backs, and we served them in many other ways which we are not able to say here. . . .

And when they began their conquest and war-making, then also we well prepared ourselves to aid them, for out came all of our war gear, our arms and provisions and all our equipment, and we not merely named someone, we went in person, we who rule, and we brought all our nobles and all of our vassals to aid the Spaniards. . . . And when they went to conquer Michoacan, Jalisco, and Colhuacan, and there at Pánuco and there at Oaxaca and Tehuantepec and Guatemala, (we were) the only ones who went along while they conquered and made war here in New Spain until they finished the conquest; we never abandoned them. . . .

Our lord sovereign, we also say and declare before you that your fathers the twelve sons of St. Francis reached us, whom the very high priestly ruler the Holy Father sent and whom you sent, both taking pity on us so that they came to teach us the gospel, to teach us the holy Catholic faith and belief, to make us acquainted with the single deity God our Lord, and likewise God favored us and enlightened us, us of Huejotzingo, who dwell in your city, so that we gladly received them. When they entered the city of Huejotzingo, of our own free will we honored them and showed them esteem. When they embraced us so that we would abandon the wicked belief in many gods, we forthwith voluntarily left it; likewise they did us the good deed (of telling us) to destroy and burn the stones and wood that we worshipped as gods, and we did it; very willingly we destroyed, demolished, and burned the temples. Also when they gave us the holy gospel, the holy Catholic faith, with very good will and desire we received and grasped it; no one frightened us into it, no one forced us, but very willingly we seized it, and they gave us all the sacraments. . . . Therefore now, in and through God, may you hear these our words, all that we say and declare before you, so that you will take pity on us, so that you will exercise on us your rulership to console us and aid us in (this trouble) with which daily we weep and are sad. We are afflicted and sore pressed, and your town and city of Huejotzingo is as if it is about to disappear and be destroyed. Here is what is being done to us: now your stewards the royal officials and the prosecuting attorney Dr. Maldonado are assessing us a very great tribute to belong to you. The tribute we are to give is 14,800 pesos in money, and also all the bushels of maize.

Our lord sovereign, never has such happened to us in all the time since your servants and vassals the Spaniards came to us,. . . But now we are taken aback and very afraid and we ask, have we done something wrong, have we somehow behaved badly and ill toward you, our lord sovereign, or have we committed some sin against almighty God? Perhaps you have heard something of our wickedness and for that reason now this very great tribute has fallen upon us, seven times exceeding all we had paid before, the 2,000 pesos. And we declare to you that it will not be long before your city of Huejotzingo completely disappears and perishes, because our fathers, grandfathers, and ancestors knew no tribute and gave tribute to no one, but were independent, and we nobles who guard your subjects are now truly very poor. Nobility is seen among us no longer; now we resemble the commoners. As they eat and dress, so do we; we have been very greatly afflicted, and our poverty has reached its culmination. Of the way in which our fathers and grandfathers and forebears were rich and honored, there is no longer the slightest trace among us.

O our lord sovereign king, we rely on you as on God the one deity who dwells in heaven, we trust in you as our father. Take pity on us, have compassion with us. May you especially remember those who live and subsist in the wilds, those who move us to tears and pity; we truly live with them in just such poverty as theirs, wherefore we speak out before you so that afterwards you will not become angry with us when your subjects have disappeared or perished. There ends this our prayer.

READING AND DISCUSSION QUESTIONS

1. What arguments does the council believe would be convincing to the Spanish king?
2. What does this petition reveal about the extent to which European colonization and domination had affected indigenous culture?

1-6 | Debating the Morality of Slavery

BROTHER LUIS BRANDAON, *Letter to Father Sandoval* (1610)

In the early modern period, colonization and its effects on native populations increasingly became a topic of discussion and debate. In addition to atrocities perpetrated against native populations such as those described by Las Casas (Document 1-4), the growing trade in African slaves raised moral concerns for some. In this March 12, 1610 letter, Brother Luis Brandaon, a Jesuit in Angola, addresses the concerns of Father Sandoval, a Catholic priest serving in Brazil. Angola, on the west coast of Africa, was a Portuguese colony that supplied Africans for the slave trade.

[March 12, 1610.]

Your Reverence writes me that you would like to know whether the negroes who are sent to your parts have been legally captured. To this I reply that I think your Reverence should have no scruples on this point, because this is a matter which has been questioned by the Board of Conscience in Lisbon, and all its members are learned and conscientious men. Nor did the bishops who were in São Thomé, Cape Verde, and here in Loando—all learned and virtuous men—find fault with it. We have been here ourselves for forty years and there have been [among us] very learned Fathers; in the Province of Brazil as well, where there have always been Fathers of our order eminent in letters, never did they consider this trade as illicit. Therefore we and the fathers of Brazil buy these slaves for our service without any scruple. Furthermore, I declare that if any one could be excused from having scruples it is the inhabitants of those regions, for since the traders who bring those negroes bring them in good faith, those inhabitants can very well buy from such traders without any scruple, and the latter on their part can sell them, for it is a generally accepted opinion that the owner who owns anything in good faith can sell it and that it can be bought. Padre Sánchez thus expresses this point in his Book of Marriage, thus solving this doubt of your Reverence. Therefore, we here are the ones who could have greater scruple, for we buy these negroes from other negroes and from people who perhaps

Brother Luis Brandaon to Father Sandoval, in *Documents Illustrative of the History of the Slave Trade to America*, vol. 1, 1441–1700, ed. Elizabeth Donnan (Washington, DC: Carnegie Institution of Washington, 1930), 123–124.

have stolen them; but the traders who take them away from here do not know of this fact, and so buy those negroes with a clear conscience and sell them out there with a clear conscience. Besides I found it true indeed that no negro will ever say he has been captured legally. Therefore your Reverence should not ask them whether they have been legally captured or not, because they will always say that they were stolen and captured illegally, in the hope that they will be given their liberty. I declare, moreover, that in the fairs where these negroes are bought there are always a few who have been captured illegally because they were stolen or because the rulers of the land order them to be sold for offenses so slight that they do not deserve captivity, but these are few in number and to seek among ten or twelve thousand who leave this port every year for a few who have been illegally captured is an impossibility, however careful investigation may be made. And to lose so many souls as sail from here—out of whom many are saved—because some, impossible to recognize, have been captured illegally does not seem to be doing much service to God, for these are few and those who find salvation are many and legally captured.

READING AND DISCUSSION QUESTIONS

1. How does Brandaon attempt to calm Sandoval's anxiety about the slave trade?
2. What does this letter tell you about the extent of the slave trade by the early seventeenth century?
3. What evidence of the Catholic Church's role in debates over slavery does this document provide?

▪ COMPARATIVE QUESTIONS ▪

1. How do these sources illustrate the extent to which European culture had an impact on native peoples?
2. In what ways did Hariot, Columbus, and Las Casas apply a European "lens" to their views of indigenous peoples?
3. What similarities between European and indigenous American society and culture can be glimpsed through the windows opened by these sources?
4. How might the authors of these various texts have assessed the advantages and costs of colonization?

2

American Experiments

1521–1700

The "age of exploration" resulted in the establishment of many different colonies in the Americas. As no single model prevailed, the sixteenth and seventeenth centuries are best understood as a period of colonial experimentation. European colonists projected onto their communities the intellectual and cultural hallmarks of the world they left behind, but the unique challenges they faced also demanded change and innovation. The New World was not "discovered" so much as it was forged through crisis and adaptation by the Europeans, Native Americans, and imported Africans who found themselves occupying common ground.

This chapter focuses on the forces that shaped colonial society and the ways that colonists interacted with their new surroundings. In the Spanish tribute colonies, Europeans extracted resources from indigenous peoples, but their efforts were met with native resistance. In New England, Governor John Winthrop's dream of a colony based on Christian charity existed alongside the realities of daily living and surviving. As plantations were established, changing systems of trade and a growing dependence on race-based slavery came to define enduring racial and economic patterns. Finally, as colonists were not settling an empty continent, in many ways their experiences were shaped by conflicts and encounters with indigenous peoples.

2-1 | Indians Resist Spanish Conquest
Testimony of Acoma Indians (1599)

The colonies that Spain established in the Americas rewarded their conquistadors with rich land from which they extracted labor and tribute from conquered indigenous peoples. Spain's process of imposing Catholicism and its cultural and political interests onto its

---

colonies, while largely successful, was sometimes met with resistance from the Indian majority. In the pueblo of Acoma in 1598, Indians attacked and killed several Spanish officials. The source included here is the official Spanish report of the incident, including the testimony from several Indians.

Statement of Indian Caoma

On this same day, February 9, the governor ordered testimony taken from an Indian through Don Tomás, a Christian Indian interpreter, who swore by God and a cross in due legal manner to declare faithfully all that might be said by this and the other Indians in their testimony. He said: "I so swear, amen."

The interpreter said that this Indian was named Caoma, a native of the pueblo of Acoma, and the captain of one of the wards of this pueblo. Not being a Christian he was not asked to take an oath. He explained through the interpreter that he was not present at Acoma when they killed the maese de campo and the others, as he had gone to the country. When he returned on the night of the day they were killed, the Indians at the pueblo told him how the maese de campo and his men came to the pueblo and asked the natives to furnish them with the maize and flour which they needed, and because they asked for such large amounts they killed them. He was very sorry for what the Indians had done and denounced them for it. Then the governor asked him to explain why it was that when the sargento mayor and the soldiers went to his pueblo to summon them to peace, the Indians, instead of submitting, attacked with arrows, stones, and clubs. He replied that they refused to come down peacefully and to be friends because they had already killed the Spaniards, but he urged the Indians, both men and women, all of whom hurled stones, to submit peacefully, but they refused.

This witness was asked to tell who dug up the two small field pieces, the horseshoes, and other iron goods that the Spaniards had buried near Acoma when they were unable to carry it further. He answered that Indians of the pueblo dug it up, carried it away, and divided it among themselves, each one taking his share. This is the truth and what he knows. He gave this testimony in the presence of Captain Alonso Gómez, his defense attorney, who signed it, together with the governor. Don Juan de Oñate. Alonso Gómez Montesinos. Before me, Juan Gutiérrez Bocanegra, secretary.

Statement of Cat-ticati

Immediately thereafter, on this same day, the governor called before him an Indian named Cat-ticati, a native of the pueblo of Acoma, who testified through the interpreter that he did not know how old he was, but perhaps about thirty-five years. He declared that he was not present when the maese de campo and the other soldiers were killed, but that he learned about it at the pueblo when he returned. They had killed them because they asked for maize, flour, and blankets.

Asked why the Indians refused to accept peace and to come down from the pueblo when the sargento mayor summoned them, he replied that they declined to submit and accept peace since they had already killed the Spaniards.

Asked why, when the sargento mayor offered them peace, they not only rejected it but shot arrows and hurled rocks and insulting words, he replied that some shot arrows and threw stones but there were some who did not want to fight. To other questions he replied that he was telling the truth. All of this took place in the presence of his defense attorney, who signed his testimony, together with the governor. Don Juan de Oñate. Alonso Gómez Montesinos. Before me, Juan Gutiérrez Bocanegra, secretary.

Testimony of Indian Taxio

This same day the governor called before him an Indian named Taxio, a native of the pueblo of Acoma, who did not know how old he was, but who seemed to be about twenty-three years.

Asked why he and the other Indians of Acoma killed the maese de campo and ten other soldiers and two servants, he said that when they began to kill them, he was at home, but when he heard the shouting that they were killing the Spaniards, he went up to the roof and stayed there and saw a dead Spaniard and that the others whom they had killed had been thrown down the rocks.

Asked why, when the sargento mayor offered the Indians peace, he and the others did not come down to accept but shot many arrows and threw rocks and cried for the Spaniards to come on and fight, he said that the old people and other leading Indians did not want peace, and for this reason they attacked with arrows and stones.

Asked why the Indian women threw rocks and helped in the fight, he said it was because they were together with the men and therefore they took part in the demonstrations and the fighting. He made this statement in the presence of the defender, who signed it. To other questions he said that he had spoken the truth, and he ratified his testimony, after it was explained to him. The interpreter did not sign this statement or the others, because he did not know how. Don Juan de Oñate. Alonso Gómez Montesinos. Before me, Juan Gutiérrez Bocanegra, secretary.

Statement of Indian Xunusta

This same day the governor called before him an Indian who, according to the interpreter, was named Xunusta, a native of the pueblo of Acoma. He did not know how old he was, but seemed to be about twenty-two years.

Asked why he and the other Indians of the pueblo had killed the maese de campo and his men, he said that the Spaniards first killed an Indian, and then all the Indians became very angry and killed them.

Asked why it was that when the sargento mayor asked them to accept peace they did not come down from the pueblo but shot many arrows and threw rocks and clubs, both men and women taking part in the fray, he said that some of the Indians wanted to make peace but others did not, and because they could not agree, they would not submit. This statement was given in the presence of their defender, who signed it, but the interpreter did not because he did not know how to write, though he ratified the testimony when it was read to him. Don Juan de Oñate. Alonso Gómez Montesinos. Before me, Juan Gutiérrez Bocanegra, secretary.

Statement of Indian Excasi

Immediately thereafter, on this same day, the governor called before him an Indian who, according to the interpreter, was named Excasi, a native of the pueblo of Acoma. He did not know his age, but seemed to be about twenty-five years.

Asked why he and the other Indians of the pueblo killed the maese de campo, two captains, eight soldiers, and two servants, he said that he did not see them killed but that he saw his people throw the bodies down the rocks. He had heard it said that they killed the Spaniards because a soldier either asked for or took a turkey.

Asked why the Indians did not accept peace when the sargento mayor appealed to them and asked them to come down and be friends, which he did many times, the Indian said that he did not want to fight, but others did, and therefore they did not submit.

Asked why they shot arrows and threw stones from the pueblo when they had been summoned to peace, he repeated what he had already said. This is the truth, and he ratified it. Done in the presence of the defender, who signed. Don Juan de Oñate. Alonso Gómez de Montesinos. Before me, Juan Gutiérrez Bocanegra, secretary.

Statement of Indian Caucachi

Immediately thereafter, on this same day, the governor called before him an Indian who, according to the interpreter, was called Caucachi, a native of the pueblo of Acoma. He did not know how old he was, but appeared to be about fifty.

Asked why he and the other Indians of the pueblo had killed the maese de campo and the other ten Spaniards and two servants, he said that the Spaniards had wounded an Acoma Indian and for this reason his people became angry and killed them.

Asked why it was that when the sargento mayor asked them to accept peace, they not only refused his offer but cried out that they wanted to fight and shot arrows and hurled stones, he said that since some of the Acomas did not wish to make friends, they began to fight. He was asked other questions, but replied that what he had said was the truth. He ratified his testimony in the presence of his defender, who signed. Don Juan de Oñate. Alonso Gómez Montesinos. Before me, Juan Gutiérrez Bocanegra, secretary.

READING AND DISCUSSION QUESTIONS

1. Whose point of view does this source express? How does that perspective shape your understanding of the event it describes?
2. What inferences can you draw about the daily relationships between the Spanish rulers and the Indians in the pueblo of Acoma?
3. Compare the testimony of these Indians. How do you explain any contradictions you find? What limitations does this source present to the historian trying to reconstruct the events it claims to describe?

2-2 | Punishing Pilgrims
Plymouth Colony Court Records (17th Century)

As we saw in the testimony from the Acoma Indians, legal sources can open a window for historians to examine the social and political dynamics within a community. The same is true when we peer into the records of colonial New England. Court records can show what values a community aspired to uphold and where those ideals slipped in practice. The records from court proceedings reproduced here are all from cases involving sexual transgressions. Our stereotypes of early New England colonists may sometimes cause us to forget that these were ordinary people facing ordinary temptations. Moreover, these particular cases raise interesting possibilities for understanding both the gendered nature of New England justice and the demographic complexity of the region in this first century of English settlement.

September 3, 1639

Mary, the wyfe of Robert Mendame, of Duxborrow, for using dallyance diuers [divers, meaning many] tymes with Tinsin, an Indian, and after committing the act of vncleanesse with him, as by his owne confession by seuerall [several] interpreters is made apparent, the Bench [meaning the Court] doth therefore censure the said Mary to be whipt at a carts tayle[1] through the townes streets, and to weare a badge vpon her left sleeue during her aboad [abode] within this gouerment; and if shee shalbe found without it abroad, then to be burned in the face with a hott iron; and the said Tinsin, the Indian, to be well whipt with a halter about his neck at the post, because it arose through the allurement [and] inticement of the said Mary, that hee was drawne therevnto.

Lisa M. Lauria, "*Sexual Misconduct in Plymouth Colony*" (1998). Published in The Plymouth Colony Archive Project. Reprinted with permission from Lisa Lauria. Accessed at http://www.histarch.illinois.edu/Plymouth/Lauria2.html#II

[1] **Carts tayle**: Cart's Tail, a form of punishment where a person was tied to the end of a cart and whipped.

December 7, 1641

Forasmuch, as Thomas Bray, of Yarmouth, a single person, and Anne, the wyfe of Francis Linceford, haue committed the act of adultery and vncleanesse, and haue diuers tymes layne in one bed together in the absence of her husband, which hath beene confessed by both parties in the publike Court, the Court doth censure them as followeth: That they be both seuerely [severely] whipt immediately at the publik post, [and] that they shall weare (whilst they remayne in the gouernment) two letters, namely, an AD, for Adulterers, daily, vpon the outside of their vppermost garment, in a most emenent place thereof; and if they shalbe found at any tyme in any towne or place within the gouerment without them so worne vpon their vppermost garment as aforesaid, that then the constable of the towne or place shall take them, or wither of them, omitting so to weare the said two letters, and shall forthwith whip them for their negligence, and shall cause them to be immediately put on againe, and so worne by them and either of them; and also that they shalbe both whipt at Yarmouth, publikly, where the offence was committed, in such fitt season as shalbe thought meete [proper] by Mr. Edmond Freeman [and] such others as are authorized for the keepeing of the Courts in these partes.

June 7, 1642

John Casley, of Barnestable, [and] Alis, his wyfe, for fornicacion before marriage, is censured, the said John to be whipt, and Alis, his wyfe, to sit in the stocks whilst her husband is in whipping; which was accordingly executed.

October 27, 1685

Hannah Bonny conuict [convicted] for fornication with John Michell, [and] also with Nimrod, negro, [and] haueing a bastard child by said Nimrod, is sentanced to be well whipt.

October 27, 1685

Nimrod, negrow, conuict [convicted] for fornication with Hannah Bonny, is sentanced to be seuerely whipt, [and] that said Nimrod pay 18 pence per weeke to said Bonny towards the maintainance of said child for a year, if it liue soe long; [and] if he, or his master in his behalfe, neglect to pay the same, the said negro to be putt out to seruice by the Deputy Gouernor soe long time, or from time to time, soe as to procure the same.

READING AND DISCUSSION QUESTIONS

1. What can you infer from these records of court proceedings about the system of values these communities were attempting to uphold? Why do you think these infractions worried them?

2. In the various cases, do you see similarities or differences in punishment for men and women and even among women? What might account for any differences you see?
3. What do the cases involving Mary Mendame and Hannah Bonny reveal about the population of colonial New England?

2-3 | English Planters in the New World

CAREL ALLARD, *English Quakers Planting Tobacco on Barbados* (1680)

Carel Allard was an engraver from a prominent Amsterdam publishing family, and this image comes from a 1680 book entitled *The Towns and Costumes of the Inhabited World*. It depicts a Quaker couple in an idealized Barbados landscape cultivating tobacco, a lucrative New World commodity much favored in England. At the time, Quakers faced persecution in England for their beliefs, so many were shipped to Barbados to work on plantations. Others arrived as missionaries and planters hoping to take part in the growing transatlantic trade. Though many initially participated in the slave trade, Quaker leaders were beginning to condemn slavery.

AKG images/British Library

READING AND DISCUSSION QUESTIONS

1. What does this image reveal about the dynamics of the transatlantic trade during the seventeenth century?
2. Identify the various figures in the image and describe the setting. What is the artist suggesting about New World labor and economy?

2-4 | Maryland Protects Religious Belief *Maryland Act of Religious Toleration* (1649)

We sometimes romanticize America's founding as having been driven by a desire for religious liberty. As Anne Hutchinson and Roger Williams discovered when they were banished from Massachusetts Bay colony, however, religious toleration went only so far. New England Puritans, for example, prized consensus and they tried to enforce orthodox religious views and practices. There was greater tolerance in the mid-Atlantic colonies whose populations were more heterogeneous. There, no single religious denomination could dominate the others so most people existed, however uneasily, with the religious pluralism that characterized those colonies. Remarkably, in Maryland, toleration became a matter of law. The Maryland Assembly passed the 1649 Toleration Act, which guaranteed religious freedom to all Christians in the colony. This was important to the colony's many Catholics, who feared persecution from the growing presence of Protestants. Protestants had recently threatened the power of the Catholic proprietor Cecilius Calvert, Lord Baltimore, and Calvert urged passage of the Toleration Act just months after the Catholic-sympathizing Charles I of England was beheaded.

Forasmuch as in a well governed and [Christian] Com[m]on Wea[l]th matters concerning Religion and the honor of God ought in the first place to bee taken, into serious consideracon and endeavoured to bee settled. Be it therefore ordered and enacted by the Right [Honorable] Cecilius Lord Baron of Baltemore absolute Lord and Proprietary of this Province with the advise and consent of this Generall Assembly. That whatsoever p[er]son or p[er]sons within this Province and the Islands thereunto belonging shall from henceforth blaspheme God, that is Curse him, or deny our Saviour Jesus Christ to bee the sonne of God, or shall deny the holy Trinity the father sonne and holy Ghost, or the Godhead of any of the said Three p[er]sons of the Trinity or the Unity of the Godhead, or shall use or utter any reproachfull Speeches, words or language concerning the said Holy Trinity, or any of the said three p[er]sons thereof, shalbe punished with death and confiscaton or forfeiture of all his or her lands and goods to the Lord Proprietary and his heires. And bee it also Enacted by the Authority and with the advise and assent aforesaid. That whatsoever p[er]son or p[er]sons shall from henceforth use or utter any reproachfull words or Speeches concerning the blessed Virgin Mary the Mother of our Saviour or the holy Apostles or Evangelists or any of them shall in such case for the first

Proceedings and Acts of the General Assembly of Maryland, ed. William Hand Browne (Baltimore: Maryland Historical Society, 1883), 244–247.

offence forfeit to the said Lord Proprietary and his heirs Lords and Proprietaries of this Province the sume of five pound Sterling or the value thereof to be Levyed on the goods and chattells of every such p[er]son soe offending, but in case such Offender or Offenders, shall not then have goods and chattells sufficient for the satisfyeing of such forfeiture, or that the same bee not otherwise speedily satisfyed that then such Offender or Offenders shalbe publiquely whipt and bee ymprisoned during the pleasure of the Lord Proprietary or the [Lieutenant] or cheife Governor of this Province for the time being. And that every such Offender or Offenders for every second offence shall forfeit tenne pound sterling or the value thereof to bee levyed as aforesaid, or in case such offender or Offenders shall not then have goods and chattells within this Province sufficient for that purpose then to bee publiquely and severely whipt and imprisoned as before is expressed. And that every p[er]son or p[er]sons before mentioned offending herein the third time, shall for such third Offence forfeit all his lands and Goods and bee for ever banished and expelled out of this Province. And be it also further Enacted by the same authority advise and assent that whatsoever p[er]son or p[er]sons shall from henceforth uppon any occasion of Offence or otherwise in a reproachful manner or Way declare call or denominate any p[er]son or p[er]sons whatsoever inhabiting residing traffiqueing trading or comerceing within this Province or within any the Ports, Harbors, Creeks or Havens to the same belonging an heritick, Scismatick, Idolator, puritan, Independant, Prespiterian popish prest, Jesuite, Jesuited papist, Lutheran, Calvenist, Anabaptist, Brownist, Antinomian, Barrowist, Roundhead, Sep[ar]atist, or any other name or terme in a reproachfull manner relating to matter of Religion shall for every such Offence forfeit and loose the some [of] tenne shillings sterling or the value thereof to bee levyed on the goods and chattells of every such Offender and Offenders, the one half thereof to be forfeited and paid unto the person and persons of whom such reproachfull words are or shalbe spoken or uttered, and the other half thereof to the Lord Proprietary and his heires Lords and Proprietaries of this Province[.] But if such p[er]son or p[er]sons who shall at any time utter or speake any such reproachfull words or Language shall not have Goods or Chattells sufficient and overt within this Province to bee taken to satisfie the penalty aforesaid or that the same bee not otherwise speedily satisfyed, that then the p[er]son or p[er]sons soe offending shalbe publickly whipt, and shall suffer imprisonmt without baile or maineprise untill he shee or they respectively shall satisfy the party soe offended or greived by such reproachfull Language by asking him or her respectively forgivenes publiquely for such his Offence before the Magistrate or cheife Officer or Officers of the Towne or place where such Offence shalbe given. And be it further likewise Enacted by the Authority and consent aforesaid That every person and persons within this Province that shall at any time hereafter p[ro]phane the Sabbath or Lords day called Sunday by frequent swearing, drunkennes or by any uncivill or disorderly recreacon, or by working on that day when absolute necessity doth not require it shall for every such first offence forfeit 2s. 6d sterling or the value thereof, and for the second offence 5s sterling or the value thereof, and for the third offence and soe for every time he shall offend in like manner afterwards 10s sterling or the value thereof. And in case such offender and offenders shall not have sufficient goods or chattells within this Province to satisfy any of the said Penalties respectively hereby imposed for prophaning the Sabbath or Lords day called Sunday as aforesaid, That in Every such case the [party] soe offending shall for the first and second offence in that kinde be imprisoned till hee or shee shall publickly in open Court before the cheife Commander Judge or Magistrate, of that County Towne or precinct where such offence shalbe committed acknowledg the Scandall and offence he hath in that respect given against God and the good and civill Governemt. of this Province And for the third offence and for every time after shall also bee publickly whipt. And whereas the inforceing of the conscience in matters of Religion hath frequently fallen out to be of dangerous Consequence in those commonwealthes where it hath been practised, And for the more quiett and peaceable governemt. of this Province, and the better to [preserve] mutuall Love and amity amongst the Inhabitants thereof. Be it Therefore also by the Lo: Proprietary with the advise and consent of this Assembly Ordeyned & enacted (except as in this [present] Act is before Declared and sett forth) that noe person or p[er]sons whatsoever within this Province, or the Islands, Ports, Harbors, Creekes, or havens thereunto belonging professing to beleive in Jesus Christ, shall from henceforth bee any waies troubled, Molested or discountenanced for or in respect of his or her religion nor in the free exercise thereof within this Province or the Islands thereunto belonging nor any way compelled to the beleife or exercise of any other Religion against his or her consent, soe as they be not unfaithfull to the Lord Proprietary, or molest or conspire against the civill Governemt. established or to bee established in this Province under him or his heires. And that all & every p[er]son and p[er]sons that shall presume Contrary to this Act and the true intent and meaning thereof directly or indirectly either in person or estate willfully to wrong disturbe trouble or molest any person whatsoever within this Province professing to beleive in Jesus Christ for or in respect of his or her religion or the free exercise thereof within this Province other than is provided for in this Act that such p[er]son or p[er]sons soe offending, shalbe compelled to pay trebble damages to the party soe wronged or molested, and for every such offence shall also forfeit 20s sterling in money or the value thereof, half thereof for the use of the Lo: Proprietary, and his heires Lords and Proprietaries of this Province, and the other half for the use of the party soe wronged or molested as aforesaid, Or if the p[ar]tie soe offending as aforesaid shall refuse or bee unable to recompense the party soe wronged, or to satisfy such fyne or forfeiture, then such Offender shalbe severely punished by publick whipping & imprisonmt during the pleasure of the Lord Proprietary, or his [Lieutenant] or cheife Governor of this Province for the tyme being without baile or maineprise[.] And bee it further alsoe Enacted by the authority and consent aforesaid That the Sheriff or other Officer or Officers from time to time to bee appointed & authorized for that purpose, of the County Towne or precinct where every particular offence in this p[re]sent Act conteyned shall happen at any time to bee comitted and whereuppon there is hereby a forfeiture fyne or penalty imposed shall from time to time distraine and seise the goods and estate of every such p[er]son soe offending as aforesaid against this p[re]sent Act or any p[ar]t thereof, and sell the same or any part thereof for the full satisfaccon of such forfeiture, fine, or penalty as aforesaid, Restoring unto the p[ar]tie soe offending the Remainder or overplus of the said goods or estate after such satisfaccon soe made as aforesaid[.]

The freemen have assented.

READING AND DISCUSSION QUESTIONS

1. What might Lord Baltimore and the Maryland Assembly have been trying to accomplish with their passage of the Toleration Act?
2. What might the Toleration Act reveal to us about the state of affairs in the colony at the time?
3. How did the events taking place in England at that time affect the decisions being made in the colonies?

2-5 | Slave Labor on the Rise

EDMUND WHITE, *Letter to Joseph Morton* (1687)

The colonies participated in a transatlantic economy regulated by a series of Navigation Acts passed by the English Parliament in the seventeenth century. While sugar, rice, and tobacco were exported to England, African slaves were imported to England's North American colonies in increasing numbers by the end of the century. Colonists experimented with different forms of labor, including using white indentured servants, before embracing a race-based slave-labor agricultural system in the Americas. In the letter reproduced here, Edmund White writes from London to South Carolina governor Joseph Morton in February 1687 expressing the advantages of "negroes" over white servants.

Sir. . . .

If anything be recoverable there my Lord Cardross told me negroes were more desirable tha[n] English servants [and] such you may have enough of from Barbadoes: or if you desire to be concerned in a small vessel from hence to Ginny [and] your port the Royall Comp[any] now gives leave uppon the allowance of 20 pr. cent or thereabouts for any vessell to trade to any of their ports [and] they furnish the cargo cheaper than others can buy [and] so the East India Comp[any] permitts ships to trade to this coast: allowing the Comp[any]

"Letter to Joseph Morton (1687)." From *The South Carolina Historical and Genealogical Magazine*, Vol. XXX, January 1929. Used by permission of the South Carolina Historical Society.

such a certain profit. Now if you [and] Mr. Grimball or any other would joyne in ordering their corresponds here to fitt out a small vessell to the byte or other port on the Coast of Ginny I understand how to manage it to the best advantage. I have twice lett ships to the Royall Comp[any] but their termes are so hard that they make the owner tak out their freight [1/3] in money [and 2/3rds] in negroes at 15 lb pr head if to Barbadoes; [and] 16 lb pr. head for other ports. Now at Barbadoes I sold the negroes but for 11 lb a head bills of exc. [and] at Nevis for 3000 lb sugr a head but the accompt is not yet cleared [and] it was A . . . er they arrived: so that losing 4 lb a head by the freight negroes there was loss by the ship [and] I gave over those voyages: If you approve not of this way or can have none to joyne [with] you, then write to Coll John Johnson at Barbados that was Major Johnson (for I understand by his son in law Capt Mercer that resides here, that he is much at the bridge though he hath a plantation) that he would do you the kindness, when any bargaine of negroes is to be had, he would buy them for you and keep them upon his plantation till he can send them you [and] this he can doe with much care [and] the negroes will be the better after they have been ashore for sometime an their work will be worth their keeping [and] he may draw upon me [and] I doubt not but he will buy of masters of ships for bills of exchange at 11 or 12 lb a head [and] that will certainly be the most profitable for you [and] you need not trouble your friends for servants from hence: you still fill up yr letters with the bad conditions of the Milkmayd I sent. I shall endeavor the next ship to gett another having lately heard of one that was willing to goe upon wages, and the same party I hope will supply me when I want one. But as to all other serv[ants] let [your] negroes be taught to be smiths shoemakers [and] carpenters [and] bricklayers: they are capable of learning anything [and] I find when they are kindly used [and] have their belly full of victualls and clothes, they are the truest servants: one Coll. Bach that came lately from Jamaica had 100 slaves upon his plantation that prayed God to bless him when he came away [and] prayed him not to dispose of the plantation for they would rather dye than serve another M[aste]r: [and] there was an instance of negroes that did hang themselves on a tree as soon as they heard the plantation was sold: so my friend promised he would not sell [and] since he is dead his widow keeps it during her lyfe; such a love this was between Mr and Mrs [and] slaves: [and] I have often thought: If they could be brought to the knowledge of Christ what a happiness it would be that they came out of their owne country.

READING AND DISCUSSION QUESTIONS

1. What does this letter reveal about the extent of the slave trade by the end of the seventeenth century?
2. What role did Barbados play in the American slave trade?
3. What can you infer from the letter about the author's attitude toward Africans? How is his point of view shaped by his assumptions about race?

2-6 | Spreading the Gospel Among the Iroquois

REV. FATHER LOUIS CELLOT, *Letter to Father François Le Mercier* (1656)

The French Jesuit mission to the Hurons and Iroquois in "New France," the region of Quebec between the Great Lakes and the St. Lawrence River, provides another example of cultural conflict and adaptation. By the mid-seventeenth century, the Jesuits had achieved some success and some fatal failures in their efforts to spread the Christian faith among North American tribes. They also developed an understanding and appreciation for native cultures. Jesuits sent letters, like this one from 1656, to report the wonder of working for God among the "Savages," but they also show the extent to which native and European cultures responded to each other.

[M]Y REVEREND FATHER,

Pax Christi.

After addressing all our vows to Heaven to implore its aid we have recourse to your Reverence to ask your holy blessing, before embarking on the most dangerous and likewise the most glorious enterprise that can be undertaken in this country. We are on the eve of our departure to go and collect what remains of the blood of the Son of God among those peoples, where we have had the happiness of shedding our own and of carrying the light of the Faith to them, although their sole design hitherto has been to extinguish it; that is, we go to establish ourselves among the Iroquois. I think that, in mentioning those Barbarians, I say all that can be said; for their name alone shows the risk which we run and the glory which will accrue to God from the execution of that design.

We are not ignorant of the fact that these Savages have eaten us with relish and have drunk with pleasure the blood of the Fathers of our Society; that their hands and their lips are still wet with it, and that the fires in which they roasted their limbs are not yet quite extinguished. We have not forgotten the conflagrations that they have kindled to consume our houses, and the cruelty that they have practiced on our bodies, which still bear its marks. We know that their whole policy consists in knowing well how to plot treachery, and to conceal all their plans for it; that no Nero or Diocletian ever declared himself so strongly against the Christians as these bloodthirsty Savages have done against us; and that the Faith would at the present moment be received among many Infidel Nations, had they not surpassed in rage and fury the greatest persecutors of Jesus Christ. We have not yet been able to dry the tears in which, for six years, our eyes have been bathed when we cast them upon the flourishing condition of the Huron Church before those Oppressors had sapped its foundations,

The Jesuit Relations and Allied Documents: Travels and Explorations of the Jesuit Missionaries in New France, 1610–1791, vol. 44, ed. Reuben Gold Thwaites (Cleveland: The Burrows Brothers, 1898), 52–65.

making Martyrs of its Pastors, and Saints of most of its members; and leaving but a very pitiful remnant, who have sought refuge under the wing of the French, the only asylum left them in their misfortune. We see that, ever since that first havoc, they have always pushed on their conquests, and have made themselves so redoubtable in this country that everything gives way before their arms. They still have strength in their hands, and perhaps treachery in their hearts; and our allies are so weakened and so reduced in numbers, that barely enough remain to preserve the names of many very populous and very important nations. Notwithstanding all that, we consider ourselves so convinced of the will of God—who, of old, turned his greatest persecutors into his most illustrious Apostles—that we have no doubt that, at the present time, he opens the door to his Preachers, that they might go and plant the faith in the very heart of his enemies, triumph over their barbarity, change those Wolves and Tigers into Lambs, and bring them into the fold of Jesus Christ.

It is not without reason that we conceive such bright hopes. The manifestations of Divine providence and the means employed by its guidance, which has so well directed matters to the point at which they have now arrived, compel us to admit that we cannot, without extreme cowardice, disappoint the expectations that God has caused to arise for us where we least expected them. Had we not observed the finger of God at the outset and in the course of this undertaking, we would have mistrusted our own zeal, and have feared that we were acting with more fervor than prudence; for all human appearances seem to contend against our resolution. But God acts so manifestly, in the whole of this matter, that no one can doubt that it is a work of his hand, the execution and the glory whereof belong solely to him. For what power other than his could force these peoples, inflated with pride on account of their victories, not only to come and seek a peace with us of which they seemed to have no need, but also to place themselves unarmed in our hands, and throw themselves at our feet, begging us to accept them as our friends, when we were so weak that we could no longer withstand them as enemies? They had but to continue, to massacre the remainder of the French Colony, for they met with hardly any resistance either from the French or from the savages, our Confederates; and, nevertheless, for over three years, they incessantly sent presents and embassies to ingratiate themselves with us, and to solicit us to make peace. Old and young, women and children, place themselves at our mercy; they enter our forts; they act confidently with us, and spare no effort to open their hearts to us, and to make us read therein that all their solicitations are as sincere as they are pressing.

They are not content with coming to us, but for a long time they invite us to go to them, and offer us the finest land that they have, and that is to be found in this New world. Neither the necessities of trade nor the hopes of our protection induce them to do all that; for they have hitherto had and still enjoy both those things with the Dutch, much more advantageously than they can ever hope to do with the French. But it is the act of God; he has, doubtless, lent an ear to the blood of the Martyrs, which is the seed of Christians, and which now causes them to spring up in this land that was watered by it. For, not only have those greatest enemies of the Faith given presents to declare that they wish to embrace it; not only have they asked for Preachers to instruct them, and publicly professed in open Council that they were Believers; but the Fathers of our Society who have passed the last winter with them have also observed so many good dispositions for the planting of a new Church among them, not only from the miraculous things that have happened there, as Your Reverence will see in the Journal, but also from the numerous first-fruits already consecrated to heaven, that we depart, with all confidence, to cause the name of Jesus Christ to resound in those lands where the Devil has always been master from the beginning of the world.

If those peoples are so anxious to have us in their country, we feel no less eagerness to leave ours, and to go among them. And this is another proof of the will of God, who disposes all things so opportunely that I find myself equally and agreeably importuned from two very different directions, on one side, by the Iroquois, who urge us; on the other, by our Fathers and Brethren, who eagerly ask to be allowed to join the party. The desire of the former and the zeal of the latter compel me to satisfy them all; and, although the former have hitherto manifested nothing but cruelty, the latter feel only an affection for them, which makes them hold life cheap, and lavish it generously, for the salvation of those who have so often sought to put them to death. . . .

Such is the state of affairs; and such are the effects of so many prayers, mortifications, fasts, alms, and good works, which have been performed in both Frances, and have caused so great a design to be conceived. But, as the undertaking is arduous and difficult of execution, we beg those pious Souls to continue their fervor, so that God may continue to pour his blessings on this country. And, for my part, I beg Your Reverence and all our Fathers and Brethren of your Province to lift your hands to heaven, while we go to declare war against Infidelity, and to fight the devil in the very heart of his country, I am, with all possible respect and submission,

Your Reverence's
Very humble and very obedient servant in Our Lord,
From Montréal, this FRANÇOIS LE MERCIER,
6th of June, 1656

READING AND DISCUSSION QUESTIONS

1. What was the author of this letter trying to accomplish?
2. How does the language of the letter reveal cultural assumptions Jesuit missionaries made about native peoples and culture?
3. What evidence does this letter provide about Jesuit success among the Iroquois?

▪ COMPARATIVE QUESTIONS ▪

1. What similarities and differences in religious practice do you see in the North American colonies?
2. What do the sources reveal about Europeans' treatment of their non-European neighbors in North America?
3. According to these sources, what were the major challenges facing Europeans settling the North American colonies?
4. To what extent did affairs in Europe affect daily life in the colonies?

PART 1

DOCUMENT SET

Developing Patterns of Atlantic World Exchange

1491–1700

CHAPTER 1
Colliding Worlds, 1491–1600

CHAPTER 2
American Experiments, 1521–1700

Imagine the sensation coursing through an Iroquois's body as he spied a European for the first time. What thrill of excitement, wonder, or terror must have seized him, transfixed by a foreboding of change and conflict? The early history of America is very much the story of such encounters. In the Atlantic world during the era of colonization, three richly diverse civilizations (Europeans, Native Americans, and Africans) were caught up in an intense exchange of goods, peoples, diseases, and ideas that would transform the lives of all involved and shape the formation of North American colonial societies.

The emerging patterns of exchange resulted in a cultural cross-fertilization as the three groups influenced and were influenced by contact with each other. Europeans and Native Americans traded foods, goods, and cultural assumptions that impacted the diets, trade networks, and worldviews of each. Enslaved Africans, brought to the Americas against their will, adapted their complex cultural traditions to New World experiences, in turn influencing both Europeans and Native Americans. The interactions left none unaffected, but the benefits were unequally felt, as enslaved Africans knew immediately and as Native Americans discovered when imported European germs decimated their numbers. The colonial societies that arose on the North American continent were forged by this dynamic exchange.

P1-1 | Spanish Conquistadors Arrive in Mexico
Drawing from the Codex Florentino (c. 1540)

This image, drawn by a native artist, illustrates the arrival in Mexico of Spanish conquistadors. This was one of two thousand drawings collected in what is known as the Codex Florentine, a twelve-volume book written during the mid-sixteenth century by Bernardino de Sahagun, a Spanish-born Franciscan friar who spent most of his life in Mexico, teaching and attempting to Christianize the Aztecs. Sahagun became fluent in the Aztec language and studied its culture and society. Native artists' images, such as this one, accompanied Sahagun's text and they narrate the history of the Aztecs and illuminate their religious practices, work, and leisure activities. This image is especially interesting as it records the arrival of cattle, horses, and pigs, animals not native to the Americas. It also reflects a more European pictorial style. The use of linear perspective and shading, for example, may indicate European influence on Aztec artists.

READING AND DISCUSSION QUESTIONS

1. Examine the image's details. What aspects of the Spanish arrival caught the attention of the Aztec artist? Why do you think the artist chose to record those details? Why, for instance, did the artist foreground the livestock?

Granger

2. In what way does this image reveal the extent of the cultural contact and exchange between native Aztecs and European colonists?
3. How might a historian use this image to discuss the European interest in Native American culture? What can the historian say about native attitudes of Spanish colonization?

P1-2 | Florida Natives Welcome the Returning French

THEODORE DE BRY, *The Natives of Florida Worship the Column Erected by Commander on His First Voyage* (1591)

Unlike the image of the Spanish arrival in Mexico in the preceding source, this engraving is of European origin—from the pen of Theodore de Bry (1528–1598), who never set foot himself in the New World—so the story it tells privileges the European perspective. Here we see the Timucua, a Native American people in what is now north Florida, welcoming the return of a group of French explorers. An earlier French explorer had erected the column as a monument to the French king, but the native people are shown worshipping it as if it were a god. The column has been wreathed with native garlands, and the foreground showcases North American foodstuffs offered to the visiting Europeans.

Construction of the first Christian church in San Miguel de Piura, and the battle of Hernando de Soto with the Indians, 1726 (engraving)/Spanish School (18th century)/INDEX Fototeca /Biblioteca Universidad, Barcelona, Spain/Bridgeman Images

READING AND DISCUSSION QUESTIONS

1. What evidence of cultural exchange between Native Americans and Europeans can you see in this illustration? What can you discern about how the artist may have valued that exchange?
2. Who do you think was the audience for this image, and what effect do you imagine the artist hoped to have on those viewing it?

P1-3 | A European Encounters the Algonquin Indians

THOMAS MORTON, *Manners and Customs of the Indians (of New England)* (1637)

While many colonists disparaged Native Americans, Thomas Morton stands out for the esteem with which he held the Algonquin people. Morton migrated to New England in 1622 and established trade with local native populations, a move that angered Puritans who assumed his relationships were tinged with immorality and godlessness. In *New English Canaan* (1637), Morton describes the exchange of native and European commodities and speculates on the advantages this trade might bring.

Of Their Traffic and Trade With One Another: Although these people have not the use of navigation, whereby they may traffic as other nations, that are civilized, use to do, yet do they barter for such commodities as they have, and have a kind of beads instead of money, to buy withal such things as they want, which they call Wampampeak; and it is of two sorts, the one is white, the other is of a violet color. These are made of the shells of fish. The white with them is as silver with us; the other as our gold; and for these beads they buy and sell, not only amongst themselves, but even with us. We have used to sell any of our commodities for this Wampampeak, because we know we can have beaver again of them for it: and these beads are current in all the parts of New England, from one end of the coast to the other.

And although some have endeavored by example to have the like made of the same kind of shells, yet none have ever, as yet, attained to any perfection in the composure of them, but that the savages have found a great difference to be in the one and the other; and have known the counterfeit beads from those of their own making; and have, and do slight them. The skins of beasts are sold and bartered, to such people as have none of the same kind in the parts where they live. Likewise they have earthen pots of divers [many] sizes, from a quart to a gallon, two or three to boil their victuals in; very strong, though they be thin like our iron pots. They have dainty wooden bowls of maple, of high price amongst them; and these are dispersed by bartering one

The Library of Original Sources, vol. 5, ed. Oliver J. Thatcher (Milwaukee: University Research Extension Co., 1907), 360–377.

with the other, and are but in certain parts of the country made, where the several trades are appropriated to the inhabitants of those parts only...

Of Their Magazines or Store Houses: These people are not without providence, though they be uncivilized, but are careful to preserve food in store against winter; which is the corn that they labor and dress in the summer. And, although they eat freely of it, while it is growing, yet have they a care to keep a convenient portion thereof to relieve them in the dead of winter (like to the ant and the bee), which they put under ground. Their barns are holes made in the earth, that will hold a hogshead [a large cask] of corn a piece in them. In these (when their corn is out of the husk and well dried) they lay their store in great baskets (which they make of bark) with mats under, about the sides, and on the top; and putting it into the place made for it, they cover it with earth; and in this manner it is preserved from destruction or putrefaction; to be used in case of necessity, and not else.

And I am persuaded, that if they knew the benefit of salt (as they may in time), and the means to make salt meat fresh again, they would endeavor to preserve fish for winter, as well as corn; and that if anything bring them to civility, it will be the use of salt, to have food in store, which is a chief benefit in a civilized commonwealth. These people have begun already to incline to the use of salt. Many of them would beg salt of me to carry home with them, that had frequented our homes and had been acquainted with our salt meats; and salt I willingly gave them, although I sold them all things else, only because they should be delighted with the use thereof, and think it a commodity of no value in itself, although the benefit was great that might be had by the use of it. . . .

Of their Acknowledgement of the Creation, and Immortality of the Soul: Although these savages are to be found without religion, law and king . . . yet are they not altogether without the knowledge of God (historically); for they have it amongst them by tradition that God made one man and one woman, bade them live together and get children, kill deer, beasts, birds, fish and fowl, and what they would at their pleasure; and that their posterity was full of evil, and made God so angry that he let in the sea upon them, and drowned the greatest part of them, that were naughty men (the Lord destroyed so); and they went to Sanaconquam, who feeds upon them (pointing to the center of the earth, where they imagine is the habitation of the devil); the other (which were not destroyed) increased the world, and when they died (because they were good) went to the house of Kytan, pointing to the setting of the sun; where they eat all manner of dainties, and never take pains (as now) to provide it. Kytan makes provision (they say) and saves them labor; and there they shall live with him forever, void of care. And they are persuaded that Kytan is he that makes corn grow, trees grow, and all manner of fruits.

And that we that use the book of common prayer do it to declare to them, that cannot read, what Kytan has commanded us, and that we do pray to him with the help of that book; and do make so much account of it, that a savage (who had lived in my house before he had taken a wife, by whom he had children) made this request to me (knowing that I always used him with much more respect than others), that I would let his son be brought up in my house, that he might be taught to read in that book; which request of his I granted; and he was a very joyful man to think that his son should thereby (as he said) become an Englishman; and then he would be a good man. I asked him who was a good man; his answer was, he that would not lie, nor steal.

READING AND DISCUSSION QUESTIONS

1. What conclusion can you draw from Morton's account about the importance of trade for both Native Americans and European colonists? What positive and negative effects does he describe?
2. What can you infer from the document about Morton's view of the long-term relationship between Algonquins and their European-colonist neighbors and the importance of trade to that relationship? How do you think Morton would interpret New England's subsequent history with Native Americans?
3. Can you identify any evidence of remaining "cultural superiority" in Morton's account of Algonquin culture?

P1-4 | The Trade in Goods and Slaves

THOMAS PHILLIPS, *A Journal of a Voyage Made in the* Hannibal (1693–1694)

This firsthand account of the African slave trade reveals the highly sophisticated cross-Atlantic network in commodity exchange that had developed by the end of the seventeenth century. Thomas Phillips, commander of the English slave ship *Hannibal*, brought European-made products to trade with African kings and chiefs in exchange for slaves, whom he then transported to St. Thomas and Barbados for sale primarily to plantation owners cultivating sugar, a prized commodity in Europe. This excerpt provides interesting descriptions of the process of trading commodities, including enslaved people, and the harrowing voyage across the Atlantic.

May the 21st. This morning I went ashore at Whidaw[1], accompany'd by my doctor and purser, Mr. Clay, the present Capt. of the East-India Merchant, his doctor and purser, and about a dozen of our seamen for our guard, arm'd, in order here to reside till we could purchase 1300 negro slaves, which was the number we both wanted, to compleat 700 for the Hannibal, and 650 for the

Documents Illustrative of the History of the Slave Trade to America, vol. 1, 1441–1700, ed. Elizabeth Donnan (Buffalo: William S. Hein & Co., 2002), 397–403, 408–410.

[1]**Whidaw**: A kingdom along the west coast of Africa in present day Benin noted for its extensive trade in slaves.

East-India Merchant, according to our agreement in our charter-parties with the royal African company; in procuring which quantity of slaves we spent about nine weeks. . . .

As soon as the king understood of our landing, he sent two of his cappasheirs[2], or noblemen, to compliment us at our factory[3], where we design'd to continue, that night . . .

We returned him [the king] thanks by his interpreter, and assur'd him how great affection our masters, the royal African company of England, bore to him, for his civility and fair and just dealings with their captains; . . . He answer'd that the African company was a very good brave man; that he lov'd him; that we should be fairly dealt with, and not impos'd upon; But he did not prove as good as his word; nor indeed (tho' his cappasheirs shew him so much respect) dare he do any thing but what they please . . . so after having examin'd us about our cargoe, what sort of goods we had, and what quantity of slaves we wanted, etc., we took our leaves and return'd to the factory, having promised to come in the morning to make our palavera, or agreement, with him about prices, how much of each of our goods for a slave.

According to promise we attended his majesty with samples of our goods, and made our agreement about the prices, tho' not without much difficulty; he and his cappasheirs exacted very high, but at length we concluded as per the latter end; . . .

When we were at the trunk, the king's slaves, if he had any, were the first offer'd to sale, which the cappasheirs would be very urgent with us to buy, and would in a manner force us to it ere they would shew us any other . . . tho' as I observ'd they were generally the worst slaves in the trunk, and we paid more for them than any others, which we could not remedy, it being one of his majesty's prerogatives: then the cappasheirs each brought out his slaves according to his degree and quality, the greatest first, etc. and our surgeon examin'd them well in all kinds, to see that they were sound wind and limb, making them jump, stretch out their arms swiftly, looking in their mouths to judge of their age; for the cappasheirs are so cunning, that they shave them all close before we see them, so that let them be never so old we can see no grey hairs in their heads or beards; and then having liquor'd them well and sleek with palm oil, 'tis no easy matter to know an old one from a middle-age one, but by the teeths decay; but our greatest care of all is to buy none that are pox'd, lest they should infect the rest aboard. . . .

When we had selected from the rest such as we liked, we agreed in what goods to pay for them, the prices being already stated before the king, how much of each sort of merchandize we were to give for a man, woman, and child, which gave us much ease, and saved abundance of disputes and wranglings; then we mark'd the slaves we had bought in the breast, or shoulder, with a hot

[2]**Cappasheirs**: Agents appointed by African chiefs or kings who were responsible for procuring slaves for trade.

[3]**Factory**: Permanent slave trading posts established along the African coast.

3. The passage cutteth not nere the trade of any prince, nor nere any of their contries or territories, and is a safe passage, and not easie to be annoyed by prince or potentate whatsoever.

4. The passage is to be perfourmed at all times of the yere, and in that respecte passeth our trades in the Levant Seas within the Straites of Juberalter, and the trades in the seas within the Kinge of Denmarkes Straite, and the trades to the portes of Norwey and of Russia, &c.; for as in the south weste Straite there is no passage in somer by lacke of windes, so within the other places there is no passage in winter by yse [ice] and extreme colde.

5. And where England nowe for certen hundreth yeres last passed, by the peculiar comoditie of wolles, and of later yeres by clothinge of the same, hath raised it selfe from meaner state to greater wealthe and moche higher honour, mighte, and power then before, to the equallinge of the princes of the same to the greatest potentates of this parte of the worlde; it cometh nowe so to passe, that by the greate endevour of the increase of the trade of wolles in Spaine and in the West Indies, nowe daily more and more multiplienge, that the wolles of England, and the clothe made of the same, will become base, and every day more base then other; which, prudently weyed, [yet] behoveth this realme, [if] it meane not to returne to former olde meanes and basenes, but to stande in present and late former honour, glorye, and force, and not negligently and sleepingly to slyde into beggery, to foresee and to plante at Norumbega or some like place, were it not for any thing els but for the hope of the vent of our woll indraped [meaning woven wool], the principall and in effecte the onely enrichinge contynueinge naturall comoditie of this realme. And effectually pursueinge that course, wee shall not onely finde on that tracte of lande, and especially in that firme northwarde (to whome warme clothe shalbe righte wellcome), an ample vente, but also shall, from the north side of that firme, finde oute knowen and unknowen ilandes and domynions replenished with people that may fully vent the aboundaunce of that our comoditie, that els will in fewe yeres waxe of none or of small value by forreine aboundaunce, &c.; so as by this enterprice wee shall shonne the ymmynent mischefe hanginge over our heades, that els muste nedes fall upon the realme, without breache of peace or sworde drawen againste this realme by any forreine state; and not offer our auncient riches to scornefull neighboures at home, nor sell the same in effecte for nothinge, as wee shall shortly, if presently it be not provaided for. The increase of the wolles of Spaine and America is of highe pollicie, with greate desire of our overthrowe, endevoured; and the goodnes of the forren wolles our people will not enter into the consideration of, nor will not beleve aughte, they be so sotted with opinion of their owne; and, yf it be not foresene and some such place of vent provided, farewell the goodd state of all degrees in this realme.

6. This enterprise may staye the Spanishe Kinge from flowinge over all the face of that waste firme of America, yf wee seate and plante there in time. . . . And England possessinge the purposed place of plantinge, her Majestie may, by the benefete of the seate, havinge wonne goodd and royall havens,

have plentie of excellent trees for mastes, of goodly timber to builde shippes and to make greate navies, of pitche, tarr, hempe, and all thinges incident for a navie royall, and that for no price, and withoute money or request. Howe easie a matter may yt be to this realme, swarminge at this day with valiant youthes, rustinge and hurtfull by lacke of employment, and havinge goodd makers of cable and of all sortes of cordage, and the best and moste connynge shipwrights of the worlde, to be lordes of all those sees, and to spoile Phillipps Indian navye, and to deprive him of yerely passage of his treasure into Europe, and consequently to abate the pride of Spaine and of the supporter of the greate Antechriste of Rome, and to pull him downe in equallitie to his neighbour princes, and consequently to cutt of the common mischefes that come to all Europe by the peculiar aboundaunce of his Indian treasure, and thiss withoute difficultie.

7. This voyadge, albeit it may be accomplished by barke or smallest pynnesse for advise or for a necessitie, yet for the distaunce, for burden and gaine in trade, the marchant will not for profitts sake use it but by shippes of greate burden; so as this realme shall have by that meane shippes of greate burden and of greate strengthe for the defence of this realme, and for the defence of that newe seate, as nede shall require, and withall greate increase of perfecte seamen, which greate princes in time of warres wante, and which kinde of men are neither nourished in fewe daies nor in fewe yeres.

8. This newe navie of mightie newe stronge shippes, so in trade to that Norumbega and to the coastes there, shall never be subjecte to arreste of any prince or potentate, as the navie of this realme from time to time hath bene in the portes of thempire, in the portes of the Base Contries, in Spaine, Fraunce, Portingale, &c., in the tymes of Charles the Emperour, Fraunces the Frenche kinge, and others; but shall be alwayes free from that bitter mischeefe, withoute grefe or hazarde to the marchaunte or to the state, and so alwaies readie at the comaundement of the prince with mariners, artillory, armor, and munition, ready to offende and defende as shalbe required.

9. The greate masse of wealthe of the realme imbarqued in the marchantes shippes, caried oute in this newe course, shall not lightly, in so farr distant a course from the coaste of Europe, be driven by windes and tempestes into portes of any forren princes, as the Spanishe shippes of late yeres have bene into our portes of the Weste Contries, &c.; and so our marchantes in respecte of private state, and of the realme in respecte of a generall safetie from venture of losse, are by this voyadge oute of one greate mischefe.

10. No forren commoditie that comes into England comes withoute payment of custome once, twise, or thrise, before it come into the realme, and so all forren comodities become derer to the subjectes of this realme; and by this course to Norumbega forren princes customes are avoided; and the forren comodities cheapely purchased, they become cheape to the subjectes of England, to the common benefite of the people, and to the savinge of greate treasure in the realme; whereas nowe the realme becomethe poore by the purchasinge of forreine comodities in so greate a masse at so excessive prices.

11. At the firste traficque with the people of those partes, the subjectes of this realme for many yeres shall chaunge many cheape comodities of these partes for thinges of highe valor there not estemed; and this to the greate inrichinge of the realme, if common use faile not.

12. By the greate plentie of those regions the marchantes and their factors shall lye there cheape, buye and repaire their shippes cheape, and shall returne at pleasure withoute staye or restrainte of forreine prince; whereas upon staies and restraintes the marchaunte raiseth his chardge in sale over of his ware; and, buyenge his wares cheape, he may mainteine trade with smalle stocke, and withoute takinge upp money upon interest; and so he shalbe riche and not subjecte to many hazardes, but shalbe able to afforde the comodities for cheape prices to all subjectes of the realme.

13. By makinge of shippes and by preparinge of thinges for the same, by makinge of cables and cordage, by plantinge of vines and olive trees, and by makinge of wyne and oyle, by husbandrie, and by thousandes of thinges there to be done, infinite nombers of the Englishe nation may be set on worke, to the unburdenynge of the realme with many that nowe lyve chardgeable to the state at home.

14. If the sea coste serve for makinge of salte, and the inland for wine, oiles, oranges, lymons, figges, &c., and for makinge of yron, all which with moche more is hoped, withoute sworde drawen, wee shall cutt the combe of the Frenche, of the Spanishe, of the Portingale, and of enemies, and of doubtfull frendes, to the abatinge of their wealthe and force, and to the greater savinge of the wealthe of the realme.

15. The substaunces servinge, wee may oute of those partes receave the masse of wrought wares that now wee receave out of Fraunce, Flaunders, Germanye, &c.; and so wee may daunte the pride of some enemies of this realme, or at the leaste in parte purchase those wares, that nowe wee buye derely of the Frenche and Flemynge, better cheape; and in the ende, for the parte that this realme was wonte to receave, dryve them oute of trade to idlenes for the settinge of our people on worke.

16. Wee shall by plantinge there inlarge the glory of the gospell, and from England plante sincere relligion, and provide a safe and a sure place to receave people from all partes of the worlde that are forced to flee for the truthe of Gods worde.

17. If frontier warres there chaunce to aryse, and if thereupon wee shall fortifie, yt will occasion the trayninge upp of our youthe in the discipline of warr, and make a nomber fitt for the service of the warres and for the defence of our people there and at home.

18. The Spaniardes governe in the Indies with all pride and tyranie; and like as when people of contrarie nature at the sea enter into gallies, where men are tied as slaves, all yell and crye with one voice, *Liberta, liberta,* as desirous of libertie and freedome, so no doubte whensoever the Queene of England, a prince of such clemencie, shall seate upon that firme of America, and shalbe reported

throughe oute all that tracte to use the naturall people there with all humanitie, curtesie, and freedome, they will yelde themselves to her government, and revolte cleane from the Spaniarde, and specially when they shall understande that she hathe a noble navie, and that she aboundeth with a people moste valiaunte for theyr defence. . . . [H]er Majestie and her subjectes may bothe enjoye the treasure of the mynes of golde and silver, and the whole trade and all the gaine of the trade of marchandize, that nowe passeth thither by the Spaniardes onely hande, of all the comodities of Europe; which trade of marchandize onely were of it selfe suffycient (withoute the benefite of the riche myne) to inriche the subjectes, and by customes to fill her Majesties coffers to the full. And if it be highe pollicie to mayneteyne the poore people of this realme in worke, I dare affirme that if the poore people of England were five times so many as they be, yet all mighte be sett on worke in and by workinge lynnen, and suche other thinges of marchandize as the trade into the Indies dothe require.

19. The present shorte trades causeth the maryner to be cast of, and ofte to be idle, and so by povertie to fall to piracie. But this course to Norumbega beinge longer, and a contynuaunce of themploymente of the maryner, dothe kepe the maryner from ydlenes and from necessitie; and so it cutteth of the principal actions of piracie, and the rather because no riche praye for them to take cometh directly in their course or any thing nere their course.

20. Many men of excellent wittes and of divers singuler giftes, overthrowen by suertishippe, by sea, or by some folly of youthe, that are not able to live in England, may there be raised againe, and doe their contrie goodd service; and many nedefull uses there may (to greate purpose) require the savinge of greate nombers, that for trifles may otherwise be devoured by the gallowes.

21. Many souldiers and servitours, in the ende of the warres, that mighte be hurtfull to this realme, may there be unladen, to the common profite and quiet of this realme, and to our forreine benefite there, as they may be employed.

22. The frye of the wandringe beggars of England, that growe upp ydly, and hurtefull and burdenous to this realme, may there be unladen, better bredd upp, and may people waste contries to the home and forreine benefite, and to their owne more happy state.

23. If Englande crie oute and affirme, that there is so many in all trades that one cannot live for another, as in all places they doe, this Norumbega (if it be thoughte so goodd) offreth the remedie.

READING AND DISCUSSION QUESTIONS

1. What conclusions can you draw about European perceptions of North America's potential from Hakluyt's arguments in support of colonization?
2. To what extent do you think Hakluyt's sixteenth-century vision of colonization was realized during the seventeenth century? What aspects of the cultural exchange between Europeans, North American natives, and Africans did he fail to anticipate?

▪ COMPARATIVE QUESTIONS ▪

1. What do these sources reveal about the challenges facing the various cultures that collided in the early period of American colonial settlement?
2. Compare European assessments of Africans and Native Americans. What differences do you see in how Europeans described these two different groups of people? How, for example, do the attitudes displayed by Christopher Columbus (Document 1-3), Rev. Father Louis Cellot (Document 2-6), and Thomas Morton (Document P1-3) toward Native Americans differ from those expressed about Africans by Edmund White (Document 2-5) and Thomas Phillips (Document P1-4)?
3. What might you rank as the most historically significant effect of the cultural exchange between Europeans, Native Americans, and Africans during the period from the mid-fifteenth century to the end of the seventeenth century? In answering this question, what definition of "historically significant" helps you to evaluate the evidence?
4. To what extent did the patterns of exchange between Europeans, Africans, and Native Americans shape the development of the North American colonies?

3

The British Atlantic World

1607–1750

Though the English colonies in North America were on the periphery of empire, they were never fully independent of or insulated from the culture, commerce, or politics of the British Atlantic world. Colonists were linked by trade to the Atlantic economy. The ocean served as a highway for the exchange of goods and ideas. As Great Britain developed its Atlantic trade, the colonies became critical partners in the imperial trade networks. Colonists participated through their consumption of English and European goods and culture. One tragic consequence of economic expansion, however, was the increased use and reliance on slave labor, the effects of which are described in two of the sources included here. Great Britain's imperial ambitions also resulted in a series of military conflicts with its European neighbors that spread to the North American colonies. Unable to avoid warfare, some colonists developed strategic alliances with Native Americans. The willingness of Native Americans to ally with the colonists had less to do with friendly feelings toward the Americans and more with their recognition of the colonists' growing power on the continent.

Since the 1688 Glorious Revolution in England, which deposed the much-despised King James II, the British colonies in North America had entered into their maturity under the new limited monarchy of William and Mary. Several sources included here hint at the growing self-consciousness of North American colonists who increasingly viewed themselves as British subjects with rights that government was bound to respect. As British governance of the colonies began tightening by the middle of the eighteenth century, colonists and their colonial assemblies guarded their authority and resisted the encroachments from London.

3-1 | Bostonians Welcome the Glorious Revolution

At the Town-House in Boston: April 18th, 1689. A Letter to Sir Edmond Andros Knight (1689)

Following the 1660 restoration of the Stuart monarchy, relations between Massachusetts Bay and England deteriorated. James II revoked the colony's charter and instituted the Dominion of New England, with the wildly unpopular and authoritarian Sir Edmund Andros appointed governor in 1686. When news of James II's overthrow reached the colonies in April 1689, Bostonians mobilized to throw off Andros's regime. The text of the broadside (or poster) reprinted here took the form of an open letter to Governor Andros signed by a number of prominent men of the city. As a result of the colonial challenge to Andros's leadership, his government fell and colonists reasserted local representative government.

At the Townhouse in Boston

April 18th, 1689

Sir,

Our Selves as well as many others the Inhabitants of this Town and Place adjacent, being surprised with the Peoples sudden taking to Arms, in the first motion whereof we were wholly ignorant, are driven by the present Exigence and Necessity to acquaint your *Excellency*, that for the Quieting and Securing of the People Inhabiting this Countrey from the imminent Dangers they many ways lie open, and are exposed unto, and for Your own safety; We judge it necessary that You forthwith Surrender, and Deliver up the Government and Fortifications to be preserved, to be Disposed according to Order and Direction from the Crown of England, which is suddenly expected may Arrive, promising all Security from Violence to Your Self, or any other of Your Gentlemen and Soldiers in Person or Estate or else we are assured they will endeavor the taking of the Fortifications by Storm, if any opposition be made.

READING AND DISCUSSION QUESTIONS

1. Why do you think these leading men of Boston chose to write an open letter in the form of a broadside to Governor Andros? What do you think this particular way of communicating with the governor suggests about their intended audience?
2. What can you infer about the motivations of the men who signed this letter?
3. To what extent does this document suggest an important turning point within the long period between 1607 and 1750 covered by this chapter?

Library of Congress, Rare Book and Special Collections Division, Printed Ephemera Collection.

3-2 | The Onondaga Pledge Support to Colonies

CANASSATEGO, *Speech Before Governor George Thomas and Commissioners* (1744)

As the colonies developed, settlers in search of land began moving farther west, away from the eastern seaboard. Frequently, this movement put them in contact with Native Americans upon whose lands they encroached. Treaties had attempted to settle land disputes, but conflict often persisted. In this source, Canassatego (c. 1684–1750), an Onondaga leader and representative of the Iroquois Confederacy, speaks to Brother Onas (the governor of Pennsylvania, George Thomas). The two leaders met in July 1744 to negotiate the Treaty of Lancaster between Virginia, Maryland, and the Iroquois. References to the French threat remind us of the persisting tensions between the two European rivals.

Brother Onas,

Yesterday you expressed your Satisfaction in having been instrumental to our meeting with our Brethren of Virginia and Maryland, we, in return, assure you, that we have great Pleasure in this Meeting, and thank you for the Part you have had in bringing us together, in order to create a good Understanding, and to clear the Road; and, in Token of our Gratitude, we present you with this String of Wampum.

Which was received with the usual Ceremony.

Brother Onas,

You was pleased Yesterday to inform us, "That War had been declared between the great King of England and the French King; that two great Battles had been fought, one by Land, and the other at Sea; with many other Particulars." We are glad to hear the Arms of the King of England were successful, and take part with you in your Joy on this Occasion. You then came nearer Home, and told us, "You had left your House, and were come thus far on Behalf of the whole People of Pensylvania to see us; to renew your Treaties, to brighten the Covenant-Chain,[1] and to confirm your Friendship with us." We approve this Proposition, we thank you for it. We own, with Pleasure, that the Covenant-Chain between us and Pensylvania is of old Standing, and has never contracted any Rust; we wish it may always continue as bright as it has done hitherto; and, in Token of the Sincerity of our Wishes, we present you with this Belt of Wampum.

Which was received with the Yo-hah.

Brother Onas,

You was pleased Yesterday to remind us of our mutual Obligation to assist each other in case of a War with the French, and to repeat the Substance of what we ought to do by our Treaties with you; and that as a War had been

---

The History of the Five Indian Nations of Canada (London: T. Osborne, 1747), 143–145.

[1] **Covenant-chain**: Term used to describe treaty alliances, often confirmed in the stringing of wampum belts.

already entered into with the French, you called upon us to assist you, and not to suffer the French to march through our Country to disturb any of your Settlements.

In answer, we assure you we have all these Particulars in our Hearts, they are fresh in our Memory. We shall never forget that you and we have but one Heart, one Head, one Eye, one Ear, and one Hand. We shall have all your Country under our Eye, and take all the Care we can to prevent any Enemy from coming into it; and, in proof of our Care, we must inform you, that before we came here, we told Onandio, our Father, as he is called, that neither he, nor any of his People, should come through our Country, to hurt our Brethren the English, or any of the Settlements belonging to them; there was Room enough at Sea to fight, there he might do what he pleased, but he should not come upon our Land to do any Damage to our Brethren. And you may depend upon our using our utmost Care to see this effectually done; and, in Token of our Sincerity, we present you with this Belt of Wampum.

Which was received with the usual Ceremony.

After some little Time the Interpreter said, Canassatego had forgot something material, and desired to mend his Speech, and to do so as often as he should omit any thing of Moment, and thereupon he added:

The Six Nations have a great Authority and Influence over sundry Tribes of Indians in Alliance with the French, and particularly over the Praying Indians, formerly a Part with ourselves, who stand in the very Gates of the French; and, to shew our further Care, we have engaged these very Indians, and other Indian Allies of the French for you. They will not join the French against you. They have have [*sic*] agreed with us before we set out. We have put the Spirit of Antipathy against the French in those People. Our Interest is very considerable with them, and many other Nations, and as far as ever it extends, we shall use it for your Service.

READING AND DISCUSSION QUESTIONS

1. What does Canassatego's speech reveal about the role Native Americans played in the disputes between British colonists and their French rivals?
2. What is Canassatego trying to accomplish with his speech?

3-3 | Virginia Tightens Slave Codes

THE GENERAL ASSEMBLY OF VIRGINIA, *An Act for Suppressing Outlying Slaves* (1691)

By the end of the seventeenth century, the British colonies in North America had transitioned from indentured servants to African slaves as their primary source of labor. In Virginia, this transition was hastened by Bacon's Rebellion, which demonstrated to colonial leaders the value of creating a permanent underclass defined by race. As Virginians struggled to make sense of slavery's social implications, the growing number of enslaved Africans in the colony presented new challenges. The Virginia legislature attempted to address some of those issues with this 1691 act.

Whereas many times negroes, mulattoes, and other slaves unlawfully absent themselves from their masters and mistresses service, and lie hid and lurk in obscure places killing hoggs and committing other injuries to the inhabitants of this dominion, for remedy whereof for the future, *Be it enacted by their majesties lieutenant governour, councell and burgesses of this present generall assembly, and the authoritie thereof, and it is hereby enacted,* that in all such cases upon intelligence of any such negroes, mulattoes, or other slaves lying out, two of their majesties justices of the peace of that county, whereof one to be of the quorum, where such negroes, mulattoes or other slave shall be, shall be impowered and commanded, and are hereby impowered and commanded to issue out their warrants directed to the sherrife of the same county to apprehend such negroes, mulattoes, and other slaves, which said sherriffe is hereby likewise required upon all such occasions to raise such and soe many forces from time to time as he shall think convenient and necessary for the effectual apprehending such negroes, mulattoes and other slaves, and in case any negroes, mulattoes or other slave or slaves lying out as aforesaid shall resist, runaway, or refuse to deliver and surrender him or themselves to any person or persons that shall be by lawfull authority employed to apprehend and take such negroes, mulattoes or other slaves that in such cases it shall and may be lawfull for such person and persons to kill and distroy such negroes, mulattoes, and other slave or slaves by gunn or any otherwaise whatsoever.

Provided that where any negroe or mulattoe slave or slaves shall be killed in pursuance of this act, the owner or owners of such negro or mulatto slave shall be paid for such negro or mulatto slave four thousand pounds of tobacco by the publique. And for prevention of that abominable mixture and spurious issue which hereafter may encrease in this dominion, as well by negroes, mulattoes, and Indians intermarrying with English, or other white women, as by their unlawfull accompanying with one another, *Be it enacted by the authoritie aforesaid, and it is hereby enacted,* that for the time to come, whatsoever English or other white man or woman being free shall intermarry with a negroe, mulatto, or Indian man or woman bond or free shall within three months after such marriage be banished and removed from this dominion forever, and that the justices of each respective countie within this dominion make it their perticular care, that this act be put in effectuall execution. *And be it further enacted by the authoritie aforesaid, and it is hereby enacted,* That if any

---

The Statutes at Large; Being a Collection of All the Laws of Virginia, From the First Session of the Legislature in the Year 1619, ed. William Waller Hening (Philadelphia: Thomas DeSilver, 1823), 86–88.

English woman being free shall have a bastard child by any negro or mulatto, she pay the sume of fifteen pounds sterling, within one moneth after such bastard child shall be born, to the Church wardens of the parish where she shall be delivered of such child, and in default of such payment she shall be taken into the possession of the said Church wardens and disposed of for five yeares, and the said fine of fifteen pounds, or whatever the woman shall be disposed of for, shall be paid, one third part to their majesties for and towards the support of the government and the contingent charges thereof, and one other third part to the use of the parish where the offence is committed, and the other third part to the informer, and that such bastard child be bound out as a servant by the said Church wardens untill he or she shall attaine the age of thirty yeares, and in case such English woman that shall have such bastard child be a servant, she shall be sold by the said church wardens, (after her time is expired that she ought by law to serve her master) for five yeares, and the money she shall be sold for divided as is before appointed, and the child to serve as aforesaid.

And forasmuch as great inconveniences may happen to this country by the setting of negroes and mulattoes free, by their either entertaining negro slaves from their masters service, or receiveing stolen goods, or being grown old bringing a charge upon the country; for prevention thereof, *Be it enacted by the authority aforesaid, and it is hereby enacted,* That no negro or mulatto be after the end of this present session of assembly set free by any person or persons whatsoever, unless such person or persons, their heires, executors or administrators pay for the transportation of such negro or negroes out of the countrey within six moneths after such setting them free, upon penalty of paying of tenn pounds sterling to the Church wardens of the parish where such person shall dwell with, which money, or so much thereof as shall be necessary, the said Church wardens are to cause the said negro or mulatto to be transported out of the countrey, and the remainder of the said money to imploy to the use of the poor of the parish.

READING AND DISCUSSION QUESTIONS

1. What specific concerns are Virginians attempting to address with this legislation?
2. What does this document suggest about the Virginia colonists' notions about race, identity, and sexual relations between different racial groups?

3-4 | Gentility and the Planter Elite

WILLIAM BYRD II, *Diary Entries* (1709–1712)

Though Virginia planters like William Byrd II lived on the periphery of the British Empire, they emulated the manners and interests of Britain's aristocratic class. Byrd was born in Virginia in 1674, but educated in London. When his father died, he returned to Virginia to manage the family lands that he inherited. Byrd's diary reveals his efforts to cultivate gentility, or correct living, through the books he read, the behavior he exhibited, and the relations he nurtured with peers and subordinates. His many references to his interactions with ship captains (and the letters they carried) reveal how information and commodities flowed around the Atlantic. Byrd's life demonstrates a growing self-consciousness among southern elites eager to fashion identities at the intersection of British and colonial cultures.

June 1709

15. I rose at 5 o'clock and read two chapters in Hebrew and some Greek in Josephus.[2] I said my prayers and ate milk for breakfast. Captain C-l-t brought me some letters from England and offered me freight in his ship. He brought a parson with him, Mr. Goodwin. He ate his breakfast here and went away about 9 o'clock. I ate dry beef for dinner, and chicken. While we were at dinner Captain M-r-n came with some more letters. He brought me a coaler recommended by Colonel Blakiston. He brought me also some goods for my wife, to an extravagant value. My letters gave me a sad prospect of the tobacco trade in England. My wife continued very ill. I sent Tommy to Williamsburg to inquire for my letters. I took a walk about the plantation. I said my prayers and had good thoughts, good humor and good health, thanks be to God Almighty, only I feared I was going to have the piles.

16. I rose at 5 o'clock and read a chapter in Hebrew and a little Greek. I neglected to say my prayers and ate milk for breakfast. Mr. Bland's boy brought me abundance of letters from Williamsburg, out of the men-of-war. I spent all the morning in reading them. My orders for being of the Council arrived among the rest. By these letters I learned that tobacco was good for nothing, that protested bills would ruin the country, that our trade with the Carolina Indians was adjusted in England, that my sister Braynes was in [prison by the cruelty of C-r-l-y], that my salary was in a fair way of being increased, that the College was like to be rebuilt by the Queen's bounty, that there was a probability of a peace next winter. I ate mutton for dinner. While we were at dinner, Colonel Harrison, Mr. Commissary, and Mr. Wormeley came to see us, but would not eat with us. They likewise brought me some letters. Captain Wilcox dined with us. His people brought me a box of [. . .] from P-r-c-r. I walked about the plantation. Mr. Wormeley and I played at billiards and I won half a crown. I said my prayers. All the company went away. I had good health, good thoughts, and good humor, thank God Almighty.

17. I rose at 5 o'clock and read some Greek in Josephus and perused some of my new books. I said my prayers, and ate milk for breakfast. I settled my accounts. We expected some company but they disappointed us. I ate roast

---

William Byrd, *The Secret Diary of William Byrd of Westover 1709–1712*, ed. Louis B. Wright and Marion Tinling (Richmond, VA: The Dietz Press, 1941).

[2] **Titus Flavius Josephus**: Roman-Jewish historian (A.D. 37–100).

mutton for dinner. In the afternoon we rode to my neighbor Harrison's where we stayed till the evening with Mr. [Gee]. Here I ate some apple pie. Mr. Harrison had the same bad account of tobacco in England and advised me to ship none by this ship. I promised to give no more than £12 per ton. He told me that several gentlemen were extremely in debt with Mr. Perry. In the evening we returned home, where we found all very well, thanks be to God Almighty. I said my prayers and had good health, good thoughts, and good humor, thanks be to God Almighty. . . .

25. I rose at 6 o'clock this morning and read two chapters in Hebrew and some Greek in Josephus. I said my prayers and ate milk for breakfast. I danced my dance. Tom S-d-s-n came from Falling Creek and told me the stone cutter was dead [w-l m-l-r]. I read some Latin and some news. I ate some bacon fraise for dinner. In the afternoon Mr. Bland's sloop brought my things from aboard Captain M-r-n's ship, which had received no damage. My man John got drunk, for which I reprimanded him severely. I walked about the plantation in the evening. I said my prayers and had good thoughts, good health, and good humor, thanks be to God Almighty. . . .

27. I rose at 5 o'clock and read two chapters in Hebrew and some Greek in Josephus. I said my prayers and ate milk for breakfast. I danced my dance. I made an invoice of the things that my wife could spare to be sold. I settled the accounts of protested bills. I ate mutton for dinner. My wife was in tears about her [cargo] but I gave her some comfort after dinner. Mr. Bland came with Henry Randolph to see me and soon after Mr. Harrison and his wife and daughter. They stayed till 7 o'clock and then went away. In the evening we took a walk [about] the plantation. I recommended myself to God in a short prayer. I had good health, good thoughts, and good humor, thanks be to God Almighty. Tom was whipped for not telling me that he was sick.

28. I rose at 5 o'clock and read two chapters in Hebrew and some Greek in Josephus. I said my prayers and ate milk for breakfast. The sloop came up with my things from Captain Browne with my goods which were not so much damaged as I expected. I was angry with the people for staying so long. They sailed away this morning with George the coaler to Falling Creek. I ate cold mutton and sallet [salad] for dinner. In the afternoon I read some news and some Latin and also some Greek in Homer. In the evening I took a walk about the plantation. I said my prayers. I had good health, good thoughts, and good humor, thanks be to God Almighty.

29. I rose at 5 o'clock and read only some Greek in Josephus, because I was hindered by Daniel who came last night from Williamsburg where the sea sloop is safe arrived, thanks be to God Almighty. Two of her men were pressed by the men-of-war, notwithstanding the proclamation. Wheat sold for about six shillings a bushel in Madeira and wine for £8 a pipe with the exchange. Captain Browne and Captain Collins came to see me. I said my prayers and ate milk for breakfast. I began to reap my wheat. I ate bacon and pork for dinner. In the afternoon Mr. Bland came to counsel the proper measures to be taken with the sloop and it was agreed he should go down to take care of the cargo and he went

accordingly and was caught in a great shower of rain. Daniel behaved himself very foolishly. In the evening the rain hindered my walking and lasted above an hour. I said my prayers. I had good health, good thoughts, and good humor, thanks be to God Almighty. . . .

February 1711

5. I rose about 8 o'clock and found my cold still worse. I said my prayers and ate milk and potatoes for breakfast. My wife and I quarreled about her pulling her brows. She threatened she would not go to Williamsburg if she might not pull them; I refused, however, and got the better of her, and maintained my authority. About 10 o'clock we went over the river and got to Colonel Duke's about 11. There I ate some toast and canary. Then we proceeded to Queen's Creek, where we found all well, thank God. We ate roast goose for supper. The women prepared to go to the Governor's the next day and my brother and I talked of old stories. My cold grew exceedingly bad so that I thought I should be sick. M. ___________ gave me some sage tea and leaves of [s-m-n-k] which made me mad all night so that I could not sleep but was much disordered by it. I neglected to say my prayers in form but had good thoughts, good humor, and indifferent health, thank God Almighty.

6. I rose about 9 o'clock but was so bad I thought I should not have been in condition to go to Williamsburg, and my wife was so kind to [say] she would stay with me, but rather than keep her from going I resolved to go if possible. I was shaved with a very dull razor, and ate some boiled milk for breakfast but neglected to say my prayers. About 10 o'clock I went to Williamsburg without the ladies. As soon as I got there it began to rain, which hindered about [*sic*] the company from coming. I went to the President's where I drank tea and went with him to the Governor's and found him at home. Several gentlemen were there and about 12 o'clock several ladies came. My wife and her sister came about 2. We had a short Council but more for form than for business. There was no other appointed in the room of Colonel Digges. My cold was a little better so that I ventured among the ladies, and Colonel Carter's wife and daughter were among them. It was night before we went to supper, which was very fine and in good order. It rained so that several did not come that were expected. About 7 o'clock the company went in coaches from the Governor's house to the capitol where the Governor opened the ball with a French dance with my wife. Then I danced with Mrs. Russell and then several others and among them the rest Colonel Smith's son, who made a sad freak. Then we danced country dances for an hour and the company was carried into another room where was a very fine collation of sweetmeats. The Governor was very gallant to the ladies and very courteous to the gentlemen. About 2 o'clock the company returned in the coaches and because the drive was dirty the Governor carried the ladies into their coaches. My wife and I lay at my lodgings. Colonel Carter's family and Mr. Blair were stopped by the unruliness of the horses and Daniel Wilkinson was so gallant as to lead the horses himself through all the dirt and rain to Mr. Blair's

house. My cold continued bad. I neglected to say my prayers and had good thoughts, good humor, but indifferent health, thank God Almighty. It rained all day and all night. The President had the worst clothes of anybody there.

7. I rose at 8 o'clock and found my cold continued. I said my prayers and ate boiled milk for breakfast. I went to see Mr. Clayton who lay sick of the gout. About 11 o'clock my wife and I went to wait on the Governor in the President's coach. We went there to take our leave but were forced to stay all day. The Governor had made a bargain with his servants that if they would forbear to drink upon the Queen's birthday, they might be drunk this day. They observed their contract and did their business very well and got very drunk today, in such a manner that Mrs. Russell's maid was forced to lay the cloth, but the cook in that condition made a shift to send in a pretty little dinner. I ate some mutton cutlets. In the afternoon I persuaded my wife to stay all night in town and so it was resolved to spend the evening in cards. My cold was very bad and I lost my money. About 10 o'clock the Governor's coach carried us home to our lodgings where my wife was out of humor and I out of order. I said a short prayer and had good thoughts and good humor, thank God Almighty. . . .

May 1712

22. I rose about 6 o'clock and read two chapters in Hebrew and some in Greek in Lucian. I said my prayers and ate boiled milk for breakfast. I danced my dance. It rained a little this morning. My wife caused Prue to be whipped violently notwithstanding I desired not, which provoked me to have Anaka whipped likewise who had deserved it much more, on which my wife flew into such a passion that she hoped she would be revenged of me. I was moved very much at this but only thanked her for the present lest I should say things foolish in my passion. I wrote more accounts to go to England. My wife was sorry for what she had said and came to ask my pardon and I forgave her in my heart but she seemed to resent, that she might be the more sorry for her folly. She ate no dinner nor appeared the whole day. I ate some bacon for dinner. In the afternoon I wrote two more accounts till the evening and then took a walk in the garden. I said my prayers and was reconciled to my wife and gave her a flourish in token of it. I had good health, good thoughts, but was a little out of humor, for which God forgive me.

READING AND DISCUSSION QUESTIONS

1. To what extent does the diary provide evidence for Byrd's self-fashioning as both a colonial American elite and a British subject?
2. From the excerpt, what can you infer about the role Byrd saw himself playing in colonial American society? What roles do you see him playing within his household, colony, and empire?

3. Why might Byrd have written and kept a diary? Do you think he expected others to read it? Evaluate the diary as a source for historians interested in understanding early-eighteenth-century Virginia society. What are its advantages and limitations?

3-5 | Colonial Commercial Economy

Two Tobacco Advertisements (eighteenth century)

Like William Byrd's diary (Document 3-4), these eighteenth-century advertisements hint at the robust colonial mercantile economy that developed during the 1700s. The colonies both produced commodities for trade, like the tobacco advertised here, and functioned as a market for goods produced elsewhere. Tobacco, in particular, was the most important export crop of Virginia during the colonial period. Estimates suggest that the colony exported twenty-two million pounds of tobacco to England in 1700. English newspaper advertisements such as the one below often extolled the health benefits of tobacco, which might suggest why the plant was in such high demand. This particular ad claimed tobacco would help "clear [the head] Of noxious Humour and the Spirits Chear." Tobacco was so integral to the colonial economy that the plant became a form of currency; planters used tobacco to pay debts, purchase goods, and measure the value of commodities, including enslaved people. Because the cultivation of tobacco grew in economic importance over the colonial period and was so labor-intensive, the demand for enslaved laborers also grew. Planters' dependence on their labor is acknowledged in Thomas Foster's tobacco advertisement, which depicts two slaves tending the plant. The text reads "Tho Fosters Best Virginia Tobacco at Winslow, who likewise distills Brandys and Waters and sells at reasonable rates."

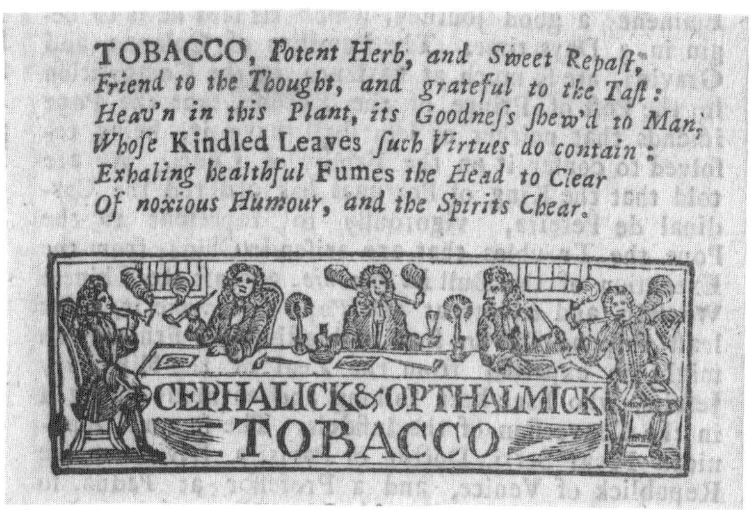

Colonial Williamsburg Foundation

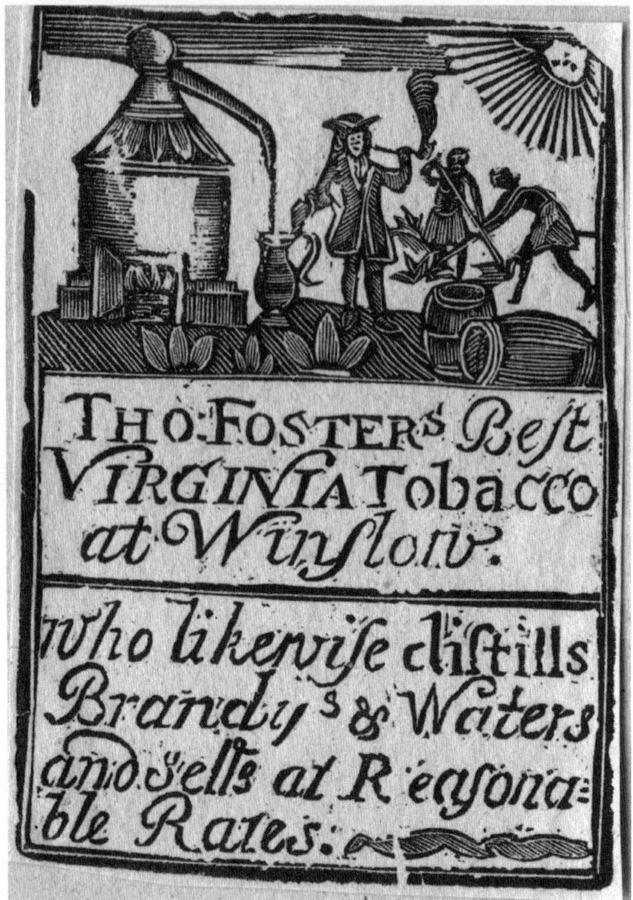

Tobacco label featuring Virginia planter and distillery (woodcut)/English School (18th century)/Virginia Historical Society, Richmond, Virginia, USA/Bridgeman Images

READING AND DISCUSSION QUESTIONS

1. What do these two advertisements suggest about the market for tobacco in the eighteenth century?
2. From the evidence provided on Thomas Foster's tobacco label, what can you infer about his role in the colonial economy and the transatlantic trade?
3. Who do you think was the target audience for these advertisements? What appeal to consumers do these advertisements make?

3-6 | Colonists Assert Their Rights

LORD CORNBURY, *Letter to the Lords of Trade* (1704)

One measure of the colonists' growing independence can be seen in the letter Lord Cornbury sent to the Lords of Trade. Cornbury was Edward Hyde, the 3rd Earl of Clarendon (1661–1723), who served as the colonial governor of New York and New Jersey from 1701 to 1708. Queen Anne removed him from office after complaints of misconduct mounted against him. (His political opponents also spread scurrilous rumors that he dressed in women's clothing.) In this letter, Cornbury discusses a number of issues, including relations with Native Americans and what he describes as the colonial assembly's "sawcy" behavior. From his perspective, the colony's legislature was challenging royal authority. The letter is also interesting for what it suggests to us about the difficulties of communication during this period when letters miscarried or were delayed by poor transportation and weeks-long sea voyages.

My Lords.

In my letter of the 30th of June last I gave Your Lord[ships] an account of the reasons why no more of my letters came safe to Your hands, occasioned by the taking of our homeward bound ships and the want [lack] of intelligence here from other parts of the Continent. I did acquaint Your Lord[ships] that I hoped to propose a remedy for the latter, at my meeting with Coll. Nicholson and Coll Seymour at which time I likewise hoped we should have seen Coll. Dudley, he having writ me word, that he would meet them here; I did intend to have proposed to them, the laying a Tax in each province by Act of Assembly, for the settling and defraying the charges of the post, which then might have gone from Boston to North Carolina; but this meeting was hindered by several accidents; first, Coll. Dudley was busy about his expedition to the Eastward, Coll. Nicholson was hindered by the sitting of the Assembly of Virginia, and as soon as the Assembly of New Yorke was over, and I thought to go into New Jersey, to the Assembly which was to sit at Burlington, I was forced to adjourn them, in order to go up to Albany where there was an alarum that the French were marching towards that place with a thousand French and Indians. I went, and when I arrived there I found the people in a very great consternation, but that was over in a few days, by the arrival of some Indians, I had sent out, to see if they could discover any number of men marching our way; at their return, they informed me they had been as far as the Lake without seeing any body, but that upon the Lake they had met some Ottawawa Indians who had informed them that three hundred French and Indians were marched with a design to attempt Northampton in New England, but that they could not find, there were

---

Documents Relative to the Colonial History of the State of New York, ed. E. B. O'Callaghan (Albany, NY: Weed, Parsons and Company, Printers, 1854), 1120–1123.

any marching our way. However, by this accident, I had an opportunity to see how far we may depend upon our own people, and the Indians too in case of need, and I must say the Militia of the County of Albany were very ready if the Ennemy had been coming; I could in eight and forty hours time have drawn together upwards of seven hundred men, reckoning the Garrison, the Militia of Albany, and that of Ulster Counties; and the Indians of the Five Nations were so ready that they all left their Castles and were coming towards Albany before I could send them any orders; at the same time that I was at Albany where I stayed but ten days, there was an Alarum at New Yorke occasioned by a Gentleman who coming from Long Island informed the Council, that ten French Men-of-war were come within Sandy hook, upon this the Gentlemen of the Council sent an express to me to desire me to make what haste I could down to New Yorke, and at the same time sent to the Collonels of the Militia in the several Counties about New Yorke to get their men ready to oppose the Ennemy. I did make all the haste I could, but before I could get to York, their fears were over, for the ten Men of Warr were dwindled away to one French privateer of fourteen Gunns who took just without Sandy hook a ship commanded by one Sinclair who was bound to this Port from England, on board of whom were all the packetts your Lord[ships] were pleased to send me, they were given into the charge of one Glenerosse a Merchant of this place who left them on Board by which means, they are fallen into the hands of the Ennemy. I can not say that the Militia of this City did their duty, for very many of the Dutchmen run away into the woods, but the Militia of Long Island deserve to be commended. . . . By this account Your Lord[ships] will perceive, how necessary it is to have a standing Force in this Province, where we are exposed to the invasions of the Enemy by sea in the Southern parts of it, and to the attacks of the French and Indians by land in the Northern parts of it. . . .

[Y]ou will perceive that the Assembly here is going into the same methods, that the Assembly's of some other Provinces upon this Continent have fallen into, who think themselves equal to the House of Commons of England, and that they are intituled [entitled] to all the same powers and priviledges, that a House of Commons in England enjoys; how dangerous it may be to suffer them to enjoy and exercise such powers, I need not tell your Lord[ships], only I shall observe that the holding of General Assembly in these parts of the world, has been settled neither by Act of Parliament in England, nor by Act of Assembly here, so that the holding General Assemblies here is purely by the grace and favour of the Crown. This I have told them often, but notwithstanding that, they will pass no Bill for the service of the Queen, nor even for their own defence, unless they can have such Clauses in, as manifestly incroach upon the prerogative [rights] of the Crown or in some measure destroy the power of the Governour . . . . it is a thing was never attempted by any of their predecessors, but as the Country increases, they grow sawcy, and no doubt but if they are allowed to go on, they will improve upon it, how far that may be of service to the Queen I leave Your Lord[ships] to Judge. . . . I intreat Your Lord[ships] to believe that I am not pleading for the laying aside of Assembly's, it is far from my thoughts, but I think it my duty to acquaint you with what I take to be the Queen's right, especially when Assembly's begin to be refractory; when I have done that, I have done my duty, and shall wait Your Lord[ships'] declarations, which I shall always punctually observe—In the mean time, I have this day dissolved the Assembly and intend to issue writts for the calling of another in March next, which I hope will behave themselves better than the last, however I am sure they can't be worse;—I am going to morrow to New Jersey to the Assembly there. I take the liberty to beg your Lord[ships] that I may have all manner of stores sent over, I have not a hundred and twenty barrells of powder left, and several of them are spoiled, I have no small arms at all, no Cartouch boxes nor paper, not one bed for the men to lye upon, but what has been peiced over and over again, not a sword in the Garrison, nor a dagger if the Enemy should attempt any thing upon our frontiers this winter, we shall not have powder enough left for salutes. I intreat Your Lord[ships] to intercede with the Queen that some presents may be sent over for the Indians, for if we must buy them here they will cost three times the price they will cost in England and sometimes the goods proper for the Indians, are not to be got here for money, such as light guns, Duffles, Strowds, Kettles, Hatchets, Stockings, Blankets and powder; and till Canada is reduced, we shall never be able to keep the Indians steady without presents. . . . I intreat you to represent our condition to Her Majesty that we may be supplyed early in the spring, else we shall be in a very poor condition even to defend ourselves if we should be attacked; however I intreat Your Lord[ships] to believe that nothing shall be wanting on my part for the Queen's service, as long as Her Majesty shall please to command me to serve her here—I am—My Lords,

Your Lord[ships'] most faithful
humble servant
CORNBURY

New York
Nov 6th 1704.

READING AND DISCUSSION QUESTIONS

1. What conclusion about the eighteenth-century circulation of news and information can you draw by analyzing Cornbury's letter?
2. How did the tensions between England and France manifest themselves locally, according to Cornbury's letter?
3. What is the nature of the complaint Cornbury makes against the Assembly of New York? To what extent was the New York Assembly exercising its "independence"?

▪ COMPARATIVE QUESTIONS ▪

1. Evaluate and synthesize the evidence from this chapter to support or challenge the argument that eighteenth-century colonists developed a growing awareness of their rights.
2. What do the sources included in this chapter reveal about the role of economics as a cause in colonial political development during the eighteenth century?
3. Compare the ways "Indians" are discussed in these documents. What might account for the differences you see?
4. How do you assess the political, social, and economic impact of slavery in this period? What may have been some of the short- or long-term effects of the growth of this system during the period?

4

Growth, Diversity, and Conflict

1720–1763

"Plenty of good land, and liberty to manage their own affairs their own way, seem to be the two great causes of the prosperity of all new colonies," argued Adam Smith in *The Wealth of Nations*. In the middle decades of the eighteenth century, the American colonies enjoyed just these favorable conditions. Parliament took a laissez-faire approach to colonial government, and the colonies grew in size, population, and demographic complexity. As settlers pushed in from the coast to establish new farms, the growing standard of living enticed Europeans to try their luck, increasing immigration and adding to the ethnic and cultural mix.

As the colonial population grew, trade between the colonies and England soared. Raw materials crossed the Atlantic in ships that returned full of the finished goods pumping out of British factories. The colonial gentry displayed their refinement through consumption, but of course not everyone had the means to do so. Class was just one dividing line in colonial America. Another was religion. In many areas throughout the colonies, religious revivalism spread widely. The Great Awakening induced religious enthusiasm and challenged conventional sources of spiritual and social authority, including the scientific emphasis of the American Enlightenment which affirmed the power of human reason to understand the workings of the natural world. Political authority, too, became contested as the French and Indian War reminded colonists that they were still a dependent part of the British Empire.

4-1 | The American Enlightenment

Benjamin Franklin's Experiments with Electricity (Turned into an 18th-Century Parlour Game) (c. 1700s)

Benjamin Franklin was an American scientist, philosopher, and statesman whose reputation in Europe made him a celebrity in the colonies. His work, including his famous experiment with a key and a kite, led to important discoveries and new understandings of the natural world, cementing his standing as one of the eighteenth century's Enlightenment figures. A religious skeptic, Franklin followed other Enlightenment men and women who explained the workings of the universe and human affairs through the scientific investigation of observable phenomena, not the teachings of scripture or the folk wisdom of the people. This eighteenth-century lithograph depicts the era's craze for electricity. Here, men and women experience electric shocks as Dr. Franklin looks on.

Benjamin Franklin's experiments with electricity (turned into an 18th-century parlour game)(color litho) /American School (18th century)/Library Company of Philadelphia, PA, USA/Bridgeman Images

READING AND DISCUSSION QUESTIONS

1. What can you infer about the artist's attitude toward the American Enlightenment? Do you think he or she was enthusiastic or skeptical about the value of Franklin's work?
2. Why do you think electricity became so fascinating to people in the eighteenth century?

4-2 | Sarah Osborn on Her Experiences During the Religious Revivals

SARAH OSBORN, *Memoirs of the Life of Mrs. Sarah Osborn* (1814)

The memoir written by Sarah Osborn (1714–1797) movingly illustrates the anguish of a woman caught in the grip of religious doubt. Born in London, Osborn emigrated to America when still a child, living in Boston, then Newport, Rhode Island, where she spent most of her life. Her husband died at sea, leaving her a widow with a small child. Despite these hardships, she persevered but experienced repeated crises of faith. In the section of her memoir excerpted here, Osborn recounts the moment of her spiritual "awakening." Osborn's account, published seventeen years after her death, reminds us that the religious revivals appealed to women whose experience of grace empowered them in a culture where women had few if any means of formal power or authority.

Thus I continued from day to day, in such ecstacies of joy, thirsting for full sanctification, and more intimate communion with God; daily asking what I should render to him for all his benefits to such an hell deserving sinner; earnestly begging that God would find out some way for me, that I might be made instrumental in advancing his kingdom and interest in the world. O, how I dreaded being an unprofitable servant. The employment I still followed seemed to encourage me to hope God intended to make use of me for the instruction of little ones; which caused me often to bless God for placing me in that calling. And though I know that in every thing I offend, and in all come short of God's glory; so that every performance has need of washing in the blood of Christ; yet it is a comfort to me, to this day, that I was enabled by grace to labour with the little souls, then committed to my charge; but desire to be humbled that I did no more. O, that I had been more faithful! Surely I longed that all the world, but especially those dear to me by the bonds of nature or friendship, might be convinced of sin, and come to a glorious Christ. I thought I could even spend and be spent for them. I thought I could travail in birth till Christ was formed in them. And when I saw any giving themselves a liberty to sin, I could not, at some times, refrain from reproving them. Some would tell me I was turned fool, and distracted, when I said I had been a vile sinner, for every body knew I had been a sober woman all my days; and yet I used to do such things too, as well as they: And what was the matter *now*? Sometimes they would say, "This fit will be over quickly." But all such answers as these, of which I had a great many, would serve to humble me yet more, and put me upon pleading for persevering grace, that I might never bring dishonor upon the name of God. And indeed, all the trials I met with, which were various, had, through the abounding goodness of God, this effect, *to quicken me yet more.*

But Satan had still a desire to sift me as wheat. He assaulted me daily; but those words of the blessed Jesus were frequently applied for my support, "I have

Memoirs of the Life of Mrs. Sarah Osborn, ed. Samuel Hopkins (Catskill, NY: N. Elliot, 1814), 33–37.

prayed for thee, that thy faith fail not." One night in particular, when watching with a dear friend, who was sick, Satan assaulted me in as furious a manner, seemingly, as though he had appeared in bodily shape, though with my bodily eyes I saw nothing. I believe the combat lasted, at least, two hours, as fierce as though I had talked with him face to face. He again ranked all my sins before my eyes, telling me it was impossible, notwithstanding my great hopes, for me ever to be saved. He was still sure of me, and would not let me go. I should surely turn back again, and worse than ever. It is impossible to relate the tenth part of the fiery darts he flung at me. But I was composed, not in the least daunted; but could prove him a liar in every thing he suggested, by scripture, which flowed into my mind, as though I had learned it all by heart. Never had I such a variety of scripture texts at my command in all my life, either before, or since. There was nothing he could allege against me, but if I knew it was true, I immediately subscribed to it; and then flew to the particular properties of the blood of Christ, which I found sufficient for me. Thus I overcame him by the blood of the Lamb; and was left, in the issue, filled with the consolations of the blessed Spirit; triumphing over Satan; blessing and praising God for delivering me out of the hand of this cruel tyrant; adoring the lovely Jesus. And thus I spent the remainder of that night. O, how sweet it was to me! I longed for more strength to praise and love; and even to be dissolved, and to be with Christ.

Thus I continued for some time, rejoicing and resolving, by assisting grace, to press forward, and by all means to make my calling and election sure. Then I wrote my experience to be communicated to the Church; and I was admitted, February 6, 1737, to partake of that holy ordinance of the Lord's Supper. But it is impossible for me to express the ecstacy of joy I was in, when I saw myself there, who was by nature a child of wrath, an heir of hell, and by practice a rebel against God, a resister of his grace, a piercer of the lovely Jesus, unworthy of the crumbs that fall; yet, through free grace, compelled to come in, and partake of children's bread. It was indeed sweet to me to feed by faith on the broken body of my dearest Lord. Surely it did humble me to the dust, and filled me with self abhorrence, as I meditated on his sufferings and death, and knew my sins to be the procuring cause. But when I came to take the cup, and by faith to apply the precious properties of the blood of Christ to my soul, the veil of unbelief seemed to drop off, and I was forced to cry out, "My Lord, and my God," when I beheld the hole in his side, and the prints of the nails. And I could not but, in the words of Peter, appeal to him, ["]Lord, thou knowest all things, thou knowest that I love thee." O then I was admitted, with the beloved disciple, to lean on his breast! O, astonishing grace, and unspeakable joy, to see God reconciled to me, in and through him; and he bidding me welcome to his table! The Holy Spirit, by his powerful influences, applied all this for my strong consolation. O, what a feast is this, when intimate communion with the glorious God is thus obtained! When strong covenant engagements with him are renewed; I being assured that he was my God, and giving myself, body and soul, to him forever, and rejoicing in him as my only portion forever more. Surely, I thought, I could never enough adore the lovely Jesus for appointing such an ordinance as this.

READING AND DISCUSSION QUESTIONS

1. How does Osborn describe the conversion experience?
2. What evidence can you see here of the reaction from others who witnessed her religious awakening?
3. Why does Osborn choose to devote so much of her memoir to her spiritual struggles? What audience was she writing for?

4-3 | The Material Lives of Colonial Americans

Estate Inventories for Mary Ripping (1745) *and Ann Stevens* (1748)

Estate inventories were legal documents created by order of a court to itemize the possessions of a person who had died for the purpose of settling his or her estate. Those conducting the inventory, often neighbors appointed by the court, listed all the possessions and gave a valuation, expressed in British pounds, shillings, and pence. (There were twelve pence to the shilling and twenty shillings to the pound.) These inventories list the goods owned by two women who died in the 1740s in York County, Virginia. Though these inventories do not indicate it, Mary Ripping and Ann Stevens were probably widows. Under the legal system of the time, they would not have owned real estate, so the inventory only includes their moveable goods, which in Mary's case included three enslaved people. By examining estate inventories, historians can recreate the material lives of colonial Americans, assess their living conditions, and speculate about the choices they made with the resources they had.

An Inventory & appraisment of the Estate of Mary Ripping decd.

Chamber in the Front House	
a Feather Bed, bolsters, pillows pr. blankets cotton Counterpane Bedsted & Curtains	£5.-.-
a Walnut looking Glass 50/. oval Table 15/	3.5.-
square Table 7/6. 1 Elbow 6 old Cane Chairs & Stool	1.7.6
cloaths press 20/. 1 pr. Doggs 5/	1.5.-
Hall.	
1 large Oak oval Table 25/. 1 Walnut do. 15/. 1 Marble Table 3 pds	5.-.-
Cane Couch & Bed 20/. Doggs 2/6 1 Looking Glass 30/	2.12.6
A Corner Cupboard with Glass door 50/. Picture of Adam, George 2/6	2.12.6
Above Stairs over the Chamber	
2 Square Tables 6 rush Chairs 1 pr. Doggs	1.6.-

Porch Chamber	
A Feather Bed, bolster, Pillows 1 blanket Quilt Bedsted	3.10.-
Other Room	
Feather Bed, bolster, pillows, rugg, blanket, bedsted Cord, Hyde Old Curtains	6.-.-
Feather bed, bolster 2 pillows, blankets, rugg, Bedstead	3.10.-
1 Pine Table 5 old Chairs	0.6.6
Cellar	
1 Pipe Madera Wine 11 bottles do	25.11.-
11 1/6 doz. Bristol Beer at 9/. P doz .	5.-.6
7 1/3 doz Port Wine at 24/.	8.16.-
1 Jugg & 4 Gall. Rum 16/. Molasses 20/	1.16.-
a Cask Vinegar 40/. 9 brass cocks 18/.	2.18.-
20½ doz. empty bottles at 24/. P Gro	2.1.-
Empty Casks 6 hhds 2 pipes 1 [Tierce?]	1.10.-
Back House below.	
Feather bed, bolster, pillows holland Sheets, Quilt, Bedsted & Curtains	2.10.-
Walnut Oval Table 20/. 1 Oak Sq: do. 10/	1.10.-
1 Sqr. looking Glass 20/. Corner Cupboard 20	2.-.-
5 old Leather Chairs 8/. Doggs & Shovel 5/	0.13.-
Middle room	
Desk 20/. Oval Table 15/. Linnen press 50/.	4.5.-
6 old leather Chairs 24/. old Cabinet 20/	2.4.-
3 old huckaback Table Cloths 26 Napkins	1.13.6
6 diaper Table Cloths 30 Towells	2.18.-
2 damask do. 30/. 5 old Table Cloths 10/	2.-.-
5 small old rushia do. 10/. 12 pillow beers 9/	0.19.-
5 pr. Sheets 45/. Cotton Counterpane 30/. 10 lb. chocolate 35/	5.10.-
4 lb. Bohea Tea 30/. 42 Oz. 18 wt. plate at 5/6 P Oz. £11.15.11	13.5.11
Carry'd Over.	£ 122.15.11
Brot. over	£ 122.15.11
1 Punch Ladle 15 /. China bowl 10/. 3 do. 7/6	1.12.6

11 China Cups & 8 Saucers 8/. 7 Earthen bowls 4/	0.12.-
6 Qt. & 2 pt. Decanters & 3 wine Glasses	1.6.-
1 pr. Doggs 10/. 14 Ivory Knives & forks 14/	1.4.-
2 doz. Earthen plates 4/. 5 Knives & forks 5/	0.9.-
2 pr. Mony Scales & weights	0.12.6
Little room	
Feather bed, blanket, bolster, pillows, Bedsted	4.-.-
Small Sqr. Table 5/. Stand 5/. 3 old Chairs 3/	0.13.-
11 brass candle Sticks 1 pr. Snuffers 22/. Doggs, Shovel & Tongs 5/	1.7.-
Tea Kettle 5/. 1 Copper Chocholate pot 2 Coffee do. 5/. 1 Coffee Mill 5/	0.15.-
1 Galln. Qt. Pt. ½ pt. 4 Gill pots 15 /. 1 Pewter Tea pot 1 bowl Sugar dish Milk pot Coffee Cups & Tea board 4/	0.19.-
1 Wigg box 1/3 1 Stone butter pot 2 Juggs 7/6	0.8.9
large cannister small do. and other Tin Ware 1 Pottle 2 qt. stone juggs about 25 lb. brown Sugar	0.12.6
Above Stairs Vizt.	
2 Cotton Counterpanes	1.5.-
Feather bed bolster pillows 1 blanket, Quilt, Bedsted Curtains &c.	6.-.-
Feather bed bolster & pillows Quilt Bedsted	3.10.-
Walnut Chest 15/. 6 rush Chairs 12/	1.7.-
Window Curtains 2/. Featherbed, bolster & pillow Rugg Bedsted Curtains & Vallens	3.2.-
Another do. without Curtains	2.5.-
5 wooden Chairs 1 small pine Table	0.10.-
2 old Chests 5/. Canvas bed 20/. 1 Still 20/	2.5.-
4 Chamber pots 3/6 Well hook 1/3 Garden Sheers 1/3.	0.6.-
7 Sack bags & 1 pr. brass Scales & Weights	0.10.-
Outhouses	
Small Sqr. Table 2 Chairs 6/. 3 Stone & 2 Earthen pots 7/6	0.13.6
Dutch Oven 35/. Do. 15/. Iron Crown 5/. 3 flat Irons 4/. 3 Milk pans 1/6	3.-.6
Grid Iron 5/. wheat Sive 2/6 Warming pan 2/6	0.10.-
66 lb. Pewter 38/7 2 dishes 6/. 1 doz. plates 12/. 15 do. 12/6	3.9.1

1 Lanthorn 1/3 rat Trap 2/6 Flesh fork & Ladle 2/6	0.6.3
Spice Mortar & Pestle 5/. Waterg pot 2/. Shovel & Tongs 2 /6	0.9.6
1 4 wheel Chair & harness for 4 horses	35.-.-
1 Iron-Jack &c & Spits 45/. 2 Iron pots 3 pr. hooks 30/	3.15.-
1 pr. Iron Doggs 20/. 1 Driping pan 2/. 1 frying pan 2/6 5 plates 10/	1.14.6
1 pr. Tongs 1/. 2 Soup Jarrs 15/. 1 Meal Tray 3/. 5 Tubbs 10/	1.9.-
1 Copper Kettle 40/. 1 fodder rope 7/6. 1 Garden rake 1/	2.8.6
1 wheel barrow 4/. 1 old Waggon & wheels £8. 6 head of cattle 6£	14.4.-
Carry'd up.	£225.7.-
Brot. up	£225.7.-
9 draught horses & Mares £40.10. Waggon & harness for 5 horses £20	60.10.-
Tumbrel & harness 1 Colt 30/	6.10.-
The Quarter	
21 Young hoggs wt. about 1100 16/. P 100	8.16.-
4 Sows & 29 pigs 30/. 8 Shoats 40/. 14 Cows 3 Calves £14.	17.10.-
3 Young Stears £3.15. 1 Bull 15/. 9 Yearlings 36/	6.6.-
1 Negro Man Will 30 £. 1 Negro Woman Nanny & Child Judith £45.	75.-.-
about 23 barrls. Corn at 6/6	7.9.6
	£407. 8. 6

The Colonial Williamsburg Foundation

An Inventory and Appraisment of Ann Stevens Estate Vizt.	
A Parcel of old Linnen £1 12 Gowns £3	£4..0..0
10 Petticoats 20/ 6 Yards Callico 12/ 7 Yards Do. 17/6	2..9..6
5 Yards Shelows 7/6 4 Handkerchiefs 8/ 1 Scarlet Cloak 10/	1..5..6
1 old Trunk and a Parcel old Linnen	0..10..0
A Parcel Womans Apparel and old Trunk	1..6..0
15 lb. Bacon 2/6 a parcel old Caps 2/6 a Mug & 2 Tumblers 2/	0..7..0
1 Bed, Bloster, 2 Pillows 1 Sheet & Quilt £2 10/1 Do. &c. £1..1..6	3..11..6
1 Bed Bolster & 2 Ruggs 15/ 1 Do. &c 10/	1..5..0

2 Bedsteads & 1 Quilting frame 7/63 dozen Bottles 6/	0..13..6
4 Iron Pots & 1 Spit	0..15..0
1 Sauce pan 1 pair bellows 1 Pestle and Morter	0..5..0
1 Parcel of old Iron 5/ 1 Table and 8 old Chairs 12/6	0..17..6
1 Tea Kettle 2/6 12 lb. old Pewter 6/ 1 lb. Cotton 1/	0..9..6
1 pr. Ear rings 4/ a Silver Thimble 2/ 1. Bed &c 40/	2..6..0
	£20..1..0

The Colonial Williamsburg Foundation

READING AND DISCUSSION QUESTIONS

1. What does the evidence from these estate inventories suggest about the relative standard of living of Ann Stevens and Mary Ripping? Were these women from the same social and economic class?
2. If we assume that individuals make conscious choices when purchasing goods, what can we say about the choices Ann and Mary made? What do their possessions say about them?
3. Though these two inventories are a limited body of evidence, what do they suggest about the material conditions of eighteenth-century colonial American society?

4-4 | Franklin Calls for Colonial Unity

BENJAMIN FRANKLIN, *Albany Plan of Union* (1754)

During the summer months of 1754, delegates from seven of Britain's North American colonies gathered in Albany, NY to discuss plans for cooperation with the Iroquois Confederation and for their mutual defense. This conference was arranged by the British government, who wanted to cement an alliance with the Iroquois and unify the colonies since relations between England and France were rapidly deteriorating. (Skirmishes against the French, which had already occurred before the Albany meeting, would lead directly to the outbreak of the French and Indian War that year.) Britain wanted an organized front to repulse French efforts to dominate the upper Ohio River Valley, a frontier region contested by both sides. One of Pennsylvania's delegates, Benjamin Franklin, offered his Albany Plan of Union, which called for a centralizing government to unite the colonies. This was not a plan for independence from Great Britain but an effort to better regulate relations among the colonies. Franklin's plan did not materialize, mostly because the colonies did not want to cede their authority. Still, the concepts it introduced would later influence the development of the American constitutional government.

Documents Illustrative of the Formation of the Union of the American States (Washington, DC: Government Printing Office, 1927).

It is proposed that humble application be made for an act of Parliament of Great Britain, by virtue of which one general government may be formed in America, including all the said colonies, within and under which government each colony may retain its present constitution, except in the particulars wherein a change may be directed by the said act, as hereafter follows.

1. That the said general government be administered by a President-General, to be appointed and supported by the crown; and a Grand Council, to be chosen by the representatives of the people of the several Colonies met in their respective assemblies.

2. That within—months after the passing such act, the House of Representatives that happen to be sitting within that time, or that shall [be] especially for that purpose convened, may and shall choose members for the Grand Council, in the following proportion, that is to say,

Massachusetts Bay	7
New Hampshire	2
Connecticut	5
Rhode Island	2
New York	4
New Jersey	3
Pennsylvania	6
Maryland	4
Virginia	7
North Carolina	4
South Carolina	4
	48

3. —who shall meet for the first time at the city of Philadelphia, being called by the President-General as soon as conveniently may be after his appointment.

4. That there shall be a new election of the members of the Grand Council every three years; and, on the death or resignation of any member, his place should be supplied by a new choice at the next sitting of the Assembly of the Colony he represented.

5. That after the first three years, when the proportion of money arising out of each Colony to the general treasury can be known, the number of members to be chosen for each Colony shall, from time to time, in all ensuing elections, be regulated by that proportion, yet so as that the number to be chosen by any one Province be not more than seven, nor less than two.

6. That the Grand Council shall meet once in every year, and oftener if occasion require, at such time and place as they shall adjourn to at the last preceding meeting, or as they shall be called to meet at by the President-General on any emergency; he having first obtained in writing the consent of seven of the members to such call, and sent duly and timely notice to the whole.

7. That the Grand Council have power to choose their speaker; and shall neither be dissolved, prorogued, nor continued sitting longer than six weeks at one time, without their own consent or the special command of the crown.

8. That the members of the Grand Council shall be allowed for their service ten shillings sterling per diem, during their session and journey to and from the place of meeting; twenty miles to be reckoned a day's journey.

9. That the assent of the President-General be requisite to all acts of the Grand Council, and that it be his office and duty to cause them to be carried into execution.

10. That the President-General, with the advice of the Grand Council, hold or direct all Indian treaties, in which the general interest of the Colonies may be concerned; and make peace or declare war with Indian nations.

11. That they make such laws as they judge necessary for regulating all Indian trade.

12. That they make all purchases from Indians, for the crown, of lands not now within the bounds of particular Colonies, or that shall not be within their bounds when some of them are reduced to more convenient dimensions.

13. That they make new settlements on such purchases, by granting lands in the King's name, reserving a quitrent to the crown for the use of the general treasury.

14. That they make laws for regulating and governing such new settlements, till the crown shall think fit to form them into particular governments.

15. That they raise and pay soldiers and build forts for the defence of any of the Colonies, and equip vessels of force to guard the coasts and protect the trade on the ocean, lakes, or great rivers; but they shall not impress men in any Colony, without the consent of the Legislature.

16. That for these purposes they have power to make laws, and lay and levy such general duties, imposts, or taxes, as to them shall appear most equal and just (considering the ability and other circumstances of the inhabitants in the several Colonies), and such as may be collected with the least inconvenience to the people; rather discouraging luxury, than loading industry with unnecessary burdens.

17. That they may appoint a General Treasurer and Particular Treasurer in each government when necessary; and, from time to time, may order the sums in the treasuries of each government into the general treasury; or draw on them for special payments, as they find most convenient.

18. Yet no money to issue but by joint orders of the President-General and Grand Council; except where sums have been appropriated to particular purposes, and the President-General is previously empowered by an act to draw such sums.

19. That the general accounts shall be yearly settled and reported to the several Assemblies.

20. That a quorum of the Grand Council, empowered to act with the President-General, do consist of twenty-five members; among whom there shall be one or more from a majority of the Colonies.

21. That the laws made by them for the purposes aforesaid shall not be repugnant, but, as near as may be, agreeable to the laws of England, and shall be transmitted to the King in Council for approbation, as soon as may be after their passing; and if not disapproved within three years after presentation, to remain in force.

22. That, in case of the death of the President-General, the Speaker of the Grand Council for the time being shall succeed, and be vested with the same powers and authorities, to continue till the King's pleasure be known.

23. That all military commission officers, whether for land or sea service, to act under this general constitution, shall be nominated by the President-General; but the approbation of the Grand Council is to be obtained, before they receive their commissions. And all civil officers are to be nominated by the Grand Council, and to receive the President-General's approbation before they officiate.

24. But, in case of vacancy by death or removal of any officer, civil or military, under this constitution, the Governor of the Province in which such vacancy happens may appoint, till the pleasure of the President-General and Grand Council can be known.

25. That the particular military as well as civil establishments in each Colony remain in their present state, the general constitution notwithstanding; and that on sudden emergencies any Colony may defend itself, and lay the accounts of expense thence arising before the President-General and General Council, who may allow and order payment of the same, as far as they judge such accounts just and reasonable.

READING AND DISCUSSION QUESTIONS

1. What are the key elements in Franklin's plan of union? How does he envision the colonies working together?
2. What need was the plan of union designed to meet?
3. Why do you think the plan failed to garner enough support to bring it into effect?

4-5 | Colonists Argue for an Alliance with Indians Against the French

State of the British and French Colonies in North America (1755)

As we saw in Chapter 3, relations between British colonists and Native Americans were strained throughout the eighteenth century. Native American peoples resented colonial encroachment, but many also realized the futility of prolonged resistance and forged

State of the British and French Colonies in North America (London: A. Millar, 1755), 69–75.

alliances when doing so suited their interests. For their part, the American colonists quickly recognized the key role that native peoples could play in defending themselves from French assaults as the French and Indian War began in 1756. In this source, published just before hostilities with France were formalized, an anonymous author argues for the necessity of befriending native peoples.

The Necessity of Using Indians in War, and of Gaining Their Friendship

The next preliminary point to be effected, is to secure the Indians in our interest; on account, as well of recovering and extending our trade, as of securing our colonies against the attack either of French or Indians.

Their way of making war and fighting is quite different from the European. They do not draw into the open field but shoot from behind trees; and are exceeding dextrous both at hitting their mark and sheltering themselves from the enemies fire or pursuit: for, there is no room for horse in countries overgrown with woods, which gave occasion to this way of fighting; and there is no overtaking them on foot they run so swiftly.

Therefore, in case of any war, either with Indians alone, or where they are auxiliaries, we must have Indians to oppose Indians. They must be fought with their own way. Regular forces being wholly unacquainted with their way of making war can be of no service against them: they are only of use to defend a fort, or to support Indian forces against regular troops. Besides, being used to fire from walls, they scorn to shoot from behind trees; and would rather die than go out of their own road to practise such a low kind of military art. Not considering that the nature of the country, which is, as it were, one continued wood, requires that way of going to war, and that of all the methods of fighting that is best which is safest.

The French of Canada know the importance of Indians on this account, and therefore never undertake any expedition without them. . . . [A]nd since they make use of them, there is still the more reason why we should; unless we had men enough of our own trained to their manner of making war.

Besides; the advantage of having the Indians our friends, may be inferred from the mischiefs they have done ourselves as well as the French; and the danger they have put the colonies in, both from within and without, when our enemies. Altho' the English, by dint of numbers, were able to support the wrongs which they did the Indians, and either destroyed or subdued them within the colonies; yet it cost them much blood and labour before they effected it, particularly in Virginia and New England; especially this last colony: where made such vigorous efforts at several times, and continued the war with so much obstinacy, even tho' much reduced by them; that the English, notwithstanding their great superiority in numbers, were scarce able to withstand them, and but for certain lucky incidents, might have been driven out of all their settlements. Those who left the country, preserve to this day their ancient animosities; and being joined by the other eastern tribes, continue to harrass the borders of the English, and do them all the mischief they can. They are now the more able to take revenge with more safety to themselves; as, having a large country to retreat in, they cannot be so easily surrounded by the English, and oppressed by numbers as they were when inclosed within the colonies, where it would have been better to have kept them by good usage. . . .

All the colony writers recommend the gaining the Indian friendship, as a matter of great importance to them. One of Carolina says, that the province is much strengthened by them; and that if trained to fire arms they would be very useful to that province, not only in case of an invasion to repel the enemy, but also by drawing other Indians to the English interest, or else destroying those who were not to be gained.

It must be confessed, that they are of great use, in either defending or invading a country. They are extremely skilful in the art of surprizing, and watching the motions of an enemy: they always know where to find you; but you never know where to find them: they disperse themselves thro' a country singly, or in very small parties, and lie on the lurch, to pick up stragglers, or procure intelligence: in which they act with an astonishing patience and indefatigableness, beyond any thing which an European could undergo; remaining in one place, and often in one posture, for whole days and weeks together, till they find an opportunity to strike their stroke, or compass their design, whatever it may be.

"Every Indian," says Mr. Kennedy,[1] "is a hunter; and as their manner of making war, by skulking, surprizing, and killing particular persons and families, is just the same as their hunting, only changing the object, every Indian is a disciplined soldier. Soldiers of this kind are always wanted in the colonies in an Indian war [or when Indians are employed] for the European military discipline is of little use in these woods." There is, therefore, an indispensible necessity of making use of Indians in our wars, unless we had men enough of our own trained in that sort of military exercise.

READING AND DISCUSSION QUESTIONS

1. What advantage does the author suggest the native peoples bring to the colonial cause?
2. What difference in warfare does the author see between European and Native American warriors?
3. What does this source suggest about the changing relationship between colonial Americans and the native peoples they encountered?

---

[1] **Mr. Kennedy**: Archibald Kennedy, the author of *The Importance of Gaining and Preserving the Friendship of Indians to the British Interest Considered* (1752).

4-6 | The North Carolina Regulators Protest British Control

Petition from the Inhabitants of Orange County, North Carolina (1770)

New tensions arose in the years immediately following the British and American victory in the French and Indian War (1754–1763). To pay Great Britain's large war debt, the British Parliament began imposing more taxes and regulations on the colonies, inciting colonial resistance. At the same time, in the western regions of colonies such as North and South Carolina, debt-laden farmers protested political, judicial, and economic policies disadvantageous to their interests. Disciplined mobs formed in these western regions to protest the use of British forces to defeat them and the prejudicial court actions that, in many cases, deprived them of their farms. This Regulator movement, though ultimately unsuccessful, revealed the class conflicts that divided colonists and pitted British subjects in America against royal representatives and their colonial dependents. While Regulators destroyed property, refused to pay taxes, and disrupted government, they also issued petitions and drew on the language of rights to plead their case.

The Humble Petition of the Inhabitants of Orange County humbly sheweth,

That as it is a Maxim in our Laws that no Law Statute or Custom which are against Gods Law or principalls of nature can be of any validity but are all null.

If therefore Laws themselves when against Reason and Justice are null and void much more the practice used by men in the Law which is contrary to the Law as well as Reason Justice and Equity ought to be condemned and surely it is against Justice Reason and Equity to exact Taxes and extort Fees that are unlawful from the poor industrious Farmers—Yet these are but a few of a great many more evils of that nature which has been of a long time our sad case and condition and to such a degree general among so many of the men of the Law that we quite despaired of any redress being to be had that way. But as you the Governor Kings Attorney Generall and other Gentlemen of the Law pledged to us your words your honours your oaths that we could and should be redressed by the Law it would be tedious as well as unnecessary to recite the world of fatigue expence and Trouble that we have been at to obtain redress in that way but in vain—for though so many of the Officers as has been convicted yet we can obtain none of our money back—but instead of refunding they still continue to take the same Fees James Watson and John Butler excepted—And notwithstanding the wheels in this work run so heavy we have so many of the Court Party against us yet we might nevertheless [have gained] our point could we have obtained Jurors of unprejudiced Men—for though the Law impowers the Justices of the Inferior Courts to appoint the Jurys yet it was to the end

"Petition of the Inhabitants of Orange County," in *The Colonial Records of North Carolina*, vol. 8, 1769 to 1771, ed. William L. Saunders (Raleigh, NC: Josephus Daniels, Printer to the State, 1890), 231–234.

they might be chosen of unprejudiced Men, this was the spirit end and design of the Law—But it has so happened that too many of our Justices are partys concerned some of them being insolvent high Sheriffs themselves and others insolvent Sheriffs securities, yet under all this disadvantage as we labored against this very unfair dealing the goodness of our course and the uprightness of our Intentions gained ground with such Justices as was not parties concerned and for some Courts past a few of the Jurors was unprejudiced Men, but at our last Inferior Court Tyree Harris and Thomas Lloyd took a most notorious and bare faced advantage of choosing the Judges [juries] on the first day of the Court contrary to the known and usual custom and have made up the Jury mostly of Men well known to be prejudiced in favor of extortionate Officers and of such Officers themselves. Tyree Harris at whose instance we suppose it was done was high Sheriff for the years 1766 & 1767, whose accounts are yet unsettled, and likely we may be sued by the Treasurer as well as the Vestry to the Court besides almost may we believe every under Sheriff he had is inditable for their Extortions and exactions of Tax[es] and most of them have already been found guilty and though they attempt to make you believe the charge against them for exacting 4d 0d & a shilling extraordinary from ignorant Men Women and in remote neighbourhoods to be a false charge yet it is not only notoriously known to be the truth by hundreds of people from whom and among whom they exacted it, but at the same time they exacted 4d more from every man in the County in the very same Tax and though this was what we had some Item of from the very beginning yet we could never come at the certainty thereof till now, we think it can be proved beyond all doubt and this is a very particular matter of great weight and moment as it was one immediate cause of the rise of the mob and for which reason we suppose the most strenuous methods has been used to hinder it from coming to light. In the next place Thomas Lloyd may also be said to be a party concerned as he is one of the insolvent Sheriffs Securities and likewise the Justice who committed H. Husband without a Warrant proof of any crime and without a Mittimus, besides all this he has been Vestry Man and Church Warden frequently these Ten years past and more during which time the Vestry accounts are unsettled and irregularly kept and large Ballances behind. Thomas Hart being the only Sheriff that ever settled which was for 1762, the particulars of whose accounts is also kept from the eyes of the public, all which is contrary to Law and for which neglect the Church Wardens and Clerks are indictable.

Mr Chief Justice you at our last Court seemed to be somewhat prejudiced against us in a speech that you made in which you signified your Jealosie that we acted through Malice, Ambition &c: But concluding if what we did was from motives to promote Justice detect Extortion &c: for the publick good that you wished us all the success imaginable and heartily concurred with us in our undertaking. Oh that you might be sincere and could but a known our hearts. However be that as it will your Speech could not but afford us consolation and encouragement to persevere for we could lay our hands on our hearts and call God to witness in ourselves that this was our whole sole end and purpose and that too out of pure necessity to keep ourselves and innocent helpless Neighbors from utter ruin our whole properties having become quite insecure as well as our characters — As the two persons who was indicted last Court for perjury by reason they had indicted and witnessed against Extortions are two honest innocent men — Yea we need say no more but that we know these two men are honest men of good characters and innocent of that charge, whereas on the contrary to pick the whole country there cannot be found men of much worse characters than many or most of those who have sworn against them. As for the objection that some pretend to make (to wit) that it is hard to find Jurymen but what is prejudiced to one side or t' other this objection has not the least foundation in Truth or Reason Absolutely no more than if a gang of horse thieves had been numerous and formidable enough to have engaged the same attention and concern of the publick — for those Extortioners and Exactors of Tax are certainly more dangerous than those Thieves and in the next place they and all who espouse their cause knowingly are as to numbers inconsiderably small, only that they have the handling the Law chiefly in their own hands — our late Elections help to prove this Diversion; we carried our Elections for Vestrymen twenty five to one — The consequence of not trying these men subject to Law is wooden shoes and uncombed hair — What sense or reason is there in saying any are prejudiced to our side for what is it we have done — we have labored honestly for our Bread and studied to defraud no man nor live on the spoils of other mens labors nor snatched the Bread out of other mens hands. Our only crime with which they can charge us is vertue in the very highest degree namely to risque our all to save our Country from Rapine and Slavery in our detecting of practices which the Law itself allows to be worse than open Robbery — It is not one in a hundred or a thousand of us who have broke one Law in this our struggle for only common Justice which it is even a shame for any Government or any set of Men in the Law once to have denyed us off — Whereas them as has acted the most legally are the most torn to pieces by the Law through malicious prosecutions carried against them.

To sum up the whole matter of our Petition in a few words it is namely these that we may obtain unprejudiced Jurys, That all extortionate Officers Lawyers and Clerks may be brought to fair Tryals — That the Collectors of publick money may be called to proper settlements of their accounts, namely the Sheriffs for the years 1764, 1765, 1766 & 1767 to which time the taxes was generally collected (a small part of the last year excepted) the refusing to settle for which or give us any satisfaction occasioned the past disturbances — If We cannot obtain this that we may have some security for our properties more than the bare humour of officers, we can see plainly that we shall not be able to live under such oppressions and to what extremities this must drive us you can as well judge of as we can ourselves, we having no other determination but to be redressed and that to be in a legal and lawful way — As we are serious and in good earnest and the Cause respects the whole Body of the people it would be loss of time to enter into arguments on particular points for though there is a few men who have the gift or art of reasoning yet every man has a feeling and knows when he has justice done him as well as the most learned.

Therefore that Justice which every man will be ashamed to own that ever he denyed us of when in his power to grant is the prayer of our Petition and your Petitioners as in duty bound shall ever pray.

Signed by 174 Subscribers.

READING AND DISCUSSION QUESTIONS

1. Identify the specific grievances that Regulators in Orange County had against the royal government of North Carolina.
2. How do the Regulators frame their argument in this petition? Who was the audience for the petition?
3. What does the Regulator movement reveal about colonial politics on the eve of the Revolution?

▪ COMPARATIVE QUESTIONS ▪

1. What were the major sources of conflict affecting colonial American society during the middle decades of the eighteenth century?
2. To what extent did religion unite or divide colonial society?
3. Why was colonial unity so difficult to achieve in these years?
4. How and to what extent did considerations of class define or enhance the conflicts of this period?
5. What do the lithograph of Franklin's electricity parlour game (Document 4-1) and Sarah Osborn's memoir of her religious revival (Document 4-2) suggest about the relationship between religion and science during the eighteenth century?

PART 2

DOCUMENT SET

The Causes and Consequences of the Peopling of North America

1607–1763

CHAPTER 3
The British Atlantic World, 1607–1750

CHAPTER 4
Growth, Diversity, and Conflict, 1720–1763

The first century and a half following the 1607 English landing at Jamestown was a period of dynamic growth, witnessing a massive movement of peoples to and within the North American colonies. Many came for some of the same reasons that had inspired fifteenth- and sixteenth-century explorers: the prospect of riches and the call of God. Increasingly, the American colonies were peopled by those expecting to stay. For various reasons, mostly connected to conditions in Europe, the colonies seemed to offer opportunities less attainable back home. This period, from 1607 to 1763, witnessed an English Civil War and the execution of a king, a series of wars between the European powers, religious persecution, and economic flux. These conditions shaped individual choices to stay or risk the uncertainties of a transatlantic crossing.

Of course, Native Americans and the enslaved Africans brought here unwillingly both experienced the European enthusiasm for migration and settlement in radically different ways. For them, this is a story of consequences more than causes. Their lives and communities were marked by this demographic phenomenon. The American Indian population suffered the impacts of disease and displacement from their lands. Enslaved people from Africa endured the loss of family, home, and identity as they were transformed from person to property. The peopling of North America during the seventeenth and eighteenth centuries enriched some but destroyed others. It also impacted the land as settlers cleared forests and planted towns, villages, and cities. Through these migrations, no one (and no place) was left untouched, as the sources in this document set show.

P2-1 | The Horrors of the Middle Passage

OLAUDAH EQUIANO, *The Interesting Narrative of the Life of Olaudah Equiano, or Gustavus Vassa, the African. Written by Himself* (1794)

Few eighteenth-century first-person accounts of slavery's Middle Passage exist, which makes Olaudah Equiano's autobiography especially valuable. Born in 1745 in Africa, but kidnapped and sold as a child into slavery, Equiano, also known as Gustavus Vassa, describes the harrowing conditions enslaved Africans endured in their forced migration across the Atlantic. Unlike most in his condition, Equiano was ultimately able to purchase his freedom and flee to Europe, where he became a leading abolitionist.

The first object which saluted my eyes when I arrived on the coast was the sea, and a slave ship, which was then riding at anchor, and waiting for its cargo. These filled me with astonishment, which was soon converted into terror, which I am yet at a loss to describe, nor the then feelings of my mind. When I was carried on board I was immediately handled, and tossed up, to see if I were found, by some of the crew; and I was now persuaded that I had got into a world of bad spirits, and that they were going to kill me. Their complexions too differing so much from ours, their long hair, and the language they spoke, which was very different from any I had ever heard, united to confirm me in this belief. Indeed, such were the horrors of my views and fears at the moment, that, if ten thousand worlds had been my own, I would have freely parted with them all to have exchanged my condition with that of the meanest slave in my own country. When I looked round the ship too, and saw a large furnace or copper boiling, and a multitude of black people of every description [chained] together, every one of their countenances expressing dejection and sorrow, I no longer doubted of my fate, and, quite overpowered with horror and anguish, I fell motionless on the deck and fainted. When I recovered a little, I found some black people about me, who I believed were some of those who brought me on board, and had been receiving their pay; they talked to me in order to cheer me, but all in vain. I asked them if we were not to be eaten by those white men with horrible looks, red faces, and long hair? They told me I was not; and one of the crew brought me a small portion of spirituous liquor in a wine glass; but, being afraid of him, I would not take it out of his hand. One of the blacks therefore took it from him and gave it to me, and I took a little down my palate, which, instead of reviving me, as they thought it would, threw me into the greatest consternation at the strange feeling it produced having never tasted any such liquor before. Soon after this, the blacks who brought me on board went off, and left me abandoned to despair. I now saw myself deprived of all chance of returning to my native country, or even the least glimpse of hope of gaining the shore, which I now

The Interesting Narrative of the Life of Olaudah Equiano, or Gustavus Vassa, The African. Written by Himself (London: Printed for and Sold by the Author, 1794), 46–57.

considered as friendly: and even wished for my former slavery, in preference to my present situation, which was filled with horrors of every kind, still heightened by my ignorance of what I was to undergo. I was not long suffered to indulge my grief; I was soon put down under the decks, and there I received such a salutation in my nostrils as I had never experienced in my life; so that with the loathsomeness of the stench, and crying together, I became so sick and low that I was not able to eat, nor had I the least desire to taste any thing. I now wished for the last friend, Death, to relieve me; but soon, to my grief, two of the white men offered me eatables; and, on my refusing to eat, one of them held me fast by the hands, and laid me across, I think, the windlass, and tied my feet, while the other flogged me severely. I had never experienced any thing of this kind before; and although not being used to the water, I naturally feared that element the first time I saw it; yet, nevertheless, could I have got over the nettings, I would have jumped over the side; but I could not; and, besides, the crew used to watch us very closely who were not chained down to the decks, lest we should leap into the water; and I have seen some of these poor African prisoners most severely cut for attempting to do so, and hourly whipped for not eating. This indeed was often the case with myself. In a little time after, amongst the poor chained men, I found some of my own nation, which in a small degree gave ease to my mind. I inquired of them what was to be done with us? They give me to understand we were to be carried to these white people's country to work for them. I then was a little revived, and thought, if it were no worse than working, my situation was not so desperate: but still I feared I should be put to death, the white people looked and acted, as I thought, in so savage a manner; for I had never seen among any people such instances of brutal cruelty; and this not only shewn towards us blacks, but also to some of the whites themselves. One white man in particular I saw, when we were permitted to be on deck, flogged so unmercifully with a large rope near the foremast, that he died in consequence of it; and they tossed him over the side as they would have done a brute. This made me fear these people the more; and I expected nothing less than to be treated in the same manner. I could not help expressing my fears and apprehensions to some of my countrymen: I asked them if these people had no country, but lived in this hollow place the ship? They told me they did not, but came from a distant one. "Then," said I, "how comes it in all our country we never heard of them?" They told me, because they lived so very far off. I then asked, where were their women? Had they any like themselves! I was told they had: "And why," said I, "do we not see them?" [T]hey answered, because they were left behind; I asked how the vessel could go? They told me they could not tell; but that there were cloth put upon the masts by the help of the ropes I saw, and then the vessel went on; and the white men had some spell or magic they put in the water when they liked in order to stop the vessel. I was exceedingly amazed at this account, and really thought they were spirits. I therefore wished much to be from amongst them, for I expected they would sacrifice me: but my wishes were vain; for we were so quartered that it was impossible for any of us to make our escape. While we staid on the coast I was mostly on deck; and one day, to my great astonishment, I saw one of these vessels coming in with the sails up. As soon as the whites saw it, they gave a great shout, at which we were amazed; and the more so as the vessel appeared larger by approaching nearer. At last she came to an anchor in my sight, and when the anchor was let go, I and my countrymen who saw it were lost in astonishment to observe the vessel stop; and were now convinced it was done by magic. Soon after this the other ship got her boats out, and they came on board of us, and the people of both ships seemed very glad to see each other. Several of the strangers also shook hands with us black people, and made motions with their hands, signifying, I suppose, we were to go to their country; but we did not understand them. At last, when the ship we were in had got in all her cargo, they made ready with many fearful noises, and we were all put under deck, so that we could not see how they managed the vessel. But this disappointment was the least of my sorrow. The stench of the hold while we were on the coast was so intolerably loathsome, that it was dangerous to remain there for any time, and some of us had been permitted to stay on the deck for the fresh air; but now that the whole ship's cargo were confined together, it became absolutely pestilential. The closeness of the place, and the heat of the climate, added to the number in the ship, which was so crouded that each had scarcely room to turn himself, almost suffocated us. This produced copious perspirations, so that the air soon became unfit for respiration, from a variety of loathsome smells, and brought on a sickness amongst the slaves, of which many died, thus falling victims to the improvident avarice, as I may call it, of their purchasers. This wretched situation was again aggravated by the galling of the chains, now become insupportable; and the filth of the necessary tubs, into which the children often fell, and were almost suffocated. The shrieks of the women, and the groans of the dying, rendered the whole a scene of horror almost inconceivable. Happily perhaps for myself I was soon reduced so low here that it was thought necessary to keep me almost always on deck; and from my extreme youth I was not put in fetters. In this situation I expected every hour to share the fate of my companions, some of whom were almost daily brought upon deck at the point of death, which I began to hope would soon put an end to my miseries. Often did I think many of the inhabitants of the deep much more happy than myself; I envied them the freedom they enjoyed, and as often wished I could change my condition for theirs. Every circumstance I met with served only to render my state more painful, and heighten my apprehensions and my opinion of the cruelty of the whites. One day they had taken a number of fishes; and when they had killed and satisfied themselves with as many as they thought fit, to our astonishment who were on the deck, rather than give any of them to us to eat, as we expected, they tossed the remaining fish into the sea again, although we begged and prayed for some as well as we could, but in vain; and some of my countrymen, being pressed by hunger, took an opportunity, when they thought no one saw them, of trying to get little privately; but they were discovered, and the attempt procured them some very severe floggings.

One day, when we had a smooth sea, and moderate wind, two of my wearied countrymen, who were chained together (I was near them at the time), preferring death to such a life of misery, somehow made through the nettings, and jumped into the sea; immediately another quite dejected fellow, who, on account of his illness, was suffered to be out of irons, also followed their example; and I believe many more would very soon have done the same, if they had not been prevented by the ship's crew who were instantly alarmed. Those of us that were the most active were, in a moment, put down under the deck; and there was such a noise and confusion amongst the people of the ship as I never heard before, to stop her, and get the boat out to go after the slaves. However, two of the wretches were drowned, but they got the other, and afterwards flogged him unmercifully, for thus attempting to prefer death to slavery. In this manner we continued to undergo more hardships than I can now relate; hardships which are inseparable from this accursed trade. —Many a time we were near suffocation, from the want of fresh air, which we were often without for whole days together. This, and the stench of the necessary tubs, carried off many. . . .

At last, we came in sight of the island of Barbadoes, at which the whites on board gave a great shout, and made many signs of joy to us. We did not know what to think of this; but, as the vessel drew nearer, we plainly saw the harbour, and other ships of different kinds and sizes: and we soon anchored amongst them off Bridge Town. Many merchants and planters now came on board, though it was in the evening. They put us in separate parcels, and examined us attentively.—They also made us jump, and pointed to the land, signifying we were to go there. We thought by this we should be eaten by these ugly men, as they appeared to us; and when, soon after we were all put down under the deck again, there was much dread and trembling among us, and nothing but bitter cries to be heard all the night from these apprehensions, insomuch that at last the white people got some old slaves from the land to pacify us. They told us we were not to be eaten, but to work, and were soon to go on land, where we should see many of our country people. This report eased us much; and sure enough, soon after we landed, there came to us Africans of all languages. We were conducted immediately to the merchant's yard, where we were all pent up together like so many sheep in a fold, without regard to sex or age. As every object was new to me, every thing I saw filled me with surprise. What struck me first was, that the houses were built with bricks, in stories, and in every other respect different from those I have seen in Africa. . . .

We were not many days in the merchant's custody before we were sold after their usual manner, which is this:—On a signal given, (as the beat of a drum), the buyers rush at once into the yard where the slaves are confined, and make choice of that parcel they like best. The noise and clamour with which this is attended, and the eagerness visible in the countenances of the buyers, serve not a little to increase the apprehension of the terrified Africans, who may well be supposed to consider them as the ministers of that destruction to which they think themselves devoted. In this manner, without scruple, are relations and friends separated, most of them never to see each other again. I remember in the vessel in which I was brought over, in the men's apartment, there were several brothers, who, in the sale, were sold in different lots; and it was very moving on this occasion to see and hear their cries at parting. O, ye nominal Christians! Might not an African ask you, learned you this from your God? Who says unto you, Do unto all men as you would men should do unto you. Is it not enough that we are torn from our country and friends to toil for your luxury and lust of gain? Must every tender feeling be likewise sacrificed to your avarice? Are the dearest friends and relations, now rendered more dear by their separation from their kindred, still to be parted from each other, and thus prevented from cheering the gloom of slavery with the small comfort of being together, and mingling their sufferings and sorrows? Why are parents to lose their children, brothers their sisters, or husbands their wives? Surely this is a new refinement in cruelty, which, while it has no advantage to atone for it, thus aggravates distress, and adds fresh horrors even to the wretchedness of slavery.

READING AND DISCUSSION QUESTIONS

1. What does Equiano's account tell us about enslaved Africans' experiences of migration from their homelands to the Americas?
2. While reading Equiano's story, what can you infer about the ways he and others like him adapted to the new social and physical environments both aboard ship and upon arrival in Barbados?

P2-2 | German Immigrant Describes Carolina Opportunities

CHRISTEN JANZEN, *Letter to His Family* (1711)

Hundreds of thousands of Europeans crossed the Atlantic during the seventeenth and eighteenth centuries to find better prospects in the Americas. English and non-English migrants, to say nothing of the enslaved Africans, created a religiously and culturally diverse North American population. German immigrants often settled in Pennsylvania, but many others took up farming in North and South Carolina. In this source, Christen Janzen, who emigrated from the Siebentaler, a region in southwestern Germany, writes home to his family to describe his new life in North Carolina.

God greet you most beloved souls, father, mother, related friends, and neighbors, always with our thousandfold greetings and obedient service. I wish you at this time to learn of my health, and to know that I must make my writing as short as I can compose it. I hope that you have the letters that I wrote from Holland and England. The most essential contents are that we came the 10th of June to New Castle in England, but the 6th I became a very sad widower.

In New Castle we lay five weeks. The 17th of July went aboard the ship and lay eight days at anchor. After that we sailed, under the all-powerful protection of

---

Christoph Von Graffenried's Account of the Founding of New Bern, ed. Vincent H. Todd (Raleigh, NC: Edwards & Broughton Printing Co., 1920), 316–320.

God, safely to land in Virginia. Also did not lose a person. A young son was born on the sea. His father's name is Benedict Kupferschmied. He worked a year for our dear brother, Christian Bürki. After that we went about a hundred hours by water and land, yet always guided and fed, and the people everywhere have done us much kindness and there is in this country no innkeeper. All go from one place to another for nothing and consider it an insult if one should wish to ask the price.

Brought here hale and hearty, the shoemaker Moritz did not die till he was on his farm. He was well on the whole journey. No one else of us Siebentaler people has died, but of the others though, three Palatines. Of the people among whom we live, however, a good many have died.

Regarding the land in general. It is almost wholly forest, with indescribably beautiful cedar wood, poplars, oaks, beech, walnut and chestnut trees. But the walnuts are very hard and full of indentations and the chestnuts very small but good. There is sassafras also, and so many other fragrant trees that I cannot describe the hundredth part. Cedar is red like the most beautiful veined cherry and smells better than the finest juniper. They are, commonly, as well as the other trees, fifty to sixty feet below the limbs.

The land in general is almost everywhere black dirt and rich soil, and everyone can get as much as he will. There are five free years. After that one is to give for an acre, which is much greater than a Juchart with us, two pennies. Otherwise it is entirely free, one's own to use and to leave to his heirs as he wishes. But this place has been entirely uninhabited, for we have not seen any signs nor heard that anything else ever was here except the so-called wild and naked Indians. But they are not wild, for they come to us often and like to get clothes of us. This is done when they pay with wild meat and leather, bacon, beans, corn, which the women plant and the men hunt; and when they, as most frequently happens, guide the Christians through the forest and show new ways. They have huts of cedar bark. Some also can speak English well. They have an idol and hold festivals at certain times. But I am sorry to say, of the true God they do not want to know anything. . . .

Wild and unplanted tree-fruits are not to be found here so good as Kocherthal[1] writes of South Carolina. I have seen no cherries yet. There are many grape-vines and many grapes on them, of which some are good to eat; and it can well be believed, if one had many together (they would do well). We are going to try to plant them for everything grows up very quickly and all fruit is of very good taste, but we do not enjoy them much yet.

We lie along a stream called Neuse. There six years ago the first (people), English, until two years ago (when) the Swiss people (came), began the cultivation. They are, as it seems to me, rather rich in cattle, all sorts of crops, the finest tree-fruit, and that, the whole year (except for) two months. From the nature of

[1] **Kocherthal**: In 1706, Joshua von Kocherthal, Lutheran pastor from southern Germany, published a pamphlet recommending South Carolina as a promising land for German settlers. Two years later he led refugees to New York under a grant from England's Queen Anne.

things we were behind in that regard, so that we do not have it yet; but we hope, through God's blessings to get it. We came shortly before Christmas and we have by God's blessing, Zioria, my son-in-law Peter Reutiger, and I, and others besides, much stronger houses than the English; have also cleared land in addition, and the most have put fences around.

It is to be hoped that now from the ground and the cattle we will get enough, through the grace of God who has always stretched out his hand helpfully and has brought us safely and unhindered through so many enemies, spiritual and worldly, and over the great sea. But one thing lies heavy on us which I cannot write without weeping, namely the lack of a true and zealous pastor. . . . We have, indeed, prayers in our houses every Sunday, but the zeal to cleanse away the canker of our old sins is so small that it is to be feared it will consume everything to the foundation, if the pitying God does not come to our help.

If it had pleased the good God to send some of our brethren and sisters or at least Christian Bürki as an instrument, as a physician of body and soul, I should have had good hopes that the light among us would not become an evil smelling lamp, for I do not believe there is a person here, either English, German, or French who would not have loved him heartily; I believe that his profession is especially good here and that he could have an estate according to his wish without doing work in the fields. For of good liquor and such medicine there is the greatest lack in this country, therefore I have a friendly request to make of you, dear brother; namely, as follows. I have married Christina Christeler, a widow of Sannen. I am her third husband. By the first she has four children. Two died in London. Her husband and one child upon the sea. But the eldest, a boy of thirteen, named Benedict Plösch, is at Mörigen in the baliwick Nidauw, staying with his deceased father's clientage. And he was alive four years ago. Her father was named Peter Christeler. Christen Walcker, who, with his wife died here in this country and left eight children, said to her that she has a rather large inheritance from her late father, left with her brother Moritz Christeler, for he has received a hundred pounds of it. When you go to Sannen to ask about it, I hope Heinrich Perret will be able to help you; for they have been nearest neighbors. And if it is as Walcker says you can take it into your hands.

Because my wife understands brewing so well and has done it for years, and the drink is very scarce here and neither money nor brewing pots are to be obtained here, otherwise I would not think of such a thing for you to do. But the pot must have two pipes but no worm; and if some reliable people should not be coming, would Mr. Ritter still be so good as to get it to me here; also four pounds worth of spice, such as ginger, pepper, safron, nutmegs, galangale,[2] cloves, each according to the proportion of the money? For here there is nothing but laurel. I have seen it on trees in the forest. But if there should be nothing to be got from the inheritance, I would most kindly beg you and my father, if he is still alive, to still help me somewhat from my own, for it is very important to me and especially to the women folks, who are very scarce here.

[2] **Galangale**: Galangale, or ganangal, is a ginger-like spice.

If only more people should wish to come, I advise that they take women with them if they want to have any, for here some of the very best men find no wives, because they are not here.

The journey is easily to be made if one can supply himself properly with old cheese, dried meat, and dried fruit, vinegar, wine, beer, and casks, butter, biscuits, in fine whatever is good to eat and feasible to transport, also a pan or kettle that is narrow at the top and broad below; for when the sea is violent the ship lies over on one side so that things are spilt. Yet I have never heard that a ship has sunk upon the high sea.

Whoever could provide himself with the things named above and should make an agreement with the ship captain that he give him liberty to cook and a good place to lie the voyage would not be hard. For we had young and old people, all are hale and hearty. Whatever one brings here in the way of wares is worth at least as much again. Linen cloth and glass would be especially needed, and is to be purchased very well in Holland.

I would have much to write. I must break off. Have patience with my bad writing, for whoever sees my hand and labor will believe that I have not written and studied much. Greet for us Christien Bürki and I should be glad if he could hear the contents of this letter.

I remain your well affectioned servant, and my parents' obedient son until death.

READING AND DISCUSSION QUESTIONS

1. What do you think Janzen's purpose was in writing this letter home to his family and friends?
2. How does Janzen's letter help you to understand the reasons why Europeans migrated to North America?
3. What are some of the advantages and disadvantages of using Janzen's letter as a source for understanding how eighteenth-century migrants adapted to their new circumstances?

P2-3 | An Indentured Servant Confesses to Murder

The Vain Prodigal Life and Tragical Penitent Death of Thomas Hellier (1680)

Thomas Hellier was a twenty-eight-year-old indentured servant who emigrated from Dorset, England, to Virginia in the late seventeenth century. His tragic story points to the disparity between the expectations that motivated his migration and the reality he faced once he arrived. While many who suffered similar disillusionment adapted to their new environments and survived as best they could, Hellier chose a different, more dreadful path: savagely murdering his masters. In time, colonists shifted from the use of indentured servants, bound for a period of seven years, to a slave-based agricultural economy, whose laborers were bound for life.

Thus had I trifled away and mis-spent my ten pounds and the price of my horse. Next, to supply necessity, I sold my Cloaths for want of money: so walking up Tower-ditch, I going in at the Eagle and Childe, enquired if there were any Ship-Captain quartered there? One replied, There was no Ship-Captain quartered in that house, but that he himself was concern'd about Seafaring matters. I enquired to what parts he was concern'd? He answered, To Virginia: So asked withal, if I were minded for that Country; if I were, I should have Meat, Drink, and Apparel, with other Necessaries provided for me. I replied, I had heard so bad a character of that Country, that I dreaded going thither, in regard I abhorred the Ax and the Haw. He told me, he would promise I should onely be employ'd in Merchants Accompts, and such Employments to which I had been bred, if they were here used.

On August the 10th, 77, I being over-perswaded, went on board the *Young Prince* Captain Robert Morris Commander; on the 5th of September ditto, the *Young Prince* weighed Anchor from the Downs; and on the 25th of October following, she arrived within the Capes of Virginia, and dropt Anchor at Newpersnews.

I was delivered into the custody and dispose of one Lewis Connor of Barmedoe hundred Virginia, who sold me off to one Cutbeard Williamson, living at a Plantation call'd Hard Labour, belonging to Westover-Parish in Charles City County Virginia: which said Williamson promised me I should be employed in Teaching his Children, and not be set to any laborious work, unless necessity did compel now and then, meerly for a short spurt. But nevertheless, though I wanted not for Cloaths nor Victuals, yet I found their dealings contrary to their fair promises; which much disheartened me. And though my labour at the Howe was very irksome, and I was however resolved to do my utmost endeavour at it; yet that which embittered my life, and made everything I took in hand burdensome to me, was the unworthy ill-usage which I received daily and hourly from my ill-tongued Mistriss; who would not only rail, swear and curse at me within doors, whenever I came into the house casting on me continually biting Taunts and bitter Flouts; but like a live Ghost would impertinently haunt me, when I was quiet in the Ground at work. And although I silently wrought as fast as she rail'd, plying my labour, without so much as muttering at her, or answering any thing good or bad; yet all the silence and observance that I could use, would not charm her vile tongue. These things burning and broyling in my Breast, tempted me to take the trip, and give my master the bag to hold; thereupon I vamped off, and got on board Capt. Larimore's ship, where I remained eleven days, or thereabouts, the Ship then riding at Warwicks-Creek Bay.

I was absent from my Master's business almost three weeks, but at length my Master hunting about, and searching to and fro, had discovered where I was, and so sending a Messenger, fetched me back home again. As I was upon my return homeward, I had a design to have knock the Messenger on the head; for which purpose I took up a great stone and carried it along in my hand a good

---

A Documentary History of American Industrial Society, vol. 1, eds. John R. Commons, Ulrich B. Phillips, Eugene A. Gilmore, Helen L. Sumner, and John B. Andrews (Cleveland: Arthur H. Clark Company, 1910), 360–365.

way, unknown to the man: but my heart failing me, I let drop that design. At length home I came, begg'd pardon of my Master for my fault, and all seemed pretty well again. But my usage proving still worse than before, my Mistress ever taunting me with her odious and inveterate Tongue, do all I would, and strive all the ways whatever I could, she, I found, was no whit pacified toward me. Whereupon I began to cast about and bethink my self, which way to rid me of that Hell upon Earth, yet still seeking if possible to weather it, but all in vain.

At last, Satan taking advantage of my secret inward regret, suggested to my vicious corrupt minde, that by ridding my Master and Mistress out of the way, I might with ease gain my Freedom, after which time I sought all opportunities to effectuate and bring to pass my said horrid contrivance: Concluding, when they were dead, I should be a Freeman. Which said execrable Project I attempted and put in execution May 24, 1678. Thus . . .

Betimes in the Morning before day, I put on my best cloaths, then got my Ax, and attempted two or three times to enter my Master's Lodging-room, still my heart failing me, I stept back again; but however at length in I rushed: A Servant-maid, who lay every night in the same Room, passed along by me the same time with her bed on her shoulder, or under her arm, to whom I offer'd no violence, but let her pass untouched; nor had I meddled with her, had she kept out of my way. From her I passed on to my Masters Bed, and struck at him with the Ax, and gave him several blows, as near as I could guess, upon the Head: I do believe I had so unhappy an aim with my hand, that I mortally wounded him the first blow. My Mistress in the interim got out of Bed, and got hold of a Chair, thinking to defend her self; and when I came toward her, struggled, but I proved to hard for her; She begg'd me to save her Life, and I might take what I would, and go my way. But all in vain, nothing would satisfie but her Life, whom I looked on as my greatest Enemy; so down she went without Mercy. The Wench to whom I intended no hurt, returned, as I suppose to rescue her Mistress; whereupon she suffer'd the same cruel Fate with the other two.

After this Tragedy I broke open a Closet, and took provision for my Journey, and rummaging my Mistress Chest, I took what I thought fit, as much as loaded a good lusty Horse; So taking my Master's Gun in my hand, away I hastened: But while the Horse stood without door, a neighbor came to the house, with an excuse to borrow the said Horse. To whom I frowning, answered very roughly, and threatening him, bid him be gone, he could not have the Horse; who departed, and (I suppose) betrayed to the other Neighbours some jealousie he had conceived, concerning some Mischief I had been doing. A Childe also belonging to the Family was run forth to betray the business. But before any body came, I was gone upon my intended progress with my Master's Horse loaded, and his gun in my hand.

After wandering the unknown Woods a tedious time, to and fro, and finding no path, I struck up towards a Plantation belonging to one Gilly, near Chickahommony Swamp, where I had a Ship-mate living; here I found a Path, and following that Path, it led me up to the house, where finding my Ship-mate, I enquir'd the nearest way to the Falls of James River: Who told me, he knew not the way, but said, he would go and enquire; so he called his Master's Son, who asked, if I would not walk into the house, and eat before I went. I said it was too early for me to eat: The said Gilly's Son-in-law came forth also, and very urgent they were to have me walk in and smoke Tobacco, seeing I would not eat. I told them, I would not smoke, but desired them to direct me my way, (still keeping my Gun in my hand, I being as shie of them, as they were watchful over me.) At last they told me, they would shew me the way; one walking before me, and the other following me, who led me to a Passage over a Water: where before I passed over, I had some occasion to lay my Gun out of my hand: Whereupon one laying hold of the Gun, said, This is a compleat Gun, and withal fired it off: Whereupon I discern'd my self surprised.

They told me I was to go no farther: So they seising me, I struggled a while, and had like to have been too hard for one of the men. But Gilly himself hearing the report of the Gun, run down toward the place; so being overpower'd, I was forced to submit to have my hands bound. Upon this seisure I was struck with silence, not having power either to confess or deny the Fact. They forthwith brought me before Mr. John Stith, the next Justice of Peace; This happened May 25, 1678. I had no power to answer the Justice to any thing, only I begg'd that I might have a Minister sent for to me, and then I should relate the whole matter. One Mr. Williams was sent to me the next morning (being Saturday) to whom I acknowledged the whole matter. After conference with the said Minister, I began by degrees to be rendred sensible of the heinousness of my horrid and bloudy Crime; for which I was Tryed at James-Town, July 26, 1678. And was Sentenced to be Hang'd in Chains the 27, ditto; according to which just Sentence, I am now deservedly to suffer here this instant 5th of August, 1678.

READING AND DISCUSSION QUESTIONS

1. What was Hellier's motivation for traveling to the colonies?
2. What can you infer about the daily life within a small plantation family from Hellier's testimony? What clues can the historian use to re-create the world Hellier entered?
3. Compare the challenges Hellier faces to those faced by other new arrivals in the colonies like Christen Janzen (Document P2-2) or Olaudah Equiano (Document P2-1).

P2-4 | Dangers of Missionary Work

GREGOIRE HURET, *The Death of Some Jesuit Fathers in Nouvelle-France* (1664)

Like Document 2-6, this image depicts Jesuit missionaries among North American native peoples. The French had colonized portions of North America during the seventeenth century. The Jesuit mission to the Huron and later the Iroquois began in the 1620s and was marked by their practice of living among the native peoples, learning their language and culture, and introducing Christian ideas and practices to individual tribal villages. They wished to immerse themselves within the lives of the native peoples, but as this image showing some Jesuit priests facing death in Nouvelle-France (New France) depicts, the results were not always what they had hoped.

The Death of Jesuit Fathers in Nouvelle-France, from 'Historiae Canadensis' by Francois Ducreux, published in 1664 (engraving) (b/w photo)/Huret, Gregoire (1606–70)/Bibliotheque Nationale, Paris, France /Bridgeman Images

READING AND DISCUSSION QUESTIONS

1. What point of view toward the native peoples does the artist seem to hold? What elements of the image help clarify this perspective?
2. In thinking about the likely audience for this image, what impact do you think the artist intended?
3. What does this image reveal about the causes and consequences of the Jesuit mission in New France?

P2-5 | Colonial Settlements Raise Indian Alarms
JAMES KENNY, *Journal* (1761–1763)

In the early 1760s, James Kenny was in charge of the trading store near Pittsburgh, in western Pennsylvania, an outpost established by the colony's Commissioners of Indian Affairs. Colonial authorities were clearly responding to the movement of white settlers to interior regions while establishing control over frontier land occupied by American Indians. As Kenny begins his diary, the North American phase of the French and Indian War was winding down. Here, he discusses colonists' encounters with American Indians.

9th.—Frederick Post came here from Tuscorawas & having a meeting with ye Indians there, before they set off (to ye Treaty) at Detroit, he let them know that the good Spirit had sent him amongst them in order to do them good & inform them in ye Christian Principels, to which they answer'd that they were very willing of his living amongst them, but not on them tearms, as they seen no better fruits or works amongst Christians than amongst themselves, but he told them that ye good spirit was with him, when he came to them in ye War time & that they had no reason to repent of his coming amongst them that time, and that now if they did not receive him on ye tearms he mentioned ye Good Spirit ordered him to leave them, and go to some others, having made them as ye head men of that Nation ye first offer & call'd for his Horse to be gone, but they would not consent to let him go, so he is now prepairing materials in order to build a House to live in, & keep School, & instruct them as far as he can or they will receive, but tells them that their hearts are not prepair'd to hear the gosple.

12th. —About this time ye Beaver King & Shingas came here & held a small council w^{t} Geo. Croughan,[3] & ye Beaver told me they would go to Philadelphia next Spring to Confirm their alliance with our Province. . . .

16th.—One Agness Miller, being a Captive amongst ye Shawnes, was delivered up here as also two other little Girls, Daughters of Charles Stuward & James McBride, taken from ye Coves, one of them being taken by Shingus & belon'd to Pisquition. Langdale had orders from Israel Pemberton to advance £20 for redeeming Agness, but she being deliver'd up cost nothing.

23^{d}—Langdale left this place and set off home, after leaving a Protest in Writing with me (as he was just going) being against all Josiah Davenports & my Actings in ye Store since ye Day he left it in order chiefly, as he told me, to clear himself if any thing happen'd in ye Goods which he said was only matter of form, as he never alledg'd any dishonesty to any of us. One Blaine ye officer which Commands at Ligonier came here. I have had no Answer as yet from ye Commiss, which gives Frederick Post some encouragement (if I am set at liberty) to go to see him to Tuscorawas.

John W. Jordan, ed., "Journal of James Kenny, 1761–1763," *The Pennsylvania Magazine of History and Biography,* vol. 37 (1913): 25–30.

[3] **Beaver King & Shingas . . . Geo. Croughan**: Beaver King (or Tamaqui) and Shingas were both leaders of the Delaware Indians. George Croughan served as deputy Indian agent in the Ohio frontier.

11[mo] *1*[st].—The Shawana Chiefs came here & Held a Treaty of Peace with Geo. Croghan where none was admitt'd but Croghan's Assistant, (Thomas Hutchins) & himself & Indians I heard they promis'd to keep in friendship with y[e] English for ever & blam'd y[e] French for drawing them away from y[e] English Intrest. . . .

12th.—Many Traders gone with Goods to Trade at y[e] Indians Towns. One Thomas Cape that was Prisoner amongst y[e] Shawanas, being taken from Cape Capen in Virginia, being set free, we have taken him to live with us. . . .

19th.—The Fort Banks here is very near raise'd which makes it look much Stronger than it was in times of more danger by accounts, y[e] front next y[e] Inhabitants being of Brick and Corners of y[e] Angles of Hewn Stone, about [?] foot High y[e] Back part next y[e] Point where y[e] two Rivers Meets being of Earth & soded all so that it grows thick of long Grass that was done last year & they have Moov'd y[e] Bank several times this Summer its four Squair with a Row of Barracks along each Squair three Rows of which are Wooden frame work & y[e] Row on y[e] Bank side next y[e] point is Brick also a large Brick House built this summer in y[e] South East Corner of y[e] Roof being now aputing on, having fine Steps at y[e] Door of Hewn free Stone, a Cellar all under it, at y[e] Bank Side of y[e] Barracks opens y[e] Doors of y[e] Magazines Vaults & Dungeons lying under y[e] Great Banks of Earth thrown out of y[e] Great Trinches all Round in these are kept y[e] Strores of Amunition &c & Prisoners that are to be tried for their Lives, in these Vaults are no light but as they carry Lanthorns, on y[e] South East Bastion stands a High Poal like a Mast & top Mast to Hoist y[e] flag on which is Hoisted on every first Day of y[e] Week from about Eleven to One o'Clock & on State Days &c there are three Wells of Water wall'd in y[e] fort, & a Squair of Clear Ground in y[e] inside of about 2 Acres.

20th.—I have been Inform'd by a Young Man that was order'd by y[e] Commanding Officer, Collonel Bouquet, (this Sumer) to Number all y[e] Dwelling Houses without y[e] Fort marking the number on each Door that there was above one Hundred Houses but y[e] Highest number I have seen by beter [account] there is 150 Houses, to take notice of I think was Seventy Eight, these being y[e] Inhabitants of Pittsburgh, where two years ago I have seen all y[e] Houses that were without ye Little Fort they had then, thrown Down, only One, which stands yet, also two that was within that little fort is now standing being y[e] Hospital now, all y[e] rest being Built since, which if y[e] Place continues to Increase near this manner it must soon be very large, which seems likely to me.

21[st].—As to y[e] Government of y[e] Place at p[re]sent y[e] Chief Laws have been Out by y[e] General's Orders, which are Viz 1[st] That all Subjects may by applying to y[e] Chief Enginear Build Houses, but none to Sell or Rent any; that no person shall buy of y[e] Indians, Horses nor Bells, &c.

11[mo] *21*[st].—To Sell no Rum or Strong Liquor nor give to Indians on Pain of having their Houses pull'd Down, & y[e] Transgressors being banished the place. There was also some time ago, restrections about Selling the Indians Powder & Lead to exceed five pounds for one man at Once of Each & that there must be no dealing in Trade after y[e] Evening Gun is fired after Sun Down. Some people have had their Houses pull'd Down for y[e] Brech of some of these Laws & themselves Banish'd.

25th.—This Day ye Provincial Soldiers Time expired, but are not discharged, y^e [Colonel] waiting for an answer whether they shall be continued over ye Winter.

27th.—Y^e Provincial Soldiers disarts without a Discharge & seems to be as willing to return, many of them as they were to List being kept to Constant Labour here at Building ye Banks of ye fort quarring Stone & Cutting Wood, which they perform'd as expeditiously as any that has work'd here & I heard that the [Colonel] should say they done an emense sight of work for ye time, so that our province has no small Share in raising ye Banks of Fort Pitt.

30th.—We have been very Busey in getting Home a Stock of fire-wood being Cut about a Mile up ye Allegheny & 150 Yards from ye River side some we haul'd with a Cart to ye River & some Carried & brought it home with a Battoe.

12mo 1st.—Many of ye Inhabitants here have hired a School Master & Subscrib'd above Sixty Pounds for this Year to him, he has about Twenty Schollars, likewise ye Soberer sort of People seemes to Long for some publick way of Worship, so ye School Master Reads ye Littany & Common Prayer on ye first Days to a Congregation of different Principels (he being a Prisbiterant) where they behave very Grave (as I hear), on ye occasion ye Children also are brought to Church as they Call it.

5th.—The Provincials are discharged & Marches off with [Colonel] Burd, this Place having but few Soldiers left in it.

Here is about 51 of ye Sennica Nation Wariors, with a Steady big Old Man, their Head, going to War against ye Cherokees. They have made a Speech at their Coming that we should not think hard of them Concerning ye Conspiracy they began this last Sumer, as that matter was Settled & they intend to live in peace with us for ye futor, & being in need of some necessaries they hop'd we would supply them as they were going against ye common Enemy to us as to them. This Nation are Said to be ye most against ye English of any of ye Six Nations. . . .

Sennica Wariors have got ye last provissions allow'd them this Day with orders to go being Supply'd with all they ask'd, they are very troublesome by crowding into ye Houses & thronging our fire Places, but behaves Civell ye Indians in General being so theevish that we are under ye necessity to watch them with ye utmost care & must be loosers after in some things unless we had as many spyes as they have thieves; this makes them fare ye worse amongst us, as we are affraid to let them Sleep in our Houses, or indulge them to tarry any longe time, but many of them are so good natured that they wont be affronted readily.

12mo 8th.—The Head Sennica Warior dealt Seven large Bucksins with me, when many of them Croud'd in ye Store being very Theivish (ye Agent being out) ye Warior seem'd not easy pleas'd with his full Pay which he took in Powder, so I gave him a Loaf of Bread which was satisfactory to them; one of them bringing a small Skin want'd Brass Wire for it, but could hardly please himself amongst a variety of sorts, telling me to hand more, which I looked upon it as a Stratagem to keep me bussie that ye others might have oppertunity to Steal something. Several of 'em want'd to get behind ye Counter but I always turn'd em back & all they got was a Handful of salt. One took out a kegg that stood behind ye door, whilst my Brother just step'd out, so I turn'd them all out & ye Hindmost stop'd by ye door & begg'd for a Little Salt, so I gave him a Handfull he being disappoint'd in Stealing of it.

READING AND DISCUSSION QUESTIONS

1. Is there anything in Kenny's account of life in western Pennsylvania that might have caused anxiety among the Native Americans living near the fort? What, for instance, might they have thought about Kenny's description of Fort Banks?
2. What does this source suggest about how the western migration of colonial peoples affected the Native American populations that they encountered?
3. How does Kenny describe the Native Americans who traded with the colonists? How would you use this source as evidence for mid-eighteenth-century Americans' attitudes toward Native Americans?

P2-6 | Making Room for Savannah

PETER GORDON, *A View of Savannah as It Stood the 29th of March 1734* (1734)

Savannah, Georgia was a planned community settled in 1733 by James Oglethorpe and a little more than a hundred other European migrants. While this 1734 engraving is an idealized view of the southern coastal city, it reflects the design Oglethorpe imposed on the city's growth. Oglethorpe established Georgia as a refuge for the poor and those of limited means and his city plan allotted equal plots to settlers as a way to ensure equality among them. Oglethorpe banned slavery from the colony and he insisted on fair trade with the neighboring Native Americans. Much of Oglethorpe's idealism did not survive (slavery was permitted in 1750), but his city plan did. This engraving, which depicts the city squares and carefully planned lots carved from the surrounding forest, hints at the environmental consequences of the peopling of North America.

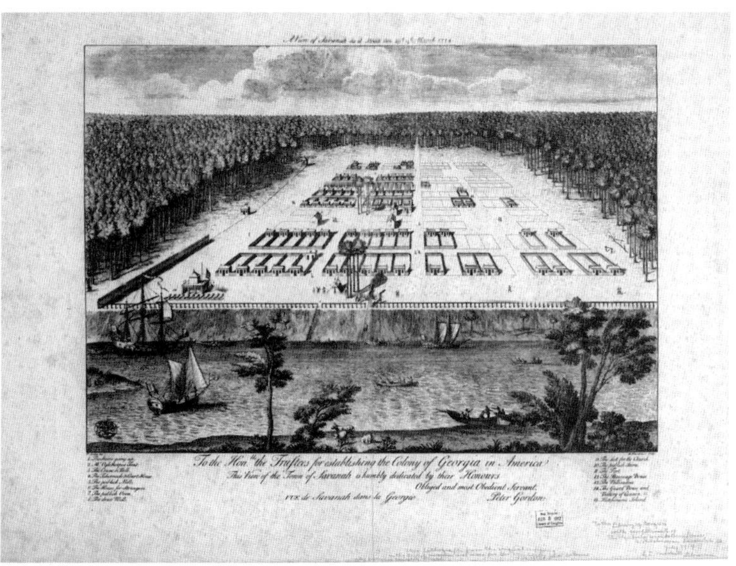

Library of Congress, Geography and Map Division.

READING AND DISCUSSION QUESTIONS

1. Examine Peter Gordon's engraving of Savannah's plan and identify the main features of Oglethorpe's vision for this new city. What aspects of the settlement do you think he prioritized?
2. What does this image suggest about the environmental impact of the settling of North America?

▪ COMPARATIVE QUESTIONS ▪

1. What do these sources suggest about the movement of various groups to and within the Americas during the era of colonization?
2. Compare the depiction of Native Americans in the image of the Jesuit Fathers (Document P2-4) and in Kenny's journal (Document P2-5). What similarities and differences do you see? What do these sources suggest about how the movement of colonial peoples affected Native American groups?
3. Compare the image of the Jesuit Fathers (Document P2-4) with Rev. Father Louis Cellot's letter to Father François Le Mercier (Document 2-6). What similarities and differences in point of view do they present regarding the causes and consequences of North American migration and settlement?
4. How did various groups adapt to their new social and physical environments? Compare the description of Native Americans in Kenny's journal (Document P2-5) with Canassatego's speech (Document 3-2).

5

The Problem of Empire

1754–1776

In late 1774, General Thomas Gage, the royally appointed governor of Massachusetts, wrote a desperate message home describing the crumbling state of colonial affairs: "Conciliating, Moderation, Reasoning is over, Nothing can be done but by forceable Means." The impasse Gage found upon taking up his duties had developed over the course of a decade. With the successful conclusion of the French and Indian War (1754–1763), the British Parliament tightened its administration of the colonies and sought to raise revenue to pay off wartime debts. Colonists who had been lightly governed before now felt the sting of Parliament's attention, and many resented the stricter colonial administration.

Richard Bland's 1766 essay, which opens this chapter, defended colonial rights and questioned Parliament's authority to legislate for the colonies. Some colonists recognized Parliament's claim of authority as legitimate, blamed excessive "liberty" for the unrest, and decried what they described as mob violence. However, by 1776, many colonists had rejected Parliament's claims of authority to legislate for them and were convinced that Britain had overstepped its rights. All that remained was some kindred loyalty to the king, but Thomas Paine's common-sense attack on monarchy destroyed even that. The ties connecting colony to empire through the person of the king had snapped. The result was revolution.

5-1 | A Virginia Planter Defends the Natural Rights of Colonies

RICHARD BLAND, *Inquiry into the Rights of the British Colonies* (1766)

The American Revolution was an extraordinary war of words. Long before Lexington and Concord, colonists fought verbal battles convincing themselves and others that the British Parliament was acting contrary to the rights of colonists. The colonists were British subjects, and they claimed their rights as such. Richard Bland (1710–1776), a Virginia planter and lawyer who was elected to the First and Second Continental Congresses, defended what he considered to be the colonists' natural rights. In his essay, written in the form of a letter to the anonymous author of a pamphlet supporting the Stamp Act, Bland argues that the rights of colonists were theirs by nature and not the gift of king or Parliament. This argument framed the debate and would eventually figure into Jefferson's bold claim in the Declaration of Independence that each was entitled to his inalienable right to life, liberty, and the pursuit of happiness.

SIR,[1]

I take the Liberty to address you, as the Author of "The Regulations lately made concerning" the Colonies, and the Taxes imposed upon "them considered." It is not to the Man, whoever you are, that I address myself; but it is to the Author of a Pamphlet which, according to the Light I view it in, endeavours to fix Shackles upon the American Colonies: Shackles which, however nicely polished, can by no Means sit easy upon Men who have just Sentiments of their own Rights and Liberties. . . .

I have undertaken to examine, with an honest Plainness and Freedom, whether the Ministry, by imposing Taxes upon the Colonies by Authority of Parliament, have pursued a wise and salutary [beneficial] Plan of Government, or whether they have exerted pernicious and definitive Acts of Power. . . .

The Question is whether the Colonies are represented in the British Parliament or not? You affirm it to be an indubitable Fact: that they are represented, and from thence you infer a Right in the Parliament to impose Taxes of every Kind upon them. You do not insist upon the *Power,* but upon the *Right* of Parliament to impose Taxes upon the Colonies. This is certainly a very proper Distinction, as *Right* and *Power* have very different Meanings, and convey very different Ideas: For had you told us that the Parliament of Great Britain have *Power,* by the Fleets and Armies of the Kingdom, to impose Taxes and to raise Contributions upon the Colonies, I should not have presumed to dispute the Point with you; but as you insist upon the *Right* only, I must beg Leave to differ from you in Opinion, and shall give my Reasons for it.

Richard Bland, *An Inquiry into the Rights of the British Colonies,* ed. Earl Gregg Swem (Richmond, VA: Appeals Press, Inc., for the Williams Parks Club, 1922), 3–7, 9–13, 21, 25–28, 30.

[1] **Sir**: Thomas Whately, British Member of Parliament (1761–1765) who supported the Stamp Act.

But I must first recapitulate your Arguments in Support of this Right in the Parliament. You say "the Inhabitants of the Colonies do not indeed choose Members of Parliament, neither are nine Tenths of the People of Britain Electors; for the Right of Election is annexed to certain Species of Property, to peculiar Franchises, and to Inhabitancy in some particular Places. . . ."

[You say that] "All British Subjects are really in the same [situation]; none are actually, all are virtually, represented in Parliament: For every Member of Parliament sits in the House not as a Representative of his own Constituents, but as one of that august Assembly by which all the Commons of Great Britain are represented. . . ."

Notwithstanding this Way of reasoning, I cannot comprehend how Men who are excluded from voting at the Election of Members of Parliament can be represented in that Assembly, or how those who are elected do not sit in the House as Representatives of their Constituents. These Assertions appear to me not only paradoxical, but contrary to the fundamental Principles of the English Constitution. . . .

Men in a State of Nature are absolutely free and independent of one another as to sovereign Jurisdiction, but when they enter into a Society, and by their own Consent become Members of it, they must submit to the Laws of the Society according to which they agree to be governed; for it is evident, by the very Act of Association, that each Member subjects himself to the Authority of that Body in whom, by common Consent, the legislative Power of the State is placed: But though they must submit to the Laws, so long as they remain Members of the Society, yet they retain so much of their natural Freedom as to have a Right to retire from the Society, to renounce the Benefits of it, to enter into another Society, and to settle in another Country; for their Engagements to the Society, and their Submission to the publick Authority of the State, do not oblige them to continue in it longer than they find it will conduce to their Happiness, which they have a natural Right to promote. This natural Right remains with every Man, and he cannot justly be deprived of it by any civil Authority. . . .

I hope I shall not be charged with Insolence, in delivering the Sentiments of an honest Mind with Freedom: I am speaking of the *Rights* of a People; *Rights* imply *Equality* in the Instances to which they belong, and must be treated without Respect to the Dignity of the Persons concerned in them. . . . I acknowledge the Parliament is the sovereign legislative Power of the British Nation, and that by a full Exertion of their Power they can deprive the Colonists of the Freedom and other Benefits of the British Constitution which have been secured to them by our Kings; they can abrogate [repeal] all their civil Rights and Liberties; but by what *Right* is it that the Parliament can exercise such a Power over the Colonists, who have as natural a Right to the Liberties and Privileges of *Englishmen* as if they were actually resident within the Kingdom? *The* Colonies are subordinate to the Authority of Parliament; subordinate I mean in Degree, but not absolutely so: For if by a Vote of the British Senate the Colonists were to be delivered up to the Rule of a French or Turkish Tyranny, they may refuse Obedience to such a Vote, and may oppose the Execution of it by Force. Great is the Power of

Parliament, but, great as it is, it cannot, constitutionally, deprive the People of their *natural* Rights; nor, in Virtue of the same Principle, can it deprive them of their *civil* Rights, which are founded in Compact, without their own Consent. . . .

[A]ccording to your Scheme, the Colonies are to be prohibited from uniting in a Representation of their general Grievances to the common Sovereign. This Moment [you say] "the British Empire in Europe and in America is the same Power; its Subjects in both are the same People; each is equally important to the other, and mutual Benefits, mutual Necessities, cement their Connexion." The next Moment [you say] "the Colonies are unconnected with each other, different in their Manners, opposite in their Principles, and clash in their Interests and in their Views, from Rivalry in Trade, and the Jealousy of Neighbourhood. This happy Division, which was effected by Accident, is to be continued throughout by Design; and all Bond of Union between them" is excluded from your vast System. *Divide et impera* [divide and conquer] is your Maxim in Colony Administration, lest "an Alliance should be formed dangerous to the Mother Country." Ungenerous Insinuation! detestable Thought! abhorrent to every Native of the Colonies! who, by an Uniformity of Conduct, have ever demonstrated the deepest Loyalty to their King, as the Father of his People, and an unshaken Attachment to the Interest of Great Britain. But you must entertain a most despicable Opinion of the Understandings of the Colonists to imagine that they will allow Divisions to be fomented between them about inconsiderable Things, when the closest Union becomes necessary to maintain in a constitutional Way their dearest Interests. . . .

I flatter myself, by what has been said, your Position of a *virtual* Representation is sufficiently refuted; and that there is really no such Representation known in the British Constitution, and consequently that the Colonies are not subject to an *internal* Taxation by Authority of Parliament.

READING AND DISCUSSION QUESTIONS

1. Why does Bland spend so much time discussing colonists' "natural" rights?
2. How does Bland's argument narrow the authority that Parliament claims over the colonies?
3. Bland accuses Parliament of adopting a policy he describes as "*Divide et impera*." What do you think he means in this context? What does he seem to anticipate the colonists' reaction to be?

5-2 | Colonists Protest Parliament's Acts

STAMP ACT CONGRESS, *Declaration of Rights* (1765)

The Stamp Act, passed by Parliament in 1765, attempted to raise revenue by requiring all colonists to pay a tax in the form of stamps affixed to all printed materials, including

---

Journal of the First Congress of the American Colonies (New York: E. Winchester, 1845), 27–29.

newspapers and legal documents. Many colonists objected to this measure, which to them seemed to depart from Parliament's traditionally limited exercise of authority. Protests quickly built momentum, resulting in the calling of the first congress, or meeting, of the colonies, which was held in New York on October 7, 1765. This Stamp Act Congress issued a "declaration of rights," which is reproduced below. Parliament, wishing to avoid conflict, repealed the Stamp Act but passed the Declaratory Act, which affirmed Parliament's authority.

The members of this congress, sincerely devoted, with the warmest sentiments of affection and duty to His Majesty's person and government, inviolably attached to the present happy establishment of the Protestant succession, and with minds deeply impressed by a sense of the present and impending misfortunes of the British colonies on this continent; having considered as maturely as time would permit, the circumstances of said colonies, esteem it our indispensable duty to make the following declarations, of our humble opinions, respecting the most essential rights and liberties of the colonists, and of the grievances under which they labor, by reason of several late acts of Parliament.

1st. That His Majesty's subjects in these colonies owe the same allegiance to the crown of Great Britain that is owing from his subjects born within the realm, and all due subordination to that august body, the Parliament of Great Britain.

2d. That His Majesty's liege subjects in these colonies are entitled to all the inherent rights and privileges of his natural born subjects within the kingdom of Great Britain.

3d. That it is inseparably essential to the freedom of a people, and the undoubted rights of Englishmen, that no taxes should be imposed on them, but with their own consent, given personally, or by their representatives.

4th. That the people of these colonies are not, and from their local circumstances cannot be, represented in the House of Commons in Great Britain.

5th. That the only representatives of the people of these colonies are persons chosen therein, by themselves; and that no taxes ever have been or can be constitutionally imposed on them but by their respective legislatures.

6th. That all supplies to the crown, being free gifts of the people, it is unreasonable and inconsistent with the principles and spirit of the British constitution for the people of Great Britain to grant to His Majesty the property of the colonists.

7th. That trial by jury is the inherent and invaluable right of every British subject in these colonies.

8th. That the late act of Parliament entitled, "An act for granting and applying certain stamp duties, and other duties in the British colonies and plantations in America, etc.," by imposing taxes on the inhabitants of these colonies, and the said act, and several other acts, by extending the jurisdiction of the courts of admiralty beyond its ancient limits, have a manifest tendency to subvert the rights and liberties of the colonists.

9th. That the duties imposed by several late acts of Parliament, from the peculiar circumstances of these colonies, will be extremely burthensome and grievous, and, from the scarcity of specie, the payment of them absolutely impracticable.

10th. That as the profits of the trade of these colonies ultimately center in Great Britain, to pay for the manufactures which they are obliged to take from thence, they eventually contribute very largely to all supplies granted there to the crown.

11th. That the restrictions imposed by several late acts of Parliament on the trade of these colonies will render them unable to purchase the manufactures of Great Britain.

12th. That the increase, prosperity, and happiness of these colonies depend on the full and free enjoyment of their rights and liberties, and an intercourse, with Great Britain, mutually affectionate and advantageous.

13th. That it is the right of the British subjects in these colonies to petition the king or either house of Parliament.

Lastly, That it is the indispensable duty of these colonies to the best of sovereigns, to the mother-country, and to themselves, to endeavor, by a loyal and dutiful address to His Majesty, and humble application to both houses of Parliament, to procure the repeal of the act for granting and applying certain stamp duties, of all clauses of any other acts of Parliament whereby the jurisdiction of the admiralty is extended as aforesaid, and of the other late acts for the restriction of the American commerce.

READING AND DISCUSSION QUESTIONS

1. How does the argument for colonial rights advanced here compare to the argument Bland made the following year, in 1766 (Document 5-1)?
2. How would you characterize the tone of this declaration of rights? Why, for instance, did the representatives of the Stamp Act Congress enumerate their points in this order?
3. The declaration discusses the "rights and liberties" of the colonists. What specific rights and liberties were they claiming?

5-3 | A Loyalist Decries the Boston Mob

PETER OLIVER, *Origin and Progress of the American Rebellion* (1781)

The repeal of the Stamp Act only temporarily calmed the storm. Parliament introduced new taxes in 1767, leading to colonial boycotts of British goods. Relations strained over the next few years as self-styled "Patriots" focused their anger at Parliament on its local representatives: those "Loyalists" in the colonies who supported Britain's policies. Many Loyalists found themselves attacked, intimidated, and physically abused. To Peter Oliver (1713–1791), chief justice of the Massachusetts Superior Court, Patriots were rebels acting with mob

Peter Oliver's Origin & Progress of the American Rebellion, ed. Douglass Adair and John A. Schutz (Stanford, CA: Stanford University Press, 1961), 152–157.

vigilantism. In his 1781 book, published after he had fled the colonies for England, Oliver included snippets, reproduced below, from Boston's newspapers detailing scenes of mob violence.

August 1774

A Mob in Berkshire assembled, & forced the Justices of the Court of common Pleas from their Seats on the Bench, and shut up the Court House, preventing any Proceedings at Law. At the same Time driving one of his Majesty's Justices of the Peace from his Dwelling House, so that he was obliged to repair to Boston for Protection by the Kings Troops.

At Taunton also, about 40 Miles from Boston, the Mob attacked the House of Daniel Leonard Esqr., one of his Majesty's Justices of the Peace; & a Barrister at Law. They fired Bullets into the House, & obliged him to fly from it to save his Life.

A Colo. [Colonel] Gilbert, a Man of Distinction & a firm Loyalist, living at Freetown, about 50 Miles from Boston, being absent about 20 Miles from his Home, was attacked by a Mob of above an 100 Men, at Midnight. But being a Man of great Bravery & Strength, he, by his single Arm, beat them all off. And on the same Night, & at the same Place, Brigadier Ruggles, a distinguished Friend of Government, & for many Years a Member of the general Assembly, was attacked by the same Mob; but by his firm Resolution he routed them all. They, in Revenge, cut his Horses Tail off & painted him all over. The Mob found that Paint was cheaper than Tar and Feathers.

September 1774

The Attorny General, Mr. Seawall, living at Cambridge, was obliged to repair to Boston under the Protection of the King's Troops. His House at Cambridge was attacked by a Mob, his Windows broke, & other Damage done; but by the Intrepidity of some young Gentlemen of the Family, the Mob were dispersed.

About the same Time Thomas Oliver Esqr. the Lieut Govr. of Massachusetts Province, was attacked in his House at Cambridge, by a Mob of 4000 Men; & as he had lately been appointed, by his Majesty, one of the new Council, they forced him to resign that Office; but this Resignation did not pacify the Mob; he was soon forced to fly to Boston for Protection. This Mob was not mixed with tag, rag & Bobtail only, Persons of Distinction in the Country were in the Mass, & as the Lieut. Governor was a Man of Distinction, he surely ought to be waited upon by a large Cavalcade & by Persons of Note.

In this Month, also, a Mob of 5000 collected at Worcester, about 50 Miles from Boston, a thousand of whom were armed. It being at the Time when the Court of Common Pleas was about sitting, the Mob made a lane, & compelled ye. Judges, Sheriff, & Gentlemen of the Bar, to pass & repass them, Cap in Hand, in the most ignominious Manner; & read their Disavowall of holding Courts under the new Acts of Parliament, no less than Thirty Times in the Procession.

Brigadier Ruggles's House at Hardwicke, about 70 Miles from Boston, was also plundered of his Guns, & one of his fine Horses poisoned.

Colo. Phips the high Sheriff of Middlesex, was obliged to promise not to serve any Processes of Courts; & retired to Boston for Protection.

A Committee, with a Justice Aikin at their Head, & a large Mob at their Heels, met at Taunton aforesaid, at Term Time, & forbid the Court of Common Pleas to sit.

Peter Oliver Esqr., a Justice of the Peace at Middleborough, was obliged by the Mob to sign an Obligation not to execute his Office under the new Acts. At the same Place, a Mr. Silas Wood, who had signed a Paper to disavow the riotous Proceedings of the Times, was dragged by a Mob of 2 or 300 Men about a Mile to a River, in Order to drown him; but one of his Children hanging around him with Cries & Tears, he was induced to recant, though, even then, very reluctantly.

The Mob at Concord, about 20 Miles from Boston, abused a Deputy Sheriff of Middlesex, & compelled him, on Pain of Death, not to execute the Precepts for a new Assembly; they making him pass through a Lane of them, sometimes walking backwards, & sometimes forward, Cap in Hand, & they beating him.

Revd. Mr. Peters, of Hebron in Connecticut, an Episcopalian Clergyman, after having his House broke into by a Mob, & being most barbarously treated in it, was stript of his Canonicals, & carried to one of their Liberty Poles, & afterwards drove from his Parish. He had applied to Governor Trumble & to some of the Magistrates, for Redress; but they were as relentless as the Mob; & he was obliged to go to England incognito, having been hunted after, to the Danger of his Life.

William Vassall Esqr., a Man of Fortune, and quite inoffensive in his publick Conduct, tho' a Loyalist, was travelling with his Lady from Boston to his Seat at Bristol, in Rhode Island Government, about 60 Miles from Boston, & were pelted by the Mob in Bristol, to the endangering of their Lives.

All the Plimouth Protestors against Riots, as also all the military Officers, were compelled by a Mob of 2000 Men collected from that County & the County of Barnstable to recant & resign their military Commissions. Although the Justices of the Peace were then sitting in the Town of Plimouth, yet the Mob ransack'd the House of a Mr. Foster, a Justice of the Court of Common Pleas, a Man of 70 Years of Age, which obliged him to fly into the Woods to secrete himself, where he was lost for some Time and was very near to the loosing of his Life. Afterwards, they deprived him of his Business, & would not suffer him to take the Acknowledgment of a Deed.

A Son of one of the East India Companies Agents being at Plimouth collecting Debts, a Mob roused him, in the Night, & he was obliged to fly out of the Town; but ye. Midnight favoured his Escape.

December 1774

A Jesse Dunbar, of Hallifax, in the County of Plimouth, an honest Drover, had bought a fat Ox of one of his Majesty's new Council, & carried it to Plimouth for sale. The Ox was hung up & skinned. He was just upon quartering it, when the Town's Committee came to the Slaughter House, & finding that the Ox was bought of one of the new Councellors, they ordered it into a Cart, & then put Dunbar into the Belly of the Ox and carted him 4 Miles, with a Mob around him, when they made him pay a Dollar after taking three other Cattle & an Horse from him. They then delivered him to another Mob, who carted him 4 Miles further, & forced another Dollar from him. The second Mob delivered him to a third Mob, who abused him by throwing Dirt at him, as also throwing the Offals, in his Face & endeavoring to cover him with it, to the endangering his Life, & after other Abuses, & carrying him 4 Miles further, made him pay another Sum of Mony. They urged the Councellors Lady, at whose House they stopped, to take the Ox; but she being a Lady of a firm Mind refused; upon which they tipped the Cart up & the Ox down into the Highway, & left it to take Care of itself. And in the Month of February following, this same Dunbar was selling Provisions at Plimouth, when the Mob seized him, tied him to his Horse's Tail, & in that Manner drove him through Dirt & mire out of the Town, & he falling down, his Horse hurt him.

In November 1774, David Dunbar of Hallifax aforesaid, being an Ensign in the Militia, a Mob headed by some of the Select Men of the Town, demand[ed] his Colours of him. He refused, saying, that if his commanding Officer demanded them he should obey, otherwise he would not part with them: upon which they broke into his House by Force & dragged him out. They had prepared a sharp Rail to set him upon; & in resisting them they seized him (by his private parts) & fixed him upon the Rail, & was held on it by his Legs & Arms, & tossed up with Violence & greatly bruised so that he did not recover for some Time. They beat him, & after abusing him about two Hours he was obliged, in Order to save his Life, to give up his Colours.

Quaere—Whether it would not have been as strictly legal to have stolen the Colours from his House, without all this Parade?

The Mob Committee, of the County of York, where Sr. William Pepperells large Estate lay, ordered that no Person should hire any of his Estates of him, nor buy any Wood of him, nor pay any Debts to him that were due to him.

One of the Constables of Hardwick, for refusing to pay the Provincial Collection of Taxes which he had gathered, to the new Receiver General of the rebel Government, was confined & bound for 36 Hours, & not suffered to lie in a Bed, & threatened to be sent to Simsbury Mines in Connecticut. These Mines being converted into a Prison, 50 Feet under Ground, where it is said that many Loyalists have suffered. The Officers Wife being dangerously ill, they suffered him to see her, after he had complied.

The aforementioned Colo. Gilbert was so obnoxious for his Attachment to Government, that the Mobs being sometimes afraid to attack him openly, some of them secretly fired Balls at him in the Woods. And as he was driving a Number of Sheep to his Farm, he was attacked by 30 or 40 of them, who robbed him of part of the Flock, but he beat the Mob off. And this same Colo. Gilbert was, some Time after, travelling on his Business, when he stopped at an Inn to bait his Horse. Whilst he was in the House, some Person lift up the Saddle from his Horse & put a Piece of a broken Glass Bottle under the Saddle; & when the Colo. mounted, the Pressure run the Glass into the Horses back, which made him frantick. The Horse threw his rider, who was so much hurt as not to recover his Senses 'till he was carried & arrived at his own House, at 3 Miles distance.

In September 1774, when the Court of Common Pleas was assembled for the Business of the Term, at Springfield, a large Mob collected, & prevented the sitting of the Court; they would not suffer Bench or Bar to enter the Court House; but obliged Bench, Sheriffs & Bar, with their Hats off, in a most humiliating Manner, to desist.

February 1775

A Number of Ladies, at Plimouth, attempted to divert their selves at the publick Assembly Room; but not being connected with the rebel Faction, the Committee Men met, and the Mob collected who flung Stones & broke the Windows & Shutters of the Room, endangering the Lives of the Company, who were obliged to break up, & were abused to their Homes.

Soon after this, the Ladies diverted their selves by riding out of Town, but were followed & pelted by the Mob, & abused with the most indecent Language.

The Honble. Israel Williams Esqr., who was appointed one of his Majesty's new Council, but had refused the Office by Reason of bodily Infirmities, was taken from his House, by a Mob, in the Night, & carried several Miles; then carried home again, after being forced to sign a Paper which they drafted; & a guard set over him to prevent his going from Home.

A Parish Clerk of an Episcopal Church at East Haddum in Connecticut, a Man of 70 Years of Age, was taken out of his Bed in a Cold Night, & beat against his Hearth by Men who held him by his Arms & Legs. He was then laid across his Horse, without his Cloaths, & drove to a considerable Distance in that naked Condition. His Nephew Dr. Abner Beebe, a Physician, complained of the bad Usage of his Uncle, & spoke very freely in Favor of Government; for which he was assaulted by a Mob, stripped naked, & hot Pitch was poured upon him, which blistered his Skin. He was then carried to an Hog Sty & rubbed over with Hogs Dung. They threw the Hog's Dung in his Face, & rammed some of it down his Throat; & in that Condition exposed to a Company of Women. His House was attacked, his Windows broke, when one of his Children was sick, & a Child of his went into Distraction upon this Treatment. His Gristmill was broke, & Persons prevented from grinding at it, & from having any Connections with him.

All the foregoing Transactions were before the Battle of Lexington, when the Rebels say that the War began.

READING AND DISCUSSION QUESTIONS

1. What propaganda value do you think these reports of violence lent to the Loyalist cause?
2. Describe the differences you see in the way Oliver depicts the Patriots and the way they presented themselves, for example, in the Stamp Act Congress (Document 5-2).
3. According to Oliver's evidence, what were the rebels attacking and why?

5-4 | Woman Loyalist Describes Patriot Menace

CHRISTIAN BARNES, *Letter to Elizabeth Smith* (June 1770)

As tensions in the colonies grew, committees of safety rapidly emerged as extralegal governments, sharing information and news and enforcing Patriot policies such as colonial boycotts of British imports. Many Loyalists worried about the activities of these unelected and unaccountable groups. In this letter from June 1770, Christian Barnes, wife of loyalist merchant Henry Barnes, wrote to her friend Elizabeth Smith about recent events. As a merchant whose livelihood depended on trade with Britain, her husband was a target of mob violence. As she notes, they both suffered at the hands of vigilantes who seized their goods and destroyed their carriage. Near the end of the letter, she comments on the fate of Thomas Preston, the British officer who was at what became known among Patriots as the Boston Massacre on March 5, 1770. Preston, whose defense lawyer was Boston Patriot and future president John Adams, was later acquitted of murder charges. Barnes and her husband fled Massachusetts in late 1775 and ultimately settled in Bristol, England.

June, 1770

Dear Mad'm,—It is long since I have dabbled in politics, and sorry I am to resume the subject . . .

The spirit of discord and confusion which has prevailed with so much violence in Boston has now begun to spread itself into the country. These poor deluded people with whom we have lived so long in peace and harmony have been influenced by the Sons of Rapin[2] to take every method to distress us. At their March meeting they entered into resolves simular [sic.] to those you have often seen in the Boston newspapers. At their next meeting they chose four inspectors,—men of the most vioulent disposition of any in the town,—to watch those who should purchase goods at the store, with intent that their names should be recorded as enimes to their country. . .

While all this was in agitation there was great outrages committed and insults offered to the importers in Boston, so that some of them have been compelled to quit the town, as not only their property but their lives were in danger. Nor are we wholly free from apprehensions of this like treetment, for they have already begun to commit outrages. The first thing that fell a sacrifice to their mallace and revenge was the coach, which caused so much decention between us. This they took the cushings out of and put them in the brook, and the next night cut the carriage to pieces. Not long after they broke the windows at the Pearl Ash Works[3]. . .

The greatest loss we have as yet met with was by a mob in Boston, who, a few nights ago, attacked a wagon-load of goods which belonged to us. They abused the driver, and cut a bag of pepper, letting it all into the street; then gathered it up

---

Letters of James Murray, Loyalist, ed. Nina Moore Tiffany (Boston, MA, 1901), 175–179.

[2] **Sons of Rapin**: She means rapine, meaning the violent seizure of another's property.

[3] **Pearl Ash Works**: Among his many commercial ventures, Henry manufactured pearl ash (potassium carbonate) which was used as a leavener for baked goods.

in their handkerchiefs and hatts, and carried it off. The rest of the load they ordered back into the publick store, of which the Well Disposed Commity keeps the key. . . the next day an effigy was hung upon a hill in sight of the House, with a paper pinned to the breast, whereon was wrote, "Henry Barnes," as infamous importer. This hung up all day, and at night they burnt it. A few nights after they stole the covering from the wagon, which was tarred to secure the goods from the weather, and the same night stole a man's horse from a neighboring stable. They dressed an image in this wagon covering, tarred the horse, saddle and bridle, placed the image upon his back, and set him loose about the town, with an infamous paper pinned to the breast, which was summed up with wishing of us all in hill. But still finding that their malice had no effect, they made a bold push and dropped an incendiary letter. . . It is not possible for me to express what I suffered upon the perusal of this letter. I could not recollect any one person that we had ever injured or even wished ill to, nor could I imagine such villany ever entered into the heart of man. . . I received a letter from Miss Cummings, which was far from being a cordial to my drooping spirits. She writes me word that one of the McMasters had been carted out of town at noonday in a most ignominious manner, and that the other two brothers had fled for their lives. That the news arrived by Hall had revived the spirit of the other party to such a degree that they had everything to fear, and that it was everybody's opinion poor Preston would be hanged. This is the officer who is in jail for the unhappy affair on the fifth of March.

A gentleman arrived from Boston in the evening and told us that Mr. Hulton's windows had been broke and the family had fled to the castle for protection. You may judge what sleep I had that night, and, indeed, ever since we have sleept in such a manner that I can hardly be called rest. It is the business of the evening to see the firearms loaded, and lights properly placed in the stores and house; and this precaution we have taken ever since we received the letter. . .

July 1st. The affair of Cutler turned out in having his goods seized and committed to the publick store, because he had purchased them of Mr. Lillie, an importer. I look upon all goods seized and committed to that store as much forfeited to the owner as if they were in the bottom of the sea. For they begin to talk of selling them at vendue[4], and distribueting the money to the poor. This will make the poor, as they call them, very assiduous in seizing everything that comes in their way, and will likewise deter people from purchasing of importers, a thing which they have never yet been able to bring to pass.

READING AND DISCUSSION QUESTIONS

1. What was this Loyalist's experience of the Revolutionary era?
2. Christian Barnes, like all women during this period, had no independent political rights so she could not have voted for either the Patriot or Loyalist cause. Yet, she was clearly seen by Patriots as a Loyalist. Why? What does her experience suggest about the fate of women generally during this period?

---

[4] **Vendue**: A public auction.

5-5 | The Danger of Too Much Liberty

THOMAS HUTCHINSON, *Letter to Thomas Whately* (1769)

As all sides attempted to understand the cause of the conflict between crown and colony, different actors diagnosed the problem in different ways. For Patriots, the culprit was Parliament's encroachment on their natural rights and liberties. For Loyalists, such as Governor Thomas Hutchinson of Massachusetts, excessive regard for their liberties encouraged colonists to act in ways contrary to their interests as subjects of the British crown. Hutchinson wrote a series of letters to Thomas Whately, a former member of Parliament and the Board of Trade. In one of those letters, reproduced below, Hutchinson offers his advice on restraining the colonists. These letters were leaked to Benjamin Franklin, then in London, and published in the Boston newspapers in 1773, inflaming the Patriots who already assumed Hutchinson was conspiring against their interests.

Boston, 20th January 1769.

Dear Sir,

You have laid me under very great obligations by the very clear and full account of proceedings in Parliament, which I received from you by Capt. Scott. You have also done much service to the people of the province. For a day or two after the ship arrived, the enemies of government gave out that their friends in Parliament were increasing, and all things would be soon on the old footing; in other words that all acts imposing duties would be repealed, the Commissioners board dissolved, the customs put on the old footing, and illicit trade be carried on with little or no hazard. It was very fortunate that I had it in my power to prevent such a false representation from spreading through the province. I have been very cautious of using your name, but I have been very free in publishing abroad the substance of your letter, and declaring that I had my intelligence from the best authority, and have in a great measure defeated the ill design in raising and attempting to spread so groundless a report. What marks of resentment the Parliament will show, whether they will be upon the province in general or particular persons, is extremely uncertain, but that they will be placed somewhere is most certain, and I add, because I think it ought to be so that those who have been most steady in preserving the constitution and opposing the licentiousness of such as call themselves Sons of Liberty will certainly meet with favor and encouragement.

This is most certainly a crisis. I really wish that there may not have been the least degree of severity beyond what is absolutely necessary to maintain, I think I may say to you the dependance which a colony ought to have upon the parent state; but if no measures shall have been taken to secure this dependance, or nothing more than some declaratory acts or resolves, it is all over with us. The friends of government will be utterly disheartened, and the friends of anarchy will be afraid of nothing be it ever so extravagant.

The Letters of Governor Hutchinson and Lieut. Governor Oliver (London: J. Wilkie, 1774), 15–17.

The last vessel from London had a quick passage. We expect to be in suspense for the three or four next weeks and then to hear our fate. I never think of the measures necessary for the peace and good order of the colonies without pain. There must be an abridgment of what are called English liberties. I relieve myself by considering that in a remove from the state of nature to the most perfect state of government there must be a great restraint of natural liberty. I doubt whether it is possible to project a system of government in which a colony 3000 miles distant from the parent state shall enjoy all the liberty of the parent state. I am certain I have never yet seen the projection. I wish the good of the colony when I wish to see some further restraint of liberty rather than the connexion with the parent state should be broken; for I am sure such a breach must prove the ruin of the colony. Pardon me this excursion, it really proceeds from the state of mind into which our perplexed affairs often throw me.

I have the honor to be with very great esteem, Sir, your most humble and most obedient servant,

THO. HUTCHINSON

READING AND DISCUSSION QUESTIONS

1. What does Hutchinson emphasize in his assessment of the political turmoil disrupting Boston?
2. How might Hutchinson have responded to Bland's argument (Document 5-1) about the natural rights of colonists?

5-6 | Thomas Paine Attacks the Monarchy

THOMAS PAINE, *Common Sense* (1776)

Much of the political argumentation in the Revolutionary period focused on whether Parliament had the authority to legislate for the colonies. Patriots rallied behind the slogan "no taxation without representation," and once they became convinced that Parliament was not their legislature, it was only their connection as subjects of the king that tethered them to the empire. Published in 1776, months before the signing of the Declaration of Independence, Thomas Paine's *Common Sense* focused on that relationship and called into disrepute the very idea of monarchy. *Common Sense* was significant for how it helped reluctant colonists sever their connection to what Paine implied was an irrational institution.

Of Monarchy and Hereditary Succession

Mankind being originally equals in the order of creation, the equality could only be destroyed by some subsequent circumstance; the distinctions of rich, and

Life and Writings of Thomas Paine, ed. Daniel Edwin Wheeler (New York: Vincent Parke and Company, 1908), 12–13, 19–20, 24, 26–32, 35–37.

poor, may in a great measure be accounted for, and that without having recourse to the harsh ill sounding names of oppression and avarice. Oppression is often the consequence, but seldom or never the means of riches; and though avarice will preserve a man from being necessitously poor, it generally makes him too timorous to be wealthy.

But there is another and greater distinction for which no truly natural or religious reason can be assigned, and that is, the distinction of men into KINGS and SUBJECTS. Male and female are the distinctions of nature, good and bad the distinctions of heaven; but how a race of men came into the world so exalted above the rest, and distinguished like some new species, is worth enquiring into, and whether they are the means of happiness or of misery to mankind.

In the early ages of the world, according to the scripture chronology, there were no kings; the consequence of which was there were no wars; it is the pride of kings which throw mankind into confusion. Holland without a king hath enjoyed more peace for this last century than any of the monarchical governments in Europe. Antiquity favors the same remark; for the quiet and rural lives of the first patriarchs hath a happy something in them, which vanishes away when we come to the history of Jewish royalty.

Government by kings was first introduced into the world by the Heathens, from whom the children of Israel copied the custom. It was the most prosperous invention the Devil ever set on foot for the promotion of idolatry. The Heathens paid divine honors to their deceased kings, and the Christian world hath improved on the plan by doing the same to their living ones. How impious is the title of sacred majesty applied to a worm, who in the midst of his splendor is crumbling into dust! . . .

To the evil of monarchy we have added that of hereditary succession; and as the first is a degradation and lessening of ourselves, so the second, claimed as a matter of right, is an insult and an imposition on posterity. For all men being originally equals, no one by birth could have a right to set up his own family in perpetual preference to all others for ever, and though himself might deserve some decent degree of honors of his contemporaries, yet his descendants might be far too unworthy to inherit them. One of the strongest natural proofs of the folly of hereditary right in kings, is, that nature disapproves it, otherwise, she would not so frequently turn it into ridicule by giving mankind an ass for a lion.

Secondly, as no man at first could possess any other public honors than were bestowed upon him, so the givers of those honors could have no power to give away the right of posterity, and though they might say "We choose you for our head," they could not, without manifest injustice to their children, say "that your children and your children's children shall reign over ours for ever." Because such an unwise, unjust, unnatural compact might (perhaps) in the next succession put them under the government of a rogue or a fool. Most wise men, in their private sentiments, have ever treated hereditary right with contempt; yet it is one of those evils, which when once established is not easily removed; many submit from fear, others from superstition, and the more powerful part shares with the king the plunder of the rest. . . .

But it is not so much the absurdity as the evil of hereditary succession which concerns mankind. Did it ensure a race of good and wise men it would have the seal of divine authority, but as it opens a door to the foolish, the wicked, and the improper, it hath in it the nature of oppression. Men who look upon themselves born to reign, and others to obey, soon grow insolent; selected from the rest of mankind their minds are early poisoned by importance; and the world they act in differs so materially from the world at large, that they have but little opportunity of knowing its true interests, and when they succeed to the government are frequently the most ignorant and unfit of any throughout the dominions. . . .

If we inquire into the business of a king, we shall find that in some countries they have none; and after sauntering away their lives without pleasure to themselves or advantage to the nation, withdraw from the scene, and leave their successors to tread the same idle round. In absolute monarchies the whole weight of business, civil and military, lies on the king; the children of Israel in their request for a king, urged this plea "that he may judge us, and go out before us and fight our battles." But in countries where he is neither a judge nor a general, as in England, a man would be puzzled to know what is his business.

The nearer any government approaches to a republic the less business there is for a king. It is somewhat difficult to find a proper name for the government of England. Sir William Meredith calls it a republic; but in its present state it is unworthy of the name, because the corrupt influence of the crown, by having all the places in its disposal, hath so effectually swallowed up the power, and eaten out the virtue of the house of commons (the republican part in the constitution) that the government of England is nearly as monarchical as that of France or Spain. . . .

[I]t is the republican and not the monarchical part of the constitution of England which Englishmen glory in, viz. the liberty of choosing an house of commons from out of their own body—and it is easy to see that when republican virtue fails, slavery ensues. Why is the constitution of England sickly, but because monarchy hath poisoned the republic, the crown hath engrossed the commons?

In England a king hath little more to do than to make war and give away places; which in plain terms, is to impoverish the nation and set it together by the ears. . . . Of more worth is one honest man to society and in the sight of God, than all the crowned ruffians that ever lived.

Thoughts on the Present State of American Affairs

In the following pages I offer nothing more than simple facts, plain arguments, and common sense; and have no other preliminaries to settle with the reader, than that he will divest himself of prejudice and prepossession, and suffer his reason and his feelings to determine for themselves; that he will put on, or rather that he will not put off, the true character of a man, and generously enlarge his views beyond the present day.

Volumes have been written on the subject of the struggle between England and America. Men of all ranks have embarked in the controversy, from different motives, and with various designs; but all have been ineffectual, and the period of debate is closed. Arms, as the last resource, decide the contest; the appeal was the choice of the king, and the continent hath accepted the challenge.

It hath been reported of the late Mr. Pelham (who tho' an able minister was not without his faults) that on his being attacked in the house of commons, on the score, that his measures were only of a temporary kind, replied, "They will last my time." Should a thought so fatal and unmanly possess the colonies in the present contest, the name of ancestors will be remembered by future generations with detestation.

The sun never shined on a cause of greater worth. 'Tis not the affair of a city, a country, a province, or a kingdom, but of a continent—of at least one eighth part of the habitable globe. 'Tis not the concern of a day, a year, or an age; posterity are virtually involved in the contest, and will be more or less affected, even to the end of time, by the proceedings now. Now is the seed time of continental union, faith and honor. The least fracture now will be like a name engraved with the point of a pin on the tender rind of a young oak; The wound will enlarge with the tree, and posterity read it in full grown characters.

By referring the matter from argument to arms, a new era for politics is struck; a new method of thinking hath arisen. All plans, proposals, &c. prior to the nineteenth of April, i.e. to the commencement of hostilities, are like the almanacks of the last year; which, though proper then, are superceded and useless now. Whatever was advanced by the advocates on either side of the question then, terminated in one and the same point, viz. a union with Great Britain; the only difference between the parties was the method of effecting it; the one proposing force, the other friendship; but it hath so far happened that the first hath failed, and the second hath withdrawn her influence. . . .

I have heard it asserted by some, that as America hath flourished under her former connexion with Great Britain, that the same connexion is necessary towards her future happiness, and will always have the same effect. Nothing can be more fallacious than this kind of argument. We may as well assert that because a child has thrived upon milk, that it is never to have meat, or that the first twenty years of our lives is to become a precedent for the next twenty. But even this is admitting more than is true, for I answer roundly, that America would have flourished as much, and probably much more, had no European power had anything to do with her. The commerce, by which she hath enriched herself are the necessaries of life, and will always have a market while eating is the custom of Europe. . . .

Much hath been said of the united strength of Britain and the colonies, that in conjunction they might bid defiance to the world. But this is mere presumption; the fate of war is uncertain, neither do the expressions mean anything; for this continent would never suffer itself to be drained of inhabitants, to support the British arms in either Asia, Africa, or Europe.

Besides, what have we to do with setting the world at defiance? Our plan is commerce, and that, well attended to, will secure us the peace and friendship of all Europe; because, it is the interest of all Europe to have America a free port. Her trade will always be a protection, and her barrenness of gold and silver secure her from invaders.

I challenge the warmest advocate for reconciliation, to shew, a single advantage that this continent can reap, by being connected with Great Britain. I repeat the challenge, not a single advantage is derived. Our corn will fetch its price in any market in Europe, and our imported goods must be paid for buy them where we will.

But the injuries and disadvantages we sustain by that connection, are without number; and our duty to mankind at large, as well as to ourselves, instruct us to renounce the alliance: Because, any submission to, or dependance on Great Britain, tends directly to involve this continent in European wars and quarrels; and sets us at variance with nations, who would otherwise seek our friendship, and against whom, we have neither anger nor complaint. As Europe is our market for trade, we ought to form no partial connection with any part of it. It is the true interest of America to steer clear of European contentions, which she never can do, while by her dependance on Britain, she is made the make-weight in the scale on British politics.

Europe is too thickly planted with kingdoms to be long at peace, and whenever a war breaks out between England and any foreign power, the trade of America goes to ruin, because of her connection with England. The next war may not turn out like the last, and should it not, the advocates for reconciliation now will be wishing for separation then, because, neutrality in that case, would be a safer convoy than a man of war. Every thing that is right or natural pleads for separation. The blood of the slain, the weeping voice of nature cries, 'tis time to part.

READING AND DISCUSSION QUESTIONS

1. Paine describes monarchy as dependent on artificial distinctions. What does he mean, and how were those distinctions created?
2. Paine invokes "the nineteenth of April." What is the significance of that date? How did what happened on that date change the relationship between king and colonists?
3. What about Paine's text might account for its widespread and immediate popularity?

▪ COMPARATIVE QUESTIONS ▪

1. From what you have read in this chapter, do you think colonists who objected to Parliament's legislative actions saw themselves as revolutionaries or as conservatives?
2. Three of the sources here—Bland's essay (Document 5-1), the declaration of the Stamp Act Congress (Document 5-2), and Paine's *Common Sense* (Document 5-6)—all represent the Patriot cause. How do their arguments and tone compare? What differences do you see, and what might account for those differences?
3. What seem to have been the major issues dividing Patriots and Loyalists? What might the sources presented in this chapter reveal as factors determining which side a person chose during the Revolutionary era?
4. To what extent did audience shape the tone, style, and substance of these documents?

6

Making War and Republican Governments

1776–1789

In March 1775, a month before fighting broke out at Lexington and Concord, Edmund Burke, a member of Parliament, advocated conciliation before the House of Commons. Having witnessed the colonists' deep-rooted devotion to liberty, Burke thought it better to make peace than to postpone the inevitability of independence. Parliament passed the Massachusetts Government Act in 1774 in response to the Boston Tea Party, revoking Massachusetts's charter, but the colonists were undaunted and protests persisted. Many in Parliament and even many Loyalists in the colonies assumed a strong hand would force colonists back into the fold, but Burke knew better.

The sources in this chapter tell the story of a revolutionary people awakening to the meaning of their rights. A "democratical" spirit touched not only those who had long enjoyed political power, but also those who had not, including women and enslaved people, many of whom began to draw on a revolutionary rhetoric. However, for some Native Americans, including Delaware Chief Buckongahelas, the colonists were petulant and violent children, not the revolutionary heroes they claimed to be. Still, in the years after the Revolution, the "democratical" spirit continued to frame Americans' arguments about citizenship and equality. Shays's Rebellion, defended in one of the sources included here, used the language of revolution to aid poor farmers facing economic collapse in the 1780s. The new Constitution, drafted in 1787, responded to these crises and, as James Madison stated, balanced conflicting interests, preserving liberties yet ensuring a stable political order.

6-1 | A Call to "Remember the Ladies"

ABIGAIL AND JOHN ADAMS, *Correspondence* (1776)

The revolution gave many people the opportunity to express themselves in a new language of rights. In a period when only propertied white males enjoyed political power, the language of revolution armed women and African Americans with the rhetorical tools to demand their own liberties. Such is the case with Abigail Adams, who wrote her husband, John, then serving at the Second Continental Congress, meeting in Philadelphia. John Adams was pivotal in moving the delegates to declare independence, and the couple's wonderfully rich letters provide a window into the buildup to that historic moment. In addition to revealing the personal hardships they endured during the Revolutionary period, the letters include the lively discussions John and Abigail shared over the place of women in the emerging republic. Abigail did not miss the opportunity to lobby for her sex, and in one letter, reproduced here, she famously instructs her husband to "remember the ladies" as he and his fellow delegates contemplate laws for the newly independent states.

Abigail Adams to John Adams

Braintree, 31 March, 1776.

I wish you would ever write me a letter half as long as I write you; and tell me if you may where your fleet are gone? What sort of defense Virginia can make against our common enemy; whether it is so situated as to make an able defense. Are not the gentry lords and the common people vassals, are they not like the uncivilized vassals Britain represents us to be? I hope their riflemen, who have shown themselves very savage and even blood-thirsty, are not a specimen of the generality of the people. I am willing to allow the colony great merit for having produced a Washington; but they have been shamefully duped by a Dunmore.

I have sometimes been ready to think that the passion for liberty cannot be equally strong in the breasts of those who have been accustomed to deprive their fellow-creatures of theirs. Of this I am certain, that it is not founded upon that generous and Christian principle of doing to others as we would that others should do unto us.

Do not you want to see Boston; I am fearful of the small-pox, or I should have been in before this time. I got Mr. Crane to go to our House and see what state it was in. I find it has been occupied by one of the doctors of a regiment, very dirty, but no other damage has been done to it. The few things which were left in it are all gone. I look upon it a new acquisition of property, a property which one month ago I did not value at a single shilling, and could with pleasure have seen it in flames.

The town in general is left in a better state than we expected, more owing to a precipitate flight than any regard to the inhabitants, though some individuals discovered a sense of honor and justice and have left the rent of the Houses in which they were, for the owners and the furniture unhurt, or, if damaged, sufficient to make it good. Others have committed abominable ravages. The mansion-house of your President is safe and the furniture unhurt whilst both

Charles Francis Adams, *Familiar Letters of John Adams and His Wife Abigail Adams, During the Revolution* (Cambridge, MA: The Riverside Press, 1875), 148–155, 158–159.

the House and Furniture of the Solicitor General have fallen a prey to their own merciless party. Surely the very fiends feel a reverential awe for virtue and patriotism, whilst they detest the parricide and traitor.

I feel very differently at the approach of spring to what I did a month ago. We knew not then whether we could plant or sow with safety, whether when we had tilled we could reap the fruits of our own industry, whether we could rest in our own cottages, or whether we should not be driven from the sea coasts to seek shelter in the wilderness; but now we feel a temporary peace, and the poor fugitives are returning to their deserted habitations.

Though we felicitate ourselves, we sympathize with those who are trembling lest the lot of Boston should be theirs. But they cannot be in similar circumstances unless pusillanimity and cowardice should take possession of them. They have time and warning given them to see the evil and shun it.

I long to hear that you have declared an independency. And, by the way, in the new code of laws which I suppose it will be necessary for you to make, I desire you would remember the ladies, and be more generous and favorable to them than your ancestors. Do not put such unlimited power into the hands of the husbands. Remember all men would be tyrants if they could. If particular care and attention is not paid to the ladies, we are determined to foment a rebellion, and will not hold ourselves bound by any laws in which we have no voice or representation.

That your sex are naturally tyrannical is a truth so thoroughly established as to admit of no dispute; but such of you as wish to be happy willingly give up the harsh title of master for the more tender and endearing one of friend. Why, then, not put it out of the power of the vicious and the lawless to use us with cruelty and indignity with impunity? Men of sense in all ages abhor those customs which treat us only as the vassals of your sex; regard us then as beings placed by Providence under your protection, and in imitation of the Supreme Being make use of that power only for our happiness.

11 April.

I take my pen and write just as I can get time; my letters will be a strange mixture. I really am "cumbered about many things," and scarcely know which way to turn myself. I miss my partner, and find myself unequal to the cares which fall upon me. I find it necessary to be the directress of our husbandry. I hope in time to have the reputation of being as a good a *farmeress* as my partner has of being a good statesman. To ask you anything about your return would, I suppose, be asking a question which you cannot answer.

Retirement, rural quiet domestic pleasures, all, all must give place to the weighty cares of state. It would be —

"Meanly poor in solitude to hide
An honest zeal, unwarped by party rage."

"Though certain pains attend the cares of state,
A good man owes his country to be great,
Should act abroad the high distinguished part,
And show, at least, the purpose of his heart."

I hope your Prussian General[1] will answer the high character which is given of him. But we, who have been bred in a land of liberty, scarcely know how to give credit to so unjust and arbitrary a mandate of a despot. To cast off a faithful servant, only for being the unhappy bearer of ill news, degrades the man and dishonors the prince. The Congress, by employing him, have shown a liberality of sentiment not confined to colonies or continents, but, to use the words of "Common Sense," have "carried their friendship on a larger scale, by claiming brotherhood with every European Christian, and may justly triumph in the generosity of the sentiment."

Yesterday, was taken and carried into Cohasset, by three whaleboats, which went from the shore on purpose, a scow from the Grenadas, laden with three hundred and fifty-four puncheons of West India rum, forty-three barrels of sugar, twelve thousand and five hundred-weight of coffee; a valuable prize. A number of Eastern sloops have brought wood into town since the fleet sailed. We have a rumor of Admiral Hopkins being engaged with a number of ships and tenders off Rhode Island, and are anxious to know the event.

Be so good as to send me a list of the vessels which sail with Hopkins, their names, weight of metal, and number of men; all the news you know, etc.

I hear our jurors refuse to serve, because the writs are issued in the King's name. Surely they are for independence.

Write me how you do this winter. I want to say many things I must omit. It is not fit "to wake the soul by tender strokes of art," or to ruminate upon happiness we might enjoy, lest absence become intolerable. Adieu.

Yours.

I wish you would burn all my letters.

John Adams to Abigail Adams

12 April, 1776.

I inclose a few sheets of paper,[2] and will send more as fast as opportunities present. . . . You will see by the papers the news, the speculations, and the political plans of the day. The ports are opened wide enough at last, and privateers are allowed to prey upon British trade. This is not independency, you know. What is? Why, government in every colony, a confederation among them all, and treaties with foreign nations to acknowledge us a sovereign state, and all that. When these things will be done, or any of them, time must discover. Perhaps the time is near, perhaps a great way off.

14 April.

You justly complain of my short letters, but the critical state of things and the multiplicity of avocations must plead my excuse. You ask where the fleet is? The inclosed papers will inform you. You ask what sort of defense Virginia can make?

[1] **Your Prussian General**: Baron de Woedtke, appointed by Congress a brigadier-general and ordered to Canada. He died soon afterward at Lake George.

[2] **Paper**: Writing paper was scarce during the occupation of Boston.

I believe they will make an able defense. Their militia and minute-men have been some time employed in training themselves, and they have nine battalions of regulars, as they call them, maintained among them, under good officers, at the Continental expense. They have set up a number of manufactories of firearms, which are busily employed. They are tolerably supplied with powder, and are successful and assiduous in making saltpetre. Their neighboring sister, or rather daughter colony of North Carolina, which is a warlike colony, and has several battalions at the Continental expense, as well as a pretty good militia, are ready to assist them, and they are in very good spirits and seem determined to make a brave resistance. The gentry are very rich, and the common people very poor. This inequality of property gives an aristocratical turn to all their proceedings, and occasions a strong aversion in their patricians to "Common Sense." But the spirit of these Barons is coming down, and it must submit. It is very true, as you observe, they have been duped by Dunmore. But this is a common case. All the colonies are duped, more or less, at one time and another. A more egregious bubble was never blown up than the story of Commissioners coming to treat with the Congress, yet it has gained credit like a charm, not only with, but against the clearest evidence. I never shall forget the delusion which seized our best and most sagacious friends, the dear inhabitants of Boston, the winter before last. Credulity and the want of foresight are imperfections in the human character, that no politician can sufficiently guard against.

You give me some pleasure by your account of a certain house in Queen Street. I had burned it long ago in imagination. It rises now to my view like a phoenix. What shall I say of the Solicitor General? I pity his pretty children. I pity his father and his sisters. I wish I could be clear that it is no moral evil to pity him and his lady. Upon repentance, they will certainly have a large share in the compassions of many. But let us take warning, and give it to our children. Whenever vanity and gayety, a love of pomp and dress, furniture, equipage, buildings, great company, expensive diversions, and elegant entertainments get the better of the principles and judgments of men or women, there is no knowing where they will stop, nor into what evils, natural, moral, or political, they will lead us.

Your description of your own *gaieté de cœur* charms me. Thanks be to God, you have just cause to rejoice, and may the bright prospect be obscured by no cloud. As to declarations of independency, be patient. Read our privateering laws and our commercial laws. What signifies a word?

As to your extraordinary code of laws, I cannot but laugh. We have been told that our struggle has loosened the bonds of government everywhere; that children and apprentices were disobedient; that schools and colleges were grown turbulent; that Indians slighted their guardians, and negroes grew insolent to their masters. But your letter was the first intimation that another tribe, more numerous and powerful than all the rest, were grown discontented. This is rather too coarse a compliment, but you are so saucy, I won't blot it out. Depend upon it, we know better than to repeal our masculine systems. Although they are in full force, you know they are little more than theory. We dare not exert our power in its full latitude. We are obliged to go fair and softly, and, in practice, you know we are the subjects. We have only the name of masters, and rather than give up this, which would completely subject us to the despotism of the petticoat, I hope General Washington and all our brave heroes would fight; I am sure every good politician would plot, as long as he would against despotism, empire, monarchy, aristocracy, oligarchy, or ochlocracy. A fine story, indeed! I begin to think the ministry as deep as they are wicked. After stirring up Tories, land-jobbers, trimmers, bigots, Canadians, Indians, negroes, Hanoverians, Hessians, Russians, Irish Roman Catholics, Scotch renegadoes, at last they have stimulated the—— to demand new privileges and threaten to rebel. . . .

15 April.

I send you every newspaper that comes out, and I send you, now and then, a few sheets of paper, but this article is as scarce here as with you. I would send a quire[3], if I could get a conveyance.

I write you now and then a line, as often as I can, but I can tell you no news but what I send in the public papers.

We are waiting, it is said, for Commissioners; a messiah that will never come. This story of Commissioners is as arrant an illusion as ever was hatched in the brain of an enthusiast, a politician, or a maniac. I have laughed at it, scolded at it, grieved at it, and I don't know but I may, at an unguarded moment, have rip'd at it. But it is vain to reason against such delusions. I was very sorry to see, in a letter from the General, that he had been bubbled with it; and still more, to see, in a letter from my sagacious friend W.,[4] at Plymouth, that he was taken in too.

My opinion is that the Commissioners and the commission have been here (I mean in America), these two months. The Governors, Mandamus Councillors, Collectors and Comptrollers, and Commanders of the army and navy, I conjecture, compose the list, and their power is to receive submissions. But we are not in a very submissive mood. They will get no advantage of us. We shall go on to perfection, I believe. I have been very busy for some time; have written about ten sheets of paper, with my own hand, about some trifling affairs, which I may mention some time or other—not now, for fear of accidents.

What will come of this labor, time will discover. I shall get nothing by it, I believe, because I never get anything by anything that I do. I am sure the public or posterity ought to get something. I believe my children will think I might as well have thought and labored a little, night and day, for their benefit. But I will not bear the reproaches of my children. I will tell them that I studied and labored to procure a free constitution of government for them to solace themselves under, and if they do not prefer this to ample fortune, to ease and elegance, they are not my children, and I care not what becomes of them. They shall live upon thin diet, wear mean clothes, and work hard with cheerful hearts and free spirits, or they may be the children of the earth, or of no one, for me.

John has genius, and so has Charles. Take care that they don't go astray. Cultivate their minds, inspire their little hearts, raise their wishes. Fix their attention upon great and glorious objects. Root out every little thing. Weed out every meanness.

[3] **Quire**: A set of folded sheets of paper.

[4] **W.**: James Warren.

Make them great and manly. Teach them to scorn injustice, ingratitude, cowardice, and falsehood. Let them revere nothing but religion, morality, and liberty.

Abby and Tommy are not forgotten by me, although I did not mention them before. The first, by reason of her sex, requires a different education from the two I have mentioned. Of this, you are the only judge. I want to send each of my little pretty flock some present or other. I have walked over this city twenty times, and gaped at every shop, like a countryman, to find something, but could not. Ask every one of them what they would choose to have, and write it to me in your next letter. From this I shall judge of their taste and fancy and discretion.

READING AND DISCUSSION QUESTIONS

1. How did the war affect the lives of ordinary Americans? What challenges did they face, as glimpsed through the letters Abigail writes to John?
2. Abigail's admonition to "remember the ladies" has become one of the most famous lines from this period. But what do you think she meant? In a period when women had no formal political power, what do you think she wanted? How does John respond?
3. To what extent does John suggest that class played a role in shaping the revolutionary struggle within the colonies?

6-2 | Enslaved Blacks Adopt the Cause of Liberty

PRINCE HALL, *Petition for Freedom to the Massachusetts Council and the House of Representatives* (1777)

John Adams observed that the Revolution had "loosened the bonds of government everywhere." A clear case of this expanding democratic spirit came from his home state, where enslaved Africans petitioned first the colonial government in 1773 and then the state legislature in January 1777 asking for their freedom. Not until 1783, by a judicial ruling, did enslaved persons in Massachusetts win their freedom when the State Supreme Judicial Court interpreted the 1780 state constitution as guaranteeing all men the right to enjoy their life and liberty. Prince Hall (1735–1807), born a slave but freed by 1770, drafted the petition at the behest of "A Great Number of Blackes."

To The Honorable Counsel & House of [Representa]tives for the State of Massachusitte [Massachusetts] Bay in General Court assembled, Jan. 13, 1777.

The petition of A Great Number of Blackes detained in a State of slavery in the Bowels of a free & Christian Country Humbly shuwith [showeth] that your Petitioners apprehend that thay have in Common with all other men a Natural and Unaliable [inalienable] Right to that freedom which the Grat Parent of the

Prince Hall, "Petition for Freedom to the Massachusetts Council and the House of Representatives," in *Collections of the Massachusetts Historical Society*, 5th series, vol. 3 (Boston: Massachusetts Historical Society, 1877), 436–437.

Unavers hath Bestowed equalley on all menkind and which they have Never forfuted by any Compact or agreement whatever—but thay wher Unjustly Dragged by the hand of cruel Power from their Derest friends and sum of them Even torn from the Embraces of their tender Parents—from A popolous Pleasant and plentiful contry and in violation of Laws of Nature and off Nations and in defiance of all the tender feelings of humanity Brough hear Either to Be sold Like Beast of Burthen & Like them Condemnd to Slavery for Life—Among A People Profesing the mild Religion of Jesus A people Not Insensible of the Secrets of Rational Being Nor without spirit to Resent the unjust endeavours of others to Reduce them to a state of Bondage and Subjection your honouer Need not to be informed that A Life of Slavery Like that of your petioners [petitioners] Deprived of Every social privilege of Every thing Requisit to Render Life Tolable is far worse then Nonexistence.

[In Imitat]ion of the Lawdable Example of the Good People of these States your petitiononers have Long and Patiently waited the Evnt of petition after petition By them presented to the Legislative Body of this state and cannot but with Grief Reflect that their Success hath ben but too similar they Cannot but express their Astonishment that It has Never Bin Consirdered that Every Principle form which Amarica has Acted in the Cours of their unhappy Dificultes with Great Briton Pleads Stronger than A thousand arguments in favowrs of your petioners they therfor humble Beseech your honours to give this petion its due weight & consideration & cause an act of the Legislatur to be past Wherby they may be Restored to the Enjoyments of that which is the Naturel Right of all men—and their Children who wher Born in this Land of Liberty may not be heald as Slaves after they arrive at the age of twenty one years so may the Inhabitance of this Stats No longer chargeable with the inconsistancey of acting themselves the part which they condem and oppose in others Be prospered in their present Glorious struggle for Liberty and have those Blessing to them, &c.

READING AND DISCUSSION QUESTIONS

1. How did the enslaved petitioners frame their request for freedom?
2. To what extent were these enslaved petitioners familiar with the revolutionary rhetoric used by the Patriots? How did they co-opt revolutionary ideas to make their argument?

6-3 | Delaware Chief Picks Side in Revolution's Family Squabble *Speech of Buckongahelas* (c. 1775)

During the French and Indian War the Delaware Chief Shingas asked a British leader: "Why do you come to fight on our land? This makes everybody believe you want to take the land from us by force and settle it." His poignant question reminds us that Native

Collections of the Illinois State Historical Library ed. H. W. Beckwith, vol. 1 (Springfield, IL: H. W. Rokker Co., 1903), 175–176.

American peoples were caught in the crosshairs of conflict as, in that war, both the British and the French enlisted Native Americans to further their cause. A decade later during the American Revolution, Native peoples again found themselves in a similar predicament, victims of a conflict not of their making, but one that directly impacted their fortunes and future. The speech reproduced below was given by the Delaware chief Buckongahelas in the mid-1770s as the revolutionary crises deepened into violence. During the colonial period, the Delaware had been forced westward into the Ohio territory as American colonists encroached on their land along the Delaware River in New Jersey. They welcomed the British Parliament's passage of the 1763 Proclamation Line limiting westward colonial expansion. When the American Revolution broke out, the Delaware feared an American victory would lead to incursions onto their land. Some Delaware tried to maintain neutrality during the Revolution. Others, like Buckongahelas, sided with the British.

"Friends!" Listen to what I say to you! You see a great and powerful nation divided! You see the father fighting against the son, and the son against the father! The father has called on his Indian children, to assist him in punishing his children, the Americans, who have become refractory. I took time to consider what I should do; whether or not I should receive the hatchet of my father to assist him. At first I looked upon it as a family quarrel, in which I was not interested. However, at length, it appeared to me that the father was in the right; and his children deserved to be punished a little. That this must be the case, I concluded from the many cruel acts his offspring had committed from time to time on his Indian children, in encroaching on their land, stealing their property, shooting at, and murdering, without cause, men, women, and children. Yes! even murdering those, who at all times had been friendly to them, and were placed for protection under the roof of their father's house—the father himself standing sentry at the door at the time. Friends! often has the father been obliged to settle, and make amends for the wrongs and mischiefs done to us by his refractory children; yet those do not grow better. No; they remain the same; and will continue to be so, as long as we have any land left us. Look back at the murders committed by the Long-knives [colonists] on many of our relations, who lived peaceable neighbors to them on the Ohio. Did they not kill them without the least provocation? Are they, do you think, better now than they were then?"

READING AND DISCUSSION QUESTIONS

1. How does Buckongahelas describe the revolutionary struggle between the British and the American colonists?
2. How does Buckongahelas explain his decision to side with the British? What factors did he find persuasive?
3. Buckongahelas said that he initially saw the revolution as a "family quarrel" that did not affect his people. Why did he change his mind? What was at stake for the Delaware Indians?

6-4 | A Republican Hero Emerges

JAMES PEALE, *General George Washington at Yorktown* (c. 1782)

Charles Willson Peale's full-length George Washington portrait helped the general become the icon of the American Revolution. Charles and his brother, James, created several versions depicting Washington in different landscapes including at the Battles of Princeton and Trenton. In this color lithograph version produced by James based on his brother's original, Washington has just defeated the British at the decisive battle at Yorktown (1781), which led swiftly to the British general Charles Cornwallis's surrender and the war's end. The Yorktown battlefield can be seen in the background. In an era before photography, artists' portraits were among the few ways people could see their heroes, and Washington's likeness was reproduced countless times.

General George Washington (1732–99) *at Yorktown, Virginia* (color litho)/Peale, James (1749–1831) (after)/PETER NEWARK'S PICTURES/Private Collection/Bridgeman Images

READING AND DISCUSSION QUESTIONS

1. What do the details Peale included in the painting tell you about his point of view toward Washington and the Battle of Yorktown?
2. What significance can you infer from Peale's decision to depict Washington leaning against the cannon with his legs crossed? How does this pose compare to more formal portraits you may have seen?
3. What conclusion about Washington's popularity can you draw from the Peale brothers' decision to produce multiple versions of the general's portrait?

6-5 | A Shaysite Defends the "Risings of the People"

DANIEL GRAY, *Address to the People of Several Towns* (1786)

The victory over the British and the establishment of the Articles of Confederation hardly settled all the challenges facing the newly independent states. The class conflict John Adams noted during the Revolutionary era (Document 6-1) persisted into the 1780s. A financial crisis following the war dealt poor debtors a difficult challenge: they could not repay debts because there was so little circulating currency, credit was tight, courts enforced judgments against them, and the state legislatures increased taxes on already strapped farmers. Resentment boiled over, and men like Daniel Shays and others attempted to shut down the courts to prevent them from foreclosing on farmers' land. These rebellions were ultimately crushed, but the insurgencies shocked many who went on to urge constitutional reforms. This process ultimately resulted in the ratification of the Constitution of the United States. In this speech at the height of the insurgency in western Massachusetts, Daniel Gray (1728–1803), chairman of the committee supporting the protests, outlines the insurgents' cause.

Worcester Dec[ember] 7th 1786

An address to the People of the Several towns in the County of Hampshire from the body now at Arms

Gentlemen, we have thought Proper to inform you of some of the principle [*sic*] Causes of the late Risings of the People, and also of their present Movement (viz)[:]

1st The Present expencive mode of Collecting Debts, which by reason of the Great Scarcity of Cash will of Necessity fill our Gaols with unhappy Debtors, and there by Hinder a respectable body of People incapable of being Serviceable Either to them selves or Community.

2dly The moneys raised by impost and Excise being appropriated to Discharge the Interest of Government Securities; (and the forreign Debt) when those Securities are in no wise subject to taxation.

3dly A Suspension of the writ of Habeas Corpes; by which those Persons who have steped forth to ascert and maintain the rights of the People are liable to be taken and Conveyed even to the most Distant Parts of the Commonwealth and there by Subject to an unjust Punishment.

Daniel Gray, "Address to the People of Several Towns," December 7, 1786.

4thly The unlimited Power granted to Justices of the Peice, thereof Deputy Sherifs, and Constables by the riot act indemnefying them in the Prosecution thereof, when Perhaps situated wholly by a principle of revenge Hatred and invy. Futhermore be it asured that this body Dispise the Idea of being instigated by british Emisaries which is so streniously Propigated by the Enimies of our Liberties, we also wish the most Proper and speedy measures may be taken to Discharge both of our foreign and Domistick Debt.

Per Order Daniel Gray {Chairman of a
{committee for
{the above Purpose

READING AND DISCUSSION QUESTIONS

1. To what extent were these insurgent farmers drawing on their Revolutionary War experiences to make the case against the policies of the state of Massachusetts?
2. How do these insurgents present themselves to their fellow citizens?
3. What does this document suggest about the economic challenges faced by the newly formed states? How did these challenges affect the daily lives of the citizens?

6-6 | Madison Defends the Constitution

JAMES MADISON, *Federalist No. 10* and *Federalist No. 51* (1787)

Events like Shays's Rebellion convinced many that the weaknesses of the Articles of Confederation were fatal. In 1787, delegates who had originally been called to a convention to propose reforms were instead pushed to draft a document that would provide an entirely new framework for government. The resulting Constitution of the United States then faced ratification battles in the state conventions. James Madison and Alexander Hamilton, both delegates to the Constitutional Convention, joined John Jay in drafting a series of eighty-five articles, published in New York newspapers and later collected under the title *The Federalist*, urging the citizens to ratify the new Constitution. In two of these articles, *Federalist No. 10* and *Federalist No. 51*, Madison addresses key criticisms leveled against the Constitution.

Federalist No. 10: James Madison, "The Same Subject Continued: The Union as a Safeguard Against Domestic Faction and Insurrection," *The New York Packet*, November 23, 1787.

Federalist No. 51: James Madison, "The Structure of the Government Must Furnish the Proper Checks and Balances Between the Different Departments," *The New York Packet*, February 8, 1788.

Federalist No. 10

AMONG the numerous advantages promised by a well-constructed Union, none deserves to be more accurately developed than its tendency to break and control the violence of faction. . . .

By a faction, I understand a number of citizens, whether amounting to a majority or a minority of the whole, who are united and actuated by some common impulse of passion, or of interest, adversed to the rights of other citizens, or to the permanent and aggregate interests of the community.

There are two methods of curing the mischiefs of faction: the one, by removing its causes; the other, by controlling its effects.

There are again two methods of removing the causes of faction: the one, by destroying the liberty which is essential to its existence; the other, by giving to every citizen the same opinions, the same passions, and the same interests.

It could never be more truly said than of the first remedy, that it was worse than the disease. Liberty is to faction what air is to fire, an aliment without which it instantly expires. But it could not be less folly to abolish liberty, which is essential to political life, because it nourishes faction, than it would be to wish the annihilation of air, which is essential to animal life, because it imparts to fire its destructive agency.

The second expedient is as impracticable as the first would be unwise. As long as the reason of man continues fallible, and he is at liberty to exercise it, different opinions will be formed. As long as the connection subsists between his reason and his self-love, his opinions and his passions will have a reciprocal influence on each other; and the former will be objects to which the latter will attach themselves. The diversity in the faculties of men, from which the rights of property originate, is not less an insuperable obstacle to a uniformity of interests. The protection of these faculties is the first object of government. From the protection of different and unequal faculties of acquiring property, the possession of different degrees and kinds of property immediately results; and from the influence of these on the sentiments and views of the respective proprietors, ensues a division of the society into different interests and parties.

The latent causes of faction are thus sown in the nature of man; and we see them everywhere brought into different degrees of activity, according to the different circumstances of civil society. A zeal for different opinions concerning religion, concerning government, and many other points, as well of speculation as of practice; an attachment to different leaders ambitiously contending for pre-eminence and power; or to persons of other descriptions whose fortunes have been interesting to the human passions, have, in turn, divided mankind into parties, inflamed them with mutual animosity, and rendered them much more disposed to vex and oppress each other than to co-operate for their common good. So strong is this propensity of mankind to fall into mutual animosities, that where no substantial occasion presents itself, the most frivolous and fanciful distinctions have been sufficient to kindle their unfriendly passions and excite their most violent conflicts. But the most common and durable source of factions has been the various and unequal distribution of property. Those who hold and those who are without property have ever formed distinct interests in society. Those who are creditors, and those who are debtors, fall under a like discrimination. A landed interest, a manufacturing interest, a mercantile interest, a moneyed interest, with many lesser interests, grow up of necessity in civilized nations, and divide them into different classes, actuated by different sentiments and views. The regulation of these various and interfering interests forms the principal task of modern legislation, and involves the spirit of party and faction in the necessary and ordinary operations of the government. . . .

It is in vain to say that enlightened statesmen will be able to adjust these clashing interests, and render them all subservient to the public good. Enlightened statesmen will not always be at the helm. Nor, in many cases, can such an adjustment be made at all without taking into view indirect and remote considerations, which will rarely prevail over the immediate interest which one party may find in disregarding the rights of another or the good of the whole.

The inference to which we are brought is, that the CAUSES of faction cannot be removed, and that relief is only to be sought in the means of controlling its EFFECTS.

If a faction consists of less than a majority, relief is supplied by the republican principle, which enables the majority to defeat its sinister views by regular vote. It may clog the administration, it may convulse the society; but it will be unable to execute and mask its violence under the forms of the Constitution. When a majority is included in a faction, the form of popular government, on the other hand, enables it to sacrifice to its ruling passion or interest both the public good and the rights of other citizens. To secure the public good and private rights against the danger of such a faction, and at the same time to preserve the spirit and the form of popular government, is then the great object to which our inquiries are directed. . . .

It may be concluded that a pure democracy, by which I mean a society consisting of a small number of citizens, who assemble and administer the government in person, can admit of no cure for the mischiefs of faction. A common passion or interest will, in almost every case, be felt by a majority of the whole; a communication and concert result from the form of government itself; and there is nothing to check the inducements to sacrifice the weaker party or an obnoxious individual. Hence it is that such democracies have ever been spectacles of turbulence and contention; have ever been found incompatible with personal security or the rights of property; and have in general been as short in their lives as they have been violent in their deaths. Theoretic politicians, who have patronized this species of government, have erroneously supposed that by reducing mankind to a perfect equality in their political rights, they would, at the same time, be perfectly equalized and assimilated in their possessions, their opinions, and their passions.

A republic, by which I mean a government in which the scheme of representation takes place, opens a different prospect, and promises the cure for which we are seeking. Let us examine the points in which it varies from pure democracy, and we shall comprehend both the nature of the cure and the efficacy which it must derive from the Union.

The two great points of difference between a democracy and a republic are: first, the delegation of the government, in the latter, to a small number of citizens elected by the rest; secondly, the greater number of citizens, and greater sphere of country, over which the latter may be extended.

The effect of the first difference is, on the one hand, to refine and enlarge the public views, by passing them through the medium of a chosen body of citizens, whose wisdom may best discern the true interest of their country, and whose patriotism and love of justice will be least likely to sacrifice it to temporary or partial considerations. Under such a regulation, it may well happen that the public voice, pronounced by the representatives of the people, will be more consonant to the public good than if pronounced by the people themselves, convened for the purpose. On the other hand, the effect may be inverted. Men of factious tempers, of local prejudices, or of sinister designs, may, by intrigue, by corruption, or by other means, first obtain the suffrages, and then betray the interests, of the people. The question resulting is, whether small or extensive republics are more favorable to the election of proper guardians of the public weal; and it is clearly decided in favor of the latter by two obvious considerations:

In the first place, it is to be remarked that, however small the republic may be, the representatives must be raised to a certain number, in order to guard against the cabals[5] of a few; and that, however large it may be, they must be limited to a certain number, in order to guard against the confusion of a multitude. Hence, the number of representatives in the two cases not being in proportion to that of the two constituents, and being proportionally greater in the small republic, it follows that, if the proportion of fit characters be not less in the large than in the small republic, the former will present a greater option, and consequently a greater probability of a fit choice.

In the next place, as each representative will be chosen by a greater number of citizens in the large than in the small republic, it will be more difficult for unworthy candidates to practice with success the vicious arts by which elections are too often carried; and the suffrages of the people being more free, will be more likely to centre in men who possess the most attractive merit and the most diffusive and established characters.

It must be confessed that in this, as in most other cases, there is a mean, on both sides of which inconveniences will be found to lie. By enlarging too much the number of electors, you render the representatives too little acquainted with all their local circumstances and lesser interests; as by reducing it too much, you render him unduly attached to these, and too little fit to comprehend and pursue great and national objects. The federal Constitution forms a happy combination in this respect; the great and aggregate interests being referred to the national, the local and particular to the State legislatures.

[5] **Cabals**: Secret schemes or plots against the government.

The other point of difference is, the greater number of citizens and extent of territory which may be brought within the compass of republican than of democratic government; and it is this circumstance principally which renders factious combinations less to be dreaded in the former than in the latter. The smaller the society, the fewer probably will be the distinct parties and interests composing it; the fewer the distinct parties and interests, the more frequently will a majority be found of the same party; and the smaller the number of individuals composing a majority, and the smaller the compass within which they are placed, the more easily will they concert and execute their plans of oppression. Extend the sphere, and you take in a greater variety of parties and interests; you make it less probable that a majority of the whole will have a common motive to invade the rights of other citizens; or if such a common motive exists, it will be more difficult for all who feel it to discover their own strength, and to act in unison with each other. Besides other impediments, it may be remarked that, where there is a consciousness of unjust or dishonorable purposes, communication is always checked by distrust in proportion to the number whose concurrence is necessary. . . .

In the extent and proper structure of the Union, therefore, we behold a republican remedy for the diseases most incident to republican government. And according to the degree of pleasure and pride we feel in being republicans, ought to be our zeal in cherishing the spirit and supporting the character of Federalists.

Federalist No. 51

TO WHAT expedient, then, shall we finally resort, for maintaining in practice the necessary partition of power among the several departments, as laid down in the Constitution? The only answer that can be given is, that as all these exterior provisions are found to be inadequate, the defect must be supplied, by so contriving the interior structure of the government as that its several constituent parts may, by their mutual relations, be the means of keeping each other in their proper places. Without presuming to undertake a full development of this important idea, I will hazard a few general observations, which may perhaps place it in a clearer light, and enable us to form a more correct judgment of the principles and structure of the government planned by the convention. In order to lay a due foundation for that separate and distinct exercise of the different powers of government, which to a certain extent is admitted on all hands to be essential to the preservation of liberty, it is evident that each department should have a will of its own; and consequently should be so constituted that the members of each should have as little agency as possible in the appointment of the members of the others. Were this principle rigorously adhered to, it would require that all the appointments for the supreme executive, legislative, and judiciary magistracies should be drawn from the same fountain of authority, the people, through channels having no communication whatever with one another. Perhaps such a plan of constructing the several departments would be less difficult in practice than it may in contemplation appear. Some difficulties, however, and some additional expense would attend the execution of it. Some deviations, therefore, from the principle must be admitted. In the constitution of the judiciary department in particular, it might be inexpedient to insist rigorously on the principle: first, because peculiar qualifications being essential in the members, the primary consideration ought to be to select that mode of choice which best secures these qualifications; secondly, because the permanent tenure by which the appointments are held in that department, must soon destroy all sense of dependence on the authority conferring them. It is equally evident, that the members of each department should be as little dependent as possible on those of the others, for the emoluments annexed to their offices. Were the executive magistrate, or the judges, not independent of the legislature in this particular, their independence in every other would be merely nominal. But the great security against a gradual concentration of the several powers in the same department, consists in giving to those who administer each department the necessary constitutional means and personal motives to resist encroachments of the others. The provision for defense must in this, as in all other cases, be made commensurate to the danger of attack. Ambition must be made to counteract ambition. The interest of the man must be connected with the constitutional rights of the place. It may be a reflection on human nature, that such devices should be necessary to control the abuses of government. But what is government itself, but the greatest of all reflections on human nature? If men were angels, no government would be necessary. If angels were to govern men, neither external nor internal controls on government would be necessary. In framing a government which is to be administered by men over men, the great difficulty lies in this: you must first enable the government to control the governed; and in the next place oblige it to control itself. A dependence on the people is, no doubt, the primary control on the government; but experience has taught mankind the necessity of auxiliary precautions. This policy of supplying, by opposite and rival interests, the defect of better motives, might be traced through the whole system of human affairs, private as well as public. We see it particularly displayed in all the subordinate distributions of power, where the constant aim is to divide and arrange the several offices in such a manner as that each may be a check on the other—that the private interest of every individual may be a sentinel over the public rights. These inventions of prudence cannot be less requisite in the distribution of the supreme powers of the State. But it is not possible to give to each department an equal power of self-defense. In republican government, the legislative authority necessarily predominates. The remedy for this inconveniency is to divide the legislature into different branches; and to render them, by different modes of election and different principles of action, as little connected with each other as the nature of their common functions and their common dependence on the society will admit. It may even be necessary to guard against dangerous encroachments by still further precautions. As the weight of the legislative authority requires that it should be thus divided, the weakness of the executive may require, on the other hand, that it should be fortified. An absolute negative on the legislature appears, at first view, to be the natural defense with which the executive magistrate should be armed. But perhaps it would be neither altogether safe nor alone sufficient. On ordinary occasions it might not be exerted with the requisite firmness, and on extraordinary occasions it might be perfidiously abused. May not this defect of an absolute negative be supplied by some qualified connection between this weaker department and the weaker branch of the stronger department, by which the latter may be led to support the constitutional rights of the former, without being too much detached from the rights of its own department? If the principles on which these observations are founded be just, as I persuade myself they are, and they be applied as a criterion to the several State constitutions, and to the federal Constitution it will be found that if the latter does not perfectly correspond with them, the former are infinitely less able to bear such a test. There are, moreover, two considerations particularly applicable to the federal system of America, which place that system in a very interesting point of view. First. In a single republic, all the power surrendered by the people is submitted to the administration of a single government; and the usurpations are guarded against by a division of the government into distinct and separate departments. In the compound republic of America, the power surrendered by the people is first divided between two distinct governments, and then the portion allotted to each subdivided among distinct and separate departments. Hence a double security arises to the rights of the people. The different governments will control each other, at the same time that each will be controlled by itself. Second. It is of great importance in a republic not only to guard the society against the oppression of its rulers, but to guard one part of the society against the injustice of the other part. Different interests necessarily exist in different classes of citizens. If a majority be united by a common interest, the rights of the minority will be insecure. There are but two methods of providing against this evil: the one by creating a will in the community independent of the majority—that is, of the society itself; the other, by comprehending in the society so many separate descriptions of citizens as will render an unjust combination of a majority of the whole very improbable, if not impracticable. The first method prevails in all governments possessing an hereditary or self-appointed authority. This, at best, is but a precarious security; because a power independent of the society may as well espouse the unjust views of the major, as the rightful interests of the minor party, and may possibly be turned against both parties. The second method will be exemplified in the federal republic of the United States. Whilst all authority in it will be derived from and dependent on the society, the society itself will be broken into so many parts, interests, and classes of citizens, that the rights of individuals, or of the minority, will be in little danger from interested combinations of the majority. In a free government the security for civil rights must be the same as that for religious rights. It consists in the one case in the multiplicity of interests, and in the other in the multiplicity of sects. The degree of security in both cases will depend on the number of interests and sects; and this may be presumed to depend on the extent of country and number of people comprehended under the same government. This view of the subject must particularly recommend a proper federal system to all the sincere and considerate friends of republican government, since it shows that in exact proportion as the territory of the Union may be formed into more circumscribed Confederacies, or States oppressive combinations of a majority will be facilitated: the best security, under the republican forms, for the rights of every class of citizens, will be diminished: and consequently the stability and independence of some member of the government, the only other security, must be proportionately increased. Justice is the end of government. It is the end of civil society. It ever has been and ever will be pursued until it be obtained, or until liberty be lost in the pursuit. In a society under the forms of which the stronger faction can readily unite and oppress the weaker, anarchy may as truly be said to reign as in a state of nature, where the weaker individual is not secured against the violence of the stronger; and as, in the latter state, even the stronger individuals are prompted, by the uncertainty of their condition, to submit to a government which may protect the weak as well as themselves; so, in the former state, will the more powerful factions or parties be gradually induced, by a like motive, to wish for a government which will protect all parties, the weaker as well as the more powerful. It can be little doubted that if the State of Rhode Island was separated from the Confederacy and left to itself, the insecurity of rights under the popular form of government within such narrow limits would be displayed by such reiterated oppressions of factious majorities that some power altogether independent of the people would soon be called for by the voice of the very factions whose misrule had proved the necessity of it. In the extended republic of the United States, and among the great variety of interests, parties, and sects which it embraces, a coalition of a majority of the whole society could seldom take place on any other principles than those of justice and the general good; whilst there being thus less danger to a minor from the will of a major party, there must be less pretext, also, to provide for the security of the former, by introducing into the government a will not dependent on the latter, or, in other words, a will independent of the society itself. It is no less certain than it is important, notwithstanding the contrary opinions which have been entertained, that the larger the society, provided it lie within a practical sphere, the more duly capable it will be of self-government. And happily for the REPUBLICAN CAUSE, the practicable sphere may be carried to a very great extent, by a judicious modification and mixture of the FEDERAL PRINCIPLE.

READING AND DISCUSSION QUESTIONS

1. Many at the time feared the divisive impact of factions, and some critics suggested these self-interested political groups would be fatal to a republic as large as the one proposed by the Constitution. How does Madison, in *Federalist No. 10*, address the concerns about factions? What unorthodox remedy does he propose?

2. In *Federalist No. 51*, Madison addresses another concern: the danger of a concentration of power in the national government. How does Madison explain the Constitution's solution to this problem?
3. In the same article, Madison argues, "If men were angels, no government would be necessary." Clearly, Madison recognized man's fallibility. How did this view of human nature shape the way the founders constructed the new form of government under the Constitution?

▪ COMPARATIVE QUESTIONS ▪

1. To what extent did the language of rights and liberties prevalent during this period touch various groups within the colonies? How did those groups use that language for their own purposes?
2. How did ideas about government change as a result of the Revolutionary War experience?
3. How might the Constitution have read had Abigail Adams, Daniel Gray, and the enslaved Africans in Massachusetts been delegates to the Philadelphia convention?
4. Do you see the American Revolution more as a radical social movement (the people demanding liberty and equality) or as a conservative political movement (colonists demanding respect for their traditional rights)? Explain.

7

Hammering Out a Federal Republic

1787–1820

The new republic, formed with the ratification of the Constitution, wrestled with the meaning of the Revolution. What did it mean to be a citizen when Americans were no longer subjects of a distant monarch? How should they behave? What might republican politics look like? For those who embraced the republic's egalitarian promise, they looked upon fine clothes and elaborate titles for officeholders as symbols of dangerous aristocratic pretensions. By contrast, others agreed with a leading Federalist who warned against the "mire of a democracy, which pollutes the morals of citizens before it swallows up their liberties." In many ways, the first decade under the Constitution was about coming to terms with conflicting interpretations of the Revolution's legacy.

The sources in this chapter highlight the conflicts that Americans faced as they struggled to understand the new political order they had created. The first two documents illustrate some of the varying political visions that emerged, while the third highlights one of the flashpoints of the 1790s: France's alleged influence over American politics. The remaining three sources address the young republic's geographical expansion and the other major foreign policy crisis of this early period: the War of 1812. As we see here, this conflict also drove domestic politics, ultimately crushing New England Federalists and ushering in an era of submerged political drama.

7-1 | Hamilton Diverges from Jefferson on the Economy

ALEXANDER HAMILTON, *Letter to Edward Carrington* (1792)

The political crisis of the 1790s was fueled by more than personality. However, two strong individuals dominated the era, and their difficult relationship helps to clarify the issues up for debate. In this selection and the next, Alexander Hamilton and Thomas Jefferson reveal some of the political disagreements that drove the early national era, mostly centered on divergent views of the economy. Hamilton's important reports on manufactures, public credit, and the national bank outlined a Federalist political-economic agenda, which Jefferson and James Madison opposed. While Hamilton's letter to Virginia political leader Edward Carrington highlights these policy disputes, it also reveals the personal dimension of the political conflicts in an era before the trappings of political party became institutionalized.

It was not till the last session that I became unequivocally convinced of the following truth: *"that Mr. Madison, cooperating with Mr. Jefferson, is at the head of a faction decidedly hostile to me and my administration; and actuated by views, in my judgment, subversive of the principles of good government and dangerous to the Union, peace, and happiness of the country."*

These are strong expressions, they may pain your friendship for one or both of the gentlemen whom I have named. I have not lightly resolved to hazard them. They are the result of a *serious alarm* in my mind for the public welfare, and of a full conviction that what I have alleged is a truth, and a truth which ought to be told, and well attended to by all the friends of the Union and efficient national government. The suggestion will, I hope, at least, awaken attention free from the bias of former prepossessions.

This conviction, in my mind, is the result of a long train of circumstances, many of them minute. To attempt to detail them all would fill a volume. I shall therefore confine myself to the mention of a few.

First.—As to the point of opposition to me and my administration.

Mr. Jefferson, with very little reserve, manifests his dislike of the funding system generally, calling in question the expediency of funding a debt at all. Some expressions, which he has dropped in my presence (sometimes without sufficient attention to delicacy), will not permit me to doubt on this point representations which I have had from various respectable quarters. I do not mean that he advocates directly the undoing of what has been done, but he censures the whole, on principles which, if they should become general, could not but end in the subversion of the system.

In various conversations, with *foreigners* as well as citizens, he has thrown censure on my *principles* of government and on my measures of administration. He has predicted that the people would not long tolerate my proceedings, and that I should not long maintain my ground. Some of those whom he *immediately*

The Works of Alexander Hamilton, ed. Henry Cabot Lodge (New York: G. P. Putnam's Sons, 1903), 517–535.

and *notoriously* moves have *even* whispered suspicions of the rectitude of my motives and conduct. In the question concerning the bank he not only delivered an opinion in writing against its constitutionality and expediency, but he did it *in a style and manner* which I felt as partaking of asperity [harshness] and ill humor toward me. As one of the trustees of the sinking fund, I have experienced in almost every leading question opposition from him. When any turn of things in the community has threatened either odium or embarrassment to me, he has not been able to suppress the satisfaction which it gave him. . . .

With regard to Mr. Madison, the matter stands thus: I have not heard, but in the one instance to which I have alluded, of his having held language unfriendly to me in private conversation, but in his public conduct there has been a more uniform and persevering opposition than I have been able to resolve into a sincere difference of opinion. I cannot persuade myself that Mr. Madison and I, whose politics had formerly so much the *same point of departure*, should now diverge so widely in our opinions of the measures which are proper to be pursued. The opinion I once entertained of the candor and simplicity and fairness of Mr. Madison's character, has, I acknowledge, given way to a decided opinion that *it is one of a peculiarly artificial and complicated kind*. . . .

Mr. Jefferson is an avowed enemy to a funded debt. Mr. Madison disavows, in public, any intention to *undo* what has been done, but, in private conversation with Mr. Charles Carroll, Senator . . . he favored the sentiment in Mr. Mercer's speech, that a Legislature had no right to *fund* the debt by mortgaging permanently the public revenues, because they had no right to bind posterity. The inference is that what has been unlawfully done may be undone.

The discourse of partisans in the Legislature, and the publication in the party newspapers, direct their main battery against the *principle* of a funded debt, and represent it in the most odious light as a perfect *Pandora's box*. . . .

Whatever were the original merits of the funding system, after having been so solemnly adopted, and after so great a transfer of property under it, what would become of the government should it be reversed? What of the national reputation? Upon what system of morality can so atrocious a doctrine be maintained? In me, I confess it excited *indignation and horror*!

What are we to think of those maxims of government by which the power of a Legislature is denied to bind the nation, by a *contract* in the affair of *property* for twenty-four years? For this is precisely the case of the debt. What are to become of all the legal rights of property, of all charters to corporations, nay, of all grants to a man, his heirs and assigns, for ever, if this doctrine be true? What is the term for which a government is in capacity to *contract*? Questions might be multiplied without end, to demonstrate the perniciousness and absurdity of such a doctrine.

In almost all the questions, great and small, which have arisen since the first session of Congress, Mr. Jefferson and Mr. Madison have been found among those who are disposed to narrow the federal authority. The question of a national bank is one example. The question of bounties to the fisheries is another. Mr. Madison resisted it on the ground of constitutionality, till it was evident, by the intermediate questions taken, that the bill would pass; and he then, under the wretched subterfuge of a change of a single word, "bounty" for "allowance," went over to the majority, and voted for the bill. On the militia bill, and in a variety of minor cases, he has leaned to abridging the exercise of federal authority, and leaving as much as possible to the States; and he lost no opportunity of *sounding the alarm*, with great affected solemnity, at encroachments, meditated on the rights of the States, and of holding up the bugbear of a faction in the government having designs unfriendly to liberty.

This kind of conduct has appeared to me the more extraordinary on the part of Mr. Madison, as I know for a certainty, it was a primary article in his creed, that the real danger in our system was the subversion of the national authority by the preponderancy of the State governments. All his measures have proceeded on an opposite supposition. . . .

In respect to foreign politics, the views of these gentlemen are, in my judgment, equally unsound and dangerous. *They have a womanish attachment to France and a womanish resentment against Great Britain.* They would draw us into the closest embrace of the former, and involve us in all the consequences of her politics; and they would risk the peace of the country in their endeavors to keep us at the greatest possible distance from the latter. This disposition goes to a length, particularly in Mr. Jefferson, of which, till lately, I had no adequate idea. Various circumstances prove to me that if these gentlemen were left to pursue their own course, there would be, in less than six months, *an open war between the United States and Great Britain.*

I trust I have a due sense of the conduct of France towards this country in the late revolution; and that I shall always be among the foremost in making her every suitable return; but there is a wide difference between this and implicating ourselves in all her politics; between bearing good-will to her and hating and wrangling with all those whom she hates. The neutral and the pacific policy appears to me to mark the true path to the United States. . . .

Mr. Jefferson, it is known, did not in the first instance cordially acquiesce in the new Constitution for the United States; he had many doubts and reserves. He left this country before we had experienced the imbecilities of the former.

In France, he saw government only on the side of its abuses. He drank freely of the French philosophy, in religion, in science, in politics. He came from France in the moment of a fermentation, which he had a share in exciting, and in the passions and feelings of which he shared both from temperament and situation.

He came here probably with a too partial idea of his own powers; and with the expectation of a greater share in the direction of our councils than he has in reality enjoyed. I am not sure that he had not peculiarly marked out for himself the department of the finances.

He came, electrified *plus* with attachment to France, and with the project of knitting together the two countries in the closest political bands.

Mr. Madison had always entertained an exalted opinion of the talents, knowledge, and virtues of Mr. Jefferson. The sentiment was probably reciprocal. A close correspondence subsisted between them during the time of Mr. Jefferson's absence from the country. A close intimacy arose upon his return.

Whether any peculiar opinions of Mr. Jefferson's concerning the public debt wrought a change in the sentiments of Mr. Madison (for it is certain that the former is more radically wrong than the latter), or whether Mr. Madison, seduced by the expectation of popularity, and possibly by the calculation of advantage to the State of Virginia, was led to change his own opinion, certain it is that a very material *change* took place, and that the two gentlemen were united in the new ideas. . . .

Attempts were made by these gentlemen, in different ways, to produce a commercial warfare with Great Britain. In this, too, they were disappointed. And, as they had the liveliest wishes on the subject, their dissatisfaction has been proportionally great; and, as I had not favored the project, I was comprehended in their displeasure.

These causes, and perhaps some others, created, much sooner than I was aware of it, a systematic opposition to me, on the part of these gentlemen. My subversion, I am now satisfied, has been long an object with them. . . .

Under the influence of all these circumstances the attachment to the government of the United States, originally weak in Mr. Jefferson's mind, has given way to something very like dislike in Mr. Madison's. It is so counteracted by personal feelings as to be more an affair of the head than of the heart; more the result of a conviction of the necessity of Union than of cordiality to the thing itself. I hope it does not stand worse than this with him.

In such a state of mind both these gentlemen are prepared to hazard a great deal to effect a change. Most of the important measures of every government are connected with the treasury. To subvert the present head of it, they deem it expedient to risk rendering the government itself odious; perhaps foolishly thinking that they can easily recover the lost affections and confidence of the people, and not appreciating, as they ought to do, the natural resistance to government, which in every community results from the human passions, the degree to which this is strengthened by the *organized rivality* [*sic*] of State governments, and the infinite danger that the national government, once rendered odious, will be kept so by these powerful and indefatigable enemies. . . .

In giving you this picture of political parties, my design is, I confess, to awaken your attention, if it has not yet been awakened, to the conduct of the gentlemen in question. If my opinion of them is founded, it is certainly of great moment to the public weal that they should be understood. I rely on the strength of your mind to appreciate men as they merit, when you have a clue to their real views.

A word on another point. I am told that serious apprehensions are disseminated in your State as to the existence of a monarchical party meditating the destruction of State and republican government. If it is possible that so absurd an idea can gain ground, it is necessary that it should be combated. I assure you, on *my private faith* and *honor* as a man, that there is not, in my judgment, a shadow of foundation for it. A very small number of men indeed may entertain theories less republican than Mr. Jefferson and Mr. Madison, but I am persuaded there is not a man among them who would not regard as both *criminal* and *visionary* any attempt to subvert the republican system of the country. Most of these men rather fear that it may not justify itself by its fruits, than feel a predilection for a different form; and their fears are not diminished by the factious and fanatical politics which they find prevailing among a certain set of gentlemen and threatening to disturb the tranquillity and order of the government.

As to the destruction of State governments, the *great* and *real* anxiety is to be able to preserve the national from the too potent and counteracting influence of those governments. As to my own political creed, I give it to you with the utmost sincerity. I am *affectionately* attached to the republican theory. I desire *above all things* to see the *equality* of political rights, exclusive of all *hereditary* distinction, firmly established by a practical demonstration of its being consistent with the order and happiness of society. . . .

I said that I was *affectionately* attached to the republican theory. This is the real language of my heart, which I open to you in the sincerity of friendship; and I add that I have strong hopes of the success of that theory; but, in candor, I ought also to add that I am far from being without doubts. I consider its success as yet a problem.

It is yet to be determined by experience whether it be consistent with that *stability* and *order* in government which are essential to public strength and private security and happiness. On the whole, the only enemy which Republicanism has to fear in this country is in the spirit of faction and anarchy. If this will not permit the ends of government to be attained under it, if it engenders disorders in the community, all regular and orderly minds will wish for a change, and the demagogues who have produced the disorder will make it for their own aggrandizement. This is the old story.

If I were disposed to promote monarchy and overthrow State governments, I would mount the hobby-horse of popularity; I would cry out "usurpation," "danger to liberty," etc., etc.; I would endeavor to prostrate the national government, raise a ferment, and then "ride in the whirlwind, and direct the storm." That there are men acting with Jefferson and Madison who have this in view, I verily believe; I could lay my finger on some of them. That Madison does *not* mean it, I also verily believe; and I rather believe the same of Jefferson, but I read him upon the whole thus: "A man of profound ambition and violent passions."

READING AND DISCUSSION QUESTIONS

1. What do Hamilton's views on the economy suggest about his larger political philosophy?
2. What is the nature of this dispute with Jefferson and Madison? How does Hamilton explain their relationship?
3. What insight about the conduct of early national politics does Hamilton's letter reveal? What does it suggest about the emergence of political parties and the role they played in national politics?

7-2 | Jefferson's Agrarian Vision for the New Republic

THOMAS JEFFERSON, *Notes on the State of Virginia* (1781)

Thomas Jefferson had a distinguished political career even before assuming the presidency in 1801. Son of a prominent Virginia family, Jefferson took his position at the front of colonial politics, serving as a member of the Second Continental Congress, governor of Virginia, minister to France, secretary of state, and vice president. While serving as secretary of state under Washington, he sparred with Hamilton over the direction of the young republic, especially with regard to the economy and whether it should be centered on agriculture or manufacturing. During the 1780s, Jefferson wrote and published his major work, *Notes on the State of Virginia*, in which he offers his own vision of America's economic future, one clearly at odds with Hamilton's views.

The Present State of Manufactures, Commerce, Interior and Exterior Trade

We never had an interior trade of any importance. Our exterior commerce has suffered very much from the beginning of the present contest. During this time we have manufactured within our families the most necessary articles of cloathing. Those of cotton will bear some comparison with the same kinds of manufacture in Europe; but those of wool, flax and hemp are very coarse, unsightly, and unpleasant: and such is our attachment to agriculture, and such our preference for foreign manufactures, that be it wise or unwise, our people will certainly return as soon as they can, to the raising [of] raw materials, and exchanging them for finer manufactures than they are able to execute themselves.

The political economists of Europe have established it as a principle that every state should endeavour to manufacture for itself: and this principle, like many others, we transfer to America, without calculating the difference of circumstance which should often produce a difference of result. In Europe the lands are either cultivated, or locked up against the cultivator. Manufacture must therefore be resorted to of necessity not of choice, to support the surplus of their people. But we have an immensity of land courting the industry of the husbandman. Is it best then that all our citizens should be employed in its improvement, or that one half should be called off from that to exercise manufactures and handicraft arts for the other? Those who labour in the earth are the chosen people of God, if ever he had a chosen people, whose breasts he has made his peculiar deposit for substantial and genuine virtue. It is the focus in which he keeps alive that sacred fire, which otherwise might escape from the face of the earth. Corruption of morals in the mass of cultivators

---

Thomas Jefferson, *Notes on the State of Virginia* (London: John Stockdale, 1787), 273–275, 289–291, 293.

is a phenomenon of which no age nor nation has furnished an example. It is the mark set on those, who not looking up to heaven, to their own soil and industry, as does the husbandman, for their subsistance, depend for it on the casualties and caprice of customers. Dependance begets subservience and venality, suffocates the germ of virtue, and prepares fit tools for the designs of ambition. This, the natural progress and consequence of the arts, has sometimes perhaps been retarded by accidental circumstances: but, generally speaking, the proportion which the aggregate of the other classes of citizens bears in any state to that of its husbandmen, is the proportion of its unsound to its healthy parts, and is a good-enough barometer whereby to measure its degree of corruption. While we have land to labour then, let us never wish to see our citizens occupied at a work-bench, or twirling a distaff. Carpenters, masons, smiths, are wanting in husbandry: but, for the general operations of manufacture, let our work-shops remain in Europe. It is better to carry provisions and materials to workmen there, than bring them to the provisions and materials, and with them their manners and principles. The loss by the transportation of commodities across the Atlantic will be made up in happiness and permanence of government. The mobs of great cities add just so much to the support of pure government, as sores do to the strength of the human body. It is the manners and spirit of a people which preserve a republic in vigour. A degeneracy in these is a canker which soon eats to the heart of its laws and constitution. . . .

It should be our endeavour to cultivate the peace and friendship of every nation, even of that which has injured us most, when we shall have carried our point against her. Our interest will be to throw open the doors of commerce, and to knock off all its shackles, giving perfect freedom to all persons for the vent of whatever they may chuse to bring into our ports, and asking the same in theirs. Never was so much false arithmetic employed on any subject, as that which has been employed to persuade nations that it is their interest to go to war. Were the money which it has cost to gain, at the close of a long war, a little town, or a little territory, the right to cut wood here, or to catch fish there, expended in improving what they already possess, in making roads, opening rivers, building ports, improving the arts, and finding employment for their idle poor, it would render them much stronger, much wealthier and happier. This I hope will be our wisdom. And, perhaps, to remove as much as possible the occasions of making war, it might be better for us to abandon the ocean altogether, that being the element whereon we shall be principally exposed to jostle with other nations: to leave to others to bring what we shall want, and to carry what we can spare. This would make us invulnerable to Europe, by offering none of our property to their prize, and would turn all our citizens to the cultivation of the earth; and, I repeat it again, cultivators of the earth are the most virtuous and independent citizens. It might be time enough to seek employment for them at sea, when the land no longer offers it. But the actual habits of our countrymen attach them to commerce. They will exercise it for themselves. Wars then must sometimes be our lot; and all the wise can do, will be to avoid that half of them which would be produced by our own follies, and our own acts of injustice; and to make for the other half the best preparations we can. Of what nature should these be? A land army would be useless for offence, and not the best nor safest instrument of defence. For either of these purposes, the sea is the field on which we should meet an European enemy. On that element it is necessary we should possess some power. To aim at such a navy as the greater nations of Europe possess, would be a foolish and wicked waste of the energies of our countrymen. It would be to pull on our own heads that load of military expence, which makes the European labourer go supperless to bed, and moistens his bread with the sweat of his brows. It will be enough if we enable ourselves to prevent insults from those nations of Europe which are weak on the sea, because circumstances exist, which render even the stronger ones weak as to us. Providence has placed their richest and most defenceless possessions at our door; has obliged their most precious commerce to pass as it were in review before us. . . .

The value of our lands and slaves, taken conjunctly, doubles in about twenty years. This arises from the multiplication of our slaves, from the extension of culture, and increased demand for lands. The amount of what may be raised will of course rise in the same proportion.

READING AND DISCUSSION QUESTIONS

1. In one of the most famous lines in *Notes*, Jefferson writes, "Those who labour in the earth are the chosen people of God." We know from his other writings that he meant yeoman farmers, who lived self-sufficiently on small farms (and that he meant white farmers, not African slaves), but why do you think he accorded farmers such respect?
2. How does this source help you to understand Jefferson's opposition to Hamilton's economic policies?

7-3 | An Anti-Jefferson Political Cartoon
The Providential Detection (c. 1790s)

During the 1790s, as the French Revolution broke out—formed around the idea of *liberté, égalité, fraternité* (liberty, equality, fraternity) and leading to the execution of the absolutist King Louis XVI—Federalists and Republicans (as Jefferson's supporters were called) took sides, interpreting the French Revolution in light of their own. Jeffersonian Republicans supported the French revolutionaries, who seemed to embrace the same republican ideals that had fueled the American Revolution. Federalists were horrified, especially after the French Revolution darkened into the Reign of Terror. In this cartoon, the artist questions Jefferson's loyalties. Dropping from Jefferson's right hand is a letter to his Italian friend Philip Mazzei in which Jefferson had criticized Federalist foreign policy. His enemies seized on this letter to accuse Jefferson of treason.

'The Providential Detection', cartoon depicting Thomas Jefferson (1743–1826) trying to destroy the Constitution (engraving)/American School (18th century)/AMERICAN ANTIQUARIAN SOCIETY/American Antiquarian Society, Worcester, Massachusetts, USA/Bridgeman Images

READING AND DISCUSSION QUESTIONS

1. Identify each of the cartoon's details and describe how the artist used them to criticize Jefferson and his political views.
2. What is the significance of the Altar to Gallic Despotism? One of the papers fueling the fire is Thomas Paine's *Age of Reason*. What do you think the artist is suggesting about Jefferson's political leanings and influences?
3. What does the title of this cartoon mean? What is the artist suggesting about Jefferson's religious faith by using the eye (at top right) and the dark figure (at bottom right)?

7-4 | Anxiety over Western Expansion

THE PANOPLIST AND MISSIONARY HERALD, *Retrograde Movement of National Character* (1818)

Land policy was another arena of political debate. Federalists supported the sale of large tracts of the western territories to ensure an orderly settlement. By contrast, once Jeffersonian Republicans took office, they worked to reduce the federal minimum on land purchases from 640 acres (which excluded everyone but wealthy speculators) to 320 acres in 1800, and to even smaller amounts in subsequent years. By 1832, the minimum plot available for sale had been reduced to 40 acres, opening the territories to yeomen farmers, the same men whom Jefferson praised as God's chosen. Not everyone agreed that the westward movement invited by territorial expansion was a good thing. In this selection, an article from a Christian monthly magazine published in 1818, the author (identified only by the initials "M.N.") describes his anxiety.

The manner in which the population is spreading over this continent has no parallel in history. The first settlers of every other country have been barbarians, whose habits and institutions were suited to a wild and wandering life. As their numbers multiplied, they have gradually become civilized and refined. The progress has been from ignorance to knowledge, from the rudeness, of savage life to the refinements of polished society. But in the settlement of North America the case is reversed. The tendency is from civilization to barbarism.

Every one knows the manner in which our new settlements are formed. Single families, sometimes single individuals, proceed from this cultivated country, and, leaving behind them the religion and institutions of their fathers, they penetrate the western forest. It is usually several years before they are able to erect a comfortable dwelling-house, and many more before they can enjoy some of the most common privileges of older settlements. During this whole period, they are from necessity without schools, without ministers, without any of that influence, or those institutions which form the sober, steady, sterling character of older parts of the country. By the time that they are able to support these institutions, long habit has made them easy without them. With many the expense is an objection; and, not unfrequently a new generation have sprung up, who are unacquainted with their value, and unwilling to make any sacrifices for their support. In such a soil we should naturally suppose that infidelity and error of every species would take root and flourish. And such is the fact. The accounts which we hear represent the state of these settlements as deplorable for ignorance and irreligion.

The tendency of the American character is then to degenerate, and to degenerate rapidly; and that not from any peculiar vice in the American people, but from the very nature of a spreading population. The population of the country is out-growing its institutions.

But would we have a more convincing evidence of this degeneracy, let us go back to the days of our fathers. It is but a few years; our aged men can almost reach the time, when they first landed on these shores. They were good men, men of prayer, upright, and perfect in their generations, men who walked with God. Go now to our western borders—and who are these without Bibles, without Sabbaths—to whom the news of a Savior was never preached—who

"Retrograde Movement of National Character," *The Panoplist and Missionary Herald,* vol. 14 (1818), 212–213.

blaspheme God day and night? Are these the sons of the pilgrims?—these the children of their prayers—these the offspring for whom they endured persecution—the perils of the sea, and the perils of the wilderness—for whom they toiled and bled to procure the blessings of the Gospel? You search history in vain for degeneracy like this. Yet this is the beginning of sorrows. Could we draw aside the veil from the future, we might see these degraded men giving birth to settlements still more remote; we might see whole nations sprung from their loins—yes, we might see these men, at whose degeneracy we are now shocked, regarded as venerable, as holy, by their still more degenerate offspring. We talk of India—of Juggernaut—of the bloody rites of Pagan worship—but who can tell, how soon our own Missouri will be a Ganges, and our own children pass through the fire to Moloch.

M. N.

READING AND DISCUSSION QUESTIONS

1. What does the author suggest will be the consequences of the rapid movement of people from the East into the western territories?
2. How do the author's views align with the political philosophies of the Federalists and Republicans?

7-5 | A Shawnee Chief Calls for Native American Unity

TECUMSEH, *Sleep Not Longer, O Choctaws and Chickasaws* (1811)

The movement west cheered some citizens of the newly formed United States and worried others, but it angered many Native Americans. Tecumseh (1768–1813), a Shawnee chief, focused Native American attention on the encroachments of whites onto native lands. In this speech to the Choctaws and the Chickasaws, he describes the threat that Americans were posing and urges a united front to turn back the intruders. Here Tecumseh announces his alliance with the British, who once again found themselves at war with the Americans in 1812. Western "war hawks," Americans who lived on the frontier and hoped to eliminate the native peoples blocking their expansion west, urged war against the British, who had supported Tecumseh's people. Tecumseh's aim was to rally his allies to join the British in attacking the common American enemy.

Horatio Bardwell Cushman, *History of the Choctaw, Chickasaw, and Natchez Indians* (Greenville, TX: Headlight Printing House, 1899), 310–314.

In view of questions of vast importance, have we met together in solemn council to-night. Nor should we here debate whether we have been wronged and injured, but by what measures we should avenge ourselves; for our merciless oppressors, having long since planned out their proceedings, are not about to make, but have and are still making attacks upon those of our race who have as yet come to no resolution. Nor are we ignorant by what steps, and by what gradual advances, the whites break in upon our neighbors. Imagining themselves to be still undiscovered, they show themselves the less audacious because you are insensible. The whites are already nearly a match for us all united, and too strong for any one tribe alone to resist; so that unless we support one another with our collective and united forces; unless every tribe unanimously combines to give a check to the ambition and avarice of the whites, they will soon conquer us apart and disunited, and we will be driven away from our native country and scattered as autumnal leaves before the wind.

But have we not courage enough remaining to defend our country and maintain our ancient independence? Will we calmly suffer the white intruders and tyrants to enslave us? Shall it be said of our race that we knew not how to extricate ourselves from the three most to be dreaded calamities—folly, inactivity and cowardice? But what need is there to speak of the past? It speaks for itself and asks, "Where to-day is the Pequod? Where the Narragansetts, the Mohawks, Pocanokets, and many other once powerful tribes of our race? They have vanished before the avarice and oppression of the white men, as snow before a summer sun. In the vain hope of alone defending their ancient possessions, they have fallen in the wars with the white men. Look abroad over their once beautiful country, and what see you now? Naught but the ravages of the pale-face destroyers meet your eyes. So it will be with you Choctaws and Chickasaws! Soon your mighty forest trees, under the shade of whose wide spreading branches you have played in infancy, sported in boyhood, and now rest your wearied limbs after the fatigue of the chase, will be cut down to fence in the land which the white intruders dare to call their own. Soon their broad roads will pass over the grave of your fathers, and the place of their rest will be blotted out forever. The annihilation of our race is at hand unless we unite in one common cause against the common foe. Think not, brave Choctaws and Chickasaws, that you can remain passive and indifferent to the common danger, and thus escape the common fate. Your people too will soon be as falling leaves and scattering clouds before their blighting breath. You too will be driven away from your native land and ancient domains as leaves are driven before the wintry storms. . . .

Sleep not longer, O Choctaws and Chickasaws . . . in false security and delusive hopes. Our broad domains are fast escaping from our grasp. Every year our white intruders become more greedy, exacting, oppressive and overbearing. Every year contentions spring up between them and our people and when blood is shed we have to make atonement whether right or wrong, at the cost of the lives of our greatest chiefs, and the yielding up of large tracts of our lands. Before the palefaces came among us, we enjoyed the happiness of unbounded freedom, and were acquainted with neither riches, wants, nor oppression. How is it now? Wants and oppressions are our lot; for are we not controlled in everything, and dare we move without asking, by your leave? Are we not being stripped day by day of the little that remains of our ancient liberty? Do they not even now kick and strike us as they do their black-faces? How long will it be before they will tie us to a post and whip us, and make us work for them in their corn fields as they do them? Shall we wait for that moment or shall we die fighting before submitting to such ignominy? . . .

Have we not for years had before our eyes a sample of their designs, and are they not sufficient harbingers of their future determinations? Will we not soon be driven from our respective countries and the graves of our ancestors? Will not the bones of our dead be plowed up, and their graves be turned into fields? Shall we calmly wait until they become so numerous that we will no longer be able to resist oppression? Will we wait to be destroyed in our turn, without making an effort worthy of our race? Shall we give up our homes, our country, bequeathed to us by the Great Spirit, the graves of our dead, and everything that is dear and sacred to us, without a struggle? I know you will cry with me, Never! Never! Then let us by unity of action destroy them all, which we now can do, or drive them back whence they came. War or extermination is now our only choice. You choose? I know your answer. Therefore, I now call on you, brave Choctaws and Chickasaws, to assist in the just cause of liberating our race from the grasp of our faithless invaders and heartless oppressors. The white usurpation in our common country must be stopped, or we, its rightful owners, be forever destroyed and wiped out as a race of people. I am now at the head of many warriors backed by the strong arm of English soldiers. Choctaws and Chickasaws, you have too long borne with grievous usurpation inflicted by the arrogant Americans. Be no longer their dupes. If there be one here to-night who believes that his rights will not sooner or later, be taken from him by the avaricious American pale-faces, his ignorance ought to excite pity, for he knows little of the character of our common foe. And if there be one among you mad enough to undervalue the growing power of the white race among us, let him tremble in considering the fearful woes he will bring down upon our entire race, if by his criminal indifference he assists the designs of our common enemy against our common country. Then listen to the voice of duty, of honor, of nature and of your endangered country. Let us form one body, one heart, and defend to the last warrior our country, our homes, our liberty, and the graves of our fathers.

Choctaws and Chickasaws, you are among the few of our race who sit indolently at ease. You have indeed enjoyed the reputation of being brave, but will you be indebted for it more from report than fact? Will you let the whites encroach upon your domains even to your very door before you will assert your rights in resistance? Let no one in this council imagine that I speak more from malice against the pale-face Americans than just grounds of complaint. Complaint is just toward friends who have failed in their duty; accusation is against enemies guilty of injustice. And surely, if any people ever had, we have good and just reasons to believe we have ample grounds to accuse the Americans of injustice; especially when such great acts of injustice have been committed by them upon our race, of which they seem to have no manner of regard, or even to reflect. They are a people fond of innovations, quick to contrive and quick to put their schemes into effectual execution, no matter how great the wrong and injury to us; while we are content to preserve what we already have. Their designs are to enlarge their possessions by taking yours in turn; and will you, can you longer dally, O Choctaws and Chickasaws? Do you imagine that that people will not continue longest in the enjoyment of peace who timely prepare to vindicate themselves, and manifest a determined resolution to do themselves right whenever they are wronged? Far otherwise. Then haste to the relief of our common cause, as by consanguinity of blood you are bound; lest the day be not far distant when you will be left single-handed and alone to the cruel mercy of our most inveterate foe.

READING AND DISCUSSION QUESTIONS

1. What parallels do you see in the way Tecumseh describes Americans and the way Americans described the British during the Revolution?
2. What arguments does Tecumseh use to rally the Choctaws and Chickasaws?
3. What can we learn from Tecumseh's speech about the consequences of American land policy in the early years of the republic?

7-6 | Cartoon Satirizing Federalist Opposition to the War of 1812

WILLIAM CHARLES, *The Hartford Convention, or Leap No Leap* (1815)

This political cartoon pokes fun at New England Federalists who opposed the War of 1812. The war revived the Federalists, who used it to mount a vicious attack on Jefferson and Madison. Jefferson's 1807 Embargo Act outraged New England Federalists, whose shipping interests suffered as a result, but his critics also ridiculed him for grasping enormous power, contrary to his own political philosophy. Madison fared no better. He was excoriated for stumbling into a war the nation was ill prepared to fight. The disgruntled Federalists met in Hartford, Connecticut to cohere their protests into a series of resolutions they intended to present to Congress. Some at the convention, including Timothy Pickering, a Massachusetts Federalist who had served as Secretary of State and in both houses of Congress, suggested New England secede from the Union. Ultimately, the Convention offered more modest proposals, but the Convention's timing worked against their interests. Soon after the convention ended, news of General Andrew Jackson's astounding victory over the British at the Battle of New Orleans, followed by news of the peace signed at Ghent, Belgium, rendered the Federalists' attack moot and seemingly unpatriotic. The party quickly dissolved.

The three figures at the cartoon's top left represent the New England states of Massachusetts, Rhode Island, and Connecticut. Timothy Pickering, depicted kneeling in prayer, says "I, Strongly and most fervently pray for the success of this great leap which will change my vulgar name into that of my Lord of Essex. God save the King." At right is the King of England, George III, who says, "O'tis my Yankey boys! Jump in my fine fellows; plenty of molasses and Codfish; plenty of goods to Smuggle; Honours, titles and Nobility into the bargain." The King's exclamation, "O'tis," is a play on the name of Harrison Gray Otis, the Massachusetts politician depicted directly above Pickering. Otis pulls the rest of New England toward secession saying, "What a dangerous leap!!! But we must jump Brother Conn."

Library of Congress

READING AND DISCUSSION QUESTIONS

1. What is the cartoonist's attitude toward the Hartford Convention? How does the political cartoon express that attitude?
2. What does the cartoonist suggest about the motivations of the key figures depicted in the cartoon? Who do you think was the intended audience for this cartoon? Why might they have found this image funny?
3. What does the Hartford Convention tell us about early national politics?

▪ COMPARATIVE QUESTIONS ▪

1. What might account for the difference in American responses to the French Revolution? What impact might those differences have had on American politics?
2. Compare and contrast the political program of the Federalists and Republicans based on the sources included in this chapter. How did the emergence of these early political parties affect American society during this time?
3. What did the two major political parties see as the source of strength for the American republic? Did they have the same or different answers?
4. To what extent were the disputes between Federalists and Republicans fueled by policy or personality?
5. How would you interpret the War of 1812? Is it the end of one era or the start of another? Did the War of 1812 introduce new issues or settle old ones?

PART 3

DOCUMENT SET

The Emergence of Democratic Ideals and a New National Identity

1754–1820

CHAPTER 5
The Problem of Empire, 1754–1776

CHAPTER 6
Making War and Republican Governments, 1776–1789

CHAPTER 7
Hammering Out a Federal Republic, 1787–1820

Upon his election as president in 1788, George Washington described his feelings as "not unlike those of a culprit who is going to the place of his execution." The period of revolution and republic-building that began with Washington's election was challenging not only for the new president but also for the newly independent nation as a whole. The American people, once freed from British rule, were challenged to create and enact a republican government and a national identity in a period when elites continued to liken ordinary folk to the "common herd." This traditional distrust of "the people" came up against the democratic ideals that energized non-elites, who increasingly regarded liberty, as Jefferson told them in the Declaration of Independence, as a birthright. Competing conceptions of national identity gave rise to tension, and yet a growing optimism trumped the difficulties Washington anticipated, creating a political environment pregnant with the confidence of the age. The emerging democratic ideals shaped values, sparked reform efforts, and produced an enduring republican culture out of a diverse population. The sources in this chapter speak to the various ways individuals understood democracy as a key component in an emerging national identity.

P3-1 | Mourning Washington

RICHARD ALLEN, *Eulogy for Washington* (1799)

When George Washington died in December 1799, the nation's outpouring of grief spoke to the unique and unifying figure he had become. This was true even to many free and enslaved African Americans despite Washington having been a slave owner himself. Richard Allen, whose eulogy for Washington appears below, was born a slave but bought his freedom and began preaching. In 1816 the African Methodist Episcopal Church ordained him as its first bishop. In this eulogy, Allen claims an American identity along with whites through their common mourning for the nation's founding father. Washington's will, which Allen alludes to here, provided for the complete emancipation of all his slaves upon his wife Martha's death.

At this time it may not be improper to speak a little on the late mournful event—an event in which we participate in common with the feelings of a grateful people—an event which causes "the land to mourn" in a season of festivity. Our father and friend is taken from us—he whom the nations honoured is "seen of men no more."

We, my friends, have particular cause to bemoan our loss. To us he has been the sympathising friend and tender father. He has watched over us, and viewed our degraded and afflicted state with compassion and pity—his heart was not insensible to our sufferings. He whose wisdom the nations revered thought we had a right to liberty. Unbiased by the popular opinion of the state in which is the memorable Mount Vernon—he dared to do his duty, and wipe off the only stain with which man could ever reproach him.

And it is now said by an authority on which I rely, that he who ventured his life in battles, whose "head was covered" in that day, and whose shield the "Lord of hosts" was, did not fight for that liberty which he desired to withhold from others—the bread of oppression was not sweet to his taste, and he "let the oppressed go free"—he "undid every burden"—he provided lands and comfortable accommodations for them when he kept this "acceptable fast to the Lord"—that those who had been slaves might rejoice in the day of their deliverance.

If he who broke the yoke of British burdens "from off the neck of the people" of this land, and was hailed his country's deliverer, by what name shall we call him who secretly and almost unknown emancipated his "bondmen and bondwomen"—became to them a father, and gave them an inheritance!

Deeds like these are not common. He did not let "his right hand know what his left hand did"—but he who "sees in secret will openly reward" such acts of beneficence.

The name of Washington will live when the sculptured marble and statue of bronze shall be crumbled into dust—for it is the decree of the eternal God that "the righteous shall be had in everlasting remembrance, but the memorial of the wicked shall rot."

Richard Allen, "Eulogy for Washington" in *Lift Every Voice: African American Oratory, 1787–1900*, eds. Philip S. Foner and Robert James Branham (Tuscaloosa: The University of Alabama Press, 1998), 57–58.

It is not often necessary, and it is seldom that occasion requires recommending the observance of the laws of the land to you, but at this time it becomes a duty; for you cannot honour those who have loved you and been your benefactors more than by taking their council and advice.

And here let me intreat you always to bear in mind the affectionate farewell advice of the great Washington—"to love your country—to obey its laws—to seek its peace—and to keep yourselves from attachment to any foreign nation."

Your observance of these short and comprehensive expressions will make you good citizens—and greatly promote the cause of the oppressed and shew to the world that you hold dear the name of George Washington.

May a double portion of his spirit rest on all the officers of the government in the United States, and all that say my Father, my Father—the chariots of Israel, and the horsemen thereof, which is the whole of the American people.

READING AND DISCUSSION QUESTIONS

1. Explain why Allen tells his African American parishioners that Washington's death was "our loss."
2. What can you infer about Allen's understanding of American citizenship? How does he describe for his congregation the marks of a "good citizen"?

P3-2 | Defining the American Character

J. HECTOR ST. JOHN DE CRÈVECOEUR, *Letters from an American Farmer* (1782)

In 1782, the same year the writer J. Hector St. John de Crèvecoeur (1735–1813) published his popular *Letters from an American Farmer*, the Continental Congress adopted the Great Seal for the United States, including the Latin motto *E pluribus unum* (Out of many, one). But one what? Congress of course intended it to mean one nation, comprising the thirteen newly independent states. For Crèvecoeur, a French-born emigrant to New York who became an American citizen, the question was more philosophical. In one of his essays, excerpted below, he attempts an answer to his most famous question: "What then is the American, this new man?"

I wish I could be acquainted with the feelings and thoughts which must agitate the heart and present themselves to the mind of an enlightened Englishman, when he first lands on this continent. . . . [A] modern society offers itself to his contemplation, different from what he had hitherto seen. It is not composed, as in Europe, of great lords who possess everything, and of a herd of people who have nothing. Here are no aristocratical families, no courts, no kings, no bishops, no ecclesiastical dominion, no invisible power giving to a few a very visible one,

J. Hector St. John Crèvecoeur, *Letters from an American Farmer* (New York: Fox, Duffield & Company, 1904), 48–50, 52–56.

no great manufacturers employing thousands, no great refinements of luxury. The rich and the poor are not so far removed from each other as they are in Europe. Some few towns excepted, we are all tillers of the earth, from Nova Scotia to West Florida. We are a people of cultivators, scattered over an immense territory, communicating with each other by means of good roads and navigable rivers, united by the silken bands of mild government, all respecting the laws, without dreading their power, because they are equitable. We are all animated with the spirit of an industry which is unfettered and unrestrained, because each person works for himself. If he travels through our rural districts he views not the hostile castle, and the haughty mansion, contrasted with the clay-built hut and miserable cabin, where cattle and men help to keep each other warm, and dwell in meanness, smoke, and indigence. A pleasing uniformity of decent competence appears throughout our habitations. . . . We have no princes, for whom we toil, starve, and bleed: we are the most perfect society now existing in the world. Here man is free as he ought to be; nor is this pleasing equality so transitory as many others are. . . .

In this great American asylum, the poor of Europe have by some means met together, and in consequence of various causes; to what purpose should they ask one another what countrymen they are? Alas, two thirds of them had no country. Can a wretch who wanders about, who works and starves, whose life is a continual scene of sore affliction or pinching penury; can that man call England or any other kingdom his country? A country that had no bread for him, whose fields procured him no harvest, who met with nothing but the frowns of the rich, the severity of the laws, with jails and punishments; who owned not a single foot of the extensive surface of this planet? No! urged by a variety of motives, here they came. Every thing has tended to regenerate them; new laws, a new mode of living, a new social system; here they are become men: in Europe they were as so many useless plants, wanting vegetative mould, and refreshing showers; they withered, and were mowed down by want, hunger, and war; but now by the power of transplantation, like all other plants they have taken root and flourished! Formerly they were not numbered in any civil lists of their country, except in those of the poor; here they rank as citizens. By what invisible power has this surprising metamorphosis been performed? By that of the laws and that of their industry. The laws, the indulgent laws, protect them as they arrive, stamping on them the symbol of adoption; they receive ample rewards for their labours; these accumulated rewards procure them lands; those lands confer on them the title of freemen, and to that title every benefit is affixed which men can possibly require. . . .

What attachment can a poor European emigrant have for a country where he had nothing? The knowledge of the language, the love of a few kindred as poor as himself, were the only cords that tied him: his country is now that which gives him land, bread, protection, and consequence: *Ubi panis ibi patria,*[1]

---

[1] ***Ubi panis ibi patria***: A Latin motto meaning "Where there is bread, there is my country."

is the motto of all emigrants. What then is the American, this new man? He is either an European, or the descendant of an European, hence that strange mixture of blood, which you will find in no other country. I could point out to you a family whose grandfather was an Englishman, whose wife was Dutch, whose son married a French woman, and whose present four sons have now four wives of different nations. *He* is an American, who, leaving behind him all his ancient prejudices and manners, receives new ones from the new mode of life he has embraced, the new government he obeys, and the new rank he holds. He becomes an American by being received in the broad lap of our great *Alma Mater.* Here individuals of all nations are melted into a new race of men, whose labours and posterity will one day cause great changes in the world. Americans are the western pilgrims, who are carrying along with them that great mass of arts, sciences, vigour, and industry which began long since in the east; they will finish the great circle. The Americans were once scattered all over Europe; here they are incorporated into one of the finest systems of population which has ever appeared, and which will hereafter become distinct by the power of the different climates they inhabit. The American ought therefore to love this country much better than that wherein either he or his forefathers were born. Here the rewards of his industry follow with equal steps the progress of his labour; his labour is founded on the basis of nature, *self-interest*; can it want a stronger allurement? Wives and children, who before in vain demanded of him a morsel of bread, now, fat and frolicsome, gladly help their father to clear those fields whence exuberant crops are to arise to feed and to clothe them all; without any part being claimed, either by a despotic prince, a rich abbot, or a mighty lord. Here religion demands but little of him; a small voluntary salary to the minister and gratitude to God; can he refuse these? The American is a new man, who acts upon new principles; he must therefore entertain new ideas, and form new opinions. From involuntary idleness, service dependence, penury, and useless labour, he has passed to toils of a very different nature, reward by ample subsistence.—This is an American.

READING AND DISCUSSION QUESTIONS

1. Crèvecoeur's book of letters was first published in London for a European audience. How did Crèvecoeur explain to that audience what made Americans a distinctive people? Which themes did he emphasize?
2. How would you summarize Crèvecoeur's understanding of American citizenship? He himself was born in France but "became an American." Assuming he meant more than completing a legal process of naturalization, what did he understand "becoming an American" to involve?
3. To what extent is Crèvecoeur's construction of American identity relevant to contemporary Americans? Compare his views with your own.

P3-3 | Women's Right to Education in the New Republic

JUDITH SARGENT MURRAY, *On the Equality of the Sexes* (1790)

The Revolution's legacy on reformers was both immediate and enduring. The growing emphasis on democratic ideals helped to shape cultural values, as did Jefferson's claim of inalienable rights to "life, liberty, and the pursuit of happiness." Growing demands for a strong and democratic nation inspired reform efforts to eradicate slavery, promote religious revival and temperance campaigns, and expand women's rights. Judith Sargent Murray's essay, written in 1779 but published in 1790, decried gender inequalities and called for equal educational opportunities for women. Murray challenged the notion that females were intellectually inferior. This was a radical statement for the time and inspired later feminist efforts to advance women's rights. Murray wrote a column for the *Massachusetts Magazine* beginning in 1792 and her play, *The Medium* (1795), was the first staged production by an American author in the United States.

Is it upon mature consideration we adopt the idea, that nature is thus partial in her distributions? Is it indeed a fact, that she hath yielded to one half of the human species so unquestionable a mental superiority? I know that to both sexes elevated understandings, and the reverse, are common. But, suffer me to ask, in what the minds of females are so notoriously deficient, or unequal. May not the intellectual powers be ranged under these four heads—imagination, reason, memory, and judgment. The province of imagination hath long since been surrendered to us, and we have been crowned and undoubted sovereigns of the regions of fancy. Invention is perhaps the most arduous effort of the mind; this branch of imagination hath been particularly ceded to us, and we have been time out of mind invested with that creative faculty. Observe the variety of fashions (here I bar the contemptuous smile) which distinguish and adorn the female world: how continually are they changing, insomuch that they almost render the wise man's assertion problematical, and we are ready to say, *there is something new under the sun*. . . .

Another instance of our creative powers, is our talent for slander; how ingenious are we at inventive scandal? what a formidable story can we in a moment fabricate merely from the force of a prolifick imagination? how many reputations, in the fertile brain of a female, have been utterly despoiled? . . . Perhaps it will be asked if I furnish these facts as instances of excellency in our sex. Certainly not; but as proofs of a creative faculty, of a lively imagination. Assuredly great activity of mind is thereby discovered, and was this activity properly directed, what beneficial effects would follow. Is the needle and kitchen sufficient to employ the operations of a soul thus organized? I should conceive not. . . . Are we deficient in reason? we can only reason from what we know, and if an opportunity of acquiring knowledge hath been denied us, the inferiority of our

Judith Sargent Murray, "On the Equality of the Sexes," in *The Massachusetts Magazine*, vol. 2 (Boston: I. Thomas and E. T. Andrews, 1790).

sex cannot fairly be deduced from thence. Memory, I believe, will be allowed us in common, since everyone's experience must testify, that a loquacious old woman is as frequently met with, as a communicative man. . . .

"But our judgment is not so strong—we do not distinguish so well."—Yet it may be questioned, from what doth this superiority, in this determining faculty of the soul, proceed. May we not trace its source in the difference of education, and continued advantages? Will it be said that the judgment of a male of two years old, is more sage than that of a female's of the same age? I believe the reverse is generally observed to be true. But from that period what partiality! how is the one exalted, and the other depressed, by the contrary modes of education which are adopted! the one is taught to aspire, and the other is early confined and limited. As their years increase, the sister must be wholly domesticated, while the brother is led by the hand through all the flowery paths of science. Grant that their minds are by nature equal, yet who shall wonder at the *apparent* superiority, if indeed custom becomes *second nature*. . . . At length arrived at womanhood, the uncultivated fair one feels a void, which the employments allotted her are by no means capable of filling. What can she do? to books she may not apply; or if she doth, *to those only of the novel kind*, lest she merit the appellation of a *learned lady*; and what ideas have been affixed to this term, the observation of many can testify. Fashion, scandal, and sometimes what is still more reprehensible, are then called in to her relief; and who can say to what lengths the liberties she takes may proceed. Meantimes she herself is most unhappy; she feels the want of a cultivated mind. . . . Now, was she permitted the same instructors as her brother, (with an eye however to their particular departments) for the employment of a rational mind an ample field would be opened. . . . A mind, thus filled, would have little room for the trifles with which our sex are, with too much justice, accused of amusing themselves, and they would thus be rendered fit companions for those, who should one day wear them as their crown. . . . Females would become discreet, their judgments would be invigorated, and their partners for life being circumspectly chosen, an unhappy Hymen would then be as rare, as is now the reverse.

Will it be urged that those acquirements would supersede our domestick duties. I answer that every requisite in female economy is easily attained; and, with truth I can add, that when once attained, they require no further *mental attention*. Nay, while we are pursuing the needle, or the superintendency of the family, I repeat, that our minds are at full liberty for reflection; that imagination may exert itself in full vigor; and that if a just foundation is early laid, our ideas will then be worthy of rational beings. . . . Should it still be vociferated, "Your domestick employments are sufficient"—I would calmly ask, is it reasonable, that a candidate for immortality, for the joys of heaven, an intelligent being, who is to spend an eternity in contemplating the works of the Deity, should at present be so degraded, as to be allowed no other ideas, than those which are suggested by the mechanism of a pudding, or the sewing the seams of a garment? . . .

Yes, ye lordly, ye haughty sex, our souls are by nature *equal* to yours; the same breath of God animates, enlivens, and invigorates us; and that we are not fallen lower than yourselves, let those witness who have greatly towered above the various discouragements by which they have been so heavily oppressed; and though I am unacquainted with the list of celebrated characters on either side, yet from the observations I have made in the contracted circle in which I have moved, I dare confidently believe, that from the commencement of time to the present day, there hath been as many females, as males, who, by the *mere force of natural powers*, have merited the crown of applause; who, *thus unassisted*, have seized the wreath of fame. . . .

The exquisite delicacy of the female mind proclaimeth the exactness of its texture, while its nice sense of honour announceth its innate, its native grandeur. And indeed, in one respect, the preeminence seems to be tacitly allowed us; for after an education which limits and confines, and employments and recreations which naturally tend to enervate the body, and debilitate the mind; after we have from early youth been adorned with ribbons, and other gewgaws, dressed out like the ancient victims previous to a sacrifice, being taught by the care of our parents in collecting the most showy materials that the ornamenting our exteriour ought to be the principal object of our attention; after, I say, fifteen years thus spent, we are introduced into the world, amid the united adulation of every beholder. . . . It is expected that with the other sex we should commence immediate war, and that we should triumph over the machinations of the most artful. We must be constantly upon our guard; prudence and discretion must be our characteristiks; and we must rise superiour to, and obtain a complete victory over those who have been long adding to the native strength of their minds, by an unremitted study of men and books, and who have, moreover, conceived from the loose characters which they have seen portrayed in the extensive variety of their reading, a most contemptible opinion of the sex. . . . If we are allowed an equality of acquirements, let serious studies equally employ our minds, and we will bid our souls arise to equal strengths. We will meet upon even ground, the despot man; we will rush with alacrity to the combat, and, crowned by success, we shall then answer the exalted expectations, which are formed. Though sensibility, soft compassion, and gentle commiseration, are inmates in the female bosom. . . . If we meet an equal, a sensible friend, we will reward him with the hand of amity, and through life we will be assiduous to promote his happiness; but from every deep laid scheme, for our ruin, retiring into ourselves, amid the flowery paths of science, we will indulge in all the refined and sentimental pleasures of contemplation: And should it still be urged, that the studies thus insisted upon would interfere with our more peculiar department, I must further reply, that *early hours*, and close application, will do wonders; and to her who is from the first dawn of reason taught to fill up time rationally, both the requisites will be easy. I grant that niggard [stingy or selfish] fortune is too generally unfriendly to the mind; and that much of that valuable treasure, time, is necessarily expended upon the wants of the body; but it should be remembered; that in embarrassed circumstances our companions have as little leisure for literary improvements, as is afforded to us; for most certainly their provident care is at least as requisite as our exertions. . . . In high life, or, in other words, where the parties are in possession of affluence, the objection respecting time is wholly obviated, and of course falls to the ground. . . . But in one respect, O ye arbiters of our fate! we confess that the superiority is indubitably yours; you are by nature formed for our protectors; we pretend not to vie with you in bodily strength; upon this point we will never contend for victory. Shield us then, we beseech you, from external evils, and in return we will transact *your* domestick affairs. Yes, *your,* for are you not equally interested in those matters with ourselves? Is not the elegancy of neatness as agreeable to your sight as to ours; is not the well favoured viand equally delightful to your taste; and doth not your sense of hearing suffer as much, from the discordant sounds prevalent in an ill regulated family, produced by the voices of children and many *et ceteras*?

CONSTANTIA

READING AND DISCUSSION QUESTIONS

1. How important were the democratic ideals of the period to shaping Murray's argument about the inequality of the sexes, which she experienced? What does her argument suggest about her vision for the new nation?
2. Who do you think Murray's audience is for this essay? What effect do you think she expected to have on the cultural values of her day?
3. Assess the historical significance of Murray's essay as an artifact of the late-eighteenth-century debate over democratic ideals and national identity.

P3-4 | A Warning for the Young Republic
George Washington's Farewell Address (1796)

In everyone's estimation, Washington was the new nation's indispensable man. His two terms as president established the working structure of the national government and created a national identity around republican ideals. Washington's neutral course in foreign affairs aimed to ensure America's separate destiny from the war-wracked fate of Europe. By embracing Hamilton's economic policies, Washington supported a national bank and established public credit, thereby creating the political institutions affirming federal power. As his term closed, he cautioned his fellow Americans in a farewell address published in 1796.

Friends and Fellow Citizens:

In looking forward to the moment which is intended to terminate the career of my public life, my feelings do not permit me to suspend the deep acknowledgment of that debt of gratitude which I owe to my beloved country for the many honors it has conferred upon me; still more for the steadfast confidence with which it has supported me; and for the opportunities I have thence enjoyed

Washington's Farewell Address, 1796 (Yale Law School's Avalon Project, avalon.law.yale.edu).

of manifesting my inviolable attachment, by services faithful and persevering, though in usefulness unequal to my zeal. If benefits have resulted to our country from these services, let it always be remembered to your praise, and as an instructive example in our annals, that under circumstances in which the passions, agitated in every direction, were liable to mislead, amidst appearances sometimes dubious, vicissitudes of fortune often discouraging, in situations in which not unfrequently want of success has countenanced the spirit of criticism, the constancy of your support was the essential prop of the efforts, and a guarantee of the plans by which they were effected. . . .

The name of American, which belongs to you in your national capacity, must always exalt the just pride of patriotism more than any appellation derived from local discriminations. With slight shades of difference, you have the same religion, manners, habits, and political principles. You have in a common cause fought and triumphed together; the independence and liberty you possess are the work of joint counsels, and joint efforts of common dangers, sufferings, and successes.

But these considerations, however powerfully they address themselves to your sensibility, are greatly outweighed by those which apply more immediately to your interest. Here every portion of our country finds the most commanding motives for carefully guarding and preserving the Union of the whole. . . .

These considerations speak a persuasive language to every reflecting and virtuous mind, and exhibit the continuance of the Union as a primary object of patriotic desire. Is there a doubt whether a common government can embrace so large a sphere? Let experience solve it. To listen to mere speculation in such a case were criminal. We are authorized to hope that a proper organization of the whole with the auxiliary agency of governments for the respective subdivisions, will afford a happy issue to the experiment. It is well worth a fair and full experiment. With such powerful and obvious motives to union, affecting all parts of our country, while experience shall not have demonstrated its impracticability, there will always be reason to distrust the patriotism of those who in any quarter may endeavor to weaken its bands.

In contemplating the causes which may disturb our Union, it occurs as matter of serious concern that any ground should have been furnished for characterizing parties by geographical discriminations, *Northern* and *Southern*, *Atlantic* and *Western*; whence designing men may endeavor to excite a belief that there is a real difference of local interests and views. One of the expedients of party to acquire influence within particular districts is to misrepresent the opinions and aims of other districts. You cannot shield yourselves too much against the jealousies and heartburnings which spring from these misrepresentations; they tend to render alien to each other those who ought to be bound together by fraternal affection. . . .

To the efficacy and permanency of your Union, a government for the whole is indispensable. . . . Sensible of this momentous truth, you have improved upon your first essay, by the adoption of a constitution of government better calculated than your former for an intimate union, and for the efficacious management of your common concerns. This government, the offspring of our own choice, uninfluenced and unawed, adopted upon full investigation and mature deliberation, completely free in its principles, in the distribution of its powers, uniting security with energy, and containing within itself a provision for its own amendment, has a just claim to your confidence and your support. Respect for its authority, compliance with its laws, acquiescence in its measures, are duties enjoined by the fundamental maxims of true liberty. The basis of our political systems is the right of the people to make and to alter their constitutions of government. But the Constitution which at any time exists, till changed by an explicit and authentic act of the whole people, is sacredly obligatory upon all. The very idea of the power and the right of the people to establish government presupposes the duty of every individual to obey the established government.

All obstructions to the execution of the laws, all combinations and associations, under whatever plausible character, with the real design to direct, control, counteract, or awe the regular deliberation and action of the constituted authorities, are destructive of this fundamental principle, and of fatal tendency. They serve to organize faction, to give it an artificial and extraordinary force; to put, in the place of the delegated will of the nation the will of a party, often a small but artful and enterprising minority of the community. . . .

However combinations or associations of the above description may now and then answer popular ends, they are likely, in the course of time and things, to become potent engines, by which cunning, ambitious, and unprincipled men will be enabled to subvert the power of the people and to usurp for themselves the reins of government, destroying afterwards the very engines which have lifted them to unjust dominion.

Towards the preservation of your government, and the permanency of your present happy state, it is requisite, not only that you steadily discountenance irregular oppositions to its acknowledged authority, but also that you resist with care the spirit of innovation upon its principles, however specious the pretexts. . . .

I have already intimated to you the danger of parties in the State, with particular reference to the founding of them on geographical discriminations. Let me now take a more comprehensive view, and warn you in the most solemn manner against the baneful effects of the spirit of party generally.

This spirit, unfortunately, is inseparable from our nature, having its root in the strongest passions of the human mind. It exists under different shapes in all governments, more or less stifled, controlled, or repressed; but, in those of the popular form, it is seen in its greatest rankness, and is truly their worst enemy.

The alternate domination of one faction over another, sharpened by the spirit of revenge, natural to party dissension, which in different ages and countries has perpetrated the most horrid enormities, is itself a frightful despotism. But this leads at length to a more formal and permanent despotism. The disorders and miseries which result gradually incline the minds of men to seek security and repose in the absolute power of an individual; and sooner or later the chief of some prevailing faction, more able or more fortunate than his competitors, turns this disposition to the purposes of his own elevation, on the ruins of public liberty. . . .

It is important, likewise, that the habits of thinking in a free country should inspire caution in those entrusted with its administration, to confine themselves within their respective constitutional spheres, avoiding in the exercise of the powers of one department to encroach upon another. . . . The necessity of reciprocal checks in the exercise of political power, by dividing and distributing it into different depositaries, and constituting each the guardian of the public weal against invasions by the others, has been evinced by experiments ancient and modern; some of them in our country and under our own eyes. To preserve them must be as necessary as to institute them. If, in the opinion of the people, the distribution or modification of the constitutional powers be in any particular wrong, let it be corrected by an amendment in the way which the Constitution designates. But let there be no change by usurpation; for though this, in one instance, may be the instrument of good, it is the customary weapon by which free governments are destroyed. The precedent must always greatly overbalance in permanent evil any partial or transient benefit, which the use can at any time yield.

Of all the dispositions and habits which lead to political prosperity, religion and morality are indispensable supports. In vain would that man claim the tribute of patriotism, who should labor to subvert these great pillars of human happiness, these firmest props of the duties of men and citizens. The mere politician, equally with the pious man, ought to respect and to cherish them. A volume could not trace all their connections with private and public felicity. Let it simply be asked: Where is the security for property, for reputation, for life, if the sense of religious obligation desert the oaths which are the instruments of investigation in courts of justice? And let us with caution indulge the supposition that morality can be maintained without religion. Whatever may be conceded to the influence of refined education on minds of peculiar structure, reason and experience both forbid us to expect that national morality can prevail in exclusion of religious principle. . . .

Observe good faith and justice towards all nations; cultivate peace and harmony with all. Religion and morality enjoin this conduct; and can it be, that good policy does not equally enjoin it?

In the execution of such a plan, nothing is more essential than that permanent, inveterate antipathies against particular nations, and passionate attachments for others, should be excluded; and that, in place of them, just and amicable feelings towards all should be cultivated. The nation which indulges towards another a habitual hatred or a habitual fondness is in some degree a slave. It is a slave to its animosity or to its affection, either of which is sufficient to lead it astray from its duty and its interest. . . .

The great rule of conduct for us in regard to foreign nations is in extending our commercial relations, to have with them as little *political* connection as possible. So far as we have already formed engagements, let them be fulfilled with perfect good faith. Here let us stop.

Europe has a set of primary interests which to us have none; or a very remote relation. Hence she must be engaged in frequent controversies, the causes of which are essentially foreign to our concerns. Hence, therefore, it must be unwise in us to implicate ourselves by artificial ties in the ordinary vicissitudes of her politics, or the ordinary combinations and collisions of her friendships or enmities.

Our detached and distant situation invites and enables us to pursue a different course. . . . It is our true policy to steer clear of permanent alliances with any portion of the foreign world. . . .

In offering to you, my countrymen, these counsels of an old and affectionate friend, I . . . may even flatter myself that they may be productive of some partial benefit, some occasional good; that they may now and then recur to moderate the fury of party spirit, to warn against the mischiefs of foreign intrigue, to guard against the impostures of pretended patriotism. . . .

Relying on its kindness in this as in other things, and actuated by that fervent love towards it, which is so natural to a man who views in it the native soil of himself and his progenitors for several generations, I anticipate with pleasing expectation that retreat in which I promise myself to realize, without alloy, the sweet enjoyment of partaking, in the midst of my fellow-citizens, the benign influence of good laws under a free government, the ever-favorite object of my heart, and the happy reward, as I trust, of our mutual cares, labors, and dangers.

United States
19th September, 1796
Geo. Washington

READING AND DISCUSSION QUESTIONS

1. Which challenges does Washington think are most threatening to the new nation? What clues in the text led to your conclusions?
2. How would you characterize Washington's point of view? Was he generally optimistic or pessimistic in his assessment of America's future?
3. Washington witnessed the development of new political institutions, like political parties, which he described as dangerous. Why does he see them as incompatible with America's national identity? What in Washington's critique is still valuable today?

P3-5 | Painting America's New Identity

EDWARD SAVAGE, *Liberty. In the Form of the Goddess of Youth, Giving Support to the Bald Eagle* (1796)

Edward Savage was a largely self-taught artist, but he gained prominence beginning in the 1790s with his portraits of George Washington, including his most famous life-sized painting of Washington and his family. Like Gilbert Stuart, who also painted portraits of the Revolutionary generation, Savage's images, including the one reproduced here, offered Americans a way of picturing or imagining their newly independent identity. In this image, Savage shows Liberty, personified by Hebe, the Greek goddess of youth, with the American eagle.

Library of Congress, Prints & Photographs Division, Reproduction number LC-DIG-ppmsca-13641(digital file from original print)LC-USZ62-15369(b&w film copy neg.)

READING AND DISCUSSION QUESTIONS

1. Identify the elements Savage included in this image. What meaning do you think they had for Savage? For instance, why do you think he chose to depict Liberty stepping on chains, a key, and a scepter?
2. What does an image like this suggest about the extent to which Americans in the 1790s shared a common understanding of their identity *as Americans*?

P3-6 | Battle of New Orleans and American Nationalism

FRANCISCO SCACKI, *A Correct View of the Battle Near the City of New Orleans* (1815)

Edward Savage's 1796 painting (Document P3-5) and Francisco Scacki's depiction of the stunning American defeat of the British at the Battle of New Orleans, the final battle of the War of 1812, were completed almost two decades apart. However, their works both participated in the celebration of American nationalism. Scacki's engraving can be seen as a reaffirmation of American independence. In both images, the artists depict the American flag topped with a liberty cap, a potent, visual symbol of liberty with roots extending back to antiquity where manumitted slaves wore the cap to indicate their free status. In this 1815 engraving, Scacki foregrounds the death of British General Edward Pakenham. His troops, in tight formation on either side, face General Jackson's troops who occupy the high ground. The text reads: "A Correct View of the Battle Near the City of New Orleans, on the Eighth of January 1815, Under the Command of Gen'l Andw Jackson, Over 10,000 British troops in which 3 of their most distinguished Generals were killed, & several wounded and upwards of 3,000 of their choisest [sic] soldiers were killed, wounded, and made Prisoners. &." The text surrounds a portrait identified as "The Brave Gen'l Andrew Jackson."

A Correct View of the Battle Near the City of New Orleans, 1815–1816 (engraving on wove paper)/Scacki, Francisco (fl.1815)/MUSEUM OF FINE ARTS, HOUSTON/Museum of Fine Arts, Houston, Texas, USA/Bridgeman Images

READING AND DISCUSSION QUESTIONS

1. What visual and textual clues point to the artist's perspective on the Battle of New Orleans? Why do you think Scacki chose to focus on the death of British General Edward Pakenham?
2. The War of 1812 was politically unpopular among some Americans, as can be seen in events such as the Hartford Convention (Document 7-6). To what extent do you think images such as this one promoted national unity? What does this image celebrate?

▪ COMPARATIVE QUESTIONS ▪

1. How did Federalists such as Washington and Alexander Hamilton (Document 7-1) conceive of America's national identity in ways different from Republicans such as Thomas Jefferson (Document 7-2)?
2. Do these sources present an optimistic or a pessimistic view of early American national identity? What factors account for the different attitudes toward America's new prospects?
3. What legacy of the Revolution's democratic values appears in the language and ideas of the sources included here?
4. Compare Richard Allen's eulogy (Document P3-1) with Peale's portrait of Washington at Yorktown (Document 6-4). What do these sources suggest about the role Washington's name and image may have played in shaping a national identity?
5. Compare Judith Sargent Murray's argument (Document P3-3) to those of Abigail Adams (Document 6-2) and Christian Barnes (Document 5-4). What do these sources suggest about the role of women and the question of gender roles in the formation of the new American identity?
6. Compare the two images in this chapter (Documents P3-5 and P3-6). To what extent were both artists attempting to achieve the same effect? What do these images suggest about emerging ideals of American nationalism in the early republic?

8

Economic Transformations

1800–1848

The British writer Harriet Martineau visited Chicago amid a "rage for speculation," during which frenzied investors bought title to unimproved land along a proposed canal route. "Storekeepers hailed them from their doors," she said, "with offers of farms, and all manner of land-lots, advising them to speculate before the price of land rose higher." More sober than most Chicagoans, Martineau predicted "a bursting of the bubble" and feared the worst: "Many a high-spirited, but inexperienced, young man; many a simple settler, will be ruined for the advantage of knaves." She wasn't wrong. The 1837 depression hit just as her book was published.

The land speculation that Martineau described as a "delusion" was one effect of the Market Revolution, an accelerating economic expansion in the years following the War of 1812. The frenzy she witnessed hit northerners pushing west and southerners seeking more fertile fields to expand cotton production. Fueled by improvements in manufacturing and in transportation, such as canals and roads, this economic expansion quickened the growth of towns and cities and encouraged consumption by making goods cheap and easily obtained. Such growth provided benefits, but also costs. The manufacturing revolution changed the work people did and resulted in growing class tensions. The boom in cotton fattened the pockets of some, but it also exploded America's racial divide, and encouraged financial innovations that enabled slavery's expansion. This chapter's sources explore the causes and consequences of the Market Revolution, a transformation that defined the social and political history of the early nineteenth century.

8-1 | Building the Economy

J. HILL, *Junction of Erie and Northern Canal* (c. 1830–1832)

Alexander Hamilton's commercial vision for the new republic flourished in the years after the War of 1812, aided by private and public investments in canals, roads, and bridges. In this scene from the early 1830s, a developing market economy is clearly under way. Canal traffic brought the Market Revolution to inland regions, encouraging trade and consumption on a scale previously unknown. The new "artificial rivers" literally changed the landscape, transforming Jefferson's agrarian world into the mill and factory economy Hamilton hoped for.

Junction of Erie and Northern Canal, engraved by J. Hill, c. 1830–32 (color litho)/American School (19th century)/NEW YORK HISTORICAL SOCIETY/Collection of the New-York Historical Society, USA/Bridgeman Images

READING AND DISCUSSION QUESTIONS

1. What point of view about the market economy does this lithograph express? Was the artist celebrating or lamenting the changes brought by the canal economy?
2. How would you use the evidence from this illustration to discuss specific changes to daily life those living along the canals might have experienced?

8-2 | In Praise of Domestic Manufacturing

THE WEEKLY REGISTER, *Home Influence* (1813)

The War of 1812 had economic origins and consequences. Here, in an article from the January 23, 1813 *Weekly Register*, published in the commercial city of Baltimore, Maryland, the author describes one effect of the war with Britain: an encouragement of domestic manufacturing. With trade curtailed because of the war, Americans were forced to wean themselves off foreign goods and rely on American manufactures. This necessity transformed into a virtue, as it became another element of republican self-reliance, industry, and pride.

The belief of years has resolved into moral certainty. It was an old opinion that the United States could never become a *really* independent, distinct and Separate nation, while so many of our necessaries, conveniences and luxuries were received from abroad. Our ablest politicians, knowing the *influence* generated by these considerations, always predicted what the declaration of war against *England* has realized; for now it is evident matter of fact, that our people on the sea board must be weaned from their late great commercial intercourse with that country, before they can possess one genuine and generous *American* feeling. To the shreds of the *old predilection* in favor of *Great Britain,* handed down from father to son, and imbibed through a multitude of mediums, such as books, business and all the circumstances of social life, is superadded the more powerful dispositions of *pecuniary interest.* In the scale of affections, the love of self preponderates; and the many thousands who grow rich by dealing in *foreign* goods must needs be under *foreign* influence. "*Where the treasure is the heart will lie also*" and it is too much the case with the *trading* world that money is the god they worship. It is not to be expected that these narrow personal feelings can be eradicated; but time and perseverance may divert them to better objects *at home.*

It is cause of rejoicing that many, very many millions of dollars have latterly been invested in *domestic manufacturing establishments,* and to observe the current of wealth still urging the erection of new and magnificent works. This mighty and increasing capital begets a new feeling; for the "treasure" is *at home.* The influence of money is wonderful; and the mind changes as the means of acquiring it are presented. Hence a powerful *home influence* is spreading itself through society, and the people are becoming more abstracted from *foreign* considerations. In the city of *Baltimore* are now sold various kinds of goods to the value of at least half million of dollars *per annum,* all of which species, five years ago, were received from *abroad*: and the pith and marrow of the matter is this, that the supply is immensely increasing, because all who deal in them find their *profit* in doing so—

"Men follow money
As bees follow honey"

The Weekly Register: Documents, Essays, and Facts, vol. 3, ed. H. Niles (Baltimore: The Franklin Press, 1813), 328–329.

And many very valuable establishments for the chief sale of *domestic goods* have sprung up in different parts of the city; while every day brings to market some *new commodity*.

It is true that the manufactures of the United States are not yet adequate to the consumption of the country; but hundreds of thousands are clothed entirely with *home-made* apparel; while many of our most important branches of mechanical industry are completely supplied with all their tools and apparatus from other work-shops among us. Our bountiful country pours forth its resources; and genius applies its productions to the wants and conveniences of life. Our progress in improvement has no parallel; nor is the increase of our population more surprising than the proceeds of our manufactures, rising in all their varied form in every direction, and pursued *with an eye to profit* in almost every farm house in the *United States*. The *merino breed* of sheep is spreading with astonishing rapidity—they are already numerous, and much attention is paid to improving the common species. The manufacture of all the coarser kinds of *cotton goods*, with some of the most delicate fabrics, may be considered as *fully established*. The western states will supply us with an abundance of *hemp* and *hempen manufactures*. The chief part of the *heavy metallic articles* are now made amongst us, while many of the lighter kinds are extensively and profitably furnished. The *woolen manufacture* keeps pace with the rest, and great investitures are made in its various departments. Ancient prejudices have yielded to the impulses of patriotism or the dictates of prudence, and it has become *fashionable* to use *home manufactures*. This is a most important point gained, for we are creatures of prejudice; and, "like blind horses in a mill," pursue the beaten track without a why or wherefore. Six years ago our whole export of *flour, beef, pork* and *provisions*, generally, did no more than pay for the *foreign* liquors we consumed: the case is materially altered—the long despised *whiskey*, rectified, and improved, has driven from the side-board *English* rum and *French* brandy, or suffers them to remain as mere monuments of former favor. Our most dashing bucks are proud to boast a *homespun coat*; and the prudent house-wife delighted exhibits her newly made table linen, sheeting, carpets, etc. This is that pride that destroys a *foreign* influence—it is an honest pride, and should be encouraged, and so indeed it is—for no man is ashamed for his apparel, though it be coarse, if it is clean and decent, and HOME-SPUN.

Seeing the importance of *domestic manufactures* in lessening our connection with the old world, corrupted and corrupting, the patriot heart leaps with joy at the speedy prospect of "reversing the tables" upon it, in making it the *necessity* of *foreign* nations to *depend* on us for those raw materials and articles of food which it was *our* object to exchange for *their* productions—*but which they must have*, not possessing within themselves the means to furnish them.—*Then* will our country stand on high ground; and wealth flow gradually in from all quarters, without subjecting us to *foreign* partialities or the *gamblings* of commerce. The trade of the country will increase; but the anxiety of the merchant will be not to receive from *Europe* the chief articles of his adventure, but to obtain of his neighbors, responsible men vouching for their good qualities and on whose faith he can recommend them abroad, all that he wants.—This time is not far distant—the *political mellenium* in America is fast approaching, and will come; though like the croaking raven, a FOREIGN INFLUENCE predicts all calamity. The righteous war for our *seamen* and our *rights*, grossly violated, is one of the grand means by which a good Providence will bring about a blessed union of the people, in directing them to look AT HOME for all they desire. Let the real *American* be of good cheer—we shall triumph by land as well as by sea; but more than all in establishing a HOME INFLUENCE that will guard and defend happy *Columbia* amidst the "throes and convulsions of the old world," when "infuriated man, th[r]ough blood and slaughter, shall seek his liberty," with horrors unprecedented.

This state of things is clearly manifested to the view of *England*. With unspeakable hatred and bitterness of spirit, like *Babylon* of old, she sees the time "when no man [in America] shall buy her merchandize any more"—and herein is the *true cause* of that rancour of party which is excited in the United States by her turbulent advocates. We should bear with that patiently, well assured that *her influence* here is at its last gasp. It will not expire without great screamings and noise; but they shall not divert us from our course. *Home manufactures*, with steady perseverance, will destroy the hydra; and when, hereafter, we shall calmly view his deformity, great will be our wonder that we bore with it so long.

READING AND DISCUSSION QUESTIONS

1. What evidence of an emerging market economy does this source provide for the early national period?
2. Besides providing goods for Americans to consume, what other benefit does the author claim will come from a strong and vibrant domestic manufacturing economy?

8-3 | A Factory Girl Remembers Mill Work

LUCY LARCOM, *Among Lowell Mill-Girls: A Reminiscence* (1889)

One effect of the enthusiasm for domestic production praised by the *Weekly Register* (Document 8-2) was the transfer of work from the home to the factory. In Lowell, Massachusetts, young Lucy Larcom (1824–1893) experienced this shift at age eleven, when family circumstances pushed her to paid employment in the textile mill. Like many of her contemporaries, Larcom was forced to sacrifice her childhood to provide much-needed income to her family. Larcom was unusual in that she developed a literary talent, publishing poetry and songs and a memoir of her childhood, an excerpt from which appears here.

Lucy Larcom, *A New England Girlhood* (Boston: Houghton Mifflin, 1889), 145–146, 152–156.

During my father's life, a few years before my birth, his thoughts had been turned towards the new manufacturing town growing up on the banks of the Merrimack. He had once taken a journey there, with the possibility in his mind of making the place his home, his limited income furnishing no adequate promise of a maintenance for his large family of daughters. From the beginning, Lowell had a high reputation for good order, morality, piety, and all that was dear to the old-fashioned New Englander's heart.

After his death, my mother's thoughts naturally followed the direction his had taken; and seeing no other opening for herself, she sold her small estate, and moved to Lowell, with the intention of taking a corporation-house for mill-girl boarders. Some of the family objected, for the Old World traditions about factory life were anything but attractive; and they were current in New England until the experiment at Lowell had shown that independent and intelligent workers invariably give their own character to their occupation. My mother had visited Lowell, and she was willing and glad, knowing all about the place, to make it our home. . . .

Our house was quickly filled with a large feminine family. As a child, the gulf between little girlhood and young womanhood had always looked to me very wide. I supposed we should get across it by some sudden jump, by and by. But among these new companions of all ages, from fifteen to thirty years, we slipped into womanhood without knowing when or how.

Most of my mother's boarders were from New Hampshire and Vermont, and there was a fresh, breezy sociability about them which made them seem almost like a different race of beings from any we children had hitherto known.

We helped a little about the housework, before and after school, making beds, trimming lamps, and washing dishes. The heaviest work was done by a strong Irish girl, my mother always attending to the cooking herself. She was, however, a better caterer than the circumstances required or permitted. She liked to make nice things for the table, and, having been accustomed to an abundant supply, could never learn to economize. At a dollar and a quarter a week for board (the price allowed for mill-girls by the corporations), great care in expenditure was necessary. It was not in my mother's nature closely to calculate costs, and in this way there came to be a continually increasing leak in the family purse. The older members of the family did everything they could, but it was not enough. I heard it said one day, in a distressed tone, "The children will have to leave school and go into the mill."

There were many pros and cons between my mother and sisters before this was positively decided. The mill-agent did not want to take us two little girls, but consented on condition we should be sure to attend school the full number of months prescribed each year. I, the younger one, was then between eleven and twelve years old.

I listened to all that was said about it, very much fearing that I should not be permitted to do the coveted work. For the feeling had already frequently come to me, that I was the one too many in the overcrowded family nest. Once, before we left our old home, I had heard a neighbor condoling with my mother because there were so many of us, and her emphatic reply had been a great relief to my mind: —

"There isn't one more than I want. I could not spare a single one of my children."

But her difficulties were increasing, and I thought it would be a pleasure to feel that I was not a trouble or burden or expense to anybody. So I went to my first day's work in the mill with a light heart. The novelty of it made it seem easy, and it really was not hard, just to change the bobbins on the spinning-frames every three quarters of an hour or so, with half a dozen other little girls who were doing the same thing. When I came back at night, the family began to pity me for my long, tiresome day's work, but I laughed and said, —

"Why, it is nothing but fun. It is just like play."

And for a little while it was only a new amusement; I liked it better than going to school and "making believe" I was learning when I was not. And there was a great deal of play mixed with it. We were not occupied more than half the time. The intervals were spent frolicking around among the spinning-frames, teasing and talking to the older girls, or entertaining ourselves with games and stories in a corner, or exploring, with the overseer's permission, the mysteries of the carding-room, the dressing-room, and the weaving-room.

I never cared much for machinery. The buzzing and hissing and whizzing of pulleys and rollers and spindles and flyers around me often grew tiresome. I could not see into their complications, or feel interested in them. But in a room below us we were sometimes allowed to peer in through a sort of blind door at the great waterwheel that carried the works of the whole mill. It was so huge that we could only watch a few of its spokes at a time, and part of its dripping rim, moving with a slow, measured strength through the darkness that shut it in. It impressed me with something of the awe which comes to us in thinking of the great Power which keeps the mechanism of the universe in motion. . . .

There were compensations for being shut in to daily toil so early. The mill itself had its lessons for us. But it was not, and could not be, the right sort of life for a child, and we were happy in the knowledge that, at the longest, our employment was only to be temporary.

When I took my next three months at the grammar school, everything there was changed, and I too was changed. The teachers were kind, and thorough in their instruction; and my mind seemed to have been ploughed up during that year of work, so that knowledge took root in it easily. It was a great delight to me to study, and at the end of the three months the master told me that I was prepared for the high school.

But alas! I could not go. The little money I could earn—one dollar a week, besides the price of my board—was needed in the family, and I must return to the mill. It was a severe disappointment to me, though I did not say so at home.

READING AND DISCUSSION QUESTIONS

1. How does Larcom's memoir help us to understand some of the effects of the Market Revolution on the lives of ordinary Americans?
2. What does Larcom see as the advantages and disadvantages of work in the factory?
3. How might Larcom's initial impression of the mill have been different if she had started as a machine worker?

8-4 | Reporting on the South's Peculiar Institution

ETHAN ANDREWS, *Slavery and the Domestic Slave-Trade* (1836)

While the Constitution ended the importation of enslaved people beginning in 1808, a thriving internal (or domestic) trade in slaves continued. Treated as property, enslaved African Americans became a tradable commodity and source of wealth for southern planters. As movable property, enslaved people were useful to planters who left exhausted farms in search of more fertile fields in the Gulf Coast states. The slave trade and accompanying cotton boom was another feature of the era's economic transformation. As a professor of ancient languages at the University of North Carolina, Ethan Andrews (1787–1858) observed firsthand the effects of slavery and the slave trade. At the behest of the American Union for the Relief and Improvement of the Colored Race, he published in 1836 a series of letters recounting his observations.

Fredericksburg, July 26, 1835.

A gentleman in this city has a female slave whom he purchased from a trader, for the purpose of preventing her separation from her husband. Her former mistress had taken some offence at her, and had sold her to the trader, with the intention of having her carried out of the state. The husband and wife were both greatly distressed, and from compassion to them this gentleman purchased her. After this trouble was over, a year or two passed quietly away, when suddenly the husband, who had belonged to the minor heirs of an estate, was seized, just as a drove of negroes were setting off for the south, and immediately hand-cuffed to prevent his escape. He had been sold some little time previously, but had not been informed of his fate, until the hour of departure arrived. The gentleman who had purchased the wife, learning the circumstances, attempted again to prevent the separation of the husband and wife, by offering to sell the latter to the trader, provided he would guarantee that they should not be separated, when sold at the south. The trader was willing to purchase her, but said he could give no such guaranty, as he always sold his slaves to those who would pay the highest price, and he supposed it possible, that for this purpose he should

E. A. Andrews, *Slavery and the Domestic Slave-Trade in the United States. In a Series of Letters Addressed to the Executive Committee of the American Union for the Relief and Improvement of the Colored Race* (Boston: Light & Stearns, 1836), 167–174, 193–196.

have to separate them. Under these circumstances, the husband, who was much attached to his wife, begged her not to leave her present situation, and thus they were finally separated.

A friend, to whom and to whose family I am indebted for many attentions, considers the final extinction of slavery as decisively indicated by the treatment which slaves now receive in the south, and particularly in Virginia, when compared with that which was common twenty or thirty years since. Even the advertisements for runaway slaves would serve to indicate a change in public sentiment, and in fact, as the same gentleman observes, are collectively a good index of the state of feeling, not only at the same place at different periods, but in different places at the same time. A Virginia advertisement usually contains a clause, stating, or implying, that the slave has run away, notwithstanding he has always been treated with the greatest indulgence; while advertisements from the extreme south are solely occupied, like those for stray oxen and horses, in describing their natural and artificial marks, their ages and habits.

He thinks, also, that in this state, slaves would have no value whatever as field-hands, were it not for the southern market. The labor performed by them is not sufficient to meet the current expenses of the plantations, at least of the more ordinary ones, and the only profit of the planter is derived from the negroes whom he raises for market.

It remains still to be determined whether, if wages were paid to the slaves in place of their present regular supplies, and in proportion to the amount of services rendered, a different result would not be obtained. That this experiment will soon be made, I have great confidence, and am inclined to believe that, if judiciously made, it will succeed.

Richmond, July 28, 1835.

In my journey yesterday from Fredericksburg to this place, I travelled with a planter, who had emigrated from North Carolina to Louisiana, where he has resided for several years, but is now about to remove from his plantation to a more healthy one in a different part of the same state. His present journey was undertaken partly for the purpose of increasing the number of his slaves; and he had just completed the purchase of one hundred and fifty-five, the entire stock of a plantation near Fredericksburg. For these he had given seventy-five thousand dollars, or about five hundred dollars, on an average, for each. They included mechanics of every kind necessary upon a great plantation. The purchaser was still young, and exhibited, in a striking degree, that promptitude and decision of character, so often observable in those accustomed early to direct their own conduct and that of others. Visions, perhaps I ought rather to say sober calculations, of boundless wealth, to be acquired by the labor of his slaves, were alluring him forward, and though naturally humane in his feelings, his kindness to the slaves will probably go no farther than to provide for their animal wants, regardless of their high destinies as moral and intelligent beings. He was not wholly without apprehension that his hopes of soon acquiring a vast fortune might be frustrated by a fall in the price of his staple production, cotton. He remarked that he should soon pay for his slaves, if the present price of cotton continued; and that he should ultimately succeed, if it did not fall below twelve and a half, or even ten cents, but that he could not afford to go below that price.

He represents the cares of the master upon an extensive plantation as very great. These are much increased in case of sickness among the slaves, as they cannot in general be depended upon to nurse one another, and the whole care of them while sick often devolves upon the master. He says "their weekly rations in Louisiana consist of eight or ten quarts of corn meal and four pounds of northern pork; for the latter of which, in the winter, bacon is commonly given to them, and molasses also is frequently substituted for the whole or a part of the pork, at the rate of a pint of the former for a pound of the latter. Some make use of salt fish instead of pork; but this is generally thought objectionable, on account of its tendency to create violent thirst. The negroes commonly choose to receive their corn-meal, rather than its equivalent in bread, that they may cook it for themselves. Rations of spirits are never given to them, except upon peculiar and rare occasions, as at *corn shucking*, and the like. It is therefore extremely rare that a negro is seen intoxicated, and still more so that he acquires a habit of intemperance."

To the inquiry, how do the slaves in Louisiana usually spend the Sabbath? he replied: "generally in complete idleness; lolling in the shade, or basking in the sun. Some of them are disposed to go to preaching, when there is an opportunity; but the greater part consider it a hardship to be compelled to attend meeting. They are universally attached to the Baptist, rather than to any other church, and seem to consider 'going into the water,' as a most essential part of religion. 'This,' he observes, 'may perhaps be attributed in part to its involving an act of self-denial, as they are doggedly averse to bathing or washing, for the purposes of cleanliness.' This indisposition to practise ablutions for the promotion of health and cleanliness, is nearly universal, and they can scarcely be more offended by anything, than by a compulsory system of bathing or of washing their clothes. If not compelled to do it, they would never wash a garment from the time when it is put on new, until it is worn out. Even house servants must be watched like children, or most of them would neglect attention to cleanliness.

"Whatever indulgences, in regard to dress or other things, custom has established, as the right of the slave, he is very particular to require; and if anything is withheld, he remembers it as his due, and asks for it, when he has an opportunity.

"The slave-traders have exacted such a profit upon their slaves, that the planters, when intending to make a considerable purchase, either come to the north for the purpose, or employ a factor to whom they allow a stipulated commission on the purchase money. By such means only, can they prevent the combinations among the traders, to keep up the prices, as the infamy of the traffic operates to prevent great competition."

A gentleman from Halifax N.C. represents the slaves as rapidly diminishing in that part of the state, by their removal to Alabama, and other southern states. In most cases, the masters emigrate with their slaves. . . .

Baltimore, July 30, 1835.

To a stranger, one of the most revolting features in American slavery is, the domestic slave-trade; and hence the inquiry is so frequently made, whether this evil at least may not be abolished. Various plans have been proposed for the purpose, but none which appear feasible; and it may well be doubted, whether this feature can ever be obliterated while the general system remains. All which it appears possible to do, is to regulate the sales in such a manner, that husbands and wives, parents and young children, shall never be separated. This, no one can deny, ought to be done; and if the system cannot exist with this innovation, it ought not to be tolerated for a single hour. The domestic relations are at the foundation of all the virtue, and consequently of all the happiness of society, and everything inconsistent with the perpetuity of these relations ought at once, everywhere, and forever, to cease. But whether even this is practicable, is a question which I confess my inability to answer. I cannot see how these separations are to be prevented, while the husband is the property of one master, and the wife and children of another, each master being wholly independent, and his slaves being considered as in the most absolute sense his property. The mode of accomplishing this change belongs to southern moralists to determine; but it is not a subject which they are at liberty to neglect, and least of all, can the christian, who acts in view of his Master's command not to separate those whom God has joined in the marriage relation, consent that such separations should be legalized by the laws of a state of which he is an active and responsible member.

When these relations are not violated, the character of the domestic slave-trade, considered as a part of the general system of slavery, depends upon the circumstances under which the transfer is made. If the condition of the slave is improved in everything essential, and especially if, with a full understanding of the nature of the transaction, he really desires the transfer, no additional wrong appears to be done by the new relation in which the parties are placed. This case, so far from being uncommon, is one which frequently occurs.

A literary friend who is a native of North Carolina, remarked to me to-day, that he could tolerate every thing else about slavery better than the shocking separations, which he saw continually caused by the removal of slaves to the south and west. When I told him that the evil seemed inseparable from slavery in such a country as this, he reluctantly assented to the position, after a moment's hesitation, in a manner that seemed to me little short of ludicrous. My meaning had been, that a system, to which such evils were necessary incidents, was intolerable; his conclusion evidently was, that if it cannot be made better, it must be submitted to with all its inconveniences.

READING AND DISCUSSION QUESTIONS

1. What evidence does Andrews's report provide for understanding both the domestic trade in slaves and the geographical movement of southern planters?
2. How does knowing that an advocacy group organized for the "relief and improvement of the colored race" commissioned Andrews's work impact how a historian might interpret the evidence it contains?

8-5 | Insuring Their Investment in Slaves

NAUTILUS MUTUAL LIFE INSURANCE COMPANY, *Policy on Robert Moody* (1847)

The previous source (Document 8-4) highlighted the tragic costs of the domestic slave trade for those enslaved people whose lives were often subject to twists of fate beyond their control. When a master died or went bankrupt, enslaved people were frequently sold off, forced to leave their families and the places they knew. In the cotton south, enslaved people were property and viewed as commodities that could be turned to cash quickly. Enslaved people were often used as collateral for loans that funded moves west or the expansion of a planter's landholdings. In a word, enslaved people were valuable, and masters wanted to protect their investments. In the 1840s, a few insurance companies expanded their businesses to include issuing policies that covered the loss of slaves. Newspapers began carrying advertisements for slave insurance underwritten by companies such as the Nautilus Mutual Life Insurance Company (now New York Life). The text of one such policy insuring the life of Robert, an enslaved man owned by Sarah E. Moody, appears below.

(No. 925) The Nautilus (Mutual Life) Insurance Company of New-York.

This Policy of Insurance Witnesseth, That The Nautilus (Mutual Life) Insurance Company of New-York, in consideration of the sum of Five dollars and eighty one cents to them in hand paid by James H. Moody, of Chesterfield Co. Virginia.

Do Assure the Life of Robert Moody of ____________ in the County of Chesterfield State of Virginia in the amount of Four Hundred & twelve dollars, for the term of One year from the 10th day of February 1847—with permission to be employed in the Clover Hill Pits.

And the said Company do hereby Promise and Agree, to and with the said assured, his executors, administrators, and assigns, well and truly to pay, or cause to be paid, the said sum insured, to the said assured his executors, administrators, or assigns, within sixty days after due notice, and proof of the death of the said slave Robert Moody.

Provided always, and it is hereby declared to be the true intent and meaning of this Policy, and the same is accepted by the assured upon these express conditions, that in case the said Robert Moody shall die upon the seas, or shall, without

---

Nautilus Mutual Life Insurance Company, Policy on Robert Moody (1847) text transcribed from image. Schomburg Center for Research in Black Culture, Manuscripts, Archives and Rare Books Division.

the consent of this Company previously obtained, and endorsed upon this Policy, pass beyond the settled limits of the United States, (excepting into the settled limits of the British Provinces of the two Canadas, Nova Scotia, or New Brunswick,) or shall, without such previous consent thus endorsed, visit those parts of the United States, which lie south of the southern boundaries of the States of Virginia and Kentucky, between the first of July and the first of November, or shall, without such previous consent thus endorsed, enter into any military or naval service whatsoever, (the militia not in actual service excepted;) or in case he shall die by his own hand, in, or in consequence of a duel, or by the hands of justice, or in the known violation of any law of these States, or of the United States, or of the said Provinces, this Policy shall be void, null, and of no effect.

And it is also Understood and Agreed, to be the true intent and meaning hereof, that if the declaration made by the said James H. Moody—guardian for Sarah E. Moody—and bearing date the Tenth day of February 1847 and upon the faith of which this agreement is made, shall be found in any respect untrue, then, in such case, this Policy shall be null and void.

N.B. If assigned, notice to be given to this Company.

In Witness Whereof, the said Nautilus (Mutual Life) Insurance Company of New-York, have, by their President and Secretary, or Actuary, signed and delivered this Contract, this Sixteenth day of February one thousand eight hundred and forty seven.

READING AND DISCUSSION QUESTIONS

1. What does this source suggest about the extent to which slavery was part of the national economy? Is it significant that the life insurance policy was issued by a New York-based company?
2. How might a historian use this insurance policy to write a history of slavery during the 1840s? What does a source such as this say about the institutionalization of slavery in this period?

8-6 | Workers Organize to Defend Their Rights

ELY MOORE, *Address Delivered Before the General Trades' Union of the City of New-York* (1833)

Ely Moore, trained as a printer, became president of the General Trades' Union when it organized in 1833 to unite New York City's skilled craftsmen from various trades into one "brotherhood" of workers. Alarmed by the factory system, these skilled workers resisted the efforts of employers to drive down wages by mechanizing production and using semiskilled or unskilled workers in their place. The labor movement scored successes through collective action, including strikes. In this address to fellow members of the Union, Moore describes what's at stake for workers in a changing economic landscape.

Ely Moore, Address Delivered Before the General Trades' Union of the City of New-York (1833).

In order to mitigate the evils that ever flow from inordinate desire and unrestricted selfishness; to restrain and chastise unlawful ambition; to protect the weak against the strong, and to establish an equilibrium of power among nations and individuals, conventional compacts were formed. These confederative associations have never been fully able to stay the march of intolerance, of mercenary ambition, or of political despotism. Even in this fair land of freedom, where liberty and equality are guaranteed to all, and where our written constitutions have so wisely provided limitations to power, and securities for rights, the *twin fiends, intolerance* and *aristocracy,* presume to rear their hateful crests! But we have no cause to marvel at this. Wherever man exists, under whatever form of government, or whatever be the structure or organization of society, this principle of his nature, selfishness, will appear, operating either for evil or for good. To curb it sufficiently by legislative enactments is impossible. Much *can* be done, however, towards restraining it within proper limits, by unity of purpose, and concert of action, on the part of the *producing classes.* To contribute toward the achievement of this great end, is one of the objects of the "General Trades' Union." Wealth, we all know, constitutes the aristocracy of this country. Happily no distinctions are known among us save what wealth and worth confer. No legal barriers are erected to protect exclusive privileges, or unmerited rank. . . . The greatest danger, therefore, which threatens the stability of our government, and the liberty of the people, is an undue accumulation and distribution of wealth. . . . We ask, then, what better means can be devised for promoting a more equal distribution of wealth, than for the producing classes to *claim,* and by virtue of union and concert, *secure their claims* to their respective portions? And why should not those who have the toil, have the enjoyment also? Or why should the sweat that flows from the brow of the labourer, be converted into a source of revenue for the support of the crafty or indolent? . . .

[A]s the line of distinction between the employer and employed is *widened,* the condition of the latter inevitably verges toward a state of vassalage, while that of the former as certainly approximates toward supremacy; and that whatever system is calculated to make the many dependent upon, or subject to, the few, not only tends to the subversion of the natural rights of man, but is hostile to the best interests of the community, as well as to the spirit and genius of our government. Fully persuaded that the foregoing positions are incontrovertible, WE, in order to guard against the encroachments of aristocracy, to preserve our natural and political rights, to elevate our moral and intellectual condition, to promote our pecuniary interests, to narrow the line of distinction between the journeyman and employer, to establish the honour and safety of our respective vocations upon a more secure and permanent basis, and to alleviate the distresses of those suffering from want of employment, have deemed it expedient to form ourselves into a "General Trades' Union." . . .

There are, doubtless, many individuals who are resolved, right or wrong, to misrepresent our principles, impeach our measures, and impugn our motives. . . . And why, let me ask, should the character of our union be obnoxious to censure? . . . I defy the ingenuity of man to point to a single measure which it recognises, that is wrong in itself, or in its tendency. What! is it wrong for men to unite for the purpose of resisting the encroachments of aristocracy? Wrong! to restrict the principle of selfishness to its proper and legitimate bounds and objects? Wrong! to oppose monopoly and mercenary ambition? Wrong! to consult the interests, and seek the welfare, of the producing classes? Wrong! to attempt the elevation of our moral and intellectual standing? Wrong! to establish the honour and safety of our respective vocations upon a more secure and permanent basis? I ask—in the name of heaven I ask—can it be wrong for men to attempt the melioration of their condition, and the preservation of their natural and political rights?

I am aware, that the charge of "illegal combination" is raised against us. The cry is as senseless, as 'tis stale and unprofitable. Why, I would inquire, have not journeymen the same right to ask their own price for their own property, or services, that employers have? or that merchants, physicians, and lawyers have? Is that equal justice, which makes it an offence for journeymen to combine for the purpose of maintaining their present prices, or raising their wages, while employers may combine with impunity for the purpose of lowering them? . . .

It is further alleged, that the "General Trades' Union" is calculated to encourage *strikes* and *turn-outs.* Now, the truth lies in the converse. Our constitution sets forth, that "Each trade or art may represent to the Convention, through their delegates, their grievances, who shall take cognizance thereof, and decide upon the same." And further, that "No trade or art shall strike for higher wages than they at present receive, without the sanction of the Convention." True, if the Convention shall, after due deliberation, decide that the members of any trade or art there represented are aggrieved, and that their demands are warrantable, then the Convention is pledged to sustain the members of such trade or art to the uttermost. Hence, employers will discover, that it is idle, altogether idle, to prolong a contest with journeymen, when they are backed by the Convention. And journeymen will perceive, that in order to obtain assistance from the Convention, in the event of a *strike,* or *turn-out,* that their claims must be founded in justice, and all their measures be so taken as not to invade the rights, or sacrifice the welfare, of employers. So far, then, from the Union encouraging strikes or turn-outs, it is destined, we conceive, to allay the jealousies, and abate the asperities, which now unhappily exist between employers and the employed.

READING AND DISCUSSION QUESTIONS

1. How does Moore describe the challenges facing skilled workers in this period of manufacturing innovation?
2. From Moore's address to workers, what can you discover about the manufacturing revolution's impact on class relations during the early nineteenth century?

COMPARATIVE QUESTIONS

1. How would you characterize the consequences of the rapid economic transformations that occurred in the United States during the first half of the nineteenth century? Were there clear beneficiaries of the economic development in this period? If so, who were they?
2. Did the economic changes that occurred during this period encourage a more or less optimistic view of American society? Consider the tone of the authors /creators of the documents in this chapter.
3. To what extent did the economic transformations of the early nineteenth century tell a regional or national story?
4. Compare the perspectives of Lucy Larcom (Document 8-3) and Ely Moore (Document 8-6) as each experienced the effects of the manufacturing revolution. What factors explain similarities and differences in the work experiences they describe?

9

A Democratic Revolution

1800–1848

Andrew Jackson's 1829 inauguration inspired a wide variety of responses. At the White House reception that followed Jackson's swearing-in, many of his political opponents recoiled at the mob scene that developed. Those who witnessed Jackson's supporters mud-stomping silk upholstered chairs and toppling china dishes predicted the Republic's collapse at the hand of mob rule. "The Majesty of the People had disappeared," said one weary observer. Jacksonians, on the other hand, heralded the inauguration as the fulfillment of the Revolutionary promise of equality and freedom. Jackson's election, they argued, was a triumph of democracy.

The contradictory reactions that Jackson's election evoked highlight the lines of political battle that would define the era. The Democrats and the Whigs, the two predominant political parties of the period, sparred over fundamental questions about the role of government, the distribution of federal and state power, and economic development. Both sides came to accept the implications of the Democratic Revolution: that the parties must court the people. The documents in this chapter highlight the political drama that divided the major parties. They also reveal the extent to which Americans embraced the language of equal rights to fuel democracy's expansion.

9-1 | Log Cabin Campaigning
Hard Cider and Log Cabin Almanac (1841)

Andrew Jackson's successful campaigns for president in 1828 and 1832 changed American politics. He positioned himself as the voice of the people and a defender of simple democratic virtues. Once Jackson's opponents organized themselves into the Whig Party, they too claimed to speak for the people and crafted campaign messages accordingly, as in one famous cartoon portraying Jackson as King Andrew I, a power-hungry royal tyrant. In the political cartoon included here, the artist shifts focus by using log cabin imagery, popular during the 1840 presidential campaign. Whig William Henry Harrison ran against incumbent president Martin Van Buren and Whigs capitalized on the era's democratic rhetoric. Here, for example, the artist utilized the log cabin image to portray Harrison as a man of the people; in fact, Harrison was the wealthy son of a signer of the Declaration of Independence and he lived in a mansion, not a log cabin. Harrison defeated Van Buren, but he died one month after taking office.

Bettmann/Getty Images

READING AND DISCUSSION QUESTIONS

1. What does this cover image for an 1841 almanac suggest about the message Whigs hoped to convey about Harrison and the party in general? Why are the images of the log cabin and hard cider important components of the Whig message?
2. What role do the two figures on the right of the image play? Kneeling is Van Buren who says: "I shall Endeavor to stop the supply." Standing behind him is former president Jackson who says: "Do so Matty for by the Etarnal its cursed sour."

9-2 | Insurgent Democrats Flex Political Power

FITZWILLIAM BYRDSALL, *The History of the Loco-Foco or Equal Rights Party* (1842)

The curiously named Loco-Foco faction within the Democratic Party is an example of the extent to which the Revolutionary-era ideals of liberty affected popular politics in this period. Increasingly, party leaders discovered how difficult it was to control rank-and-file members. In the scene described here, the Loco-Foco (or the Equal Rights Party), a working men's splinter group of Democrats led by Joel Curtis, crashes a party meeting managed by Tammany Hall, the name of the traditional party leadership. Disgruntled, the party bosses leave the hall and turn off the gaslights. The insurgents light "loco-focos," a kind of match, to keep the meeting going. The passage ends with a list of resolutions adopted at the meeting. These resolutions illustrate the radicalism of this group. Their opposition to the Second Bank, however, was a standard part of the Jacksonian political program.

Everything being arranged, the sovereign people are again called upon to approve or disapprove the acts of their nominating (appointing) committee. At the hour named, the doors of the great room are opened from the inside, to the congregated hundreds on the outside;—when lo! the actors by some secret passage are already on the stage and perfect in their parts. Order being partially obtained, the tickets are read, the vote is taken and declared in the affirmative; the farce is over, the meeting is adjourned, and the "regular ticket" is announced next day to those who always submit to the majority, and never vote any other.

The clock has just struck seven, and the doors of Tammany Hall are opening for the democracy. What a mass of human beings rush forward into the room! Yet they are late, for George D. Strong,[1] who came up the back stairs, has already

F. Byrdsall, The History of the Loco-Foco or Equal Rights Party, Its Movements, Conventions and Proceedings, with Short Characteristic Sketches of Its Prominent Men (New York: Clement & Packard, 1842), 24–27.

[1] **George D. Strong**: President of Commercial Bank.

nominated Isaac L. Varian,[2] who also ascended by the same way, for the chair, and the latter is hastening towards it before the question is heard by a fifth part of the crowd. Joel Curtis is nominated as the room is filling up, and the loud "aye" of the Equal Rights Democracy calls him to the chair. The honest working-man approaches it, and now begins the contest between monopoly and its opponents. There is a struggle of gladiators on the platform around the chair;—the loudest vociferations are heard, and Tammany trembles with intestine war. The contest at length becomes more furious; men are struggling with each other as if for empire, while the multitude in the body of the room are like the waves of a tempestuous sea. But who is he, that man of slender form and youthful appearance, the foremost in the struggle? Equal Rights men, your chief should be a man of stalwart frame; but there is hope, for your cause is good, and the indomitable spirit of equality is in that slender man. "Cheers for Ming!"—What! is that the office-holder? He who is always up with every rising of the people? *He* openly dares the majesty of monopoly, even in its temple;—*he* disregards the tenure of his office, for the elevating principle of Equality of Rights—the honest war-cry of "opposition to all monopolies" have aroused the democratic enthusiasm of his heart, and he counts not the cost. It is so!—he is unconsciously, for the occasion, and the time being, the natural hero of humanity, striving with all his energy of character to place Joel Curtis in the chair, as the representative of the masses. Unquestionably it is a contest for empire between man and monopoly.

Behold! a broad banner is spread before the eyes of the vast assemblage, and all can read its inscription: "*Joel Curtis, the Anti-Monopolist chairman.*"

The efforts of Isaac L. Varian and the monopoly democracy are futile to obtain order, or to read their ticket of nominations so as to be heard, or any decision had thereon. They are struck with amazement at the sight of another banner with the inscription "*Anti-Monopolist Democrats are opposed to Gideon Lee,*[3] *Ringgold, West, and Conner*";[4] and another with "*We go all gold but Ringgold.*" What a desecration of the usages! . . .

But behold—there is the broadest banner of all, and it is greeted with cheers. It is the whole of the anti-monopoly ticket for Congress and the Legislature, so that all can see and read where none can distinctly hear. The shouts of the Equal Rights' Democracy are still more deafening. But heartfelt cheers are given to that banner which declares for Leggett: "*The Times must change ere we desert our Post.*"

The struggle is drawing towards a close. Isaac L. Varian believes the evidence presented to his senses, and in attempting to leave the chair, to which he is forcibly held down by George D. Strong and a member of the Common Council since dead, he exclaims, "Let me get out, gentlemen, we are in the minority here!" They held him fast;—but there! the chair is upset, and Isaac L. Varian is thrown

---

[2] **Isaac L. Varian**: A bank director.

[3] **Gideon Lee**: President of Leather Manufacturers' Bank.

[4] **Ringgold, West, and Conner**: Bank partisans.

from it. Instantly Joel Curtis, the true-hearted workingman is in it, both by right and fact, while two banners speak to the democracy, "Don't adjourn"—"Sustain the chair." There is clapping of hands and triumphant cheers. What can the discomfited do?

They have done it. When they got down stairs they turned off the gas. It is half-past seven, and the darkness of midnight is in Tammany Hall. Nothing but the demon spirit of monopoly, in its war upon humanity, could have been wicked enough to involve such an excited throng in total darkness.

"Let there be light, and there is light!" A host of fire-fly lights are in the room—loco-foco matches are ignited, candles are lit, and they are held up by living and breathing chandeliers. It is a glorious illumination! There are loud and long plaudits and huzzas, such as Tammany never before echoed from its foundations.

Reader, if this were not a victory over Monopoly, a blow, at least, was struck upon the hydra-headed monster, from which it never recovered.

The anti-monopoly ticket was enthusiastically adopted by the apparently undiminished multitude. Resolutions of the same character were passed, from which we select the following:

"*Resolved*—That, in a free state, all distinctions but those of merit are odious and oppressive, and ought to be discouraged by a people jealous of their liberties.

"*Resolved*—That all laws which directly or indirectly infringe the free exercise and enjoyment of equal rights and privileges by the great body of the people, are odious, unjust, and unconstitutional in their nature and effect, and ought to be abolished.

"*Resolved*—For all amounts of money, gold and silver are the only legitimate, substantial, and proper, circulating medium of our country.

"*Resolved*—That perpetuities and monopolies are offensive to freedom, contrary to the genius and spirit of a free state and the principles of commerce, and ought not to be allowed.

"*Resolved*—That we are in favor of a strict construction of the Constitution of the United States, and we are therefore opposed to the United States Bank, as being unconstitutional and opposed to the genius and spirit of our democratic institutions, and subversive of the great and fundamental principles of equal rights and privileges, asserted in the charter of our liberties.

"*Resolved*—That we are opposed to all bank charters granted by individual states, because we believe them founded on, and as giving an impulse to principles of speculation and gambling, at war with good morals and just and equal government, and calculated to build up and strengthen in our country the odious distribution of wealth and power against merit and equal rights; and every good citizen is bound to war against them as he values the blessings of free government.

"*Resolved*—That we receive the Evening Post with open arms to the bosom of the Democratic family, and that the efforts of its talented editors must and shall receive our uncompromising support."

READING AND DISCUSSION QUESTIONS

1. The Loco-Focos were Democrats, yet they stormed a Democratic Party meeting and took over its leadership positions under the banner of "anti-monopoly." What criticism of traditional party leadership were they making?
2. How would you summarize the political program the Loco-Focos championed?
3. In the last resolution, the Loco-Focos praise the *Evening Post*. What value do you think they believed the newspaper played in party politics?

9-3 | President Defeats Monopoly Threat

ANDREW JACKSON, *Veto Message Regarding the Bank of the United States* (1832)

Andrew Jackson's famous attack on the Second Bank of the United States symbolized one of the key policy differences between Democrats and Whigs. Led by Henry Clay, the Whigs' American System supported building canals, roads, bridges, and banks to encourage economic development. Many Democrats opposed using government funds to support these projects. Like the Loco-Foco faction within his own party, Jackson thundered against the "monster bank's" monopoly power, which profited private investors who earned interest on federal revenue deposited in the bank. When Clay tried to make the bank's recharter an issue in the 1832 presidential election, Jackson called his bluff. In the document excerpted below, Jackson explains to Congress the reasons for his veto.

WASHINGTON, July 10, 1832.

To the Senate:

The bill "to modify and continue" the act entitled "An act to incorporate the subscribers to the Bank of the United States" was presented to me on the 4th July instant. Having considered it with that solemn regard to the principles of the Constitution which the day was calculated to inspire, and come to the conclusion that it ought not to become a law, I herewith return it to the Senate, in which it originated, with my objections.

The present corporate body, denominated the president, directors, and company of the Bank of the United States, will have existed at the time this act is intended to take effect twenty years. It enjoys an exclusive privilege of banking under the authority of the General Government, a monopoly of its favor and support, and, as a necessary consequence, almost a monopoly of the foreign and domestic exchange. The powers, privileges, and favors bestowed upon it in the original charter, by increasing the value of the stock far above its par value, operated as a gratuity of many millions to the stockholders.

A Compilation of the Messages and Papers of the Presidents Prepared Under the Direction of the Joint Committee on Printing, of the House and Senate Pursuant to an Act of the Fifty-Second Congress of the United States (New York: Bureau of National Literature, 1897), 1139–1141, 1144–1146, 1152–1154.

Every monopoly and all exclusive privileges are granted at the expense of the public, which ought to receive a fair equivalent. The many millions which this act proposes to bestow on the stockholders of the existing bank must come directly or indirectly out of the earnings of the American people. It is due to them, therefore, if their Government sell monopolies and exclusive privileges, that they should at least exact for them as much as they are worth in open market. The value of the monopoly in this case may be correctly ascertained. The twenty-eight millions of stock would probably be at an advance of 50 per cent, and command in market at least $42,000,000, subject to the payment of the present bonus. The present value of the monopoly, therefore, is $17,000,000, and this the act proposes to sell for three millions, payable in fifteen annual installments of $200,000 each.

It is not conceivable how the present stockholders can have any claim to the special favor of the Government. The present corporation has enjoyed its monopoly during the period stipulated in the original contract. If we must have such a corporation, why should not the Government sell out the whole stock and thus secure to the people the full market value of the privileges granted? Why should not Congress create and sell twenty-eight millions of stock, incorporating the purchasers with all the powers and privileges secured in this act and putting the premium upon the sales into the Treasury? . . .

Is there no danger to our liberty and independence in a bank that in its nature has so little to bind it to our country? The president of the bank has told us that most of the State banks exist by its forbearance. Should its influence become concentered, as it may under the operation of such an act as this, in the hands of a self-elected directory whose interests are identified with those of the foreign stockholders, will there not be cause to tremble for the purity of our elections in peace and for the independence of our country in war? Their power would be great whenever they might choose to exert it; but if this monopoly were regularly renewed every fifteen or twenty years on terms proposed by themselves, they might seldom in peace put forth their strength to influence elections or control the affairs of the nation. But if any private citizen or public functionary should interpose to curtail its powers or prevent a renewal of its privileges, it can not be doubted that he would be made to feel its influence. . . .

If we must have a bank with private stockholders, every consideration of sound policy and every impulse of American feeling admonishes that it should be purely American. Its stockholders should be composed exclusively of our own citizens, who at least ought to be friendly to our Government and willing to support it in times of difficulty and danger. So abundant is domestic capital that competition in subscribing for the stock of local banks has recently led almost to riots. To a bank exclusively of American stockholders, possessing the powers and privileges granted by this act, subscriptions for $200,000,000 could be readily obtained. . . .

It is maintained by the advocates of the bank that its constitutionality in all its features ought to be considered as settled by precedent and by the decision of the Supreme Court. To this conclusion I can not assent. Mere precedent is a dangerous source of authority, and should not be regarded as deciding questions of constitutional power except where the acquiescence of the people and the States can be considered as well settled. . . .

If the opinion of the Supreme Court covered the whole ground of this act, it ought not to control the coordinate authorities of this Government. The Congress, the Executive, and the Court must each for itself be guided by its own opinion of the Constitution. Each public officer who takes an oath to support the Constitution swears that he will support it as he understands it, and not as it is understood by others. It is as much the duty of the House of Representatives, of the Senate, and of the President to decide upon the constitutionality of any bill or resolution which may be presented to them for passage or approval as it is of the supreme judges when it may be brought before them for judicial decision. The opinion of the judges has no more authority over Congress than the opinion of Congress has over the judges, and on that point the President is independent of both. The authority of the Supreme Court must not, therefore, be permitted to control the Congress or the Executive when acting in their legislative capacities, but to have only such influence as the force of their reasoning may deserve. . . .

The principle here affirmed is that the "degree of its necessity," involving all the details of a banking institution, is a question exclusively for legislative consideration. A bank is constitutional, but it is the province of the Legislature to determine whether this or that particular power, privilege, or exemption is "necessary and proper" to enable the bank to discharge its duties to the Government, and from their decision there is no appeal to the courts of justice. Under the decision of the Supreme Court, therefore, it is the exclusive province of Congress and the President to decide whether the particular features of this act are necessary and proper in order to enable the bank to perform conveniently and efficiently the public duties assigned to it as a fiscal agent, and therefore constitutional, or unnecessary and improper, and therefore unconstitutional.

Without commenting on the general principle affirmed by the Supreme Court, let us examine the details of this act in accordance with the rule of legislative action which they have laid down. It will be found that many of the powers and privileges conferred on it can not be supposed necessary for the purpose for which it is proposed to be created, and are not, therefore, means necessary to attain the end in view, and consequently not justified by the Constitution. . . .

Under such circumstances the bank comes forward and asks a renewal of its charter for a term of fifteen years upon conditions which not only operate as a gratuity to the stockholders of many millions of dollars, but will sanction any abuses and legalize any encroachments. . . .

The bank is professedly established as an agent of the executive branch of the Government, and its constitutionality is maintained on that ground. Neither upon the propriety of present action nor upon the provisions of this act was the Executive consulted. It has had no opportunity to say that it neither needs nor wants an agent clothed with such powers and favored by such exemptions. There is nothing in its legitimate functions which makes it necessary or proper. Whatever interest or influence, whether public or private, has given birth to this act, it can not be found either in the wishes or necessities of the executive department, by which present action is deemed premature, and the powers conferred upon its agent not only unnecessary, but dangerous to the Government and country.

It is to be regretted that the rich and powerful too often bend the acts of government to their selfish purposes. Distinctions in society will always exist under every just government. Equality of talents, of education, or of wealth can not be produced by human institutions. In the full enjoyment of the gifts of Heaven and the fruits of superior industry, economy, and virtue, every man is equally entitled to protection by law; but when the laws undertake to add to these natural and just advantages artificial distinctions, to grant titles, gratuities, and exclusive privileges, to make the rich richer and the potent more powerful, the humble members of society—the farmers, mechanics, and laborers—who have neither the time nor the means of securing like favors to themselves, have a right to complain of the injustice of their Government. There are no necessary evils in government. Its evils exist only in its abuses. If it would confine itself to equal protection, and, as Heaven does its rains, shower its favors alike on the high and the low, the rich and the poor, it would be an unqualified blessing. In the act before me there seems to be a wide and unnecessary departure from these just principles.

Nor is our Government to be maintained or our Union preserved by invasions of the rights and powers of the several States. In thus attempting to make our General Government strong we make it weak. Its true strength consists in leaving individuals and States as much as possible to themselves—in making itself felt, not in its power, but in its beneficence; not in its control, but in its protection; not in binding the States more closely to the center, but leaving each to move unobstructed in its proper orbit.

Experience should teach us wisdom. Most of the difficulties our Government now encounters and most of the dangers which impend over our Union have sprung from an abandonment of the legitimate objects of Government by our national legislation, and the adoption of such principles as are embodied in this act. Many of our rich men have not been content with equal protection and equal benefits, but have besought us to make them richer by act of Congress. By attempting to gratify their desires we have in the results of our legislation arrayed section against section, interest against interest, and man against man, in a fearful commotion which threatens to shake the foundations of our Union. It is time to pause in our career to review our principles, and if possible revive that devoted patriotism and spirit of compromise which distinguished the sages of the Revolution and the fathers of our Union. If we can not at once, in justice to interests vested under improvident legislation, make our Government what it ought to be, we can at least take a stand against all new grants of monopolies and exclusive privileges, against any prostitution of our Government to the advancement of the few at the expense of the many, and in favor of compromise and gradual reform in our code of laws and system of political economy.

I have now done my duty to my country. If sustained by my fellow citizens, I shall be grateful and happy; if not, I shall find in the motives which impel me ample grounds for contentment and peace. In the difficulties which surround us and the dangers which threaten our institutions there is cause for neither dismay nor alarm. For relief and deliverance let us firmly rely on that kind Providence which I am sure watches with peculiar care over the destinies of our Republic, and on the intelligence and wisdom of our countrymen. Through His abundant goodness and their patriotic devotion our liberty and Union will be preserved.

ANDREW JACKSON

READING AND DISCUSSION QUESTIONS

1. What arguments against the bank does Jackson think the American people will find persuasive?
2. Why does Jackson see the bank as a threat to "our liberty and independence"? Do you think he believed a threat existed, or do you think he was playing politics?
3. What does Jackson see as the role of the Supreme Court in relationship to the other branches of government?

9-4 | Whig Leader Campaigns Against Jacksonians

HENRY CLAY, *Speech on the Presidential Election* (1840)

In July 1840, when Henry Clay delivered this campaign speech to Whig partisans in Virginia, he was one of the party's leaders in the U.S. Senate and remained a bitter foe of former president Andrew Jackson. Though Jackson had been out of office for more than three years, Clay continued his attack on him and his successor, President Martin Van Buren, who was seeking a second term against the Whig nominee, William Henry Harrison. Here, Clay lays out the case against the Democrats by outlining Whig priorities.

Here, friends and fellow-citizens, let us pause and contemplate this stupendous structure of executive machinery and despotism, which has been reared in our young republic. The executive branch of the government is a unit; throughout all its arteries and veins there is to be but one heart, one head, one will. . . . An absolute obedience to his will is secured and enforced by the power of dismissing them[5] at his pleasure, from their respective places. . . . The constitution and laws

---

The Life and Speeches of Henry Clay, vol. 2 (New York: Greeley & McElrath, Tribune Office, 1844), 426–427, 432–441.

[5] *executive branch officials.

of the United States are to be executed in the sense in which the President understands them—although that sense may be at variance with the understanding of every other man in the United States. . . . [I]f an act of Congress be passed, in his opinion, contrary to the constitution, or if a decision be pronounced by the courts, in his opinion, contrary to the constitution or the laws, that act or that decision the President is not obliged to enforce, and he could not cause it to be enforced, without a violation, as is pretended, of his official oath. . . . The command of the army and navy being already in the President, and having acquired a perfect control over the treasury of the United States, he has consummated that frightful union of purse and sword, so long, so much, so earnestly deprecated by all true lovers of civil liberty. And our present Chief Magistrate stands solemnly and voluntarily pledged, in the face of the whole world, to follow in the footsteps and carry out the measures and the principles of his illustrious predecessor! . . .

If this be not practical despotism, I am not capable of conceiving or defining it. . . .What are the positions of the two great parties of the present day? Modern democracy has reduced the federal theory of a strong and energetic executive to practical operation. It has turned from the people, the natural ally of *genuine* democracy, to the executive, and, instead of vigilance, jealousy and distrust, has given to that department all its confidence, and made to it a virtual surrender of all the powers of government. The recognised maxim of royal infallibility is transplanted from the British monarchy into modern American democracy, and the President can do no wrong! . . .

The whigs of 1840 stand where the republicans of 1798 stood, and where the whigs of the revolution were, battling for liberty, for the people, for free institutions, against power, against corruption, against executive encroachments, against monarchy. . . .

If this state of things were to remain—if the progress of executive usurpation were to continue unchecked, hopeless despair would seize the public mind, or the people would be goaded to acts of open and violent resistance. But, thank God, the power of the President, fearful and rapid as its strides have been, is not yet too great for the power of the elective franchise; and a bright and glorious prospect, in the election of WILLIAM HENRY HARRISON, has opened upon the country. . . .

The first, and in my opinion, the most important object which should engage the serious attention of a new administration, is that of circumscribing the executive power, and throwing around it such limitations and safe-guards as will render it no longer dangerous to the public liberties. . . .

With the view, therefore, to the fundamental character of the government itself, and especially of the executive branch, it seems to me that, either by amendments of the constitution, when they are necessary, or by remedial legislation when the object falls within the scope of the powers of Congress, there should be, 1st. A provision to render a person ineligible to the office of President of the United States, after a service of one term. . . .

2d. That the veto power should be more precisely defined, and be subjected to further limitations and qualifications. . . .

3d. That the power of dismission from office should be restricted, and the exercise of it be rendered responsible. . . .

4th. That the control over the treasury of the United States should be confided and confined exclusively to Congress; and all authority of the President over it, by means of dismissing the Secretary of the Treasury, or other persons having the immediate charge of it, be rigorously precluded. . . .

And 5th. That the appointment of members of Congress to any office, or any but a few specific offices, during their continuance in office, and for one year thereafter, be prohibited. . . .

These are the subjects, in relation to the permanent character of the government itself, which, it seems to me, are worthy of the serious attention of the people, and of a new administration. There are others, of an administrative nature, which require prompt and careful consideration.1st. The currency of the country, its stability and uniform value, and, as intimately and indissolubly connected with it, the assurance of the faithful performance of the fiscal services necessary to the government should be maintained and secured by exercising all the powers requisite to those objects with which Congress is constitutionally invested. . . .

Without banks I believe we cannot have a sufficient currency; without a Bank of the United States, I fear we cannot have a sound currency. . . .

2d. That the public lands, in conformity with the trusts created expressly or by just implication, on their acquisition, be administered in a spirit of liberality towards the new states and territories, and in a spirit of justice towards all the States. . . .

3d. That the policy of protecting and encouraging the productions of American industry, entering into competition with the rival productions of foreign industry, be adhered to and maintained on the basis of the principles and in the spirit of the compromise of March, 1833.

Protection and national independence are, in my opinion, identical and synonymous. . . . Who, with just pride and national sensibility, can think of subjecting the products of our industry to all the taxation and restraints of foreign powers, without effort on our part to counteract their prohibitions and burdens by suitable countervailing legislations? . . .

4th. That a strict and wise economy, in the disbursement of the public money be steadily enforced; and that, to that end, all useless establishments, all unnecessary offices and places, foreign and domestic, and all extravagance, either in the collection or expenditure of the public revenue, be abolished and repressed. . . .5th. The several States have made such great and gratifying progress in their respective systems of internal improvement, and have been so aided by the distribution under the deposite act, that, in future the election of new roads and canals should be left to them with such further aid only from the general government as they would derive from the payment of the last instalment under that act, from an absolute relinquishment of the right of Congress to call upon them to refund the previous instalments, and from their equal and just quotes, to be received by a future distribution of the nett proceeds from the sales of the public lands. And 6th. That the right to slave property, being guarantied by the constitution, and recognized as one of the compromises incorporated in that instrument by our ancestors, should be left where the constitution has placed it, undisturbed and unagitated by Congress. . . . Whether the[se] salutary reforms . . . will be effected or considered, depends upon the issue of that great struggle which is now going on throughout all this country. This contest has had no parallel since the period of the revolution. In both instances there is a similarity of object. That was to achieve, this is to preserve the liberties of the country. Let us catch the spirit which animated, and imitate the virtues which adorned our noble ancestors. . . . Our opponents are powerful in numbers and in organization active, insidious, and possessed of ample means, and wholly unscrupulous in the use of them. . . . And allow me to conjure you not to suffer yourselves to be diverted, deceived, or discouraged by the false rumors which will be industriously circulated, between the present time and the period of the election, by our opponents. They will put them forth in every variety and without number, in the most imposing forms, certified and sworn to by conspicuous names. They will brag, they will boast, they will threaten. Regardless of all their arts, let us keep steadily and faithfully, and fearlessly at work.

READING AND DISCUSSION QUESTIONS

1. How does Clay define the contest between Jacksonian Democrats and the Whigs?
2. What does the tone of Clay's attack on Jackson suggest about the nature of politics during the 1830s and 1840s?
3. From the list of priorities Clay includes here, how would you characterize the Whig political philosophy during the 1840s?

9-5 | Poking Fun at Van Buren
Capitol Fashions for 1837 (1837)

With the revolutions in printing technology, cartoons became an effective weapon in the divisive political campaigns of the antebellum period. Both the Democrats and the Whigs employed cheaply produced newspapers and other campaign materials to rally voters with images of their party's standard-bearers and opponents. In this cartoon, the artist lampoons President Martin Van Buren for clothing himself in Andrew Jackson's policies. Notice the regal robes he wears and the "specie circular" and "Indian claims" under Van Buren's feet. The winged creature seems to be anointing Van Buren's head with a "shin plaster," or the worthless paper money issued by banks.

Universal History Archive/Getty Images

READING AND DISCUSSION QUESTIONS

1. Analyze the elements of this cartoon. What do you infer about the artist's political perspective? Who was the intended audience? What effect do you think the artist expected the image to have?
2. How might a historian use cartoons like this one to understand popular politics during the 1830s? What does the image suggest about how political parties used the press to spread their ideas?
3. How do Van Buren's regal robes and the references to the "specie circular" and "Indian claims" hint at the political issues dividing Whigs and Democrats?

9-6 | Native American Women Urge Resistance to Removal Policy
CHEROKEE WOMEN, *Petition* (1821 [1831?])

Andrew Jackson saw himself as the protector of the people, but his treatment of Native Americans reveals the limits of his vision. Jackson justified his policy of Indian removal, which resulted in the infamous Trail of Tears, as necessary to "protect" Indians from white encroachment by removing them from eastern lands and resettling them in the interior. Native Americans saw the move differently. In this petition, published in 1831 in *The Cherokee Phoenix*, a tribal newspaper, Cherokee women denounced the Indian removal policy.

October 17, 1821 [1831?]

To the Committee and Council,

We the females, residing in Salequoree and Pine Log, believing that the present difficulties and embarrassments under which this nation is placed demands a full expression of the mind of every individual, on the subject of emigrating to Arkansas, would take upon ourselves to address you. Although it is not common for our sex to take part in public measures, we nevertheless feel justified in expressing our sentiment on any subject where our interest is as much at stake as any other part of the community.

We believe the present plan of the General Government to effect our removal West of the Mississippi, and thus obtain our lands for the use of the State of Georgia, to be highly oppressive, cruel and unjust. And we sincerely hope there is no consideration which can induce our citizens to forsake the land of our fathers of which they have been in possession from time immemorial, and thus compel us, against our will, to undergo the toils and difficulties of removing with our helpless families hundreds of miles to unhealthy and unproductive country. We hope therefore the Committee and Council will take into deep consideration our deplorable situation, and do everything in their power to avert such a state of things. And we trust by a prudent course their transactions with the General Government will enlist in our behalf the sympathies of the good people of the United States.

READING AND DISCUSSION QUESTIONS

1. How do these Cherokee women craft their petition against the federal government's policy of removal?
2. What conclusions about the extent and limits of women's political power in this period can you draw from this source? How significant do you think it is that the Cherokee women issued a petition?

The Cherokee Removal: A Brief History with Documents, eds. Theda Perdue and Michael D. Green (Boston: Bedford/St. Martin's, 2005), 134.

▪ COMPARATIVE QUESTIONS ▪

1. What conclusions can you draw from the sources in this chapter about the extent of "democratization" during the Jacksonian era? To what degree did different groups of people during these years benefit from this egalitarian ethos?
2. Contrast the competing political philosophies spurring the Whig and Democratic parties during the 1830s and 1840s. How did these policy disputes manifest themselves?
3. Compare the enthusiasm for party politics as demonstrated by the Democrats and Whigs in this chapter's sources with the attitude toward parties expressed by James Madison in *Federalist No. 10* (Document 6-6) and George Washington in his *Farewell Address* (Document P3-4). How might you explain the differences you see?
4. What can you infer about the argument historians make when they label the years 1800 to 1848 a Democratic Revolution? What comparison do you see between these years and those years of the American Revolution during the 1770s?

10

Religion, Reform, and Culture

1820–1848

"The Americans combine the notions of religion and liberty so intimately in their minds," noted Alexis de Tocqueville in the 1830s, "that it is impossible to make them conceive of one without the other." The antebellum religious revivals stressed a person's freedom to choose God's gift of salvation. Life everlasting became a matter of choice and not, as the Calvinists had proclaimed, the prerogative of God alone. Religious enthusiasm also inspired new religious sects, denominations, and utopian communities, like Joseph Smith's Mormonism. The spiritual excitement of the era combined with Jefferson's "inalienable right" to pursue one's happiness to produce a powerful devotion to individualism that had widespread repercussions.

This theme of individualism also influenced culture, politics, and reform. The transcendentalists used this ideal in creative ways, inspiring utopian communities and the campaign for women's rights. The political dimension of individualism, as glimpsed in the Jacksonian era, also liberated urban culture from the constraints of upper-class "respectability." Some, particularly advocates of women's and African American rights, used the language of individualism to strike blows against gender and racial discrimination and slavery. Others quickly saw the limits, even dangers, of excessive individualism: political turmoil, sectionalism, and social discord.

10-1 | A Transcendentalist View of Women's Rights

MARGARET FULLER, *Woman in the Nineteenth Century* (1845)

Margaret Fuller (1810–1850) was nurtured among the New England literary and philosophical circle known as the transcendentalists, and along with Ralph Waldo Emerson and others she became one of its leading interpreters. In this selection, from her 1845 book, *Woman in the Nineteenth Century*, Fuller reveals the extent of her philosophical commitment to transcendentalism and to gender equality, a stand in line with, but more radical than, calls for women's suffrage.

Of all its banners, none has been more steadily upheld, and under none have more valor and willingness for real sacrifices been shown, than that of the champions of the enslaved African. And this band it is, which, partly from a natural following out of principles, partly because many women have been prominent in that cause, makes, just now, the warmest appeal in behalf of Woman.

Though there has been a growing liberality on this subject, yet society at large is not so prepared for the demands of this party, but that its members are, and will be for some time, coldly regarded as the Jacobins of their day.

"Is it not enough," cries the irritated trader, "that you have done all you could to break up the national union, and thus destroy the prosperity of our country but now you must be trying to break up family union, to take my wife away from the cradle and the kitchen-hearth to vote at polls, and preach from a pulpit? Of course, if she does such things, she cannot attend to those of her own sphere. She is happy enough as she is. She has more leisure than I have,—every means of improvement, every indulgence."

"Have you asked her whether she was satisfied with these *indulgences*?"

"No, but I know she is. She is too amiable to desire what would make me unhappy, and too judicious to wish to step beyond the sphere of her sex. I will never consent to have our peace disturbed by any such discussions."

"Consent—you? it is not consent from you that is in question—it is assent from your wife."

"Am not I the head of my house?"

"You are not the head of your wife. God has given her a mind of her own."

"I am the head, and she the heart."

"God grant you play true to one another, then! I suppose I am to be grateful that you did not say she was only the hand. If the head represses no natural pulse of the heart, there can be no question as to your giving your consent. Both will be of one accord, and there needs but to present any question to get a full

---

Margaret Fuller Ossoli, *Woman in the Nineteenth Century and Kindred Papers Relating to the Sphere, Condition, and Duties of Woman* (Boston: Brown, Taggard and Chase, 1860), 28–30, 115–116, 174–176.

and true answer. There is no need of precaution, of indulgence, nor consent. But our doubt is whether the heart does consent with the head, or only obeys its decrees with a passiveness that precludes the exercise of its natural powers, or a repugnance that turns sweet qualities to bitter, or a doubt that lays waste the fair occasions of life. It is to ascertain the truth that we propose some liberating measures."

Thus vaguely are these questions proposed and discussed at present. But their being proposed at all implies much thought, and suggests more. Many women are considering within themselves what they need that they have not, and what they can have if they find they need it. Many men are considering whether women are capable of being and having more than they are and have, and whether, if so, it will be best to consent to improvement in their condition. . . .

The especial genius of Woman I believe to be electrical in movement, intuitive in function, spiritual in tendency. She excels not so easily in classification, or recreation, as in an instinctive seizure of causes, and a simple breathing out of what she receives, that has the singleness of life, rather than the selecting and energizing of art.

More native is it to her to be the living model of the artist than to set apart from herself any one form in objective reality; more native to inspire and receive the poem, than to create it. In so far as soul is in her completely developed, all soul is the same; but in so far as it is modified in her as Woman, it flows, it breathes, it sings, rather than deposits soil, or finishes work; and that which is especially feminine flushes, in blossom, the face of earth, and pervades, like air and water, all this seeming solid globe, daily renewing and purifying its life. Such may be the especially feminine element spoken of as Femality. But it is no more the order of nature that it should be incarnated pure in any form, than that the masculine energy should exist unmingled with it in any form.

Male and female represent the two sides of the great radical dualism. But, in fact, they are perpetually passing into one another. Fluid hardens to solid, solid rushes to fluid. There is no wholly masculine man, no purely feminine woman. . . .

But if you ask me what offices they [women] may fill, I reply—any. I do not care what case you put; let them be sea-captains, if you will. I do not doubt there are women well fitted for such an office, and, if so, I should be as glad to see them in it, as to welcome the maid of Saragossa, or the maid of Missolonghi, or the Suliote heroine, or Emily Plater.[1]

I think women need, especially at this juncture, a much greater range of occupation than they have, to rouse their latent powers. A party of travellers lately visited a lonely hut on a mountain. There they found an old woman,

[1] **Saragossa . . . Plater**: Fuller draws from early-nineteenth-century European history, including the Spanish and Greek wars for independence and the 1830 Polish uprising, to identify these examples of female valor.

who told them she and her husband had lived there forty years. "Why," they said, "did you choose so barren a spot?" She "did not know; *it was the man's notion*."

And, during forty years, she had been content to act, without knowing why, upon "the man's notion." I would not have it so.

In families that I know, some little girls like to saw wood, others to use carpenters' tools. Where these tastes are indulged, cheerfulness and good-humor are promoted. Where they are forbidden, because "such things are not proper for girls," they grow sullen and mischievous.

Fourier[2] had observed these wants of women, as no one can fail to do who watches the desires of little girls, or knows the ennui that haunts grown women, except where they make to themselves a serene little world by art of some kind. He, therefore, in proposing a great variety of employments, in manufactures or the care of plants and animals, allows for one third of women as likely to have a taste for masculine pursuits, one third of men for feminine.

Who does not observe the immediate glow and serenity that is diffused over the life of women, before restless or fretful, by engaging in gardening, building, or the lowest department of art? Here is something that is not routine, something that draws forth life towards the infinite.

I have no doubt, however, that a large proportion of women would give themselves to the same employments as now, because there are circumstances that must lead them. Mothers will delight to make the nest soft and warm. Nature would take care of that; no need to clip the wings of any bird that wants to soar and sing, or finds in itself the strength of pinion for a migratory flight unusual to its kind. The difference would be that all need not be constrained to employments for which some are unfit.

I have urged upon the sex self-subsistence in its two forms of self-reliance and self-impulse, because I believe them to be the needed means of the present juncture.

I have urged on Woman independence of Man, not that I do not think the sexes mutually needed by one another, but because in Woman this fact has led to an excessive devotion, which has cooled love, degraded marriage, and prevented either sex from being what it should be to itself or the other.

I wish Woman to live, first for God's sake. Then she will not make an imperfect man her god, and thus sink to idolatry. Then she will not take what is not fit for her from a sense of weakness and poverty. Then, if she finds what she needs in Man embodied, she will know how to love, and be worthy of being loved.

By being more a soul, she will not be less Woman, for nature is perfected through spirit.

---

[2] **Fourier**: Charles Fourier, French philosopher and reformer, advocated for women's rights and inspired the development of several utopian communities in America, including Brook Farm in West Roxbury, Massachusetts.

READING AND DISCUSSION QUESTIONS

1. To what extent did Fuller's claim that there is "no wholly masculine man, no purely feminine woman" challenge prevailing ideas of men and women's roles in nineteenth-century society?
2. Paying attention to the language Fuller uses in making her argument, what evidence of transcendentalism's influence can you identify? Are there particular words or phrases that help you see her writing as having been influenced by transcendentalist ideas?

10-2 | Mormon Leader's Vision of Religious Community

JOSEPH SMITH, *History of Joseph Smith, the Prophet* (c. 1830s)

The competing claims of religious truth that emerged from the proliferating denominations of the era liberated some from the constraints of the church, but alienated others, including Joseph Smith (1805–1844). Reared in western New York during the revivals of the 1820s, Smith was unsatisfied with the churches he knew. Spiritually driven, Smith experienced visions foretelling the arrival of a new gospel of God, which under his personal leadership bloomed into the church of Mormonism.

During this time of great excitement my mind was called up to serious reflection and great uneasiness; but though my feelings were deep and often poignant, still I kept myself aloof from all these parties, though I attended their several meetings as often as occasion would permit. In process of time my mind became somewhat partial to the Methodist sect, and I felt some desire to be united with them; but so great were the confusion and strife among the different denominations, that it was impossible for a person young as I was, and so unacquainted with men and things, to come to any certain conclusion who was right and who was wrong. My mind at times was greatly excited, the cry and tumult were so great and incessant. The Presbyterians were most decided against the Baptists and Methodists, and used all the powers of both reason and sophistry to prove their errors, or, at least, to make the people think they were in error. On the other hand, the Baptists and Methodists in their turn were equally zealous in endeavoring to establish their own tenets and disprove all others.

In the midst of this war of words and tumult of opinions, I often said to myself, What is to be done? Who of all these parties are right; or, are they all wrong together? If any one of them be right, which is it, and how shall I know it? While I was laboring under the extreme difficulties caused by the contests

---

Joseph Smith, *History of the Church of Jesus Christ of Latter-Day Saints, Period I. History of Joseph Smith, the Prophet,* an introduction and notes by B. H. Roberts (Salt Lake City: Church of Jesus Christ of Latter-Day Saints, 1902), 3–7, 9–13.

of these parties of religionists, I was one day reading the Epistle of James, first chapter and fifth verse, which reads:

> If any of you lack wisdom, let him ask of God, that giveth to all men liberally, and upbraideth not; and it shall be given him.

. . . I at length came to the determination to "ask of God," concluding that if he gave wisdom to them that lacked wisdom, and would give liberally, and not upbraid, I might venture. So, in accordance with this, my determination to ask of God, I retired to the woods to make the attempt. . . . I kneeled down and began to offer up the desires of my heart to God. I had scarcely done so, when immediately I was seized upon by some power which entirely overcame me, and had such an astonishing influence over me as to bind my tongue so that I could not speak. Thick darkness gathered around me, and it seemed to me for a time as if I were doomed to sudden destruction. But, exerting all my powers to call upon God to deliver me out of the power of this enemy which had seized upon me, and at the very moment when I was ready to sink into despair and abandon myself to destruction—not to an imaginary ruin, but to the power of some actual being from the unseen world, who had such marvelous power as I had never before felt in any being—just at this moment of great alarm, I saw a pillar of light exactly over my head, above the brightness of the sun, which descended gradually until it fell upon me.

It no sooner appeared than I found myself delivered from the enemy which held me bound. When the light rested upon me I saw two Personages, whose brightness and glory defy all description, standing above me in the air. One of them spake unto me, calling me by name and said, pointing to the other—

"THIS IS MY BELOVED SON, HEAR HIM."

My object in going to inquire of the Lord was to know which of all the sects was right, that I might know which to join. No sooner, therefore, did I get possession of myself, so as to be able to speak, than I asked the Personages who stood above me in the light, which of all the sects was right (for at this time it had never entered into my heart that all were wrong)—and which I should join. I was answered that I must join none of them, for they were all wrong; and the Personage who addressed me said that all their creeds were an abomination in His sight: that those professors were all corrupt; that "they draw near to me with their lips, but their hearts are far from me; they teach for doctrines the commandments of men: having a form of godliness, but they deny the power thereof." He again forbade me to join with any of them: and many other things did he say unto me, which I cannot write at this time. When I came to myself again, I found myself lying on my back, looking up into heaven. When the light had departed, I had no strength; but soon recovering in some degree, I went home. And as I leaned up to the fireplace, mother inquired what the matter was. I replied, "Never mind, all is well—I am well enough off." I then said to my mother, "I have learned for myself that Presbyterianism is not true."

. . . Some few days after I had this vision, I happened to be in company with one of the Methodist preachers, who was very active in the before-mentioned religious excitement; . . . and I took occasion to give him an account of the vision which I had had. I was greatly surprised at his behavior; he treated my communication not only lightly, but with great contempt, saying it was all of the devil, that there were no such things as visions or revelations in these days; that all such things had ceased with the Apostles, and that there would never be any more of them. I soon found, however, that my telling the story had excited a great deal of prejudice against me among professors of religion, and was the cause of great persecution, which continued to increase. . . .

Chapter II: The Visitation of Moroni— Existence of the Book of Mormon Made Known

I continued to pursue my common vocations in life until the twenty-first of September, one thousand eight hundred and twenty-three, all the time suffering severe persecution at the hands of all classes of men, both religious and irreligious, because I continued to affirm that I had seen a vision.

During the space of time which intervened between the time I had the vision and the year eighteen hundred and twenty-three . . . I was left to all kinds of temptations; and, mingling with all kinds of society, I frequently fell into many foolish errors, and displayed the weakness of youth, and the foibles of human nature; which, I am sorry to say, led me into divers temptations, offensive in the sight of God. . . .

In consequence of these things, I often felt condemned for my weakness and imperfections; when, on the evening of the above-mentioned twenty-first of September, after I had retired to my bed for the night, I betook myself to prayer and supplication to Almighty God. . . . While I was thus in the act of calling upon God, I discovered a light appearing in my room, which continued to increase until the room was lighter than at noonday, when immediately a personage appeared at my bedside, standing in the air, for his feet did not touch the floor. He had on a loose robe of most exquisite whiteness. It was a whiteness beyond anything earthly I had ever seen; nor do I believe that any earthly thing could be made to appear so exceedingly white and brilliant. His hands were naked, and his arms also, a little above the wrist; so, also, were his feet naked, as were his legs, a little above the ankles. His head and neck were also bare. I could discover that he had no other clothing on but this robe, as it was open, so that I could see into his bosom. Not only was his robe exceedingly white, but his whole person was glorious beyond description, and his countenance truly like lightning. The room was exceedingly light, but not so very bright as immediately around his person.

When I first looked upon him, I was afraid; but the fear soon left me. He called me by name, and said unto me that he was a messenger sent from the presence of God to me, and that his name was Moroni; that God had a work for me to do; and that my name should be had for good and evil among all nations, kindreds, and tongues, or that it should be both good and evil spoken of among all people. He said there was a book deposited, written upon gold plates, giving an account of the former inhabitants of this continent, and the source from whence they sprang. He also said that the fullness of the everlasting Gospel was contained in it, as delivered by the Savior to the ancient inhabitants; also, that there were two stones in silver bows—and these stones, fastened to a breastplate, constituted what is called the Urim and Thummim—deposited with the plates; and the possession and use of these stones were what constituted "Seers" in ancient or former times; and that God had prepared them for the purpose of translating the book. . . .

Again, he told me, that when I got those plates of which he had spoken—for the time that they should be obtained was not yet fulfilled—I should not show them to any person; neither the breastplate with the Urim and Thummim; only to those to whom I should be commanded to show them; if I did I should be destroyed. While he was conversing with me about the plates, the vision was opened to my mind that I could see the place where the plates were deposited, and that so clearly and distinctly that I knew the place again when I visited it.

After this communication, I saw the light in the room begin to gather immediately around the person of him who had been speaking to me, and it continued to do so until the room was again left dark, except just around him; when, instantly I saw, as it were, a conduit open right up into heaven, and he ascended till he entirely disappeared, and the room was left as it had been before this heavenly light had made its appearance.

READING AND DISCUSSION QUESTIONS

1. What does Smith's account suggest about the historical context of religion during the 1820s and 1830s? How would you characterize Smith's perspective on the existing religious denominations of his day?
2. How might you account for the timing of Smith's visions, the first of which occurred in 1820 when Smith was only fourteen? What details from his biography, as he shares them here, shed light on his life and his early visions?
3. How might a historian explain the success of Smith's ministry during the 1820s and 1830s?

10-3 | A Night at the Museum

Advertisement for the American Museum (1845)

The transcendentalist world inhabited by Margaret Fuller—airy, abstract, intellectual—contrasts sharply with the view on display in this 1845 advertisement for P. T. Barnum's American Museum. Barnum was one of the great showmen of the nineteenth century and a pioneer in the art of entertainment. He beguiled Americans with exhibits featuring such curiosities as the Feejee Mermaid (in reality, the upper body of a monkey sewn onto the body of a fish) and such people as Joice Heth (whom he advertised as the 161-year-old nurse of George Washington). In this advertisement, Barnum highlights his orangutan exhibit featuring Mad'le Fanny, whom he claimed was "the nearest approach to humanity of ANY ANIMAL ever yet discovered. She is indeed," the advertisement continues, "the Connecting link between Man and Brute!!!! possessing as many of the characteristics of the one as the other." Patrons could also visit the well-named Madame Rockwell, "an eminent Petrologist!" Barnum described her as a "Lady, who by Looking Into a Rock, which to common eyes is perfectly opaque, is capable of Foretelling Future Events! Relating those that are Past!! Describing Diseases! Revealing Mysteries, &c. !!!" For twenty-five cents, patrons could consult with her privately. Barnum's exhibits, more entertaining than educational, became popular amusements in the growing and diversifying cities of antebellum America.

TCS 65. Houghton Library, Harvard University

READING AND DISCUSSION QUESTIONS

1. By reading Barnum's advertisement for his American Museum, what can you infer about American urban culture during the 1840s?
2. What advertising techniques does Barnum use to attract people to his museum? What assumptions about his audience's taste and desires is he making?

10-4 | Attacking the Legal Disabilities of Women

SARAH GRIMKÉ, *Letters on the Equality of the Sexes and the Condition of Woman* (1837)

Like Margaret Fuller, Sarah Grimké (1792–1873) also championed women's rights by fighting an uphill battle against the prejudices of her day. In her famous series of essays written as letters to her sister, Grimké attacked conventional religious doctrines that had subordinated women. Born into a slave-owning family in South Carolina, she embraced abolitionism and the Quaker faith. In this essay, Grimké targets the legal prescriptions against women, the same ones that prevented women's education and her dream of becoming a lawyer.

Concord, 9th Mo., 6th, 1837

My Dear Sister,—There are few things which present greater obstacles to the improvement and elevation of woman to her appropriate sphere of usefulness and duty, than the laws which have been enacted to destroy her independence, and crush her individuality; laws which, although they are framed for her government, she has had no voice in establishing, and which rob her of some of her *essential rights.* Woman has no political existence. With the single exception of presenting a petition to the legislative body, she is a cipher in the nation; or, if not actually so in representative governments, she is only counted, like the slaves of the South, to swell the numbers of law-makers who form decrees for her government, with little reference to her benefit, except so far as her good may promote their own. . . . These laws bear with peculiar rigor on married women. Blackstone,[3] in the chapter entitled "Of husband and wife," says:—

> By marriage, the husband and wife are one person in law; that is, *the very being, or legal existence of the woman* is suspended during the marriage, or at least is incorporated and consolidated into that of the husband under whose wing, protection and cover she performs everything. . . .

Here now, the very being of a woman, like that of a slave, is absorbed in her master. All contracts made with her, like those made with slaves by their owners, are a mere nullity. Our kind defenders have legislated away almost all our legal rights, and in the true spirit of such injustice and oppressions, have kept us in ignorance of those very laws by which we are governed. They have persuaded us, that we have no rights to investigate the laws, and that, if we did, we could not comprehend them. . . .

Th[e] law that "a wife can bring no action," &c., is similar to the law respecting slaves. "A slave cannot bring a suit against his master, or any other person, for an injury—his master, must bring it." So if any damages are recovered for an

Sarah M. Grimké, *Letters on the Equality of the Sexes, and the Condition of Woman* (Boston: Isaac Knapp, 1838), 74–83.

[3] **Blackstone**: Sir William Blackstone, English jurist and author of Commentaries on the Laws of England, a legal treatise on the common law that influenced the development of American jurisprudence.

injury committed on a wife, the husband pockets it; in the case of the slave, the master does the same.

> In criminal prosecutions, the wife may be indicted and punished separately, unless there be evidence of coercion from the fact that the offense was committed in the presence, or by the command of her husband. A wife is excused from punishment for theft committed in the presence, or by the command of her husband.

It would be difficult to frame a law better calculated to destroy the responsibility of woman as a moral being, or a free agent. Her husband is supposed to possess unlimited control over her; and if she can offer the flimsy excuse that he bade her steal, she may break the eighth commandment with impunity, as far as human laws are concerned. . . .

Such a law speaks volumes of the abuse of that power which men have vested in their own hands. Still the private examination of a wife, to know whether she accedes to the disposition of property made by her husband is, in most cases, a mere form; a wife dares not do what will be disagreeable to one who is, in his own estimation, her superior, and who makes her feel, in the privacy of domestic life, that she has thwarted him. . . .

What a mortifying proof this law affords, of the estimation in which woman is held! She is placed completely in the hands of a being subject like herself to the outbursts of passion, and therefore unworthy to be trusted with power. Perhaps I may be told respecting this law, that it is a dead letter, as I am sometimes told about the slave laws; but this is not true in either case. The slaveholder does kill his slave by moderate correction, as the law allows; and many a husband, among the poor, exercises the right given him by the law, of degrading women by personal chastisement. And among the higher ranks, if actual imprisonment is not resorted to, women are not unfrequently restrained of the liberty of going to places of worship by irreligious husbands, and of doing many other things about which, as moral and responsible beings, they should be the sole judges. . . .

And farther, all the avails of her labor are absolutely in the power of her husband. All that she acquires by her industry is his; so that she cannot, with her own honest earnings, become the legal purchaser of any property. If she expends her money for articles of furniture, to contribute to the comfort of her family, they are liable to be seized for her husband's debts. . . .

> The laws above cited are not very unlike the slave laws of Louisiana.
>
> "By the marriage, the husband is absolutely master of the profits of the wife's land during the coverture, and if he has had a living child, and survives the wife, he retains the whole of those lands, if they are estates of inheritance, during his life; but the wife is entitled only to one third if she survives, out of the husband's estates on inheritance. But this she has, whether she has had a child or not. With regard to the property of women, there is taxation without representation; for they pay taxes without having the liberty of voting for representatives."

And this taxation, without representation, be it remembered, was the cause of our Revolutionary war, a grievance so heavy, that it was thought necessary to purchase exemption from it at an immense expense of blood and treasure, yet the daughters of New England, as well as of all the other States of this free Republic, are suffering a similar injustice—but for one, I had rather we should suffer any injustice or oppression, than that my sex should have any voice in the political affairs of the nation.

The laws I have quoted, are, I believe, the laws of Massachusetts, and, with few exceptions, of all the States in the Union. . . . That the laws which have generally been adopted in the United States, for the government of women, have been framed almost entirely for the exclusive benefit of men, and with a design to oppress women, by depriving them of all control over their property, is too manifest to be denied. . . .

As these abuses do exist, and women suffer intensely from them, our brethren are called upon in this enlightened age, by every sentiment to honor, religion and justice, to repeal these unjust and unequal laws, and restore to woman those rights which they have wrested from her. Such laws approximated too nearly to the laws enacted by slaveholders for the government of their slaves, and must tend to debase and depress the mind of that being, whom God created as a help meet for man, or "helper like unto himself," and designed to be his equal and his companion. Until such laws are annulled, woman never can occupy that exalted station for which she was intended by her Maker. . . .

The various laws which I have transcribed leave women very little more liberty, or power, in some respects, than the slave. "A slave," says the civil code of Louisiana, "is one who is in the power of a master, to whom he belongs. He can possess nothing, nor acquire anything, but what must belong to his master." I do not wish by any means to intimate that the condition of free women can be compared to that of slaves in suffering, or in degradation; still, I believe the laws which deprive married women of their rights and privileges, have a tendency to lessen them in their own estimation as moral and responsible beings, and that their being made by civil law inferior to their husbands, has a debasing and mischievous effect upon them, teaching them practically the fatal lesson to look unto man for protection and indulgence.

Ecclesiastical bodies, I believe, without exception, follow the example of legislative assemblies, in excluding women from any participation in forming the discipline by which she is governed. The men frame the laws, and, with few exceptions, claim to execute them on both sexes. In ecclesiastical, as well as civil courts, woman is tried and condemned, not by a jury of her peers, but by beings, who regard themselves as her superiors in the scale of creation. Although looked upon as an inferior, when considered as an intellectual being, woman is punished with the same severity as man, when she is guilty of moral offenses. Her condition resembles, in some measure, that of the slave, who, while he is denied the advantages of his more enlightened master, is treated with even greater rigor of the law. Hoping that in the various reformations of the day, women may be relieved from some of their legal disabilities, I remain,

Thine in the bonds of womanhood,

SARAH M. GRIMKÉ

READING AND DISCUSSION QUESTIONS

1. What comparisons does Grimké see in the condition of women and slaves in antebellum America? How does she describe both in relation to the law?
2. Compare Grimké's attitude toward religion with the spiritual or transcendentalist perspective of Margaret Fuller (Document 10-1). Do the two writers see religion in the same way, as a help or a hindrance to women?

10-5 | Abolitionist Decries Slavery's Dehumanizing Power

DAVID WALKER, Preamble to *Walker's Appeal in Four Articles* (1830)

In his powerful *Appeal to the Coloured Citizens of the World*—first published in 1829, with two further editions published in 1830—David Walker (c. 1796–1830) offers a scorching attack on American slavery. Born free in North Carolina, Walker moved north, spending most of his short life in Boston, where he quickly became a leading abolitionist, deriding popular colonization plans embraced by many whites that aimed to send blacks "back" to Africa, a continent few African Americans, free or slave, had ever seen. Walker's preamble, excerpted here, is directed to a black audience who, he argues, must awaken to the cruelties of slavery and the hypocrisy of America and lead the charge for freedom.

My dearly beloved Brethren and Fellow Citizens.

Having travelled over a considerable portion of these United States, and having, in the course of my travels, taken the most accurate observations of things as they exist—the result of my observations has warranted the full and unshaken conviction, that we, (coloured people of these United States,) are the most degraded, wretched, and abject set of beings that ever lived since the world began; and I pray God that none like us ever may live again until time shall be no more. They tell us of the Israelites in Egypt, the Helots in Sparta, and of the Roman Slaves, which last were made up from almost every nation under heaven, whose sufferings under those ancient and heathen nations, were, in comparison with ours, under this enlightened and Christian nation, no more than a cypher—or, in other words, those heathen nations of antiquity, had but little more among them than the name and form of slavery; while wretchedness and endless miseries were reserved, apparently in a phial, to be poured out upon our fathers, ourselves and our children, by *Christian* Americans!

These positions I shall endeavour, by the help of the Lord, to demonstrate in the course of this *Appeal*, to the satisfaction of the most incredulous mind—and may God Almighty, who is the Father of our Lord Jesus Christ, open your hearts to understand and believe the truth.

David Walker, *Walker's Appeal in Four Articles* (Boston: Revised and Published by David Walker, 1830), 3–5.

The *causes*, my brethren, which produce our wretchedness and miseries, are so very numerous and aggravating, that I believe the pen only of a Josephus or a Plutarch, can well enumerate and explain them. Upon subjects, then, of such incomprehensible magnitude, so impenetrable, and so notorious, I shall be obliged to omit a large class of, and content myself with giving you an exposition of a few of those, which do indeed rage to such an alarming pitch, that they cannot but be a perpetual source of terror and dismay to every reflecting mind.

I am fully aware, in making this appeal to my much afflicted and suffering brethren, that I shall not only be assailed by those whose greatest earthly desires are, to keep us in abject ignorance and wretchedness, and who are of the firm conviction that Heaven has designed us and our children to be slaves and *beasts of burden* to them and their children. I say, I do not only expect to be held up to the public as an ignorant, impudent and restless disturber of the public peace, by such avaricious creatures, as well as a mover of insubordination—and perhaps put in prison or to death, for giving a superficial exposition of our miseries, and exposing tyrants. But I am persuaded, that many of my brethren, particularly those who are ignorantly in league with slaveholders or tyrants, who acquire their daily bread by the blood and sweat of their more ignorant brethren—and not a few of those too, who are too ignorant to see an inch beyond their noses, will rise up and call me cursed—Yea, the jealous ones among us will perhaps use more abject subtlety, by affirming that this work is not worth perusing, that we are well situated, and there is no use in trying to better our condition, for we cannot. I will ask one question here.—Can our condition be any worse?—Can it be more mean and abject? If there are any changes, will they not be for the better though they may appear for the worst at first? Can they get us any lower? Where can they get us? They are afraid to treat us worse, for they know well, the day they do it they are gone. But against all accusations which may or can be preferred against me, I appeal to Heaven for my motive in writing—who knows that my object is, if possible, to awaken in the breasts of my afflicted, degraded and slumbering brethren, a spirit of inquiry and investigation respecting our miseries and wretchedness in this Republican Land of Liberty!!!!!!

READING AND DISCUSSION QUESTIONS

1. Upon what basis does Walker seek to challenge American slavery? Why do you think he believes his argument has persuasive power?
2. What obstacles does Walker acknowledge facing in launching his attack? Were you surprised by some of them and, if so, why?

10-6 | Race and American Popular Culture
Jim Crow Jubilee (1847)

In the early 1830s, New Yorker Thomas Dartmouth Rice began performing on stage as Jumping Jim Crow, a caricature he popularized of an enslaved black man. Rice, a white man, painted his face black, wore threadbare clothes, and danced and sang songs in an exaggerated dialect meant to lampoon African Americans. It was a hit. His shows, and those of his imitators, became immensely popular, especially among the white working-class audiences of northern cities. Jim Crow became a stock character throughout the nineteenth century. After the Civil War, the name came to describe the system of racial segregation that persisted into the mid-twentieth century. This source is the cover of sheet music for "Jim Crow Jubilee," a collection of "Negro Melodies" arranged for the piano. Many middle-class families in the 1840s owned pianos, and they would have purchased sheet music for use at home.

Sheridan Libraries/Levy/Gado/Getty Images

READING AND DISCUSSION QUESTIONS

1. What does this image suggest about white attitudes toward African Americans during this period? How are African Americans portrayed?
2. What argument about American culture during the 1840s can you make by analyzing this artifact? What does it suggest about American culture that sheet music was produced with these images?

▪ COMPARATIVE QUESTIONS ▪

1. What ideal of American society emerges when you compare the various reformers highlighted in this chapter?
2. What were the limits or obstacles reformers encountered in the antebellum period?
3. How important was religion in shaping antebellum reform efforts?
4. Which do you think was the stronger appeal during this period: the idea of American individualism or the idea of community? Explain.

11

Imperial Ambitions

1820–1848

Catching the spirit of the times, a young Walt Whitman asked in 1846: "What has miserable, inefficient Mexico—with her superstition, her burlesque upon freedom, her actual tyranny by the few over the many—what has she to do with the great mission of peopling the new world with a noble race? Be it ours, to achieve that mission!" America's poet of democracy spoke the language of Manifest Destiny, the ideology of expansion that caused the U.S.-Mexico War (1846–1848), fueled the subsequent sectional crisis, and led ultimately to the Civil War. America's territorial ambitions were fueled by northerners seeking market opportunities and homesteads and by southern planters seeking to expand the slave-cotton economy. But their ambitions were met by Native Americans and Europeans whose presence staked competing claims on the plains and the West.

With the land in the Old South growing exhausted from decades of intensive planting, many southerners embraced territorial expansion to seek more fertile fields to grow their slave-produced cotton empires. This impacted the politics of the era, but it had lasting consequences on the lives of enslaved people whose fate became increasingly determined by the economics of the plantation economy. Remarkably, African Americans, both free and enslaved, built a world of their own within the expanding empire of oppression.

11-1 | Southern Hospitality on Display

SUSAN DABNEY SMEDES, *Memorials of a Southern Planter* (1887)

The planter class in the Old South cultivated a self-image as benevolent stewards whose sense of *noblesse oblige* (the idea that those of high social rank are obligated to help those of low rank) led naturally to their open hospitality and gentle nurturing of their "servants," a common euphemism for slaves. The reality was frequently at odds with the romance they created. The image was part of their broader appreciation of the differences they drew between themselves and northerners, whom they frequently viewed as less genteel, more cold-fisted capitalists intruding into their affairs. Susan Smedes's memoir of her father, Thomas Smith Gregory Dabney, is a classic example of the genre: a flattering portrait of a "good master" who treated his slaves as family, and whose love and affection was returned by the grateful servants. Here, Smedes remembers holiday celebrations at Burleigh, her father's plantation in Lebanon, Mississippi, where he had moved his family in the early 1830s, part of the migration of planters in search of more productive soil.

A Southern Planter

. . . Managing a plantation was something like managing a kingdom. The ruler had need of a great store, not only of wisdom, but of tact and patience as well.

When there was trouble in the house the real kindness and sympathy of the servants came out. They seemed to anticipate every wish. In a thousand touching little ways they showed their desire to give all the comfort and help that lay in their power. They seemed to claim a right to share in the sorrow that was their master's, and to make it their own. It was small wonder that the master and mistress were forbearing and patient when the same servants who sorrowed with them in their affliction should, at times, be perverse in their days of prosperity. Many persons said that the Burleigh servants were treated with overindulgence. It is true that at times some of them acted like spoiled children, seeming not to know what they would have. Nothing went quite to their taste at these times. The white family would say among themselves, "What is the matter now? Why these martyr-like looks?" Mammy Maria usually threw light on these occasions. She was disgusted with her race for posing as martyrs when there was no grievance. . . .

Holiday Times on the Plantation

A life of Thomas Dabney could not be written without some reference to the Christmas at Burleigh. It was as looked forward to not only by the family and by friends in the neighborhood and at a distance, but by the house and plantation servants. The house was crowded with guests, young people and older ones too. . . . On one of the nights during the holidays it was his custom to invite his

---

Susan Dabney Smedes, *Memorials of a Southern Planter* (Baltimore: Cushings & Bailey, 1887), 115–117, 160–163.

former overseer and other plain neighbors to an eggnog-party. In the concoction of this beverage he took a hand himself, and the freedom and ease of the company, as they saw the master of the house beating his half of the eggs in the great china bowl, made it a pleasant scene for those who cared nothing for the eggnog. . . .

Sometimes, not often, there was a Christmas-tree,—on one occasion one for the colored Sunday-school. One Christmas everybody hung up a sock or stocking; a long line, on the hall staircase. There were twenty-two of them, white silk stockings, black silk stockings, thread and cotton and woollen socks and stockings. And at the end of the line was, side by side with the old-fashioned home-spun and home-knit sock of the head of the house, the dainty pink sock of the three-weeks-old baby.

Who of that company does not remember the morning scramble over the stockings and the notes in prose and poetry that tumbled out!

Music and dancing and cards and games of all sorts filled up a large share of the days and half the nights. The plantation was as gay as the house. The negroes in their holiday clothes were enjoying themselves in their own houses and in the "great house" too. A visit of a day to one of the neighboring towns was considered by them necessary to the complete enjoyments of the holidays.

They had their music and dancing too. The sound of the fiddles and banjos, and the steady rhythm of their dancing feet, floated on the air by day and night to the Burleigh house. But a time came when this was to cease. The whole plantation joined the Baptist church. Henceforth not a musical note nor the joyful motion of a negro's foot was ever again heard on the plantation. "I done buss' my fiddle an' my banjo, an' done fling 'em 'way," the most music-loving fellow on the place said to the preacher, when asked for his religious experience. It was surely the greatest sacrifice of feeling that such a race could make. Although it was a sin to have music and dancing of their own, it was none to enjoy that at the "great house." They filled the porches and doors, and in serried ranks stood men, women, and children, gazing as long as the music and dancing went on. Frequently they stood there till the night was more than half gone. In the crowd of faces could be recognized the venerable ones of the aged preachers, surrounded by their flocks. . . .

On Christmas mornings the servants delighted in catching the family with "Christmas giff!" "Christmas giff!" betimes in the morning. They would spring out of unexpected corners and from behind doors on the young masters and mistresses. At such times there was an affectionate throwing off of the reserve and decorum of every-day life.

"Hi! ain't dis Chris'mus?" one of the quietest and most low-voiced of the maid-servants asked, in a voice as loud as a sea-captain's. One of the ladies of the house had heard an unfamiliar and astonishingly loud laugh under her window, and had ventured to put an inquiring head out.

In times of sorrow, when no Christmas or other festivities gladdened the Mississippi home, the negroes felt it sensibly. "It 'pears so lonesome; it mak' me feel bad not to see no comp'ny comin'," our faithful Aunt Abby said on one of these occasions. Her post as the head maid rendered her duties onerous when the house was full of guests. We had thought that she would be glad to have a quiet Christmas, which she could spend by her own fireside, instead of attending to the wants of a houseful of young people.

In the presence of the guests, unless they were old friends, the dignity of the family required that no light behavior should be indulged in, even though it were Christmas. In no hands was the dignity of the family so safe as with negro slaves. A negro was as proud of the "blood" of his master and mistress as if it had been his own. Indeed, they greatly magnified the importance of their owners, and were readily affronted if aspersion of any sort were cast on their master's family. It was very humiliating to them, for they are all aristocrats by nature, to belong to what they call "poor white trash."

Our steady Lewis was often sent to take us to evening entertainments, on account of his being so quiet and nice in his ways. On one of these occasions he became so incensed that he refused to set his foot on that plantation again. Mammy Maria informed us of the cause of Lewis's anger. One of the maids in the house in which we were spending the evening had insulted him by saying that her mistress wore more trimming on her clothes than his young ladies did!

READING AND DISCUSSION QUESTIONS

1. Analyze and evaluate Smedes's description of the family's relationship with the slaves living and working at Burleigh. What point of view about the slaves' feelings toward the family does she emphasize?
2. From the portrait Smedes offers of her father, what do you imagine his reaction would have been had one of his slaves escaped?
3. Analyze the role hospitality played in shaping a southern planter's perception of his roles and responsibilities on the plantation and within the broader community. To what extent did his welcoming generosity have political implications? What role did slaves play in the hospitality of the plantation?

11-2 | Private Life of Enslaved African Americans

Slave Songs of the United States (1867) and *Slaves Dance to Their Own Music on a Southern Plantation* (c. 1852)

Enslaved African Americans left few written records like diaries or letters, so historians' attempts to re-create their spiritual and intellectual world are fraught with difficulties. The two sources included here, the lyrics from a slave spiritual and an 1850s lithograph of slave life on a plantation, provide tantalizing clues to the world enslaved African Americans were able to create despite the limitations of slavery. Masters sometimes encouraged Christian conversion among slaves, underscoring passages defending slavery as the punishment for sin, but slaves adapted Protestant Christianity to their own purposes. They rejected the interpretation to obey one's master, which whites emphasized, for a gospel of deliverance and communal salvation as seen in this spiritual, "Michael Row the Boat Ashore." Even though the image depicts a white person's interpretation of slave life, it reveals the role music played in shaping what leisure they had.

William Francis Allen, Charles Pickard Ware, and Lucy McKim Garrison, *Slave Songs of the United States* (New York: A. Simpson & Co., 1867), 23–24.

Michael Row the Boat Ashore

Michael row de boat ashore, Hallelujah!
Michael boat a gospel boat, Hallelujah!
I wonder where my mudder deh [there].
See my mudder on de rock gwine home.
On de rock gwine home in Jesus' name.
Michael boat a music boat.
Gabriel blow de trumpet horn.
O you mind your boastin' talk.
Boastin' talk will sink your soul.
Brudder, lend a helpin' hand.
Sister, help for trim dat boat.
Jordan stream is wide and deep.
Jesus stand on t'oder side.
I wonder if my maussa deh.
My fader gone to unknown land.
O de Lord he plant his garden deh.
He raise de fruit for you to eat.
He dat eat shall neber die.
When de riber overflow.
O poor sinner, how you land?
Riber run and darkness comin'.
Sinner row to save your soul.

Slaves dance to their own music on a Southern plantation, c. 1852 (color litho)/American School (19th century) /PETER NEWARK'S PICTURES/Private Collection/Bridgeman Images

READING AND DISCUSSION QUESTIONS

1. What challenges and opportunities do historians face in using these types of sources as historical evidence? How are songs, as sources, different from diaries or letters?
2. What historical argument about the lives of slaves can you make by analyzing and interpreting the lyrics of slave songs and images of slave life?
3. What kinds of imagery do the song lyrics evoke? What kinds of messages do the lyrics convey?

11-3 | The Lure of the West

LANSFORD HASTINGS, *The Emigrants' Guide to Oregon and California* (1845)

While many southerners pushed westward to expand the slave-cotton economy, others sought escape and riches in the far West, encouraged by books like Lansford Hastings's *The Emigrants' Guide to Oregon and California*. An example of "booster" literature, the guide provided practical advice about routes to follow, items to bring, and destinations to settle. Guides such as this were sometimes embroidered with exaggeration. In this case, Hastings, who had made an overland trek to Oregon in 1842, hoped to entice emigrants to California, then still a province of Mexico. His hopes for an independent republic of California ended when Mexico ceded California to the United States as part of the 1848 Treaty of Guadalupe Hidalgo, which ended the U.S.-Mexico War.

The settlements and improvements, which are disconnected with the forts and missions, are chiefly at the Wallammette valley, the Fualitine plains, and the Wallammette falls. The settlement at the Wallammette valley, is at present, the most extensive settlement in the country. It contains about one hundred families, who have extensive farms, and who are otherwise comfortably situated. Each of the farmers in this valley, generally have, from one hundred to five hundred acres of land under fence, and in a good state of cultivation, upon which, they grow annually, from five hundred to a thousand bushels of wheat for exportation, besides beans, peas and potatoes, turnips and various other vegetables, which they grow in great abundance. They also usually rear cattle, horses, sheep and hogs, in large numbers; each farmer generally having, from fifty to five hundred head of cattle, from ten to one hundred head of horses, and as many sheep and hogs; for all of which, the continued, annual emigration, affords an ample market. . . . In the winter of 1843, a town was laid off, near the falls, which has since improved, with unparalleled rapidity. . . . In the autumn of 1843, there were fifty three buildings in this town,

Lansford W. Hastings, *The Emigrants' Guide, to Oregon and California, Containing Scenes and Incidents of a Party of Oregon Emigrants* (Cincinnati: George Conclin, 1845; rept., Bedford, MA: Applewood Books, n.d.), 55–59.

among which, were four stores, four mills, two of which were flouring mills, one public-house, one black smith's shop and various other mechanic's shops; a church was also in contemplation, and in fact, commenced. Many of the lots, which were obtained gratuitously, only the spring previous, were then worth at least, one thousand dollars each, and their value was daily increasing, with the improvements of the town. Such were the improvements of Oregon City, in the autumn of 1843, but about eight months, after its emergent appearance. Oregon City is situated upon a very favorable site for a town, and it is, beyond a doubt, destined to become a place of very considerable manufacturing and commercial importance. . . . For the present, and until other towns spring up, emigrants will, in a great measure, concentrate at this place, especially merchants, mechanics and those of the learned professions. But other towns are already, springing into existence, as additional evidences of the unbounded energy and enterprise of American citizens. . . .

The buildings in Oregon City, are, with a few exceptions, framed and well-finished. Including saw and flouring mills, there are now fourteen in Oregon, many of which, are doing a very extensive and profitable business; and there are innumerable sites for mills and other machinery, which are destined, soon to be occupied. There are perhaps, very few countries which afford more numerous, or more advantageous sites for the most extensive water power than Oregon. The people of this territory, in their anxiety to provide for their individual necessities, and to promote their individual interests, have paid but very little attention to the making of roads, and other public improvements. Traveling and transportation, are, as yet, chiefly on horseback, and by water, but from the nature of the soil however, there can be no difficulty, in making good roads, and thereby, rendering intercommunication easy, and transportation cheap, throughout all portions of the country. The foregoing facts, in reference to the improvements of Oregon, afford a few evidences of the very enterprising character of the Oregon emigrants; but a further evidence is found in the fact of their having recently sent to New York for a printing-press and a steam-engine, which will be received sometime during the next summer or autumn; when the same energy and enterprise that procured them, will soon put them into extensive and successful operation. . . .

In every thing that tends to the advancement of the interests of the country, there appears to be a hearty co-operation, between the gentlemen of the Hudson Bay Company, and the American citizens. As one instance of extraordinary, and entire devotion to the best interest of the country, the whole community, with one unanimous voice, determined to abandon the use of all alcoholic or inebriating liquors; and to prevent their introduction or sale, under any state of circumstances. In this measure, the gentlemen of the company perform a very efficient part, and although their own store-houses are full of intoxicating liquors, they sell none to any person. . . . This certainly speaks volumes, for the morality and intelligence of the citizens of Oregon, and it is, no doubt, the chief cause of all that order and quiet, which so universally prevail, throughout all the different settlements.

A kindness and hospitality exist, among those pioneers of the west, which is almost unparalleled. Upon the arrival of emigrants, in the country, immediate arrangements are made by the former settlers, to provide them with houses and provisions, and every aid is rendered them in making their selections of lands, and procuring houses for themselves. . . .

There are several powerful and warlike tribes of Indians, occupying each of the different sections. The principal tribes inhabiting the Eastern section, are the Shoshonies, or Snakes, the Black-feet, and the Bonarks. The Nezpercies also frequent this section, but their country is properly in the Middle section, where they are principally found. The Indians of this section are much less advanced in civilization, than those of the other sections. They are all said to be friendly, excepting the Black-feet, who have always been hostile. Emigrants, however, very seldom meet with them, in traveling to Oregon, by the way of Fort Hall, as their country lies far to the north of that route. They are not to be dreaded, however, when met by a large party of whites; even forty or fifty armed men, are ample to deter them from any hostile movements. They should always be considered, and treated as enemies, whatever may be their pretensions of friendship. . . . Petit larceny is the most common offence committed at these places, while grand larceny, and robbery are constantly being committed by them elsewhere; but as they are "friendly," murder is an offence which they seldom commit.

READING AND DISCUSSION QUESTIONS

1. What can you infer about Hastings's audience from the details he chose to share about migrating to the Oregon and California territories?
2. What conclusions can you draw from this source about the experience of traveling in the mid-nineteenth century?
3. Compare Hastings's book with modern travel guides (or Web sites) you may have seen or used. How do you interpret the differences you see?

11-4 | Romanticizing the Frontier

GEORGE CALEB BINGHAM, *The Jolly Flatboatmen* (1846)

While Lansford Hastings's guide (Document 11-3) provided practical advice to travelers heading west, the paintings of George Caleb Bingham offered viewers a visual celebration of the American frontier. Though he was born in Virginia, Bingham grew up in Missouri and taught himself to paint. In the mid-1840s, as "Manifest Destiny" captured the imaginations of many Americans, Bingham began painting canvasses depicting life on the Missouri and Mississippi rivers. His romanticizing of this frontier experience no doubt appealed to those enthralled by the West and its promise of riches, independence, and adventure. In this painting, one of Bingham's most popular works, he portrays a group of boatmen in a moment of leisure as they float their way downriver.

The Jolly Flatboatmen, 1846 (oil on canvas)/Bingham, George Caleb (1811–79)/National Gallery of Art, Washington DC, USA/Bridgeman Images

READING AND DISCUSSION QUESTIONS

1. Reproductions of Bingham's painting sold by the thousands in the two decades after he completed it. Why do you think that was the case? What is it about this image that may have struck a chord with so many viewers?
2. Bingham's painting is a celebration of the American frontier, but what did he leave out of his image? Do you think the real boatmen on the Missouri and Mississippi rivers would have identified with his depiction of their lives?

11-5 | Two Views of the War with Mexico

JOHN D. SLOAT, *To the Inhabitants of California* (1846), and GENERAL FRANCISCO MEJIA, *A Proclamation at Matamoros* (1846)

In 1846, General Francisco Mejia was the commander of Mexico's military forces at Matamoros, a city on the southern bank of the Rio Grande, opposite the U.S. troops that President James K. Polk had ordered forward to provoke a war with Mexico. The United States and Mexico disputed the southern border of Texas, recently annexed by the United States as its twenty-eighth state. Once hostilities broke out, Commodore John

D. Sloat of the U.S. Navy stationed off California, then a province of Mexico, landed at Monterey and claimed California as a territory of the United States. These sources present conflicting perspectives on the cause of the U.S. war with Mexico.

To the Inhabitants of California

The central government of Mexico having commenced hostilities against the United States of America, by invading its territory and attacking the troops of the United States stationed on the north side of the Rio Grande, and with a force of seven thousand men, under the command of General Arista, which army was totally destroyed and all their artillery, baggage, &c., captured on the 8th and 9th of May last, by a force of two thousand three hundred men, under the command of General Taylor, and the city of Matamoras taken and occupied by the forces of the United States; and the two nations being actually at war by this transaction, I shall hoist the standard of the United States at Monterey immediately, and shall carry it throughout California.

I declare to the inhabitants of California, that although I come in arms with a powerful force, I do not come among them as an enemy to California; on the contrary, I come as their best friend as henceforward California will be a portion of the United States, and its peaceable inhabitants will enjoy the same rights and privileges they now enjoy; together with the privileges of choosing their own magistrates and other officers for the administration of justice among themselves, and the same protection will be extended to them as to any other State in the Union. They will also enjoy a permanent government under which life, property and the constitutional right and lawful security to worship the Creator in the way most congenial to each one's sense of duty will be secured, which unfortunately the central government of Mexico cannot afford them, destroyed as her resources are by internal factions and corrupt officers, who create constant revolutions to promote their own interests and to oppress the people. Under the flag of the United States California will be free from all such troubles and expense, consequently the country will rapidly advance and improve both in agriculture and commerce; as of course the revenue laws will be the same in California as in all other parts of the United States, affording them all manufactures and produce of the United States, free of any duty, and all foreign goods at one quarter of the duty they now pay, a great increase in the value of real estate and the products of California may also be anticipated.

With the great interest and kind feelings I know the government and people of the United States possess towards the citizens of California, the country cannot but improve more rapidly than any other on the continent of America. Such of the inhabitants of California, whether natives or foreigners, as may not be disposed to accept the high privileges of citizenship, and to live peaceably under the government of the United States, will be allowed time to dispose of

---

JOHN D. SLOAT, To the Inhabitants of California (1846), and GENERAL FRANCISCO MEJIA, A Proclamationat Matamoros (1846) from Taylor, Z., Scott, W., & Trist, N. P. (1848). Messages of the President of the United States: With the Correspondence, Therewith Communicated, Between the Secretary of War and Other Officers of the Government, on the Subject of the Mexican War (No. 60). Wendell and Van Benthuysen, printers.

their property and to remove out of the country, if they choose, without any restriction, or remain in it, observing strict neutrality.

With full confidence in the honor and integrity of the inhabitants of the country, I invite the judges, alcaldes,[1] and other civil officers, to retain their offices and to execute their functions as heretofore, that the public tranquility may not be disturbed; at least, until the government of the territory can be more definitely arranged.

All persons holding titles to real estate, or in quiet possession of lands under a color of right, shall have those titles and rights guarantied to them.

All churches, and the property they contain, in possession of the clergy of California, shall continue in the same rights and possessions they now enjoy.

All provisions and supplies of every kind, furnished by the inhabitants for the use of United States ships and soldiers, will be paid for at fair rates, and no private property will be taken for public use without just compensation at the moment.

JOHN D. SLOAT,
Commander-in-chief of the United States naval forces in the Pacific ocean.
United States Flag-ship Savannah, Harbor of Monterey, July 7, 1846.

A Proclamation by the General-in-Chief of the Forces Assembled Against the Enemy, to the Inhabitants of This Department and the Troops Under His Command

FELLOW-CITIZENS: The annexation of the department of Texas to the United States, projected and consummated by the tortuous policy of the cabinet of the Union, does not yet satisfy the ambitious desires of the degenerate sons of Washington. The civilized world has already recognized in that act all the marks of injustice, iniquity, and the most scandalous violation of the rights of nations. Indelible is the stain which will for ever darken the character for virtue falsely attributed to the people of the United States; and posterity will regard with horror their perfidious conduct, and the immorality of the means employed by them to carry into effect that most degrading depredation. The right of conquest has always been a crime against humanity; but nations jealous of their dignity and reputation have endeavoured at least to cover it by the splendour of arms and the prestige of victory. To the United States, it has been reserved to put in practice dissimulation, fraud, and the basest treachery, in order to obtain possession, in the midst of peace, of the territory of a friendly nation, which generously relied upon the faith of promises and the solemnity of treaties.

The cabinet of the United States does not, however, stop in its career of usurpation. Not only does it aspire to the possession of the department of Texas, but it covets also the regions on the left bank of the Rio Bravo. Its army, hitherto for some time stationed at Corpus Christi, is now advancing to take possession of a large part of Tamaulipas; and its vanguard has arrived at the Arroya Colorado, distant eighteen leagues from this place. What expectations, therefore, can the

[1] **Alcalde**: A local judicial and administrative officer.

Mexican government have of treating with an enemy, who, whilst endeavouring to lull us into security, by opening diplomatic negotiations, proceeds to occupy a territory which never could have been the object of the pending discussion? The limits of Texas are certain and recognized; never have they extended beyond the river Nueces; notwithstanding which, the American army has crossed the line separating Tamaulipas from that department. Even though Mexico could forget that the United States urged and aided the rebellion of the former colonists, and that the principle, giving to an independent people the right to annex itself to another nation, is not applicable to the case, in which the latter has been the protector of the independence of the former, with the object of admitting it into its own bosom; even though it could be accepted as an axiom of international law, that the violation of every rule of morality and justice might serve as a legitimate title for acquisition; nevertheless, the territory of Tamaulipas would still remain beyond the law of annexation, sanctioned by the American Congress; because that law comprises independent Texas, the ground occupied by the rebellious colony, and in no wise includes other departments, in which the Mexican government has uninterruptedly exercised its legitimate authority.

Fellow-countrymen: With an enemy which respects not its own laws, which shamelessly derides the very principles invoked by it previously, in order to excuse its ambitious views, we have no other resource than arms. We are fortunately always prepared to take them up with glory, in defence of our country; little do we regard the blood in our veins, when we are called on to shed it in vindication of our honour, to assure our nationality and independence. If to the torrent of devastation which threatens us it be necessary to oppose a dike of steel, our swords will form it; and on their sharp points will the enemy receive the fruits of his anticipated conquest. If the banks of the Panuco have been immortalized by the defeat of an enemy, respectable and worthy of the valour of Mexico, those of the Bravo shall witness the ignominy of the proud sons of the north, and its deep waters shall serve as the sepulchre for those who dare to approach it. The flames of patriotism which burns in our hearts will receive new fuel from the odious presence of the conquerors; and the cry of Dolores and Iguala[2] shall be re-echoed with harmony to our ears, when we take up our march to oppose our naked breasts to the rifles of the hunters of the Mississippi.

FRANCISCO MEJIA,
Matamoros, March 18, 1846.

READING AND DISCUSSION QUESTIONS

1. Compare how each of these sources describes the conflict between the United States and Mexico. What is the cause of the conflict each identifies?
2. To what extent does each author tailor his message to the specific audience he is addressing? What can you infer about the audience from the language of each source?

[2] **Dolores and Iguala**: Two Mexican cities traditionally associated with the beginning and the end of the Mexican War for Independence (1810–1821).

11-6 | An Attack on Polk's Mexican Policy

RICHARD DOYLE, *The Land of Liberty* (1847)

Punch was a British magazine known for its satire and pointed cartoons. Published in London beginning in 1841, the magazine also covered events in the United States and, as is shown in this 1847 cartoon, it did not shy away from making fun of American policies and politicians. During the 1840s, Britain and the United States disputed territorial claims in the Pacific Northwest, but they brokered a settlement in June 1846 defining the northern boundary of the United States at the forty-ninth parallel. By that point, President James K. Polk, the relaxed figure in the cartoon's foreground, had already persuaded Congress to declare war on Mexico. This cartoon is *Punch*'s commentary on Polk's foreign and domestic policies.

"The Land of Liberty," cartoon from *Punch Magazine*, 1847 (engraving) (b/w photo)/Doyle, Richard (1824–83)/Private Collection/Bridgeman Images

READING AND DISCUSSION QUESTIONS

1. Analyze the elements of this cartoon. What can you infer about the cartoonist's attitude toward President Polk?
2. What policies of the Polk administration is the cartoonist singling out? Why, for example, is he referencing both the U.S.-Mexico War and slavery?
3. What is the significance of the "Texas" and "Oregon" sheets of paper at Polk's elbow? Why is his leg resting on the overturned bust of Washington?

▪ COMPARATIVE QUESTIONS ▪

1. Chapters 8 to 11 have covered the same time period but through different thematic lenses. Assess this chapter's theme of territorial expansion as one of the era's overlapping revolutions. What makes territorial expansion a revolutionary idea?
2. Compare the sources in this chapter to explain what motivated the territorial ambitions we see from the 1820s to the 1840s.
3. To what extent does the concept of Manifest Destiny provide a useful historical context for understanding the territorial expansion that drove the political conflict of the mid-nineteenth century?
4. Compare Henry Clay's 1840 campaign speech (Document 9-4) with the anti-Polk political cartoon from *Punch* magazine (Document 11-6). Explain to what extent these sources share a similar political perspective.

PART 4

DOCUMENT SET

Environment and Identity in an Age of Revolutions

1800–1848

The profound political, economic, and social transformations we associate with the first half of the nineteenth century took place within a physical context shaped by North America's environment, geography, and climate. America was largely an agricultural nation, and its climate and geography drove economic and political decisions and forged distinctive regional identities. The rocky soil and short growing season of the Northeast, for example, discouraged the adoption of the plantation system, which took root instead on the arable soils of the more temperate southern states.

Americans chose to interpret, preserve, manage, or exploit the natural world in ways that reflected the different physical environments they faced. Most often, nature presented challenges to overcome, as was the case for farmers who had to clear the land of trees before sowing seeds or canal workers who had to dig ditches to enable waterborne commerce. Nature also provided riches in the form of agricultural bounty and deposits of minerals and precious metals, which Americans commoditized to fuel their growing economy. The landscape could also inspire with its transcendent beauty. Americans' complex interaction with nature both constrained and shaped the lives they led and the world they created.

P4-1 | Commerce Overcomes Nature's Obstacles
Process of Excavation, Erie Canal, Lockport (c. 1820s)

The decade of the 1820s was a "canal era" in America's economic development. The Erie Canal was completed in 1825, connecting New York's Hudson River to the Great Lakes, a distance of more than three hundred miles. Its success inspired other efforts, and soon "artificial rivers" transporting goods and people more quickly than had ever been possible before connected the nation's interior regions. These internal improvements had obvious economic benefits, but they were also marvels of engineering and labor. As this 1820s lithograph shows, the building of canals pitted human ingenuity and effort against the obstacles of geography imposed by nature.

From The New York Public Library

READING AND DISCUSSION QUESTIONS

1. What evidence does this image provide for understanding the relationship between America's commercial development and the natural world?
2. To what extent does the confidence of canal builders as shown here reflect the historical context of the 1820s Market Revolution?
3. What can you infer about the artist's attitude toward nature from this illustration of workers moving rock to create a canal?

P4-2 | Cultivating the "Garden of Graves"

JOSEPH STORY, *Address Delivered on the Dedication of the Cemetery at Mount Auburn* (1831)

The rural cemetery movement in America began in the early 1830s when Jacob Bigelow's idea of domesticating a landscape into a parklike setting for the final repose of the deceased won approval and resulted in the opening outside Boston of the Mount Auburn Cemetery. This idealization of nature ran counter to earlier landscape manipulations of the eighteenth century, which had emphasized formal, symmetrical plans. At Mount Auburn and similar sites that followed, the living were intended to enjoy the cemetery as a place of recreation and leisure in a cultivated setting "improved" by man's design and management. Massachusetts native Joseph Story, associate justice of the Supreme Court, participated in the dedication ceremonies opening Mount Auburn, where he was interred when he died in 1845.

A rural Cemetery seems to combine in itself all the advantages, which can be proposed to gratify human feelings, or tranquillize human fears; to secure the best religious influences, and to cherish all those associations, which cast a cheerful light over the darkness of the grave.

And what spot can be more appropriate than this for such a purpose? Nature seems to point it out with significant energy, as the favourite retirement for the dead. There are around us all the varied features of her beauty and grandeur—the forest-crowned height; the abrupt acclivity; the sheltered valley; the deep glen; the grassy glade, and the silent grove. Here are the lofty oak, the beech, that "wreathes its old fantastick roots so high," the rustling pine, and the drooping willow;—the tree, that sheds its pale leaves with every autumn, a fit emblem of our own transitory bloom; and the evergreen, with its perennial shoots, instructing us, that "the wintry blast of death kills not the buds of virtue." Here is the thick shrubbery, to protect and conceal the new-made grave; and there is the wild-flower creeping along the narrow path, and planting its

Joseph Story, *An Address Delivered on the Dedication of the Cemetery at Mount Auburn, September 24, 1831* (Boston: Joseph T. & Edwin Buckingham, 1831), 16–22.

seeds in the upturned earth. All around us there breathes a solemn calm, as if we were in the bosom of a wilderness, broken only by the breeze as it murmurs through the tops of the forest, or by the notes of the warbler pouring forth his matin or his evening song.

Ascend but a few steps, and what a change of scenery to surprise and delight us. We seem, as it were, in an instant, to pass from the confines of death to the bright and balmy regions of life. Below us flows the winding Charles, with its rippling current, like the stream of time hastening to the ocean of eternity. In the distance, the City,—at once the object of our admiration and our love,—rears its proud eminences, its glittering spires, its lofty towers, its graceful mansions, its curling smoke, its crowded haunts of business and pleasure, which speak to the eye, and yet leave a noiseless loneliness on the ear. Again we turn, and the walls of our venerable University rise before us, with many a recollection of happy days passed there in the interchange of study and friendship, and many a grateful thought of the affluence of its learning, which has adorned and nourished the literature of our country. Again we turn, and the cultivated farm, the neat cottage, the village church, the sparkling lake, the rich valley, and the distant hills, are before us through opening vistas; and we breathe amidst the fresh and varied labours of man.

There is, therefore, within our reach, every variety of natural and artificial scenery, which is fitted to awaken emotions of the highest and most affecting character. We stand, as it were, upon the borders of two worlds; and as the mood of our minds may be, we may gather lessons of profound wisdom by contrasting the one with the other, or indulge in the dreams of hope and ambition, or solace our hearts by melancholy meditations.

Who is there that in the contemplation of such a scene, is not ready to exclaim, with the enthusiasm of the Poet,

Mine be the breezy hill, that skirts the down,
Where a green, grassy turf is all I crave,
With here and there a violet bestrown,
Fast by a brook, or fountain's murmuring wave,
And many an evening sun shine sweetly on my grave.

And we are met here to consecrate this spot, by these solemn ceremonies, to such a purpose. The Legislature of this Commonwealth, with a parental foresight, has clothed the Horticultural Society with authority (if I may use its own language) to make a perpetual dedication of it, as a Rural Cemetery or Burying-Ground, and to plant and embellish it with shrubbery, and flowers, and trees, and walks, and other rural ornaments. And I stand here, by the order and in behalf of this Society, to declare that, by these services, it is to be deemed henceforth and for ever so dedicated. Mount Auburn, in the noblest sense, belongs no longer to the living, but to the dead. It is a sacred, it is an eternal trust. It is consecrated ground. May it remain forever inviolate!

What a multitude of thoughts crowd upon the mind in the contemplation of such a scene. How much of the future, even in its far distant reaches, rises before us with all its persuasive realities. Take but one little narrow space of time, and how affecting are its associations! Within the flight of one half century, how many of the great, the good, and the wise will be gathered here! How many in the loveliness of infancy, the beauty of youth, the vigour of manhood, and the maturity of age, will lie down here, and dwell in the bosom of their mother earth! The rich and the poor, the gay and the wretched, the favourites of thousands, and the forsaken of the world, the stranger in his solitary grave, and the patriarch surrounded by the kindred of a long lineage! How many will here bury their brightest hopes, or blasted expectations! How many bitter tears will here be shed! How many agonizing sighs will here be heaved! How many trembling feet will cross the pathways, and returning, leave behind them the dearest objects of their reverence or their love!

And if this were all, sad indeed, and funereal would be our thoughts; gloomy, indeed, would be these shades, and desolate these prospects.

But—thanks be to God—the evils, which he permits, have their attendant mercies, and are blessings in disguise. The bruised reed will not be laid utterly prostrate. The wounded heart will not always bleed. The voice of consolation will spring up in the midst of the silence of these regions of death. The mourner will revisit these shades with a secret, though melancholy pleasure. The hand of friendship will delight to cherish the flowers, and the shrubs, that fringe the lowly grave, or the sculptured monument. The earliest beams of the morning will play upon these summits with a refreshing cheerfulness; and the lingering tints of evening hover on them with a tranquilizing glow. Spring will invite thither the footsteps of the young by its opening foliage; and Autumn detain the contemplative by its latest bloom. The votary of learning and science will here learn to elevate his genius by the holiest studies. The devout will here offer up the silent tribute of pity, or the prayer of gratitude. The rivalries of the world will here drop from the heart; the spirit of forgiveness will gather new impulses; the selfishness of avarice will be checked; the restlessness of ambition will be rebuked; vanity will let fall its plumes; and pride, as it sees "what shadows we are, and what shadows we pursue," will acknowledge the value of virtue as far, immeasurably far, beyond that of fame. . . .

Let us banish then, the thought, that this is to be the abode of a gloom, which will haunt the imagination by its terrors, or chill the heart by its solitude. Let us cultivate feelings and sentiments more worthy of ourselves, and more worthy of Christianity. Here let us erect the memorials of our love, and our gratitude, and our glory. Here let the brave repose, who have died in the cause of their country. Here let the statesman rest, who has achieved the victories of peace, not less renowned than war. Here let genius find a home, that has sung immortal strains, or has instructed with still diviner eloquence. Here let learning and science, the votaries of inventive art, and the teacher of the philosophy of nature come. Here let youth and beauty, blighted by premature decay, drop, like tender blossoms, into the virgin earth; and here let age retire, ripened for the harvest. Above all, here let the benefactors of mankind, the good, the merciful, the meek, the pure in heart, be congregated; for to them belongs an undying praise. And let us take comfort, nay, let us rejoice, that in future ages, long after we are gathered to the generations of other days, thousands of kindling hearts will here repeat the sublime declaration, "Blessed are the dead, that die in the Lord, for they rest from their labors; and their works do follow them."

READING AND DISCUSSION QUESTIONS

1. From Story's dedication, what can you infer about emerging American attitudes toward nature in the 1830s? What values does Story ascribe to the landscape?
2. How does Story summarize the benefits of this cultivated cemetery for both the living and the dead? What interaction with the landscape does Story anticipate his audience will experience?

P4-3 | Soil and Slaves in the Old South

A PLANTER, *Agricultural Prospects of Virginia* (1835)

By the time a Virginia planter wrote this article for the *Farmer's Reporter*, a monthly agricultural magazine, the farms of the state had been under cultivation for two centuries. Tobacco had been the staple crop during the colonial period, but in the late eighteenth century the economy shifted to cotton. New strains of cotton seed made its cultivation viable in those newly opened regions of the Southwest where native peoples had been expelled. The cotton economy boomed. Except in the Old South. This Virginia planter identifies some of the factors worrying him, including the exhaustion of the soil that diminished crop yields and the high demand for slaves in the Cotton Belt. This enticed some Virginia planters to sell their slaves rather than continue to plant crops on exhausted soil. As the plantation system became less lucrative for those in eastern Virginia, this Virginia planter wondered what might come of his "country."

For the Farmers' Register.
Agricultural Prospects of Virginia.

In viewing the effects of the system of agriculture pursued in eastern Virginia, the most careless observer will be struck with surprise, in comparing the small proportion of land in actual cultivation, with that which is lying waste and unimproved; and it will be increased will more when he reflects how small a part of the farm is regularly manured and kept in good condition, and fit for tillage. None of the farms afford manure enough to replace the produce taken from the fields, and keep them constantly increasing in fertility. The small quantity which is saved from the stable, farm pen, and other sources

"Agricultural Prospects of Virginia." In *The Farmers' Register,* pp. 762–764. Vol. 2. 1835.

being insufficient for the farm, is generally applied to the tobacco lots, or some favorite spot, while the rest of the farm is neglected, though perhaps regularly cultivated and grazed, or permitted to lie waste, yielding nothing but a scanty subsistence to a few half-starved cattle. The fences being thrown down, it soon becomes common pasturage, gullied, or grown up in pine barrens; its owner is restricted to a narrower limit in his system of exhaustion and destruction, until, becoming too much confined, or too much indebted, he sells out, and removes to a more fertile and cheaper soil in the west. Thousands are travelling the same road urged by the same causes. The educated, active, and enterprising young men, despairing of success with this example before them, are leaving the state very rapidly, to seek their fortunes in the west and south; and besides all this, the traders are carrying off our slaves in great numbers and thus annually diminishing in the ratio of the numbers carried off, the quantity of produce which would otherwise be made, and the prosperity of the country. The tide of emigration is regularly increasing from all classes; as if the angel of desolation had cursed the land, and imbued the people with a hatred to the place of their nativity. . . .

The present exhausted state of the country has been generally ascribed to the employment of *slave labor;* which, it is said, will always arrest the progress of improvement, because the slaves have not the capacity, nor do they feel interested to become skilful in their occupation. But the slovenly and negligent management visible on most farms need not necessarily belong to the state of slavery existing among us, as is proved by the high state of cultivation of the lands on James river, and in various small sections of almost every county in eastern Virginia. There is scarcely a person who is not acquainted with some farms cultivated to the very best advantage; and these exceptions prove that bad management, though a general, is not necessarily attendant upon the employment of slave labor. It can, therefore, offer no material obstruction to improved and successful cultivation.

The progress of rapid improvement has been opposed by that attachment to old customs, and disinclination to change old plans, which are almost as strong feelings with us as in those countries where it was regarded and punished as sacrilege, to depart from the occupation of their fathers. The first settlers of our state exhausted one piece of ground by continual cropping, then cleared and tended another piece of fresh land; and when that was exhausted, proceeded to a third. They preferred this, to raising manure, when land could be purchased for a few shillings per acre, and perhaps it was the cheapest course. Yet when lands have risen in value, and there is no reason to justify the same system of husbandry, it still prevails in many places, and is followed, "because their fathers made money in that way." The west, however, is now their resort, after ruining one piece of land by this destructive course. . . .

Besides these natural difficulties, which are incident to the cultivation of every country, there is one which is peculiar to our own state, and has generally been overlooked. I refer to the demand for slaves in the west and south, which materially affects the prosperity of our own state. . . .

It is well known to every person, that the greater fertility of the soils in the west and south, their suitability to the production of cotton and sugar will always enable the farmers of those sections to give a higher price for negroes, than the farmers of our own state—for the simple and obvious reason, that they can make larger profits from the produce of their labor. These profits, other things being equal, are almost always greatest in newly settled countries; and are here greatly increased by the superior fertility of the soil, and the enhanced value of its productions. So much larger are the profits of slave labor there, that they sell for nearly double the price which we can afford to give for them. The effect of this is already plainly perceptible; our slaves are carried there by thousands, and we cannot even enter into competition with them for their purchase. . . The farmers having poor lands will see that they can make greater profits by selling than by working them; hence they will sell all they can spare, stop the cultivation of the poor shills and confine themselves to the richest spots; the residue of the plantation being left to waste and lie unproductive. Such must be the fate of all the poor spots when the wages of labor are too high to enable the farmer to make some profit by working them; for it is absurd to suppose that any person will employ his capital or his labor, where it yields him no profit. . . What then, must be the necessary consequence? As we are, from adventitious circumstances, compelled to give more for negroes than they are really worth, and as this high price is entirely independent of the profits of their labor, their profits will be diminished. The farmer here will make smaller profits by agriculture upon all qualities of land, which cannot for the reasons before stated, make the slaves fall in price. For however small his profits here, that does not lower his price. The value of land must of necessity be reduced when the profits derived from its cultivation are lessened from any causes; capital will in consequence be withdrawn from that employment and invested in more productive stock. The poorest shills, yielding the smallest produce, will first be turned out of cultivation, instead of being reclaimed or improved. And while the general profits of farming are lessened, the farmer, so far from being compensated for improving his poor land, is scarcely rewarded when working his richest. When there are any two markets for labor in one of which double the price can be given, which can be afforded in the other, it is self-evident, that the labor will always be purchased where its price is the highest; and the market which cannot afford to pay so high, will always be depressed under the disadvantage of having to pay for labor higher than it is worth to them, and thus deduct from their profits. Thus the western and southern markets for our slaves, offer the greatest and most serious obstruction to the progress of improvement.

A Planter

Ashland, Halifax, VA,
Feb. 5, 1835

READING AND DISCUSSION QUESTIONS

1. Summarize the argument this Virginia planter makes regarding the prospects of the Old South. What factors does he cite in assessing Virginia's future?
2. What role did environmental factors play in shaping the economic viability of the plantation system in the Old South, according to this source?

P4-4 | A Woman's Perspective on the Overland Journey West

EMMELINE B. WELLS, *Diary* (1846)

The bucolic setting Joseph Story (Document P4-2) described contrasts with the unforgiving landscape through which Emmeline Wells journeyed in the mid-1840s, part of a Mormon exodus leaving Nauvoo, Illinois. The Mormons, or Latter-day Saints, a Christian denomination founded in 1830 by Joseph Smith (Document 10-2), were persecuted for their beliefs and practices. At Nauvoo in 1844 and 1845, a political crisis precipitated the Mormon flight westward to Utah. Wells fled with her family, keeping a diary that not only describes some of the trials they endured but also highlights the environmental factors that constrained and shaped her experiences heading west.

Sun. March 1, 1846

In the morning I awakened out of a sound sleep and saw Mary was preparing breakfast and the word was be ready to go at twelve o'clock we took breakfast; picked up and packed off as soon as possible, I rode with Orson in his wagon, about one o'clock we took up a line of march and left Sugar Creek, travelled over a very bad muddy road, reached the encampment about four o'clock, formed a line with the wagons, pitched their tents, made their fires and soon had a place fitted and prepared to pass the night. We are all happy and contented as yet and determined to go ahead.

Mon. March 2, 1846

This morning was warm and sunny the most pleasant day we have had since we left the city we stared behind the principal part of the teams. the first hill we came to a balking horse they had in the family wagon began to show his obstinacy and hindered us considerably we went on about seven miles and camped in a hollow with Br. Kimball's company Joseph's teams had gone on with the company ahead of us. and he was obliged to tent with his father. Sarah and I had a bed in the wagon and slept first-rate.

Tues. March 3, 1846

This morning [we] arose early and Sarah Ann taking her mother in her carriage and Joseph on horse back beside them went on to overtake their teams.

Diary (1846). Emmeline B. Wells' Diary, vol. 1 (Vault MSS 510) Perry Special Collections, Lee Library, Brigham Young University, Provo, Utah. Used by permission.

After breakfast Loenza Maria and I took a walk in the woods just behind the tent we found stems of strawberry leaves green and fresh I intend to keep them as a memorial of the time when we returned we found they were about starting Ann and I came up the hill which was very long on foot seated our selves on a prostrate log and here I am at the present time scribbling. We reached the place of encampment about noon having travelled 3 miles finding almost all of the teams had gone we proceeded on our journey together with Joseph he having waited for our coming. About ____________ miles ride brought us to Farmington a very pritty Western town. Here we saw thirty or more loafers loitering around the Groceries &c. Porter Rockwell on his mule rode up among them all armed and equipped which seemed to excite some of them considerably there being those there who knew him and they were overheard talking by themselves in a low tone of shooting &c. saying there would never be a better chance however nothing occurred of consequence. From the village we had a very bad road it was so dreadful muddy and crooked. Some of us walked along on the bank of the. Des moine considerable distance the roads being so exceedingly bad the horses could scarcly draw their loads. It was after dark when we came in sight of the camp and a dismal looking [place] it is the tents are all huddled in together and the [horses and] wagons are interspersed some are singing and laughing some are praying children crying &c. every sound may be heard from one tent to another; it is late and I must retire.

Wednesday March 4, 1846

We have stopped all day in order to recruit the teams they being nearly tired out after dragging through the mud. We have washed mended visited &c. It has been a very pleasant day.

Thursday March 5, 1846

This morn we started at ten o' clock. I walked perhaps a mile and a half along the shore of the Desmoine river when Porter came riding on his mule and said that [one of] Mr Whitney wagons had broke down I then went back to the wagons they were not yet up the first hill they took the load from the broken wagon and put it on another and hitched on the horses. We travelled about three miles and came to the village of Bonaparte a very pretty Western town here we forded the river; it was very bad travelling and continued to grow worse; we went about a mile farther and camped on the bank of the river where we have an excellent view of Bona. The rest of the company have gone on about two miles farther there are only the two families camped here.

Friday March 6, 1846

This morning at ten o clock we were again on the road which we found very muddy and bad until we came to the prairie there it was better. We arrived at the camp about three in the P.M. having travelled about eight miles the teams were very tired and so were some of the folks, we found they were on very damp ground by the side of a little muddy brook. After the tents were pitched Mr Whitney and Orson made a rustic bedstead of poles for Sarah.

Saturday March 7, 1846

This morning about the time we were ready to start a man by the name of Cochrun came and laid claim to a yoke of oxen belonging to Mr W. said they strayed or were stolen from him three years before to avoid trouble Mr. M paid him his price which was thirty dollars in gold. This day we have had rather better roads we travelled about nine miles and camped in a pleasant valley by a small stream of water about three miles from the principal encampment.

Sunday March 8, 1846

Today we have been detained in consequence of Sarah's being sick she has a fine boy her father has named this place the Valley of David in honor of the child it is situated in Iowa [2½ miles East of Richardson's] Point Chequest township Van Buren Co. At evening Brigham & Heber came down from the camp with Mary Ann Young & Vilate Kimball their wives, and, took supper and blessed the child; it has been a lovely day, warm and beautiful.

Monday March 9, 1846

About noon William Kimball came with an easy carriage, to convey S____________ to the camp; she started about two o'clock Horace and I rode in the buggy behind them, the teams followed after, all arrived in safety about four o'clock. Pitched their tents on the side hill, next to Dr. Kimball, the tents here in rows like [a] city; it is really a houseless village. Just at dusk the band commenced playing and some of the young people collected and amused themselves by dancing.

Tuesday March 10, 1846

This is a stormy day, a part of the camp intended to have moved on but it impossible; it is very muddy without yet the tents seem to be quite dry. Tuesday night at twelve o'clock the tent hooks on one side gave way and the tent pole leaned but from being on guard saved it from falling. The rain is pouring down in torrents here and there it sprinkles through the tent yet we keep a good fire and are quite comfortable.

Wednesday March 11, 1846

Today I slept till one o'clock after being up all night the rain had beat through the tent and wet my pillow and the quilts but I did not take cold Mrs W. has been quite [unwell] all day Sarah gets along finely. Horace has gone to Keosaugua to a concert I am sitting up again tonight.

Thursday March 12, 1846

It has been an unpleasant day at times a slow drizzly rain and then thick clouds gloomy and dismal they are all asleep around me Sarah is not quite so well to night.

March 19, 1846

We continued in this place being prevented by the mud until Thursday the 19. we then proceeded on our journey Sarah had an ox wagon fixed to ride in we left about eleven o'clock we had not gone far before S____________ began to grow sick from the easy rocking of the wagon and she was no better until we arrived at the stopping place

Friday March 20, 1846

This day has been cold and chilly we had a stove fixed in the wagon and a bed for Sarah; her mother, and I rode there with her we had pretty good road all day travelled about fouteen miles stopped in a mean damp place Sarah stayed in in her wagon and had a fire all night.

Saturday March 21, 1846

This morning we started at ten o'clock had a pretty decent road most of the way travelled eleven miles and camped in a pleasant place almost at the outside of the camp it has been a dark gloomy day.

Sunday March 22, 1846

This morning about nine o'clock we left the camp went about a mile and came to the bottoms they were not so bad as we had anticipated after we got across the bottom we went into the wood came in sight of the camp crossed the Chariton river here the scene was indescribable some in a boat teams wading through and men dragging them up the hill with a long rope the banks were very steep and muddy and the road very bad for a mile beyond one very long steep hill where they had to double team just at the top of the hill was the camp we came on beyond all the rest so we might be a little more retired. it is quite a pleasant situation here we all rejoice that we came over the river today for it rains very hard we have had some thunder and lightning this evening we have only travelled about five miles. This is Sarah's birthday.

Monday March 23, 1846

This has been a stormy day we were obliged to tarry on account of the weather about two in the afternoon we had some hail they fell as large or larger than buckshot it continued to rain through the night.

Tuesday March 24, 1846

Today as yesterday is rainy and unpleas[ant] very exceedingly muddy at evening Sarah thought it being so very wet and damp it would be more comfortable in her wagon so they prepared it and about four in the afternoon she left the tent.

Wednesday March 25, 1846

Last night considerable snow fell this morning was quite cold some snow has fallen during the day very muddy Mrs. Whitney has taken up her abode in the family wagon two or three doors from Sarah this evening Horace has been playing on his flute sounded very melodious at a little distance.

READING AND DISCUSSION QUESTIONS

1. Evaluate the historical context of Wells's westward migration in the 1840s. What evidence can you find of the environmental factors impacting the overland journey of men and women during this period?
2. To what extent do you think Wells's interaction with the environment, geography, and climate of the territory she traversed contributed to her Mormon identity as part of a distinct people? What role might environmental factors play in shaping identity?

P4-5 | Commentary on "Civilization" and the Native American

GEORGE CATLIN, *Wi-jun-jon—Pigeon's Egg Head: Going to and Returning from Washington* (c. 1837–1839) and *Letters and Notes* (1841)

To what extent does their environment shape individuals? Artist George Catlin (1796–1872) was clearly exploring this theme when he painted a double portrait of Wi-jun-jon (whose name he mistranslated as Pigeon's Egg Head), showing the Assiniboine leader coming to Washington to meet President Andrew Jackson and then returning to his tribe in the northern plains. Catlin created a career for himself as a painter and a chronicler of Native American people and culture, producing more than six hundred works depicting North and South American natives. As he toured with his canvases across the United States and throughout Europe, Catlin also wrote several books. His account of the event behind his portrait of Wi-jun-jon appeared in his two-volume collection of letters and notes published in 1841.

Letters and Notes (1841). *Letters and Notes on the Manners, Customs, and Condition of the North American Indians* by George Catlin, Volume. Wiley and Putnam, 161 Broadway, New York. 1841, pp. 195–199.

Wi-jun-jon, 1838/UNIVERSAL IMAGES GROUP/Bridgeman Images

Wi-jun-jon (the Pigeon's Egg Head) was a brave and a warrior of the Assinneboins—young—proud—handsome—valiant, and graceful. He had fought many a battle, and won many a laurel. The numerous scalps from his enemies' heads adorned his dress, and his claims were fair and just for the highest honours that his country could bestow upon him; for his father was chief of the nation. . . .

Well, this young Assinneboin, the "Pigeon's Egg Head," was selected by Major Sanford, the Indian Agent, to represent his tribe in a delegation which visited Washington city under his charge in the winter of 1832. With this gentleman, the Assinneboin, together with representatives from several others of those North Western tribes, descended the Missouri river, several thousand miles, on their way to Washington. . . . I was in St Louis at the time of their arrival, and painted their portraits while they rested in that place. *Wi-jun-jon* was the first. . . .

He was dressed in his native costume, which was classic and exceedingly beautiful . . .; his leggings and shirt were of the mountain goat skin, richly garnished with quills of the porcupine, and fringed with locks of scalps, taken from his enemies' heads. Over these floated his long hair in plaits, that fell nearly to the ground; his head was decked with the war-eagle's plumes—his robe was of the skin of the young buffalo bull, richly garnished and emblazoned with the battles of his life; his quiver and bow were slung, and his shield, of the skin of the bull's neck.

I painted him in this beautiful dress, and so also the others who were with him; and after I had done, Major Sanford went on to Washington with them, where they spent the winter.

Wi-jun-jon was the foremost on all occasions—the first to enter the levee—the first to shake the President's hand, and make his speech to him—the last to extend the hand to them, but the first to catch the smiles and admiration of the gentler sex. He travelled the giddy maze, and beheld amid the buzzing din of civil life, their tricks of art, their handiworks, and their finery; he visited their principal cities—he saw their forts, their ships, their great guns, steamboats, balloons, &c. &c.; and in the spring returned to St. Louis, where I joined him and his companions on their way back to their own country.

Through the politeness of Mr. Chouteau, of the American Fur Company, I was admitted (the only passenger except Major Sanford and his Indians) to a passage in their steamboat, on her first trip to the Yellow Stone; and when I had embarked, and the boat was about to depart, *Wi-jun-jon* made his appearance on deck, in a full suit of regimentals! He had in Washington exchanged his beautifully garnished and classic costume, for a full dress "en militaire." . . . It was, perhaps, presented to him by the President. It was broadcloth, of the finest blue, trimmed with lace of gold; on his shoulders were mounted two immense epaulettes; his neck was strangled with a shining black stock, and his feet were pinioned in a pair of waterproof boots, with high heels, which made him "step like a yoked hog."

On his head was a high-crowned beaver hat, with a broad silver lace band, surmounted by a huge red feather, some two feet high; his coat collar stiff with lace, came higher up than his ears, and over it flowed, down towards his haunches—his long Indian locks, stuck up in rolls and plaits, with red paint. . . .

A large silver medal was suspended from his neck by a blue ribbon—and across his right shoulder passed a wide belt, supporting by his side a broad sword. . . .

On his hands he had drawn a pair of white kid gloves, and in them held, a blue umbrella in one, and a large fan in the other. In this fashion was poor Wi-jun-jon metamorphosed, on his return from Washington; and, in this plight was he strutting and whistling Yankee Doodle, about the deck of the steamer that was wending its way up the mighty Missouri, and taking him to his native land again; where he was soon to light his pipe, and cheer the wigwam fire-side, with tales of novelty and wonder. . . .

After Wi-jun-jon had got home, and passed the usual salutations among his friends, he commenced the simple narration of scenes he had passed through, and of things he had beheld among the whites; which appeared to them so much like fiction, that it was impossible to believe them, and they set him down as an impostor. "He has been, (they said,) among the whites, who are great liars, and all he has learned is to come home and tell lies." He sank rapidly into disgrace in his tribe; his high claims to political eminence all vanished; he was reputed worthless—the greatest liar of his nation; the chiefs shunned him and passed him by as one of the tribe who was lost; yet the ears of the gossipping portion of the tribe were open, and the campfire circle and the wigwam fireside, gave silent audience to the whispered narratives of the "travelled Indian."

The next day after he had arrived among his friends, the superfluous part of his coat, (which was a laced frock), was converted into a pair of leggings for his wife; and his hat-band of silver lace furnished her a magnificent pair of garters. The remainder of the coat, curtailed of its original length, was seen buttoned upon the shoulders of his brother, over and above a pair of leggings of buckskin; and *Wi-jun-jon* was parading about among his gaping friends, with a bow and quiver slung over his shoulders, which, *sans coat,* exhibited a fine linen shirt with studs and sleeve buttons. His broadsword kept its place, but about noon, his boots gave way to a pair of garnished moccasins; and in such plight he gossipped away the day among his friends, while his heart spoke so freely and so effectually from the bung-hole of a little keg of whiskey, which he had brought the whole way, (as one of the choicest presents made him at Washington), that his tongue became silent. . . .

Two days' revel of this kind, had drawn from his keg all its charms; and in the mellowness of his heart, all his finery had vanished, and all of its appendages, except his umbrella, to which his heart's strongest affections still clung, and with it, and under it, in rude dress of buckskin, he was afterwards to be seen, in all sorts of weather, acting the fop and the beau as well as he could, with his limited means.

READING AND DISCUSSION QUESTIONS

1. What can you infer about the artist's attitude toward native people?
2. From the details Catlin shares of Wi-jun-jon's trip to Washington, what do you think he understood to be the effects of "civilization" on native peoples?
3. Imagine the trip to Washington from Wi-jun-jon's perspective. How do you think his identity as an Assiniboine leader was both affirmed and changed by his time in the nation's capital?

P4-6 | Creating a Heaven on Earth

ALBERT BRISBANE, *A Concise Exposition of the Doctrine of Association* (1843)

Albert Brisbane (1809–1890) became a disciple of French social reformer Charles Fourier and during the 1840s popularized his "associational" ideas for a new organization of society. Fourier promoted small, self-sustaining communities with residents reflecting the range of human personality types, resulting in a utopian society of social harmony. Both he and Brisbane were reacting to the rampant individualism they associated with market-based and urban societies. Brisbane's promotion of Fourier's ideas led to the establishment of many (short-lived) Fourierist communities throughout the United States.

The destiny of man is to be happy on this earth, but not in our subversive societies, characterised by indigence and discord. The realisation of happiness requires a different social order; . . .

. . . we ask how it has happened that the present social system, termed Civilisation, has not been the object of scientific investigation. Had its mechanism been analysed, it would necessarily have been discovered that it is full of complication and waste, and devoid of the three principle characteristics which mark all Nature's operations: ECONOMY OF MEANS, DISTRIBUTIVE JUSTICE, UNITY OF SYSTEM; characteristics which should not be banished from the social relations of man.

But Civilisation in its various branches is based upon the incoherent, conflicting efforts of individuals, between whom, not only no connection and combination exist, but on the contrary opposition and competition full of hatred and envy. If we take Agriculture, for example, the present condition of which calls so loudly for association and organisation, we find it pursued by isolated families, mostly without the necessary capital or credit, or the proper implements, and who only vie with each other in an ignorant and injudicious use and application of the soil. Human labour also is miserably misapplied; for, in the absence of combination between those isolated families, no appropriate adaptation of ages and sexes to functions and occupations suited to them can take place. Women, for example, are absorbed in a monotonous repetition of the trivial and degrading occupations of the kitchen and needle;—degrading because they have to be so continually repeated and on so small a scale. Moreover three-fourths of the labour of children, who are naturally very active, are wasted, owing to the absence of association between neighbouring households, who, if united, could organise minor branches of industry adapted to their strength and capacity, which besides being a pleasure to them, would develop their instincts and talents.

Albert Brisbane, A Concise Exposition of the Doctrine of Association (1843) Social Destiny of Man: Association and Reorganization of Industry by Albert Brisbane. Philadelphia: Published by CF Stollmeyer, 1840.

The root then of social incoherence is to be found in our system of separate households, or as many distinct houses as there are families, which is the essence of complication and waste. It absorbs the time, as we observed, of one sex or one-half of the human race, in an unproductive function, which has to be gone through with as many times as there are families. The monotony of such an operation so eternally and uselessly repeated, (uselessly because in association one vast kitchen with every commodity would replace the two or three hundred little kitchens of the present system,) must be fatiguing beyond conception, and its endurance must require all the patience of the female character. Let not the system be excused by saying that the character of woman is particularly adapted to it. It is not so: her destiny is not to waste her life in a kitchen, or in the petty cares of a household. Nature made her the equal of man, and equally capable of shining with him in industry and in the cultivation of the arts and sciences; —not to be his inferior, to cook and sew for him, and live dependently at his board. No class could bring so many well founded complaints against the social mechanism as women, for they are truly its slaves. There is no hope of a change for the better but in association; which, by simplifying nineteen twentieths of the present household complication, would throw open to them the broad field of human activity, now occupied to their exclusion by man alone. . . .

If we wish to find the most perfect picture of waste and disorder, we must search for it in our large cities. It is there that we will find our *cut-up* system, in which every thing is reduced to the measure and selfishness of the individual, producing an incoherence and complication, which might properly be termed a combination for the production of evil; for it would seem as if thing's were so organized, as to cause the greatest possible number of evils, and ensure their most rapid propagation. . . .

What absence of order, in an architectural point of view, on the part of society, not to be able to plan its buildings, so as to answer the wants of the community for twenty years in advance! The widening, straightning and lenghtning of streets form another gigantic item of waste. All these abuses arise from the fact that in planing our cities and towns, no system, no method exists. There is no adaptation of architecture to our wants and requirements; our houses are as little suited to our physical welfare, as our social laws are to our attraction and passions. . . .

Supppose that, out of three persons living together, one alone was engaged in producing, while the other two were idle: it is very evident that the active laborer could not alone produce enough to maintain himself and the other two comfortably. But if we suppose in addition, that each has a separate house, has his meals prepared separately in his own dwelling, the small product of the producer would not go near as far as if they lived together, and economized their means; to the loss caused by the idleness of two inactive persons, is to be added the waste of separate and complicated preparations. This is a perfect illustration of the present state of things. One-third of the population produce; two-thirds are non-producers. Instead of uniting and associating for the purpose of making the insufficient product of the labor of the active third go as far as possible, the most excessive complication and waste takes place, there being as many separate houses, kitchens, cooks, fires, &c. as there are families. . . . Eight millions of French live upon chesnuts and such trash; out of a population of thirty-two millions, twenty-two millions have but about six cents a day to live upon and defray all expenses. Twenty-five millions drink no wine, although France supplies the world with wine. It is to be remarked that in the most civilized countries, those in which industry is carried to the greatest perfection, their population are subjected to the severest labor, and are often the most miserable. The peasantry of Portugal, Austria, and even Russia are less harrassed by anxiety, and better supplied with food than are those of France and England. In this view of different countries, we must not overlook our own; nearly three millions of negro producers, whose labor pays for our imported luxuries, are merely supplied with their physical wants. We may well say with Fourier: "Can a more frightful disorder than that which exists upon this Globe be conceived. One-half of the earth is invaded by wild beasts, or savages, which is about the same thing; as to the other half which is under cultivation, we see three-quarters of it occupied by Barbarians who enslave the producers and women, and who in every respect violate justice and reason. There remains consequently an eighth of the Globe in possession the civilized, who boast of their improvements while giving to indigence and corruption their fullest development."

But to return to our subject: if we accept and approve of the system which allots to each family a separate house, we must approve of the effects which result from such a system. With four hundred families and four hundred separate dwellings, all the cares and duties attendant upon providing for a household, must be gone through with four hundred times, until the complication becomes frightful. Four hundred persons must be sent to market, to make four hundred separate purchases, who lose time enough in selecting articles wanted, and in bargaining, to produce them nearly. The four hundred houses imply that there are four hundred *dark holes,* called kitchens, in which four hundred *poor creatures* must pass their time over a hot fire in the middle of summer. Four hundred monotonous meals are prepared, three-fourths of them badly so, which give rise to as many discords as there are dishes. As neither mistresses nor servants are satisfied in this system, the former scold, and the latter are indifferent or faithless. If an ox is killed, it is cut up and disposed of in an infinite number of little lots; every hogshead of sugar, every box of tea has to be retailed out pound by pound; this excess of complication increases ten-times the number of butchers and dealers necessary, whose intermediate profits are a heavy indirect tax upon the consumer. The more we go into these details, the more we shall be convinced, that with this waste and want of system, individual economies are illusive, and that the mass must suffer poverty and privation under the best of governments.

READING AND DISCUSSION QUESTIONS

1. What can you infer about Brisbane's attitude toward the social and economic conditions in the United States that he observed in the 1830s and 1840s?
2. What relationship between environment and the individual did Brisbane assume to exist? How was the association model he promoted intended to improve society?

■ COMPARATIVE QUESTIONS ■

1. Compare the multiple perspectives of the sources in this chapter to identify similarities and differences in attitudes toward nature. What positive and negative associations with the environment emerge from these sources?
2. To what extent did environmental factors such as geography and climate constrain and shape Americans' actions?
3. Analyze and evaluate Albert Brisbane's associational communities (Document P4-6) by comparing his views to Joseph Story's comments about the rural cemetery (Document P4-2). How does each evoke a sense of place? What similarities and differences in point of view toward the environment does each express?
4. What effect might the consideration of environmental factors have on a historian's interpretation of America's past? How, for instance, might the political or economic interpretation of the early nineteenth century compare to an interpretation from an environmental perspective?

12

Sectional Conflict and Crisis

1844–1860

In his March 1845 inaugural address, President James K. Polk told his fellow citizens that the republican system "may be safely extended" over the entire continent and that the "bonds of our Union, so far from being weakened, will become stronger." As a political prognosticator, Polk failed. His forecast opened the most divisive period in American history, and his expansionist policies, which resulted in a war with Mexico, so far from strengthening the bonds of Union, led to its collapse.

The central political question of the period was slavery's extension into the territories. This issue gained currency as more Americans pushed west. The end of the U.S.-Mexico War opened additional territory to white settlers, and the 1849 discovery of gold ignited the imaginations of many seeking a quick route to the American dream. This chapter opens in the West with a diary written by a white woman who experienced the interplay of races and cultures during the expansionist decade of the 1840s. During the next decade, a series of political crises polarized Americans like never before. One of the flashpoint events was the publication in 1852 of Harriet Beecher Stowe's novel *Uncle Tom's Cabin; or, Life Among the Lowly*. This chapter presents two reviews of the novel, from southern and northern publications. A second flashpoint came with the 1857 Supreme Court ruling in *Dred Scott v. Sandford*. The famed abolitionist and escaped slave Frederick Douglass offered a scorching critique of the Court's decision. These and other events led partisans north and south to attribute to each other tyrannical motives, either to spread a Slave Power conspiracy (if you were a northerner) or to crush constitutional rights to property (if you were a southerner). In the process, compromises were struck and dissolved. Some political parties were destroyed and others born, and the bonds of Union were strained. By the time Abraham Lincoln was elected president in 1860, southern leaders had convinced themselves that only secession from the Union would save their cherished rights. Then came the war.

12-1 | On the Santa Fe Trail

SUSAN SHELBY MAGOFFIN, *Diary* (1846)

The diary that Susan Magoffin (1827–1855) wrote in 1846 provides a rare female account of the westward migration into Mexico's northern provinces, the region near Santa Fe that, with the Treaty of Guadalupe Hidalgo (1848), would soon become territory of the United States. Magoffin accompanied her merchant husband, Samuel, from Independence, Missouri, along the Santa Fe trail. Along the way she encountered General Stephen Kearny, the American officer whose troops defeated Manuel Armijo, the governor of New Mexico, that year. Americans like Samuel Magoffin saw opportunity in Mexico. This constituency for expansion faced opposition in the era's partisan (and sectional) debates. The diary entries reproduced here begin on Saturday, August 8, 1846, when Susan was just nineteen years old.

Camp No. 1. Saturday 8th. Second start. Left the Fort last evening at 6 o'clock, came six miles up the River to where we leave it finally. I am now entirely out of "The States," into a new country. The crossing of the Arkansas was an event in my life, I have never met with before; the separating me from my own dear native land. That which I love and honour as truly as any whole-souled son or daughter of the fair and happy America, (for the U. S. are considered to possess that bright name above) ever did. Perhaps I have left it for not only the first, but the last time. Maybe I am never to behold its bright and sunny landscape, its happy people, my countrymen, again. It is better always to look on the *bright* side, and it is certainly *wiser* to rely more fully on the Wisdom and Goodness of Providence. . . .

Tuesday 18th. . . . An other company of soldiers has come up today and an express too from Gen. Kearny now about entering Santa Fé. The news he brings is not less favourable than we have formerly received.

A negotiation is being carried on between the two Generals through brother James, who has the confidence of the Mexican Gen. so completely, we may look for pleasant results, and if any thing should go wrong we will be rather the first to receive a warning if it is necessary to remain from Santa Fé, and though we are behind now, if it is necessary to return to the U. S., we will be first. . . .

Down the Santa Fe Trail and Into Mexico: The Diary of Susan Shelby Magoffin, 1846–1847, Stella M. Drumm, ed., Lincoln: Yale University Press, 1926. Used with permission.

Thursday 27. Near San Miguel. We have passed through some two or three little settlements today similar to the Vegas, and I am glad to think that much is accomplished of my task. It is truly shocking to my modesty to pass such places with gentlemen.

The women slap about with their arms and necks bare, perhaps their bosoms exposed (and they are none of the prettiest or whitest) if they are about to cross the little creek that is near all the villages, regardless of those about them, they pull their dresses, which in the first place but little more than cover their calves — up above their knees and paddle through the water like ducks, sloshing and spattering every thing about them. Some of them wear leather shoes, from the States, but most have buckskin mockersins, Indian style.

And it is repulsive to see the children running about perfectly naked, or if they have on a chimese it is in such ribbands it had better be off at once. I am constrained to keep my veil drawn closely over my face all the time to protect my blushes. . . .

The news from Santa Fé is that A[r]mijo has fled, and Gen. Kearny, who is in possession of his house, is fortifying the city — so we may just fix ourselves there for the winter. . . .

Santa Fé. August 31st 1846. It is really hard to realize it, that I am here in my own house, in a place too where I once would have thought it folly to think of visiting. I have entered the city in a year that will always be remembered by my countrymen; and under the "Star-spangled banner" too, the first American lady, who has come under such auspices, and some of our company seem disposed to make me the first under any circumstances that ever crossed the Plains. . . .

Though Gen. Kearny has come in and taken entire possession, seated himself in the former Governor's chair, raised the American flag and holds Santa Fé as a part of the United States, still he has not molested the habits, religion &c. of the people, who so far are well pleased with their truly republican governor. . . .

I had made up my mind that the Gen. was quite a different man in every respect; he is small of statue, very agreeable in conversation and manners, conducts himself with ease, can receive and return compliments, a few of which I gave him. . . . He says as he is the Gov. now I must come under his government, and at the same time he places himself at my command, to serve me when I wish will be his pleasure &c. This I am sure is quite flattering, *United States General No. 1* entirely at my disposal, ready and will feel himself flattered to be my servant. . . .

Thursday 3rd. Una Senora [a lady] called to see me today, *mi alma* was in and interpreted for me, so my tongue was *vale nada* [no account]. Her name I do not know as yet, but her *lengua* [tongue] I do, for she kept in constant motion all the time of her visit, which lasted an hour and a half, very fashionable! She is a good old lady I dare say; speaks in favour of the foreigners, and without hesitation says Gen A[r]mijo is a *ladrón* [thief] and coward. . . .

We are having fine protection near us in case of danger; the soldiers have made an encampment on the common just opposite our house, and though we are situated rather "out of town," we have as much noise about us as those who reside in the center of the city. —We have constant rhumours that Gen. A[r]mijo has raised a large fource of some five or six thousand men, in the South, and is on his march to retake possession of his kingdom. The news has spread a panic among many of his former followers, and whole families are fleeing, lest on his return they should be considered as traitors and treated accordingly.

In other families there is mourning and lamentations, for friends they may never again see on earth. A day or two before Gen. Kearny arrived, A[r]mijo collected a fource of some three thousand men to go out and meet him, and even assembled them ready for a battle in the canon some twelve miles from town, but suddenly a trembling for his own personal safety seized his mind, and he dispersed his army, which if he had managed it properly could have entirely disabled the Gen's troops by blockading the road &c. and *fled himself!* While all these men, the citizens of Santa Fé and the adjacent villages, were assembled in the canon, and their families at home left entirely destitute of protection, the Nevijo [Navaho] Indians came upon them and carried off some twenty families. Since Gen. K.—arrived and has been so successful, they have petitioned him to make a treaty with them, which he will not consent to till they return their prisoners, which 'tis probable they will do thro' fear, as they deem the Gen. something almost superhuman since he has walked in so quietly and taken possession of the pallace of the great A[r]mijo, their former fear.

READING AND DISCUSSION QUESTIONS

1. How would you use this diary as evidence to help explain the growing sectional divisions of the 1840s and 1850s?
2. How would you characterize Susan Magoffin's attitude toward the Mexicans whom she encounters on her trek to Santa Fe? What might her perspective suggest about race relations during this period?

12-2 | Opposing Slavery's Expansion into the Territories

JOHN L. MAGEE, *Forcing Slavery Down the Throat of a Freesoiler Cartoon* (1856)

When Congress failed to pass the Wilmot Proviso (intended to outlaw slavery in the territory acquired in the U.S.-Mexico War), disgruntled antislavery northerners abandoned the Whig and Democratic parties and formed the Free Soil Party. Free Soilers opposed the expansion of slavery into the territories, wishing to keep the territories open to free white men. In this political cartoon from 1856, the artist is commenting on recent events in Kansas, where antislavery men, like the Free Soiler restrained in the image, were attacked. The man at the far left is Stephen A. Douglas, the senator whose "popular sovereignty" proposal in the Kansas-Nebraska Act left the decision regarding slavery's expansion into those territories up to the people.

Forcing Slavery Down the Throat of a Freesolier, 1856 (litho)/Magee, John L. (b. c. 1820) NEW YORK HISTORICAL SOCIETY/Collection of the New-York Historical Society, USA/Bridgeman Images

READING AND DISCUSSION QUESTIONS

1. What political point is the cartoonist making by depicting Stephen Douglas, Franklin Pierce, James Buchanan, and Lewis Cass—all of whom were Democratic candidates in the 1856 presidential election—shoving an enslaved African American down the throat of a Free Soil partisan?
2. What is the historical significance of the "Democratic Platform" planks on which Buchanan and Cass are standing? They read: Kansas, Cuba, and Central America.
3. What impact do you think the cartoonist was hoping to have on the election?

12-3 | Two Views of *Uncle Tom's Cabin*

Southern Press Review (1852) and *The National Era* (1852)

Harriet Beecher Stowe achieved incomparable prominence when she published *Uncle Tom's Cabin; or, Life Among the Lowly* in 1852. Her novel dramatized the lives of enslaved people, and in particular, the title character. Uncle Tom experienced the depraved and lethal cruelty of his owner Simon Legree, but Stowe depicted Tom as Christ-like in his suffering. In one of the most famous scenes, and one that was frequently dramatized on stage, the fugitive slave Eliza flees with her infant child and, crossing the Ohio River by jumping from ice floe to ice floe, she reaches safety. This scene was particularly affecting to northern antislavery readers in light of the 1850 Fugitive Slave Act, which required Americans to participate in the capture and return of escaped slaves. The novel sold hundreds of thousands of copies and its popularity in the North alarmed southerners. The two sources printed here offer conflicting assessments of the novel, and their disagreements reflect the growing sectional discord that led to war.

Southern Press Review

"Uncle Tom's Cabin" is an anti-slavery novel. It is a caricature of slavery. It selects for description the most odious features of slavery—the escape and pursuit of fugitive slaves, the sale and separation of domestic slaves, the separation of husbands and wives, parents and children, brothers and sisters. It portrays the slaves of the story as more moral, intelligent, courageous, elegant and beautiful than their masters and mistresses; and where it concedes any of these qualities to the whites, it is to such only as are, even though slaveholders, opposed to slavery. Those in favor of slavery are slave-traders, slave-catchers, and the most weak, depraved, cruel and malignant of beings and demons. . . .

Now, what is the value of a work of fiction in this controversy? What would be its value even if even [every] incident it contains were founded on fact, as the writer intimates? Why, just nothing at all. Every man who is accustomed to reason is familiar with the artifice of a discomfited antagonist. When refuted in argument, when overwhelmed with evidence, he insists on relating an anecdote, or telling a story—he retreats into fiction, or cites a particular instance although everyone capable of reasoning knows that any proposition can be maintained, or any institution be overthrown, if the citation of particular incidents is accepted as argument. Government, society, law, civilization itself would fall in an hour, if we were to listen to the stories of the wrong and ruin that incidentally or exceptionally attend them. Do not murderers escape—are not the innocent sometimes put to death under the administration of criminal law? And yet, who would abolish it, even if hundreds of novels were written to illustrate its defects, or under pretence of exposing its enormity? Do we not find bad men with wealth, or good men in want—then why not have a novel to prove it and to insist on the abolition of property? Nay, there is religion itself, whose institutions cannot be divested of superstition, hypocrisy and fanaticism. How many romances could be written and have been written to illustrate these latter? Yet must we abolish religion?

The Southern Press (June 15, 1852).

The National Era (April 15, 1852).

Mrs. Stowe may have seen, during her residence in Cincinnati, in the arrival and departure of emigrants, and in the trade and navigation of the Ohio and Mississippi, more families separated forever; she must know that from that single city more husbands, brothers, sons and fathers have gone voluntarily, as she calls it, from wives, mothers and children, and, in the pursuit of trade, met with untimely death by fevers and cholera on the river, or in the wilderness, leaving their families to suffer from want, their children to perish from neglect, than probably all who have separated by the slave trade. Why don't she write a romance against emigration, and navigation and commerce? They are all permitted by our laws.

But Mrs. Stowe complains that slavery gives to one man the power over another to do these things. Well, does not freedom, as she calls it? Cannot the landlord of Cincinnati turn out a family from his dwelling if unable to pay the rent? Cannot those who have food and raiment refuse them to such as are unable to buy? And does not Mrs. Stowe herself virtually do these very things? Suppose a poor man were to present himself to her and say, "Madam, I am a poor man with a large family, and we are destitute. And unless you prevent it, I shall be compelled to-morrow to hire myself as a hand on a flatboat to New Orleans, and besides exposing myself to the cholera and yellow fever, leave my wife in delicate health, my oldest daughter to the dangers of a large city without a protector, and my young ones to the diseases that depopulate the infancy of this place every summer. Now, I have read your novel, and I understand that you have already received a large fortune by the copy-right of it. Now, we are equals—except that I have none of your education, and that is not my fault. Yet somehow or other the laws of this freesoil State allow you to keep thousands of dollars in bank which you do not need, whilst I, for the want of a small part of it, am doomed to separation from all that I hold dear." We doubt whether Mrs. Stowe would recognize the cogency of this argument. But if she would, the laws of the country do not.

The National Era

For thrilling delineation of character, and power of description, this work is unrivalled. It has been denominated, and with truth, THE STORY OF THE AGE! The fact that ten thousand copies have been sold in two weeks is evidence sufficient of its unbounded popularity. Three paper mills are constantly at work, manufacturing the paper, and three power presses are working twentyfour hours per day, in printing it, and more than one hundred bookbinders are incessantly plying their trade, to bind them, and still it has been impossible as yet to supply the demand. Testimonials of the strongest kind, numerous enough to fill a volume, have already appeared in the public journals. We have room only for the following, from the Congregationalist of the 2d inst.:

"We conceive, then, that in writing 'Uncle Tom's Cabin,' Mrs. Harriet Beecher Stowe has done more to diffuse real knowledge of the facts and workings of American Slavery, and to arouse the sluggish nation to shake off the curse, and abate the wrong, than has been accomplished by all the orations, and anniversaries, and arguments, and documents, which the last ten years have been the witness of. Let nobody be afraid of it because it does not claim to be a memoir, or a table of statistics. It is the interlacing of a thousand memoirs, and the very quintessence of infinite statistics. It takes no extreme views. It does not seek to seize upon the most horrible atrocities, and brand the whole system as worse than it is. It is fair, and generous, and calm, and candid. A slaveholder might read it without anger, but not easily without a secret abhorrence of the system which he himself upholds. It brings out, quietly and collaterally, those incidental features of servitude which are usually little thought of, but which are the overflow of its cup of abominations. We look upon the writing of this book as providential, and upon it as the best missionary God has yet sent into the field to plead for his poor and oppressed children at the South. Such a book was a necessity of the age, and had to be written, and we are grateful to God that he put the writing of it into the hands of one who has interwoven Evangelical influences with every page of its narrative, and compressed many a Gospel sermon into its field and fireside converse. Its appeal to our sympathies is genuine. It artlessly pictures facts, and the facts make us feel. We have never read a story of more power. We doubt if anybody has. The human being who can read it through with dry eyes, is commended to Barnum."

READING AND DISCUSSION QUESTIONS

1. How do the two reviews assess the merits of Stowe's novel?
2. What is the nature of the critique the *Southern Press* reviewer makes? How, for instance, does this reviewer compare slavery to the market economy of the north?
3. What do these two reviews suggest to historians about the power of novels in shaping a society's cultural and political debates? To what extent do you think novels are useful sources for historians interpreting the past?

12-4 | Attacking the Slave Power Conspiracy

CHARLES SUMNER, *The Crime of Kansas* (1856)

Northern antislavery activists like Massachusetts senator Charles Sumner (1811–1874) railed against fellow senator Stephen Douglas's "solution" to the slavery extension issue, which called for popular sovereignty, or allowing the people to decide. Though democratic, the plan opened the possibility of slavery extending into regions where it had never gone before. The rush of both abolitionists and proslavery men into the territories to claim a majority resulted in bloody conflict, a violent prelude to the 1861 Civil War. When the proslavery Kansas constitution was recognized as the legitimate government, Sumner described the outcome as a "crime against humanity."

[B]efore entering upon the argument, I must say something of a general character, particularly in response to what has fallen from senators who have raised themselves to eminence on this floor in championship of human wrongs; I mean the Senator from South Carolina [Mr. Butler], and the Senator from Illinois [Mr. Douglas], who, though unlike as Don Quixote and Sancho Panza, yet, like this couple, sally forth together in the same adventure. I regret much to miss the elder Senator from his seat; but the cause, against which he has run a tilt, with such activity of animosity, demands that the opportunity of exposing him should not be lost; and it is for the cause that I speak. The Senator from South Carolina has read many books of chivalry, and believes himself a chivalrous knight, with sentiments of honor and courage. Of course he has chosen a mistress to whom he has made his vows, and who, though ugly to others, is always lovely to him; though polluted in the sight of the world, is chaste in his sight;—I mean the harlot, Slavery. For her his tongue is always profuse with words. Let her be impeached in character, or any proposition made to shut her out from the extension of her wantonness, and no extravagance of manner or hardihood of assertion is then too great for this Senator. The frenzy of Don Quixote in behalf of his wench Dulcinea del Toboso is all surpassed. The asserted rights of Slavery, which shock equality of all kinds, are cloaked by a fantastic claim of equality. If the slave States cannot enjoy what, in mockery of the great fathers of the Republic, he misnames equality under the constitution,—in other words, the full power in the National Territories to compel fellow-men to unpaid toil, to separate husband and wife, and to sell little children at the auction block,—then, sir, the chivalric Senator will conduct the State of South Carolina out of the Union! Heroic knight! Exalted Senator! A second Moses come for a second exodus!

But, not content with this poor menace, which we have been twice told was "measured," the senator, in the unrestrained chivalry of his nature, has undertaken to apply opprobrious words to those who differ from him on this floor. He calls them "sectional and fanatical"; and opposition to the usurpation in Kansas he denounces as "an uncalculating fanaticism." To be sure these charges lack all grace of originality, and all sentiment of truth; but the adventurous Senator does not hesitate. He is the uncompromising, unblushing representative on this floor of a flagrant *sectionalism*, which now domineers over the Republic; and yet with a ludicrous ignorance of his own position,—unable to see himself as others see him,—or with an effrontery which even his white head ought not to protect from rebuke, he applies to those here who resist his sectionalism the very epithet which designates himself. The men who strive to bring back the government to its original policy, when Freedom and not Slavery was national, while Slavery and not freedom was sectional, he arraigns as *sectional*. This will not do. It involves too great a perversion of terms. I tell that Senator that it is to himself,

Speech of Hon. Charles Sumner, in the Senate of the United States, 19th and 20th May, 1856 (Boston: John P. Jewett & Company, 1856), 9–10, 12–14.

and to the "organization" of which he is the "committed advocate," that this epithet belongs. I now fasten it upon them. For myself, I care little for names; but, since the question has been raised here, I affirm that the Republican party of the Union is in no just sense *sectional*, but, more than any other party, *national*; and that it now goes forth to dislodge from the high places of the government the tyrannical sectionalism of which the senator from South Carolina is one of the maddest zealots.

But I have not done with the senator. There is another matter, regarded by him of such consequence, that he interpolated it into the speech of the senator from New Hampshire [Mr. Hale] and also announced that he had prepared himself with it, to take in his pocket all the way to Boston, when he expected to address the people of that community. On this account, and for the sake of truth, I stop for one moment, and tread it to the earth. The North, according to the senator, was engaged in the slave trade, and helped to introduce slaves into the Southern States; and this undeniable fact he proposed to establish by statistics, in stating which, his errors surpassed his sentences in number. But I let these pass for the present, that I may deal with his argument. Pray, sir, is the acknowledged turpitude of a departed generation to become an example for us? And yet the suggestion of the senator, if entitled to any consideration in this discussion, must have this extent. I join my friend from New Hampshire in thanking the senator from South Carolina for adducing this instance; for it gives me an opportunity to say, that the northern merchants, with homes in Boston, Bristol, Newport, New York, and Philadelphia, who catered for Slavery during the years of the slave trade, are the lineal progenitors of the northern men, with homes in these places, who lend themselves to Slavery in our day; and especially that all, whether north or south, who take part, directly or indirectly, in the conspiracy against Kansas, do but continue the work of the slave-traders, which you condemn. It is true—too true, alas!—that our fathers were engaged in this traffic; but that is no apology for it. And, in repelling the authority of this example, I repel also the trite argument founded on the earlier example of England. It is true that our mother country, at the peace of Utrecht, extorted from Spain the Assiento Contract, securing the monopoly of the slave-trade with the Spanish Colonies, as the whole price of all the blood of great victories; that she higgled at Aix-la-Chapelle for another lease of this exclusive traffic; and again, at the treaty of Madrid, clung to the wretched piracy. It is true, that in this spirit the power of the mother country was prostituted to the same base ends in her American colonies, against indignant protests from our fathers. All these things now rise up in judgment against her. Let us not follow the senator from South Carolina to do this very evil to-day, which in another generation we condemn.

As the senator from South Carolina is the Don Quixote, the senator from Illinois [Mr. Douglas] is the squire of slavery, its very Sancho Panza, ready to do all its humiliating offices. This senator, in his labored address, vindicating his labored report—piling one mass of elaborate error upon another mass—constrained himself, as you will remember, to unfamiliar, decencies of speech. Of that address I have nothing to say at this moment, though before I sit down I shall show something of its fallacies. But I go back now to an earlier occasion, when, true to his native impulses, he threw into this discussion, "for a charm of powerful trouble," personalities most discreditable to this body. I will not stop to repel the imputations which he cast upon myself; but I mention them to remind you of the "sweltered venom sleeping got," which, with other poisoned ingredients, he cast into the cauldron of this debate. Of other things I speak. Standing on this floor, the senator issued his rescript, requiring submission to the usurped power of Kansas; and this was accompanied by a manner—all his own—such as befits the tyrannical threat. Very well. Let the senator try. I tell him now that he cannot enforce any such submission. The senator, with the slave power at his back, is strong; but he is not strong enough for this purpose. He is bold. He shrinks from nothing. Like Danton, he may cry, *"l'audace, l'audace, toujours l'audace!"*[1] but even his audacity cannot compass this work. The senator copies the British officer, who, with boastful swagger, said that with the hilt of his sword he would cram the "stamps" down the throats of the American people; and he will meet a similar failure. He may convulse this country with civil feud. Like the ancient madman, he may set fire to this temple of Constitutional Liberty, grander than Ephesian dome;[2] but he cannot enforce obedience to that tyrannical usurpation.

The senator dreams that he can subdue the North. He disclaims the open threat, but his conduct still implies it. How little that senator knows himself, or the strength of the cause which he persecutes! He is but a mortal man; against him is an immortal principle. With finite power he wrestles with the infinite, and he must fall. Against him are stronger battalions than any marshaled by mortal man—the inborn, ineradicable, invincible sentiments of the human heart; against him is nature in all her subtle forces; against him is God. Let him try to subdue these.

READING AND DISCUSSION QUESTIONS

1. Would you define the issues Sumner raised in his speech as short- or long-term causes of the Civil War? Explain your answer.
2. After delivering this speech, Sumner was savagely beaten with a cane on the floor of the U.S. Senate, sustaining injuries that incapacitated him for years. How did Sumner's speech and the response to it reflect the broader historical context of the 1850s?

[1] ***"L'Audace, l'audace, toujours l'audace!"***: French revolutionary Georges-Jacques Danton reputedly uttered this line, misquoted by Sumner, meaning, "We need audacity, yet more audacity, and always audacity."

[2] **Ephesian dome**: An elaborate and grand sixth-century temple built in Ephesus (modern-day Turkey), burned to the ground two hundred years later by an arsonist, who hoped his act of destruction would secure his lasting fame.

12-5 | Douglass Reacts to Dred Scott Decision

FREDERICK DOUGLASS, *Dred Scott v. Sandford* (1857)

Few Supreme Court cases have been as divisive as *Dred Scott v. Sandford*, which ruled against Dred Scott, an enslaved African American who sued his master for his freedom after he had been taken into territories where slavery was banned. Chief Justice Roger B. Taney not only ruled that slaves were property, not people, but also invalidated the Missouri Compromise of 1820, which barred slavery in much of the Louisiana Purchase. This legal triumph for slaveholders inflamed abolitionists, who feared slavery's spread throughout the nation. In this speech, famed abolitionist Frederick Douglass, himself an escaped slave, offers a characteristically eloquent and defiant assessment of the Court's decision.

This infamous decision of the Slaveholding wing of the Supreme Court maintains that slaves are within the contemplation of the Constitution of the United States, property; that slaves are property in the same sense that horses, sheep, and swine are property; that the old doctrine that slavery is a creature of local law is false; that the right of the slaveholder to his slave does not depend upon the local law, but is secured wherever the Constitution of the United States extends; that Congress has no right to prohibit slavery anywhere; that slavery may go in safety anywhere under the star-spangled banner; that colored persons of African descent have no rights that white men are bound to respect; that colored men of African descent are not and cannot be citizens of the United States.

You will readily ask me how I am affected by this devilish decision—this judicial incarnation of wolfishness? My answer is, and no thanks to the slaveholding wing of the Supreme Court, my hopes were never brighter than now. I have no fear that the National Conscience will be put to sleep by such an open, glaring, and scandalous tissue of lies as that decision is, and has been, over and over, shown to be. The Supreme Court of the United States is not the only power in this world. It is very great, but the Supreme Court of the Almighty is greater. . . Your fathers have said that man's right to liberty is self- evident. There is no need of argument to make it clear. The voices of nature, of conscience, of reason, and of revelation, proclaim it as the right of all rights, the foundation of all trust, and of all responsibility. Man was born with it. It was his before he comprehended it. The deed conveying it to him is written in the center of his soul, and is recorded in Heaven. . . To decide against this right in the person of Dred Scott, or the humblest and most whip-scarred bondman in the land, is to decide against God. It is an open rebellion against God's government. . . .

Jefferson said that he trembled for his country when he reflected that God is just, and his justice cannot sleep forever. The time may come when even the crushed worm may turn under the tyrant's feet. Goaded by cruelty, stung by a

---

Two Speeches by Frederick Douglass; One on West India Emancipation, Delivered at Canandaigua, Aug. 4th, and the Other on the Dred Scott Decision, Delivered in New York on the Occasion of the Anniversary of the American Abolition Society, May, 1857. Rochester, NY: C. P. Dewey, Printer, 1857), 31–34, 38, 40–41, 46.

burning sense of wrong, in an awful moment of depression and desperation, the bondman and bondwoman at the south may rush to one wild and deadly struggle for freedom. Already slaveholders go to bed with bowie knives, and apprehend death at their dinners. Those who enslave, rob, and torment their cooks, may well expect to find death in their dinner-pots.

The world is full of violence and fraud, and it would be strange if the slave, the constant victim of both fraud and violence, should escape the contagion. He, too, may learn to fight the devil with fire, and for one, I am in no frame of mind to pray that this may be long deferred. . . .

But I come now to the great question as to the constitutionality of slavery. The recent slaveholding decision, as well as the teachings of anti-slavery men, make this a fit time to discuss the constitutional pretensions of slavery. . . .

Neither in the preamble nor in the body of the Constitution is there a single mention of the term slave or slave holder; slave master or slave state, neither is there any reference to the color, or the physical peculiarities of any part of the people of the United States. Neither is there anything in the Constitution standing alone, which would imply the existence of slavery in this country.

We, the people—not we, the white people—not we, the citizens, or the legal voters—not we, the privileged class, and excluding all other classes but we, the people; not we, the horses and cattle, but we the people—the men and women, the human inhabitants of the United States, do ordain and establish this Constitution, &c.

I ask, then, any man to read the Constitution, and tell me where, if he can, in what particular that instrument affords the slightest sanction of slavery? Where will he find a guarantee for slavery? Will he find it in the declaration that no person shall be deprived of life, liberty, or property, without due process of law? Will he find it in the declaration that the Constitution was established to secure the blessing of liberty? Will he find it in the right of the people to be secure in their persons and papers, and houses, and effects? Will he find it in the clause prohibiting the enactment by any State of a bill of attainder?

These all strike at the root of slavery, and any one of them, but faithfully carried out, would put an end to slavery in every State in the American Union.

Take, for example, the prohibition of a bill of attainder. That is a law entailing on the child the misfortunes of the parent. This principle would destroy slavery in every State of the Union.

The law of slavery is a law of attainder. The child is property because its parent was property, and suffers as a slave because its parent suffered as a slave. Thus the very essence of the whole slave code is in open violation of a fundamental provision of the Constitution, and is in open and flagrant violation of all the objects set forth in the Constitution. . . .

The Constitution knows all the human inhabitants of this country as "the people." It makes, as I have said before, no discrimination in favor of, or against, any class of the people, but is fitted to protect and preserve the rights of all, without reference to color, size, or any physical peculiarities. Besides, it has been shown. . . that in eleven out of the old thirteen States, colored men were legal voters at the time of the adoption of the Constitution.

In conclusion, let me say, all I ask of the American people is, that they live up to the Constitution, adopt its principles, imbibe its spirit, and enforce its provisions. When this is done, the wounds of my bleeding people will be healed, the chain will no longer rust on their ankles, their backs will no longer be torn by the bloody lash, and liberty, the glorious birthright of our common humanity, will become the inheritance of all the inhabitants of this highly favored country.

READING AND DISCUSSION QUESTIONS

1. How does Douglass assess the potential impact of the Court's decision on the antislavery movement? Is he optimistic or despairing? Explain.
2. How does Douglass counter the Court's central argument concerning the constitutionality of slavery?
3. What audience do you think Douglass was hoping to reach? What do you think Douglass wanted his audience to feel and to do in response to the Court's decision?

12-6 | A Southern Woman Reacts to Lincoln's Election

KEZIAH GOODWIN HOPKINS BREVARD, *Diary* (1860–1861)

Born and raised in South Carolina, Keziah Brevard (1803–1886) was an educated and determined woman. Widowed in 1842, she managed and expanded her late husband's estate, becoming one of the region's leading planters, cultivating more than 2,600 acres with the labor of 209 enslaved African Americans. In her diary from late 1860 and early 1861, she notes the election of President Abraham Lincoln, a Republican from Illinois. Like many southerners, her anxiety about Republican intentions toward the issue of slavery colored her reaction to Lincoln's election and pushed her toward secession.

[*September*] *15th Saturday* . . . This night, if reports are true, had been set apart to cut us off—Oh God, because we own slaves—Lord thou knowest our hearts—save us for a calmer end & let us never cease to think & to bless thee for thy loving kindness—Lord, save this our good country & make us *all* & *every one*, bond & free, to love thee & do thy will as good servants—*we* are *all* thy servants—all in thy hands—Oh save us.

Glenn M. Linden, *Voices from the Gathering Storm: The Coming of the American Civil War* (Wilmington, DE: Scholarly Resources, Inc., 2001), 222–227.

18 . . . Oh my God I have so many little things to unnerve me—I wish I was prepared to die & could go to my God. I wish to be kind to my negroes—but I receive little but impudence from Rosanna & Sylvia—it is a truth if I am compelled to speak harshly to them—after bearing every thing from them I get impudence—Oh my God give me fortitude to do what is right to these then give me firmness to go no farther—At my death it is my solemn desire that Tama—Sylvia—Mack—Maria & Rosanna be sold—I cannot think of imposing such servants on any one of my heirs.

[*October*] *13th Saturday* . . .—it is time for us to shew the rabble of the North we are not to be murdered in cold blood because we own slaves—there are no doubts but thousands would have prefered being born in this beautiful country without the encumbrance—but they have been transmitted down to us & what can we do with them?—free such a multitude of half barbarians in our midst—no—no—we must sooner give up our lives than submit to such a degradation—From the time I could reason with myself I wished there was a way to get rid of them—but not free them in our midst yet. They are not prepared for freedom, many of them set no higher value on themselves than the beasts of the field do—I know a family in five miles of me where there are six women who have & have had children for thirty years back & not one of them but have [been] bastards & only one ever had a husband. . . . That wretch John Brown—if he had come as one of christ's Apostles & preached down sin he might have been the instrument of good—but he come to cut our throats because we held property we could not do otherwise with—was preposterous—Did God set the children of Israel to cutting their masters' throats to flee [free] them from bondage—no—no—he brought them out of Egypt in his own peculiar way & he can send Africa's sons & daughters back when he knows they are ready for their exode. I own many slaves & many of the females are of the lowest cast—making miserable their own fellow servants by medling with the husbands of others—. . . This is a dirty subject—& had I not thought of those cruel abolitionists who wish to free such people in our midst I would not have spoken this truth here.

[9th November] Oh My God!!! This morning heard that Lincoln was elected—I had prayed that God would thwart his election in some way & I prayed for my *Country*—Lord we know not what is to be the result of this—but I do pray if there is to be a crisis—that we all lay down our lives sooner than free our slaves in our midst—no soul on this earth is more willing for justice than I am, but the idea of being mixed up with free blacks is *horrid*!! I must trust in God that he will not forget us as unworthy as we are—Lord save us—*I would give my life to save my Country*. I have never been opposed to giveing up slavery if we could send them out of our Country—. . . but the die is cast—"Caesar has past the Rubicon."[3] We now have to act, God be with us is my prayer & let us all be willing to die rather than free our slaves in their present uncivilized state.

[3] **"Caesar has past the Rubicon"**: Reference to Julius Caesar, first century B.C. Roman general who crossed the Rubicon River with his troops to seize Rome. When one crosses the Rubicon, it means he or she has passed the point of no return.

[*December*] *Monday 10th* . . . I hope & trust in God as soon as Secession is carried out—we of the South begin to find a way to get all the Negroes sent back to Africa & let the generations to come after us live in more peace than we do—I can't see how we are ever to be safe with them in our midst—I wish every soul of them were in Africa contented in their own homes—let us begin on corn bread & live in peace & security—as long as they are here & number so many more than the whites there is no safety any way—Men of the South—I fear our end is near & the Yankeys will glory over their work. I do hate a Northern Abolitionist—Lord forgive me—but who can love those whose highest ambition is to cut our throats.

28 Friday Mrs. James H. Adams with Janie, Laura, Carry, Ellen & Jim spent the day with Goodwyn & myself—Randy's little Jane with them. They brought this morning's paper with them, the "Guardian," from it we read that Ft. Moultrie[4] had been evacuated on the 27th & the Ft. was on fire at 5 O'clock thursday evening. God alone knows the design of it—we are all in the dark as to the future—Oh that this strife could be ended for the good of the whole country—I know not what to think, certainly awful troubles seem hanging over us—

[*January*] *Thursday 10* . . . Last night we received the news of the Star of the West—from Charleston—O God put it into the hearts of the Northern people to do right & let us once more shew to the world we can yield to all that is right in thy sight—We have never invaded Northern rights—all we want is *right* in its plainest sense.

Wednesday 30 Oh my God I see nothing ahead but trouble—Our country will pass from bad to worse—the South never would be united or it might have sent Douglass [Stephen Douglas] instead of Lincoln—if she could have been united 'twould have been far better for her—I do hope if we have Civil war—that God will take me before the first drop of blood is shed—O God canst thou, wilt thou not spare us—I do not say we deserve it—no—no—slavery ever will make trouble I care not where found—I wish I had been born without them with a sufficiency to keep me from want in as good a country as this with our liberal religion —

February 28th . . . Now what of my country?—a few short days & we shall hear from Lincoln's lips what we may expect—if he makes war on us the whole body of men No. & So. should rise against him & make a blow at the man himself who would dare to bring such trouble on this land won by the blood of our fore fathers from British encroachments. If the N. should be let loose on us, the fanatics will run mad with joy & tongues cannot tell where the scene will end—. . . Now what of my country?—a few short days & we shall hear from Lincoln's lips what we may expect had a son to mix my blood with *negro blood*—Oh such a sin would [be] & is disheartening to Christian Mothers—

Monday [March] 4th . . . I pray that Lincoln's administration may disappoint his friends & his opposers—his friends are black republicans, our enemies—they must have dreadful hearts to wish to cut our throats because we are sinners—as

[4] **Ft. Moultrie**: By the time Brevard is writing, federal troops had been sent from Fort Moultrie on Sullivan's Island in Charleston harbor to nearby Fort Sumter.

if they were pure & undefiled—no surer sign of what deceivers they are than to see how self conceited they are—God can punish every sinner & will do it—perhaps many of them may yet have their eyes opened to the enormity of *their own* sins—if not in this world [then] in the next. Blessed be the Lord God Almighty who will make each answer for their own sins—& this will be like mill-stones to many deceivers. Thankful I am that I have a just God to go before & not Northern fanatics nor black Republicans—Lord let me have right feelings towards them because it [is] thy will, we should forgive our enemies. 'Tis hard for us to feel right towards those who sent John Brown (that Devil) to cut our throats—

April 2nd . . . O Lord let me not murmur—I am sorry our once strong country is now severed & I believe forever—for I see no disposition in the stubborn North to yield any thing from advantage—& the South thought she would make the North succumb to her—*I* never thought it—& have ever thought we have began troubles for ourselves & cannot see how we are to be one tittle better off than we were—if all the South had gone united we might have maintained ourselves—but six states only—we are doomed I fear to be the division of the Old United States. O my God *help us—help us*—Let me not live to see these six states disagree & I fear it very much.

April 3rd Wednesday . . . I still fear So. Ca. cannot be pleased—I do not love her disposition to cavil at every move—My heart has never been in this breaking up of the Union—but if we could be united lovingly & firmly, I will cling to my dear native land—for I love my country—but I hate contention:—too many are waiting for the loaves & fishes, South as well as North—

[*April 11*] How thankful I am—my Country is still spared—Lord save us & make us better—I pray that all things will be ordered for peace. How changeable my feelings are—sometimes buoyed with a hope of good times (this is momentary), then I can see & hear nothing to hang my hopes on—Why are they stubborn about the forts if they have any thought of reconciliation?

[13th April] Spent Sunday at home—had two little negroes sick—sent for Dr Taylor—he came in the afternoon & gave me the news from Charleston—Said Ft. Sumpter had been taken—Col. Anderson surrendered—he lost 9 or ten men—So. Ca. not one—Oh my God I thank thee for spareing blood here—Lord 'twas hard the citizens of Charleston should be rendered so miserable by that Fort—I am thankful it is no longer there a terror, but Oh my God we may still tremble for we have enemies in our midst—Oh God send them away to a land they love better than ours & Oh devise a way for our peace & safety & let the praise be thine—for who can doubt but thou didst so order it. A few months ago & 'twas said man could not take Ft. Sumpter unless walking over five or ten thousand dead—it has been taken—& not *one* life lost of those who aided in taking it—My God the work is thine & if we serve the[e] truthfully thou wilt save us—Oh save us & make us still a united contented people—we wish no ill to the North—all we ask is that they leave us to ourselves or gra[n]t us privileges & laws that will protect us—My God be with all thy dear Children—Oh how desolate many are now—Husbands & sons gone to the scenes of war—to save their [country].

READING AND DISCUSSION QUESTIONS

1. Based on your analysis and evaluation of Brevard's diary, what inferences and conclusions can you draw about southern reactions to Lincoln's election in 1860? How do you explain Brevard's particular reaction?
2. What point of view does Brevard express in her diary? What are the advantages and limitations to using diaries as historical evidence?

▪ COMPARATIVE QUESTIONS ▪

1. Compare multiple perspectives over time on the issue of slavery's expansion by identifying similarities and differences in the views of Charles Sumner (Document 12-4), David Walker (Document 10-5), and Frederick Douglass (Document 12-5).
2. Evaluate and synthesize the evidence in this chapter to construct a persuasive historical argument explaining why the Civil War broke out in 1861.
3. Compare the perspectives of Susan Magoffin (Document 12-1) and Keziah Brevard (Document 12-6). To what extent was their point of view shaped by factors of race, class, and gender? What trace of those factors can you find in their writings?
4. If the authors of the texts in this chapter could have voted in the election of 1844, which resulted in James Polk's victory and an endorsement of territorial expansion, how do you think each would have voted? What factors inform your conclusions?

13

Bloody Ground: The Civil War

1861–1865

In the fading months of war, during his second inaugural address, Abraham Lincoln expressed the hope that the war would end "with malice toward none; with charity for all." It was an audacious wish, given the carnage of the four bloody years of war, and a hope dimmed by his martyrdom at the hands of an assassin just six weeks later. The peace he envisioned would have to overcome the strains of war. The economy of the South suffered miserable setbacks, reversing fortunes and exacerbating the impoverishment of those already on the margins. The war overturned the political and social structure of southern communities and polarized opinions between the sections. Northerners squabbled with northerners, and southerners with other southerners, heightening the challenge of finding common ground to build the just and lasting peace Lincoln wanted. Slavery, as Lincoln said, was "the cause of the war," and its destruction was the war's crowning achievement. The struggle to achieve freedom, initially won with Lincoln's Emancipation Proclamation, then generally by the Thirteenth Amendment, changed the lives of former slaves. At the same time, it transformed the two societies at war, leaving no one untouched.

13-1 | View of Southern Women's Role in War *Sowing and Reaping* (1863)

Frank Leslie's Illustrated Newspaper, a weekly New York literary and news magazine, published this two-panel cartoon in 1863 in the wake of the "bread riots" in Richmond, Virginia. Two years into the war, the Confederate homefront felt the pinch of high inflation. In April 1863, Richmond's working-class women sought relief, but, when denied, a crowd of them began attacking the city's businesses, chanting "Bread or blood!" The riot was quickly put down, and city officials eventually expanded poor relief, but the riot was a blow to Confederate morale and signaled fading enthusiasm for the war.

Library of Congress, Prints & Photographs Division, Reproduction number LC-USZ62-47636 (b&w film copy neg.)

READING AND DISCUSSION QUESTIONS

1. The lines beneath the images read (on the left) "Southern Women Hounding Their Men on to Rebellion" and (on the right) "Southern Women Feeling the Effects of Rebellion and Creating Bread Riots." How would you describe the newspaper's perspective on women's role in the war effort?
2. *Frank Leslie's Illustrated Newspaper* was published in New York. How do you think a Richmond newspaper would have covered the same event?
3. What does the bread riot suggest about the impact of war on the homefront? To what extent do you think events on the homefront influenced events on the battlefield?

13-2 | A Witness to the War's Terrible Toll

AMBROSE BIERCE, *What I Saw of Shiloh* (1881)

Joining the war were many young Union and Confederate soldiers filled with romantic notions of battlefield glory and adventure, perhaps encouraged by the pleas of the women as depicted in this chapter's first document. Those who saw battle quickly replaced its charm with the dread reality of blood and death. Ambrose Bierce was a sergeant-major in the Union army when a battle near the Shiloh Meeting House in southwestern Tennessee broke out on April 6, 1862. Bierce survived this Union victory, but he witnessed its costs. Years after the war, as nostalgic veterans' memoirs were being published, Bierce wrote this unvarnished account of the battle.

Owing to the darkness, the storm and the absence of a road, it had been impossible to move the artillery from the open ground about the Landing. The privation was much greater in a moral than in a material sense. The infantry soldier feels a confidence in his cumbrous arm quite unwarranted by its actual achievements in thinning out the opposition. There is something that inspires confidence in the way a gun dashes up to the front, shoving fifty or a hundred men to one side as if it said, "Permit *me*!" Then it squares its shoulders, calmly dislocates a joint in its back, sends away its twenty-four legs and settles down with a quiet rattle which says as plainly as possible, "I've come to stay." There is a superb scorn in its grimly defiant attitude, with its nose in the air; it appears not so much to threaten the enemy as deride him.

Our batteries were probably toiling after us somewhere; we could only hope the enemy might delay his attack until they should arrive. "He may delay his defense if he likes," said a sententious young officer to whom I had imparted this natural wish. He had read the signs aright; the words were hardly spoken when a group of staff officers about the brigade commander shot away in divergent lines as if scattered by a whirlwind, and galloping each to the commander of a regiment gave the word. There was a momentary confusion of tongues, a thin line of skirmishers detached itself from the compact front and pushed forward, followed by its diminutive reserves of half a company each—one of which platoons it was my fortune to command. When the straggling line of skirmishers had swept four or five hundred yards ahead, "See," said one of my comrades, "she moves!" She did indeed, and in fine style, her front as straight as a string, her reserve regiments in columns doubled on the center, following in true subordination; no braying of brass to apprise the enemy, no fifing and drumming to amuse him; no ostentation of gaudy flags; no nonsense. This was a matter of business.

In a few moments we had passed out of the singular oasis that had so marvelously escaped the desolation of battle, and now the evidences of the previous

---

day's struggle were present in profusion. The ground was tolerably level here, the forest less dense, mostly clear of undergrowth, and occasionally opening out into small natural meadows. Here and there were small pools—mere discs of rainwater with a tinge of blood. Riven and torn with cannon-shot, the trunks of the trees protruded bunches of splinters like hands, the fingers above the wound interlacing with those below. Large branches had been lopped, and hung their green heads to the ground, or swung critically in their netting of vines, as in a hammock. Many had been cut clean off and their masses of foliage seriously impeded the progress of the troops. The bark of these trees, from the root upward to a height of ten or twenty feet, was so thickly pierced with bullets and grape that one could not have laid a hand on it without covering several punctures. None had escaped. How the human body survives a storm like this must be explained by the fact that it is exposed to it but a few moments at a time, whereas these grand old trees had had no one to take their places, from the rising to the going down of the sun. Angular bits of iron, concavo-convex, sticking in the sides of muddy depressions, showed where shells had exploded in their furrows. Knapsacks, canteens, haversacks distended with soaken and swollen biscuits, gaping to disgorge, blankets beaten into the soil by the rain, rifles with bent barrels or splintered stocks, waist-belts, hats and the omnipresent sardine-box—all the wretched debris of the battle still littered the spongy earth as far as one could see, in every direction. Dead horses were everywhere; a few disabled caissons, or Umbers, reclining on one elbow, as it were; ammunition wagons standing disconsolate behind four or six sprawling mules. Men? There were men enough; all dead apparently, except one, who lay near where I had halted my platoon to await the slower movement of the line—a Federal sergeant, variously hurt, who had been a fine giant in his time. He lay face upward, taking in his breath in convulsive, rattling snorts, and blowing it out in sputters of froth which crawled creamily down his cheeks, piling itself alongside his neck and ears. A bullet had clipped a groove in his skull, above the temple; from this the brain protruded in bosses, dropping off in flakes and strings. I had not previously known one could get on, even in this unsatisfactory fashion, with so little brain. One of my men whom I knew for a womanish fellow, asked if he should put his bayonet through him. Inexpressibly shocked by the cold-blooded proposal, I told him I thought not; it was unusual, and too many were looking.

READING AND DISCUSSION QUESTIONS

1. Analyze the details of the Battle of Shiloh that Bierce provides. What perspective does he have?
2. How might the historian use this source to write the history of the battle? As a source, what limitations does it present? What other types of sources might the historian consult?
3. This account was published nearly two decades after the battle. Why do you think Bierce wrote it? What impact do you think he intended?

13-3 | A Battlefield View of the Cost of War

CORNELIA HANCOCK, *Letters of a Civil War Nurse* (1863)

While the economic costs of the war were visible in the unplowed fields, unsold cotton bales, and bread riots, the emotional sacrifices were borne by the families who experienced the brutalities of war and the loss of life. Cornelia Hancock witnessed the effects of that brutality while nursing soldiers back to health or toward as peaceful a death as possible. In her letters home, she recounts her experiences in the field hospitals following the major battle at Gettysburg, Pennsylvania, in July 1863, one of the turning-point battles of the war.

Gettysburg, Pa. July 7th, 1863.

My dear cousin

I am very tired tonight; have been on the field all day—went to the 3rd Division 2nd Army Corps. I suppose there are about five hundred wounded belonging to it. They have one patch of woods devoted to each army corps for a hospital. I being interested in the 2nd, because Will [her brother] had been in it, got into one of its ambulances, and went out at eight this morning and came back at six this evening. There are no words in the English language to express the sufferings I witnessed today. The men lie on the ground; their clothes have been cut off them to dress their wounds; they are half naked, have nothing but hard-tack to eat only as Sanitary Commissions, Christian Associations, and so forth give them. I was the first woman who reached the 2nd Corps after the three days fight at Gettysburg. I was in that Corps all day, not another woman within a half mile. Mrs. Harris was in first division of 2nd Corps. I was introduced to the surgeon of the post, went anywhere through the Corps, and received nothing but the greatest politeness from even the lowest private. You can tell Aunt that there is every opportunity for "secesh" sympathizers to do a good work among the butternuts;[1] we have lots of them here suffering fearfully. To give you some idea of the extent and numbers of the wounds, four surgeons, none of whom were idle fifteen minutes at a time, were busy all day amputating legs and arms. I gave to every man that had a leg or arm off a gill of wine, to every wounded in Third Division, one glass of lemonade, some bread and preserves and tobacco—as much as I am opposed to the latter, for they need it very much, they are so exhausted.

I feel very thankful that this was a successful battle; the spirit of the men is so high that many of the poor fellows said today, "What is an arm or leg to whipping Lee out of Penn." I would get on first rate if they would not ask me to write to their wives; that I cannot do without crying, which is not pleasant to

---

South After Gettysburg: Letters of Cornelia Hancock from the Army of the Potomac, 1863–1865, ed. Henrietta Stratton Jaquette (Philadelphia: University of Pennsylvania Press, 1937), 7–20.

[1] **Butternuts**: An extreme faction of the Peace Democrats.

either party. I do not mind the sight of blood, have seen limbs taken off and was not sick at all.

CORNELIA

3rd Division—2nd Army Corps Hospital
Gettysburg, Pa. July 26th—Sunday.

My dear mother

Today is Sunday but there is no semblance of it here. It is now about five o'clock in the morning. Our hospital has been moved and our stores have given out. There is nothing to cook with, hence I have nothing to do, and, therefore, have time to write. Such days will come here that we have to see our wounded men fed with dry bread and poor coffee; and I can tell you it is hard to witness some cursing for food, some praying for it. It seems to be no one's fault but will happen. All the luxuries that the men get come through the Christian Commission, Sanitary, Ladies Aid, etc. I would give anything to have a barrel of butter, and some dried rusk[2] that I have seen in our parlor. I wish you would get up something of the kind and have Mrs. Jones requested to forward to me. I should think it would be as satisfactory for me to have them as for them to be sown broadcast on the land. I could make a report of everything I received and write to the Society.

I received a silver medal from the soldiers which cost twenty dollars. I know what thee will say—that the money could have been better laid out. It was very complimentary though. One of the soldiers has a sword that he found on the battlefield, which he is going to give to me before I come home. If they were only where they could buy I should be so loaded with baggage, I should never be able to get home. I shall not come home, unless I get sick, while this hospital lasts. I have two men detailed to wait on me, which suits of course. They are now fixing up nice little tables and all such things all around the tent. I have eight wall tents full of amputated men. The tents of the wounded I look right out on—it is a melancholy sight, but you have no idea how soon one gets used to it. Their screams of agony do not make as much impression on me now as the reading of this letter will on you. The most painful task we have to perform here, is entertaining the friends who come from home and see their friends all mangled up. I do hate to see them. Soldiers take everything as it comes, but citizens are not inured. You will think it is a short time for me to get used to things, but it seems to me as if all my past life was a myth, and as if I had been away from home seventeen years. What I do here one would think would kill at home, but I am well and comfortable. When we get up early in the morning, our clothes are so wet that we could wring them. On they go, and by noon they are dry.

From thy affectionate daughter —
C. HANCOCK

[2] **Dried rusk**: A dried biscuit.

General Hospital—Aug. 8th, 1863.

My dear Sallie[3]

It is well that thee is persevering enough to write to me without an answer for it is almost impossible for me to find time to write. In the morning before breakfast, before the men wake up, is the time we write, for as soon as the men are awake, they want something and continue in that state until late at night. Our hospital is on rising ground, divided off into six avenues, and eighteen tents holding twelve men each on each avenue. We call four tents a ward and name them by a letter; mine is ward E. The water is excellent and there is order about everything. I like it a great deal better than the battlefield, but the battlefield is where one does most good. I shall go to the front if there comes another battle, if not we shall stay in this hospital until fall. If thee was here thee would be very useful to run errands. I make friends with every one on the ground and get on first rate. Sallie S. I hear has passed away. But as surely as I live it does not seem to me as if I should ever make any account of death again. I have seen it disposed of in such a summary manner out here.

It is now about nine o'clock, every tent has a light in it, and a lot of groaning sick men. Our cook-house alone is a sight; they have meals cooked for thirteen hundred men, so you may know that they have to have the pots middling size. If you ever saw anything done on a large scale, it is done so here. There are many sights here, but the most melancholy one is to see the wounded come in in a long train of ambulances after night fall. I must be hardhearted though, for I do not feel these things as strangers do. What is the war news? I do not know the news at all. I never read the papers now, which is a slight change for me. I look at it in this way that I am doing all a woman can do to help the war along, and, therefore, I feel no responsibility. If people take an interest in me because I am a heroine, it is a great mistake for I feel like anything but a heroine.

Miss Dix was in camp today and stuck her head in the tents, but she does not work at all, and her nurses are being superseded very fast. I think we have some excellent nurses; we must have at least thirty women in the whole hospital. I have one tent of Johnnies[4] in my ward, but I am not obliged to give them anything but whiskey.

I have no doubt that most people think I came into the army to get a husband. It is a capital place for that, as there are very many nice men here, and all men are required to give great respect to women. There are many good-looking women here who galavant around in the evening, and have a good time. I do not trouble myself much with the common herd. There is one man who is my right-hand man; he is about nineteen years old—is a hospital steward and will do anything to accommodate.

THY AUNT, CORNELIA

[3] **Sallie**: Her niece.

[4] **Johnnies**: Refers to Johnny Reb, a nickname for Confederate soldiers. A Union soldier was sometimes referred to as Billy Yank.

Camp Letterman Hospital—Gettysburg,
Aug. 14th, 1863.

My dear mother
I received thy letter this morning and was glad to get it; letters are the desideratum in this part of the world. I am regularly installed in the General Hospital now, and like it better even than the Corps Hospital. The main reason for my staying, aside from duty, is that I am so well, if it only lasts. I feel like a new person, eat onions, potatoes, cucumbers, anything that comes up and walk as straight as a soldier, feel life and vigor which you well know I never felt at home. The place here is very healthy. I cannot explain it, but I feel so erect, and can go steadily from one thing to another from half past six o'clock in the morning until ten o'clock at night, and feel more like work at ten than when I got up at home.

My Twelve dollars per month from the government, if it should come, would pay my washing, and that is all the expense I am at, at present. I got a barrel of pads and dried fruit, and handkerchiefs to-day from express office. I have not received the box from the Salem ladies yet but I expect I shall.

From thy affectionate daughter —
C. HANCOCK

Camp Letterman, General Hospital,
Aug. 17, 1863.

Dear mother
I always spend my evenings in the post office. I am alive and well, doing duty still in the general hospital. I do think military matters are enough to aggravate a saint. We no sooner get a good physician than an order comes to remove, promote, demote or something. Everything seems to be done to aggravate the wounded. They do not get any butter; there is certainly a want of generalship somewhere for there is surely enough butter in the United States to feed these brave wounded. There are many hardships that soldiers have to endure that cannot be explained unless experienced. I have nothing to do in the hospital after dark which is well for me—all the skin is off my toes, marching so much. I am not tired of being here, feel so much interest in the men under my charge. The friends of men who have died seem so grateful to me for the little that it was in my power to do for them. I saw a man die in half a minute from the effects of chloroform; there is nothing that has affected me so much since I have been here; it seems almost like deliberate murder. His friends arrived to-day but he had to be buried before they came. Every kind of distress comes upon the friends of soldiers.

We have a nice table, meals regularly, and the nicest roast beef every day, cornbread too.

To think there is not one of the men under my care that can get up yet! How patient they are though, never complain and lay still from day to day—how different from sick men at home. I am published on the walls of the tent as the

"Lady-nurse." All kinds of conversation go on here every day. . . . Tell father that I have my shoes greased and do everything in army style.

From thy daughter,
C. HANCOCK

READING AND DISCUSSION QUESTIONS

1. Analyze Hancock's letters as a historical source. Consider her audience and what you think was her purpose in writing. What argument about women's experiences during wartime can you make based on the evidence contained in her letters?
2. What conclusions can you draw, based on Hancock's letters, about the effect of war on the lives of soldiers and their families?

13-4 | Political Divisions over Freeing the Slaves

ABRAHAM LINCOLN, *Emancipation Proclamation* (1863), and JEFFERSON DAVIS, *President's Message* (1863)

Abraham Lincoln's Emancipation Proclamation, which he announced in September 1862, became official on January 1, 1863. It declared free all those enslaved persons within states then in rebellion against the United States. Jefferson Davis, president of the Confederate States of America, responded to Lincoln's measure with a message he sent to the Confederacy's Senate and House of Representatives, condemning emancipation.

Emancipation Proclamation

Whereas, on the twenty-second day of September, in the year of our Lord one thousand eight hundred and sixty-two, a proclamation was issued by the President of the United States, containing, among other things, the following, to wit:

"That on the first day of January, in the year of our Lord one thousand eight hundred and sixty-three, all persons held as slaves within any State or designated part of a State, the people whereof shall then be in rebellion against the United States, shall be then, thenceforward, and forever free; and the Executive

Abraham Lincoln, *Emancipation Proclamation,* The Avalon Project (avalon.law.yale.edu/19th_century/emancipa.asp).

The War of the Rebellion: A Compilation of the Official Records of the Union and Confederate Armies, series 2, vol. 5, part 1 (Washington, DC: Government Printing Office, 1898–1899), 807–808.

Government of the United States, including the military and naval authority thereof, will recognize and maintain the freedom of such persons, and will do no act or acts to repress such persons, or any of them, in any efforts they may make for their actual freedom.

"That the Executive will, on the first day of January aforesaid, by proclamation, designate the States and parts of States, if any, in which the people thereof, respectively, shall then be in rebellion against the United States; and the fact that any State, or the people thereof, shall on that day be, in good faith, represented in the Congress of the United States by members chosen thereto at elections wherein a majority of the qualified voters of such State shall have participated, shall, in the absence of strong countervailing testimony, be deemed conclusive evidence that such State, and the people thereof, are not then in rebellion against the United States."

Now, therefore I, Abraham Lincoln, President of the United States, by virtue of the power in me vested as Commander-in-Chief, of the Army and Navy of the United States in time of actual armed rebellion against the authority and government of the United States, and as a fit and necessary war measure for suppressing said rebellion, do, on this first day of January, in the year of our Lord one thousand eight hundred and sixty-three, and in accordance with my purpose so to do publicly proclaimed for the full period of one hundred days, from the day first above mentioned, order and designate as the States and parts of States wherein the people thereof respectively, are this day in rebellion against the United States, the following, to wit:

Arkansas, Texas, Louisiana, (except the Parishes of St. Bernard, Plaquemines, Jefferson, St. John, St. Charles, St. James Ascension, Assumption, Terrebonne, Lafourche, St. Mary, St. Martin, and Orleans, including the City of New Orleans) Mississippi, Alabama, Florida, Georgia, South Carolina, North Carolina, and Virginia, (except the forty-eight counties designated as West Virginia, and also the counties of Berkley, Accomac, Northampton, Elizabeth City, York, Princess Ann, and Norfolk, including the cities of Norfolk and Portsmouth[)], and which excepted parts, are for the present, left precisely as if this proclamation were not issued.

And by virtue of the power, and for the purpose aforesaid, I do order and declare that all persons held as slaves within said designated States, and parts of States, are, and henceforward shall be free; and that the Executive government of the United States, including the military and naval authorities thereof, will recognize and maintain the freedom of said persons.

And I hereby enjoin upon the people so declared to be free to abstain from all violence, unless in necessary self-defence; and I recommend to them that, in all cases when allowed, they labor faithfully for reasonable wages.

And I further declare and make known, that such persons of suitable condition, will be received into the armed service of the United States to garrison forts, positions, stations, and other places, and to man vessels of all sorts in said service.

And upon this act, sincerely believed to be an act of justice, warranted by the Constitution, upon military necessity, I invoke the considerate judgment of mankind, and the gracious favor of Almighty God.

In witness whereof, I have hereunto set my hand and caused the seal of the United States to be affixed.

Done at the City of Washington, this first day of January, in the year of our Lord one thousand eight hundred and sixty three, and of the Independence of the United States of America the eighty-seventh.

By the President: Abraham Lincoln
William H. Seward, Secretary of State.

Message from Jefferson Davis to the Confederate Congress

The public journals of the North have been received containing a proclamation dated on the first day of the present month signed by the President of the United States in which he orders and declares all slaves within ten States of the Confederacy to be free, except such as are found in certain districts now occupied in part by the armed forces of the enemy.

We may well leave it to the instincts of that common humanity which a beneficent Creator has implanted in the breasts of our fellowmen of all countries to pass judgment on a measure by which several millions of human beings of an inferior race, peaceful and contented laborers in their sphere, are doomed to extermination, while at the same time they are encouraged to a general assassination of their masters by the insidious recommendation "to abstain from violence unless in necessary self-defense." Our own detestation of those who have attempted the most execrable measure recorded in the history of guilty man is tempered by profound contempt for the impotent rage which it discloses. So far as regards the action of this Government on such criminals as may attempt its execution I confine myself to informing you that I shall unless in your wisdom you deem some other course more expedient deliver to the several State authorities all commissioned officers of the United States that may hereafter be captured by our forces in any of the States embraced in the proclamation that they may be dealt with in accordance with the laws of those States providing for the punishment of criminals engaged in exciting servile insurrection. The enlisted soldiers I shall continue to treat as unwilling instruments in the commission of these crimes and shall direct their discharge and return to their homes on the proper and usual parole.

JEFF'N DAVIS

READING AND DISCUSSION QUESTIONS

1. Compare the views toward emancipation revealed in Lincoln's proclamation and Davis's response. How do their views reflect the historical context of race relations in the mid-nineteenth century?
2. Summarize Lincoln's policy toward enslaved African Americans and the states in rebellion against the Union. Upon what ground did he justify his emancipation policy? How radical do you consider Lincoln's policy at the time?
3. What does Davis's message reveal about his strategy for dealing with Lincoln's Emancipation Proclamation? What is the veiled threat Davis makes regarding the Confederacy's policy respecting Union efforts to enforce emancipation?

13-5 | Voices of Freedom
African American Letters During the Civil War (1863–1864)

This collection of letters from Hannah Johnson, a northern African American woman living in Buffalo, NY; Annie Davis, an enslaved woman from Maryland; and Spotswood Rice, an African American soldier living in Missouri, offers poignant testimony to the horrors of slavery, the joy of emancipation, and the righteous indignation of those who suffered under the institution's terror. Abraham Lincoln's Emancipation Proclamation took effect on January 1, 1863 and it freed those enslaved people within the states then in rebellion. Unfortunately, most of those enslaved had to wait for the arrival of federal troops to enforce the proclamation. Many masters kept news of the proclamation from their slaves. Even when freedom came, it was not a swift or easy transition. Congress established the Freedman's Bureau in 1865 to provide aid to former slaves, including medical care and educational opportunities. African Americans, however, took charge of their own freedom: they donated money to establish schools, they pushed for civil rights, and they fought to reunite divided families. Letters such as the ones included here demonstrate the active role they played in securing their freedom. Two of these letters, written to Lincoln, show the faith many African Americans invested in the president and his emancipation policies. The two letters from Rice, one to his daughters and the second to one of his daughter's owners, are filled with understandable rage. Together, they all show the extent to which African Americans understood the larger significance of the Civil War: a bloody strike for justice.

Hannah Johnson to Abraham Lincoln, July 31, 1863

Buffalo [N.Y.] July 31 1863

Excellent Sir My good friend says I must write to you and she will send it My son went in the 54th regiment. I am a colored woman and my son was strong and able as any to fight for his country and the colored people have as much to fight for as any. My father was a Slave and escaped from Louisiana before I was born morn forty years agone. I have but poor edication but I never went to schol.

Freedmen and Southern Society Project, University of Maryland, College Park, www.freedmen.umd.edu

but I know just as well as any what is right between man and man. Now I know it is right that a colored man should go and fight for his country, and so ought to a white man. I know that a colored man ought to run no greater risques than a white, his pay is no greater his obligation to fight is the same. So why should not our enemies be compelled to treat him the same. Made to do it.

My son fought at Fort Wagoner but thank God he was not taken prisoner, as many were I thought of this thing before I let my boy go but then they said Mr. Lincoln will never let them sell our colored soldiers for slaves, if they do he will get them back quck he will retallyate and stop it. Now Mr Lincoln dont you think you oght to stop this thing and make them do the same by the colored men—they have lived in idleness all their lives on stolen labor and made savages of the colored people, but they now arc so furious because they are proving themselves to be men, such as have come away and got some edication. It must not be so. You must put the rebels to work in State prisons to making shoes and things. if they sell our colored soldiers, till they let them all go. And give their wounded the same treatment. it would seem cruel. but their no other way, and a just man must do hard things sometimes, that shew him to be a great man. They tell me some do you will take back the Proclamation, don't do it. When you are dead and in Heaven, in a thousand years that action of yours will make the Angels sing your praises I know it. Ought one man to own another, law for or not, who made the law, surely the poor slave did not. so it is wicked, and a horrible Outrage, there is no sense in it. because a man has lived by robbing all his life and his father before him. should he complain because the stolen things found on him are taken. Robbing the colored people of their labor is but a small part of the robbery their souls arc almost taken, they are made bruits of often. You know all about this

Will you see that the colored men fighting now, are fairly treated. You ought to do this, and do it at once, Not let the thing run along meet it quickly and manfully. and stop this. mean cowardly cruelty. We poor oppressed ones, appeal to you, and ask fair play. Yours for Christs sake

Hannah Johnson

Annie Davis to Abraham Lincoln, August 25, 1864

Belair [Md.] Aug 25th 1864

Mr president—It is my Desire to be free. to go to see my people on the eastern shore. my mistress wont let me— you will please let me know if we are free. and what i can do. I write to you for advice. please send me word this week. or as soon as possible and oblidge.

Annie Davis

Spotswood Rice to His Children, September 3, 1864

[Benton Barracks Hospital, St. Louis, Mo. Sptember 3, 1864]

My Children I take my pen in hand to rite you A few lines to let you know that I have not forgot you and that I want to see you as bad as ever now my Dear

Children I want you to be contented with whatever may be your lots be assured that I will have you if it cost me my life on the 28th of the mounth. 8 hundred White and 8 hundred blacke solders expects to start up the rivore to Glasgow and above there thats to be jeneraled by a jeneral that will give me both of you when they Come I expect to be with, them and expect to get you both in return. Dont be uneasy my children I expect to have you. If Diggs dont give you up this Government will and I feel confident that I will get you Your Miss Kaitty said that I tried to steal you But I'll let her know that god never intended for man to steal his own flesh and blood. If I had no cofidence in God I could have confidence in her But as it is If I ever had any Confidence in her I have none now and never expect to have And I want her to remember if she meets me with ten thousand soldiers she [will?] meet her enemy I once [thought] that I had some respect for them but now my respects is worn out and have no sympathy for Slaveholders. And as for her cristianantty I expect the Devil has Such in hell You tell her from me that She is the frist Christian that I ever hard say that aman could Steal his own child especially out of human bondage

You can tell her that She can hold to you as long as she can I never would expect to ask her again to let you come to me because I know that the devil has got her hot set againsts that that is write now my Dear children I am a going to close my letter to you Give my love to all enquiring friends tell them all that we are well and want to see them very much and Corra and Mary receive the greater part of it you sefves and dont think hard of us not sending you any thing I you father have a plenty for you when I see you Spott & Noah sends their love to both of you Oh! My Dear children how I do want to see you

[Spotswood Rice]

Spotswood Rice to Kittey Diggs, September 3, 1864

[Benton Barracks hospital, St. Louis, Mo. September 3, 1864]

I received a leteter from Cariline telling me that you say I tried to steal to plunder my child away from you now I want you to understand that mary is my Child and she is a God given rite of my own and you may hold on to hear as long as you can but I want you to remembor this one thing that the longor you keep my Child from me the longor you will have to bum in hell and the qwicer youll get their for we are now makeing up a bout one thoughsand blacke troops to Come up tharough and wont to come through Glasgow and when we come wo [woe] be to Copperhood rabbels[5] and to the Slaveholding rebbels for we dont expect to leave them there root neor branch but we thinke how ever that we that have Children in the hands of you devels we will trie your [vertues?] the day that we enter Glasgow I want you to understand kittey diggs that where

[5] **Copperhood rabbels**: Rice means Copperhead rebels. Copperhead was a name given to anti-war/peace faction of the northern Democratic Party who favored compromise with the South. Many Copperheads blamed abolitionists for provoking war.

ever you and I meets we are enmays to each orthere I offered once to pay you forty dollers for my own Child but I am glad now that you did not accept it Just hold on now as long as you can and the worse it will be for you you never in you life befor I came down hear did you give Children any thing not eny thing whatever not even a dollers worth of expens—now you call my children your pro[per]ty—not so with me—my Children is my own and I expect to get them and when I get ready to come after mary I will have bout a powrer and autherity to bring hear away and to exacute vengencens on them that holds my Child you will then know how to talke to me I will assure that and you will know how to talk rite too I want you now co just hold on to hear if you want to iff your conchosence tells thats the road go that road and what it will brig you to kittey diggs I have no fears about geting mary out of your hands this whole Government gives chear to me and you cannot help your self

Spotswood Rice

READING AND DISCUSSION QUESTIONS

1. What do these letters reveal about their authors? How do their experiences compare? What accounts for similarities and differences in their circumstances?
2. All of these letters were written after Lincoln's Emancipation Proclamation became effective on January 1, 1863. What do these letters suggest about the impact of the Proclamation on African Americans?
3. Rice had been a slave but he enlisted in the Union Army seven months before writing these letters. What do you imagine was Kitty Diggs's response to reading Rice's letter to her? Where do you think his confidence came from?

13-6 | Redistributing the Land to Black Refugees

WILLIAM T. SHERMAN, *Special Field Order No. 15* (1865)

Union major general William T. Sherman was instrumental in forcing the defeat of the Confederacy. His notorious "march to the sea" across Georgia destroyed the Confederacy's resources and liberated tens of thousands of enslaved Africans who trailed Sherman's troops. His Special Field Order No. 15, issued in January 1865, aimed to deal with the challenge of displaced former slaves. Once Andrew Johnson assumed the presidency upon Lincoln's death, he reversed Sherman's policy.

William T. Sherman, Special Order Number 15, in *War of the Rebellion: Official Records of the Union and Confederate Armies*, ed. United States War Department (Washington, DC: Government Printing Office, 1880), 60–62.

In the Field, Savannah, Ga., January 16th, 1865.

I. The islands from Charleston, south, the abandoned rice fields along the rivers for thirty miles back from the sea, and the country bordering the St. Johns river, Florida, are reserved and set apart for the settlement of the negroes now made free by the acts of war and the proclamation of the President of the United States.

II. At Beaufort, Hilton Head, Savannah, Fernandina, St. Augustine and Jacksonville, the blacks may remain in their chosen or accustomed vocations—but on the islands, and in the settlements hereafter to be established, no white person whatever, unless military officers and soldiers detailed for duty, will be permitted to reside; and the sole and exclusive management of affairs will be left to the freed people themselves, subject only to the United States military authority and the acts of Congress. By the laws of war, and orders of the President of the United States, the negro is free and must be dealt with as such. He cannot be subjected to conscription or forced military service, save by the written orders of the highest military authority of the Department, under such regulations as the President or Congress may prescribe. Domestic servants, blacksmiths, carpenters and other mechanics, will be free to select their own work and residence, but the young and able-bodied negroes must be encouraged to enlist as soldiers in the service of the United States, to contribute their share towards maintaining their own freedom, and securing their rights as citizens of the United States.

Negroes so enlisted will be organized into companies, battalions and regiments, under the orders of the United States military authorities, and will be paid, fed and clothed according to law. The bounties paid on enlistment may, with the consent of the recruit, go to assist his family and settlement in procuring agricultural implements, seed, tools, boots, clothing, and other articles necessary for their livelihood.

III. Whenever three respectable negroes, heads of families, shall desire to settle on land, and shall have selected for that purpose an island or a locality clearly defined, within the limits above designated, the Inspector of Settlements and Plantations will himself, or by such subordinate officer as he may appoint, give them a license to settle such island or district, and afford them such assistance as he can to enable them to establish a peaceable agricultural settlement. The three parties named will subdivide the land, under the supervision of the Inspector, among themselves and such others as may choose to settle near them, so that each family shall have a plot of not more than (40) forty acres of tillable ground, and when it borders on some water channel, with not more than 800 feet water front, in the possession of which land the military authorities will afford them protection, until such time as they can protect themselves, or until Congress shall regulate their title. The Quartermaster may, on the requisition of the Inspector of Settlements and Plantations, place at the disposal of the Inspector, one or more of the captured steamers, to ply between the settlements and one or more of the commercial points heretofore named in orders, to afford the settlers the opportunity to supply their necessary wants, and to sell the products of their land and labor.

IV. Whenever a negro has enlisted in the military service of the United States, he may locate his family in any one of the settlements at pleasure, and acquire a homestead, and all other rights and privileges of a settler, as though present in person. In like manner, negroes may settle their families and engage on board the gunboats, or in fishing, or in the navigation of the inland waters, without losing any claim to land or other advantages derived from this system. But no one, unless an actual settler as above defined, or unless absent on Government service, will be entitled to claim any right to land or property in any settlement by virtue of these orders.

V. In order to carry out this system of settlement, a general officer will be detailed as Inspector of Settlements and Plantations, whose duty it shall be to visit the settlements, to regulate their police and general management, and who will furnish personally to each head of a family, subject to the approval of the President of the United States, a possessory title in writing, giving as near as possible the description of boundaries; and who shall adjust all claims or conflicts that may arise under the same, subject to the like approval, treating such titles altogether as possessory. The same general officer will also be charged with the enlistment and organization of the negro recruits, and protecting their interests while absent from their settlements; and will be governed by the rules and regulations prescribed by the War Department for such purposes.

VI. Brigadier General R. SAXTON is hereby appointed Inspector of Settlements and Plantations, and will at once enter on the performance of his duties. No change is intended or desired in the settlement now on Beaufort [Port Royal] Island, nor will any rights to property heretofore acquired be affected thereby.

By Order of Major General W. T. Sherman

READING AND DISCUSSION QUESTIONS

1. Summarize the policy regarding freed slaves that Sherman announced in January 1865. What need did he identify as pressing for those newly liberated former slaves?
2. To what extent do you see Sherman's order as part of the civil rights history of the United States? Do you see Sherman's order as a radical innovation or as limited in its scope? Explain.

▪ COMPARATIVE QUESTIONS ▪

1. Analyze and evaluate Sherman's policy regarding land redistribution (Document 13-6). How does it compare to other sources related to land as a meaningful part of citizenship? Consider, for instance, Thomas Jefferson's comments about land (Document 7-2) and Lansford Hastings's encouragement to migrants (Document 11-3).

2. Analyze the diverse evidence from the primary sources collected in this chapter to determine the cost of war on American society. Were there any positive outcomes from the war experience? If so, what were they?
3. What can you infer from the evidence here concerning the impact of war on the lives of women? How might you account for differences in women's experiences and attitudes toward the war?
4. To what extent did midcentury ideas about race and slavery inform the various perspectives on wartime society contained in these sources?

14

Reconstruction

1865–1877

The Civil War sparked more questions than it settled. While the Thirteenth Amendment to the Constitution unambiguously decided the question of slavery, practical issues concerning freedmen's rights persisted. In the face of white southern resistance and northern fatigue, the national government created federal agencies to help freedmen transition from slavery to freedom, a journey that was burdened by persistent racism. Opposition came from those who continued to believe African Americans were either incapable of self-government—much less governing the state—or were susceptible to the political manipulation of northern opportunists. Policymakers faced other perplexing questions regarding the relationship of the former Confederate states to the Union and the social, economic, and political challenges facing a defeated South. Though this political turmoil led to a presidential impeachment, exacerbated strained relationships between the North and South, and gave birth to white-hooded violence, one undeniable truth stood out: African Americans were free.

14-1 | President Focuses on Work of Reconstruction

ABRAHAM LINCOLN, *Last Public Address* (1865)

On the night of April 11, 1865, Abraham Lincoln spoke to a joy-filled crowd gathered at the White House to celebrate the surrender of Robert E. Lee's Confederate army, a sign of the war's imminent end. Lincoln took the occasion to address the work ahead. In this speech, Lincoln discussed Louisiana's recent legislative efforts and, by doing so, signaled his approach to Reconstruction. John Wilkes Booth was in the audience that night and heard Lincoln speak. Three days later, at Ford's Theatre, he aimed a pistol at the back of Lincoln's head and pulled the trigger.

We meet this evening, not in sorrow, but in gladness of heart. The evacuation of Petersburg and Richmond, and the surrender of the principal insurgent army, give hope of a righteous and speedy peace whose joyous expression can not be restrained. In the midst of this, however, He from whom all blessings flow, must not be forgotten. A call for a national thanksgiving is being prepared, and will be duly promulgated. Nor must those whose harder part gives us the cause of rejoicing, be overlooked. Their honors must not be parcelled out with others. I myself was near the front, and had the high pleasure of transmitting much of the good news to you; but no part of the honor, for plan or execution, is mine. To Gen. Grant, his skilful officers, and brave men, all belongs. The gallant Navy stood ready, but was not in reach to take active part.

By these recent successes the re-inauguration of the national authority—reconstruction—which has had a large share of thought from the first, is pressed much more closely upon our attention. It is fraught with great difficulty. Unlike a case of a war between independent nations, there is no authorized organ for us to treat with. No one man has authority to give up the rebellion for any other man. We simply must begin with, and mould from, disorganized and discordant elements. Nor is it a small additional embarrassment that we, the loyal people, differ among ourselves as to the mode, manner, and means of reconstruction.

As a general rule, I abstain from reading the reports of attacks upon myself, wishing not to be provoked by that to which I can not properly offer an answer. In spite of this precaution, however, it comes to my knowledge that I am much censured for some supposed agency in setting up, and seeking to sustain, the new State government of Louisiana. In this I have done just so much as, and no more than, the public knows. In the Annual Message of Dec. 1863 and accompanying Proclamation, I presented a plan of re-construction (as the phrase goes) which, I promised, if adopted by any State, should be acceptable to, and sustained by, the Executive government of the nation. I distinctly stated that this was not the only plan which might possibly be acceptable; and I also distinctly protested that the Executive claimed no right to say when, or whether members should be admitted to seats in Congress from such States. This plan was, in advance, submitted to the then Cabinet, and distinctly approved by every member of it. One of them suggested that I should then, and in that connection, apply

Abraham Lincoln Online (www.abrahamlincolnonline.org/lincoln/speeches/last.htm).

the Emancipation Proclamation to the theretofore excepted parts of Virginia and Louisiana; that I should drop the suggestion about apprenticeship for freed-people, and that I should omit the protest against my own power, in regard to the admission of members to Congress; but even he approved every part and parcel of the plan which has since been employed or touched by the action of Louisiana. The new constitution of Louisiana, declaring emancipation for the whole State, practically applies the Proclamation to the part previously excepted. It does not adopt apprenticeship for freed-people; and it is silent, as it could not well be otherwise, about the admission of members to Congress. So that, as it applies to Louisiana, every member of the Cabinet fully approved the plan. The message went to Congress, and I received many commendations of the plan, written and verbal; and not a single objection to it, from any professed emancipationist, came to my knowledge, until after the news reached Washington that the people of Louisiana had begun to move in accordance with it. From about July 1862, I had corresponded with different persons, supposed to be interested, seeking a reconstruction of a State government for Louisiana. When the message of 1863, with the plan before mentioned, reached New-Orleans, Gen. Banks wrote me that he was confident the people, with his military co-operation, would reconstruct, substantially on that plan. I wrote him, and some of them to try it; they tried it, and the result is known. Such only has been my agency in getting up the Louisiana government. As to sustaining it, my promise is out, as before stated. But, as bad promises are better broken than kept, I shall treat this as a bad promise, and break it, whenever I shall be convinced that keeping it is adverse to the public interest. But I have not yet been so convinced.

I have been shown a letter on this subject, supposed to be an able one, in which the writer expresses regret that my mind has not seemed to be definitely fixed on the question whether the seceding States, so called, are in the Union or out of it. It would perhaps, add astonishment to his regret, were he to learn that since I have found professed Union men endeavoring to make that question, I have purposely forborne any public expression upon it. As appears to me that question has not been, nor yet is, a practically material one, and that any discussion of it, while it thus remains practically immaterial, could have no effect other than the mischievous one of dividing our friends. As yet, whatever it may hereafter become, that question is bad, as the basis of a controversy, and good for nothing at all—a merely pernicious abstraction.

We all agree that the seceded States, so called, are out of their proper relation with the Union; and that the sole object of the government, civil and military, in regard to those States is to again get them into that proper practical relation. I believe it is not only possible, but in fact, easier to do this, without deciding, or even considering, whether these States have ever been out of the Union, than with it. Finding themselves safely at home, it would be utterly immaterial whether they had ever been abroad. Let us all join in doing the acts necessary to restoring the proper practical relations between these States and the Union; and each forever after, innocently indulge his own opinion whether, in doing the acts, he brought the States from without, into the Union, or only gave them proper assistance, they never having been out of it.

The amount of constituency, so to speak, on which the new Louisiana government rests, would be more satisfactory to all, if it contained fifty, thirty, or even twenty thousand, instead of only about twelve thousand, as it does. It is also unsatisfactory to some that the elective franchise is not given to the colored man. I would myself prefer that it were now conferred on the very intelligent, and on those who serve our cause as soldiers. Still the question is not whether the Louisiana government, as it stands, is quite all that is desirable. The question is, "Will it be wiser to take it as it is, and help to improve it; or to reject, and disperse it?" "Can Louisiana be brought into proper practical relation with the Union sooner by sustaining, or by discarding her new State government?"

Some twelve thousand voters in the heretofore slave-state of Louisiana have sworn allegiance to the Union, assumed to be the rightful political power of the State, held elections, organized a State government, adopted a free-state constitution, giving the benefit of public schools equally to black and white, and empowering the Legislature to confer the elective franchise upon the colored man. Their Legislature has already voted to ratify the constitutional amendment recently passed by Congress, abolishing slavery throughout the nation. These twelve thousand persons are thus fully committed to the Union, and to perpetual freedom in the state—committed to the very things, and nearly all the things the nation wants—and they ask the nation[']s recognition and it's [*sic*] assistance to make good their committal. Now, if we reject, and spurn them, we do our utmost to disorganize and disperse them. We in effect say to the white men "You are worthless, or worse—we will neither help you, nor be helped by you." To the blacks we say "This cup of liberty which these, your old masters, hold to your lips, we will dash from you, and leave you to the chances of gathering the spilled and scattered contents in some vague and undefined when, where, and how." If this course, discouraging and paralyzing both white and black, has any tendency to bring Louisiana into proper practical relations with the Union, I have, so far, been unable to perceive it. If, on the contrary, we recognize, and sustain the new government of Louisiana the converse of all this is made true. We encourage the hearts, and nerve the arms of the twelve thousand to adhere to their work, and argue for it, and proselyte for it, and fight for it, and feed it, and grow it, and ripen it to a complete success. The colored man too, in seeing all united for him, is inspired with vigilance, and energy, and daring, to the same end. Grant that he desires the elective franchise, will he not attain it sooner by saving the already advanced steps toward it, than by running backward over them? Concede that the new government of Louisiana is only to what it should be as the egg is to the fowl, we shall sooner have the fowl by hatching the egg than by smashing it? Again, if we reject Louisiana, we also reject one vote in favor of the proposed amendment to the national Constitution. To meet this proposition, it has been argued that no more than three fourths of those States which have not attempted secession are necessary to validly ratify the amendment. I do not commit myself against this, further than to say that such a ratification would be questionable, and sure to be persistently questioned; while a ratification by three-fourths of all the States would be unquestioned and unquestionable.

I repeat the question, "Can Louisiana be brought into proper practical relation with the Union *sooner* by *sustaining* or by *discarding* her new State Government?"

What has been said of Louisiana will apply generally to other States. And yet so great peculiarities pertain to each state, and such important and sudden changes occur in the same state; and withal, so new and unprecedented is the whole case, that no exclusive, and inflexible plan can be safely prescribed as to details and colatterals [*sic*]. Such exclusive, and inflexible plan, would surely become a new entanglement. Important principles may, and must, be inflexible.

In the present "*situation*" as the phrase goes, it may be my duty to make some new announcement to the people of the South. I am considering, and shall not fail to act, when satisfied that action will be proper.

READING AND DISCUSSION QUESTIONS

1. How would you characterize Lincoln's policy toward Reconstruction? Does Lincoln come across as an idealist, like Radical Republicans, or a pragmatist who accepted compromise for the sake of progress?
2. What can you infer about Louisiana's recent experience that angered some, encouraged others, and led to Lincoln's support and approval?
3. What about his speech do you think provoked John Wilkes Booth, a southerner and Confederate sympathizer, to murder Lincoln?

14-2 | A Freed Family's Dream of Landownership

BETTY POWERS, *Federal Writers' Project Interview* (c. 1936)

Betty Powers was eight or nine years old when the Civil War ended. She was born a slave on a Texas plantation and shared in her family's jubilation when slavery ended. Seventy years later, she was interviewed by the New Deal's Federal Writers' Project, which conducted oral histories with former slaves. Despite her "head mis'ry," which she claimed impaired her memory, she recalled poignant details of her family's life in slavery and their transition to freedom with a farm of their own.

What for you wants dis old nigger's story 'bout de old slavery days? 'Tain't worth anythin'. I's jus' a hard workin' person all my life and raised de family and done right by 'em as best I knowed. To tell the truf 'bout my age, I don't know 'zactly. I 'members de war time and de surrender time. O's old 'nough to fan flies off de white folks and de tables when surrender come. If you come 'bout five year ago, I could telt you lots more, but I's had de head mis'ry.

Library of Congress, *Born in Slavery: Slave Narratives from the Federal Writers' Project, 1936–1938*, Texas Narratives, vol. 16, part 3, 190–192.

I's born in Harrison County, 'bout twenty-five miles from Marshall. Mass's name am Dr. Howard Perry and next he house am a li'l buildin' for he office. De plantation an awful big one, and miles long, and more'n two hundred slaves was dere. Each cabin have one family and dere am three rows of cabins 'bout half a mile long.

Mammy and pappy and us twelve chillen live in one cabin, so mammy has to cook for fourteen people, 'sides her field work. She am up way befo' daylight fixin' breakfast and supper after dark, with de pine knot torch to make de light. She cook on de fireplace in winter and in de yard in summer. All de rations measure out Sunday mornin' and it have to do for de week. It am not 'nough for heavy eaters and we has to be real careful or we goes hungry. We has meat and cornmeal and 'lasses and 'taters and peas and beans and milk. Dem short rations causes plenty trouble, 'cause de niggers has to steal food and it am de whippin' if dey gets cotched. Dey am in a fix if dey can't work for bein' hungry, 'cause it am de whippin' den, sho', so dey has to steal, and most of 'em did and takes de whippin'. Dey has de full stomach, anyway.

De babies has plenty food, so dey grow up into strong, portly men and women. Dey stays in de nursery whilst dey mammies works in de fields, and has plenty milk with cornbread crumble up in it, and potlicker, too, and honey and 'lasses on bread.

De massa and he wife am fine, but de overseer am tough, and he wife, too. Dat woman have no mercy. You see dem long ears I has? Dat's from de pullin' dey gits from her. De field hands works early and late and often all night. Pappy makes de shoes and mammy weaves, and you could hear de bump, bump of dat loom at night, when she done work in de field all day.

Missy know everything what go on, 'cause she have de spies 'mongst de slaves. She purty good, though. Sometimes de overseer tie de nigger to a log and lash him with de whip. If de lash cut de skin, dey puts salt on it. We ain't 'low to go to church and has 'bout two parties a year, so dere ain't much fun. Lawd, Lawd, most dem slaves too tired to have fun noway. When all dat work am finish, dey's glad to git in de bed and sleep.

Did we'uns have weddin's? White man, you knows better'n dat. Dem times, cullud folks am jus' put together. De massa say, "Jim and Nancy, you go live together," and when dat order give, it better be done. Dey thinks nothin' on de plantation 'bout de feelin's of de women and dere ain't no 'spect for dem. De overseer and white mens took 'vantage of de women like dey wants to. De woman better not make no fuss 'bout sich. If she do, it am de whippin' for her. I sho' thanks the Lawd surrender done come befo' I's old 'nough to have to stand for sich. Yes, sar, surrender saves dis nigger from sich.

When de war am over, thousands of sojers passes our place. Some camps nearby, and massa doctors dem. When massa call us to say we's free, dere am a yardful of niggers. He give every nigger de age statement and say dey could work on halves or for wages. He 'vises dem to stay till dey git de foothold and larn how to do. Lots stays and lots goes. My folks stays 'bout four years and works on shares. Den pappy buys de piece of land 'bout five miles from dere.

De land ain't clear, so we'uns al pitches in and clears it and builds de cabin. Was we'uns proud? There 'twas, our place to do as we pleases, after bein' slaves.

Dat sho' am de good feelin'. We works live beavers puttin' de crop in, and my folks stays dere till dey dies. I leaves to git married de next year and I's only thirteen years old, and marries Boss Powers.

We'uns lives on rent land nearby for six years and has three chillen and den he dies. After two years I marries Henry Ruffins and has three more chillen, and he dies in 1911. I's livin' with two of dem now. I never took de name of Ruffins, 'cause I's dearly love Powers and can't stand to give up he name. Powers done make de will and wrote on de paper, "To my beloved wife, I gives all I has." Wasn't dat sweet of him?

I comes to Fort Worth after Ruffin dies and does housework till I's too old. Now I gits de $12.00 pension every month and dat help me git by.

READING AND DISCUSSION QUESTIONS

1. How does Powers's account help historians understand the period of Reconstruction from the perspective of social history, or the history of ordinary people?
2. Analyze and evaluate the details Powers recalls about her fellow slaves' experiences to understand the contrast she draws with her life in the era after slavery. How do those details help you understand the meaning of freedom as former enslaved people experienced it?
3. How does the context of this historical source, an oral history recorded decades after the events it describes, impact your assessment of its utility as evidence for the Civil War and Reconstruction eras?

14-3 | A Former Slave Owner Complains of "Negro Problem"

FRANCES BUTLER LEIGH, *Letter to a Friend in England* (1867)

While Betty Powers experienced the era of Reconstruction with the optimism of the newly freed, Frances Butler Leigh wrote defiant and discouraging letters from her father's Sea Island plantation on St. Simon's Island, Georgia. She and her father, divorced years earlier from Leigh's mother, the British actress and antislavery advocate Frances Kemble, moved from Philadelphia to the plantation just after the war ended in a failed effort to keep the family's estate afloat. Within a few years, she sold the plantation and moved to England, where in 1883 she wrote *Ten Years on a Georgia Plantation Since the War*, a memoir defending the Old South

S. Simon's Island: June 23, 1867

Dearest S ——, We are, I am afraid, going to have terrible trouble by-and-by with the Negroes, and I see nothing but gloomy prospects for us ahead. The unlimited power that the war has put into the hands of the present government at Washington seems to have turned the heads of the party now in office, and they don't know where to stop. The whole South is settled and quiet, and the

Frances Butler Leigh, *Ten Years on a Georgia Plantation Since the War* (London: Richard Bentley & Son, Publishers in Ordinary to her Majesty the Queen, 1883), 66–71.

people too ruined and crushed to do anything against the government, even if they felt so inclined, and all are returning to their former pursuits, trying to rebuild their fortunes and thinking of nothing else. Yet the treatment we receive from the government becomes more and more severe every day, the last act being to divide the whole South into five military districts, putting each under the command of a United States general, doing away with all civil courts and law. Even D —— who you know is a Northern republican, says it is most unjustifiable, not being in any way authorised by the existing state of things, which he confesses he finds very different from what he expected before he came. If they would frankly say they intend to keep us down, it would be fairer than making a pretence of readmitting us to equal rights, and then trumping up stories of violence to give a show of justice to treating us as the conquered foes of the most despotic Government on earth, and by exciting the negroes to every kind of insolent lawlessness, to goad the people into acts of rebellion and resistance.

The other day in Charleston, which is under the command of that respectable creature General S ——, they had a firemen's parade, and took the occasion to hoist a United States flag, to which this modern Gesler[1] insisted on everyone raising his cap as he passed underneath. And by a hundred other such petty tyrannies are the people, bruised and sore, being roused to desperation; and had this been done directly after the war it would have been bad enough, but it was done the other day, three years [sic] after the close of the war.

The true reason is the desire and intention of the Government to control the elections of the South, which under the constitution of the country they could not legally do. So they have determined to make an excuse for setting aside the laws, and in order to accomplish this more fully, each commander in his separate district has issued an order declaring that unless a man can take an oath that he had not voluntarily borne arms against the United States Government, nor in any way aided or abetted the rebellion, he cannot vote. This simply disqualifies every white man at the South from voting, disfranchising the whole white population, while the negroes are allowed to vote *en masse.*

This is particularly unjust, as the question of negro voting was introduced and passed in Congress as an amendment to the constitution, but in order to become a law a majority of two-thirds of the State Legislatures must ratify it, and so to them it was submitted, and rejected by all the Northern States with two exceptions, where the number of negro voters would be so small as to be harmless. Our Legislatures are not allowed to meet, but this law, which the North has rejected, is to be forced upon us, whose very heart it pierces and prosperity it kills. Meanwhile, in order to prepare the negroes to vote properly, stump speakers from the North are going all through the South, holding political meetings for the negroes, saying things like this to them: "My friends, you will have your rights, won't you?" ("Yes," from the negroes.) "Shall I not go back to

[1] **Gesler**: Gessler, the legendary tyrant in the fifteenth-century folktale William Tell who made the people bow to his hat, placed on a pole; Tell refused and was forced to shoot an arrow through an apple resting atop the head of his son.

Massachusetts and tell your brothers there that you are going to ride in the street cars with white ladies if you please?" ("Yes, yes," from the crowd.) "That if you pay your money to go to the theatre you will sit where you please, in the best boxes if you like?" ("Yes," and applause.) This I copy verbatim from a speech made at Richmond the other day, since which there have been two serious negro riots there, and the General commanding had to call out the military to suppress them.

These men are making a tour through the South, speaking in the same way to the negroes everywhere. Do you wonder we are frightened? I have been so forcibly struck lately while reading Baker's "Travels in Africa," and some of Du Chaillu's lectures,[2] at finding how exactly the same characteristics show themselves among the negroes there, in their own native country, where no outside influences have ever affected them, as with ours here. Forced to work, they improve and are useful; left to themselves they become idle and useless, and never improve. Hard ethnological facts for the abolitionists to swallow, but facts nevertheless.

It seems foolish to fill my letter to you with such matters, but all this comes home to us with such vital force that it is hard to write, or speak, or think of anything else, and the one subject that Southerners discuss whenever they meet is, "What is to become of us?"

Affectionately yours,
F——

READING AND DISCUSSION QUESTIONS

1. Compare Leigh's point of view concerning slaves and slavery with the perspective of Susan Dabney Smedes (Document 11-1). How might you account for the differences you see in their assessments of the Old South? What factors might have shaped each viewpoint?
2. From Leigh's letter, what conclusions can you draw regarding the challenges facing the national government in mending the political divisions between northern and southern states and between the federal and state or local governments in the South?

14-4 | Challenges of Southern Reconstruction
Three Photographs of Richmond, Virginia (1864–1865)

The Civil War was a human tragedy. Historians now think the Civil War death toll topped 750,000 people. A comparable percentage today would be approximately 6.5 million deaths. That staggering human cost was compounded by the physical destruction of those places that witnessed many of the war's decisive battles, and nearly all of them were in the South. In the three-part photo essay included here, we see several scenes from Richmond, Virginia, the Confederate capital and one of the South's important manufacturing cities. Though photographs show only what a photographer chooses to highlight and thus capture just part of the story, these images give us a sense of the immense physical toll caused by the war.

[2] **Baker's . . . lectures**: Leigh may be referring to Samuel White Baker's 1855 book *Eight Years' Wandering in Ceylon* and to Paul du Chaillu's 1861 *Explorations and Adventures in Equatorial Africa*.

Aerial view of Richmond, 1864
Hulton Archive/Getty Images

Crippled Locomotive, Richmond & Petersburg Railroad Depot, American Civil War, Richmond, Virginia, USA, 1865 (b/w photo)/American Photographer (19th century)/GLASSHOUSE IMAGES/Private Collection/Bridgeman Images

Ruined Buildings in Burnt District, Richmond, Virginia, USA, 1865 (b/w photo) /American Photographer (19th century)/GLASSHOUSE IMAGES/Bridgeman Images

READING AND DISCUSSION QUESTIONS

1. Describe the scenes captured by these photographers. What story of the Civil War do they tell?
2. Who do you imagine these photographs were intended for? Do you think the photographers were sympathetic to southerners?
3. Given the destruction recorded in these images, what challenges did the South face in its effort to recover from the Civil War? How do images like these help us understand the history of the Reconstruction period?

14-5 | Nast Lampoons Freedmen's Government

THOMAS NAST, *Colored Rule in a Reconstructed State* (1874)

Political cartoons developed sophistication in the years after the Civil War largely through the talents of the influential artist Thomas Nast (1840–1902), whose compositions effectively captured a frustrated electorate's disgust. In this image, Nast plays on then-common stereotypes and foregrounds the pervasive assumptions northern and southern whites held about black political incompetence and corruption. Many white South Carolinians popularized these beliefs in their effort to redeem state government from the African American majority that controlled the legislature.

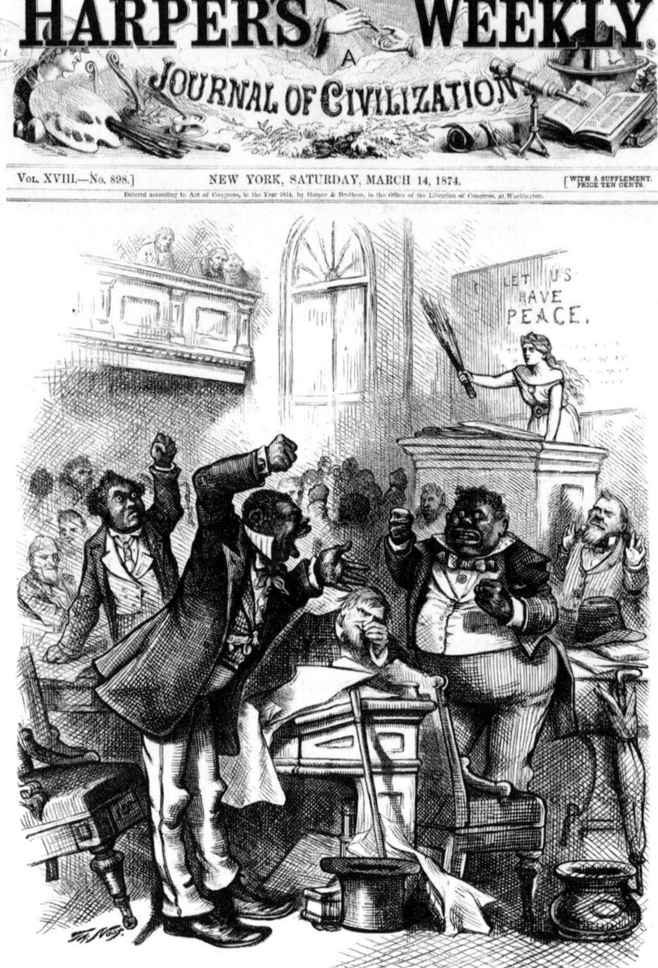

HARPER'S WEEKLY
A JOURNAL OF CIVILIZATION

Vol. XVIII.—No. 898.] NEW YORK, SATURDAY, MARCH 14, 1874. [WITH A SUPPLEMENT. PRICE TEN CENTS.

Entered according to Act of Congress, in the Year 1874, by Harper & Brothers, in the Office of the Librarian of Congress, at Washington.

COLORED RULE IN A RECONSTRUCTED(?) STATE.—[See Page 242.]
(THE MEMBERS CALL EACH OTHER THIEVES, LIARS, RASCALS, AND COWARDS.)
Columbia. "You are Aping the lowest Whites. If you disgrace your Race in this way you had better take Back Seats."

Library of Congress, LC-USZ62-102256

READING AND DISCUSSION QUESTIONS

1. Analyze and evaluate Nast's image to identify the racial stereotypes it conveys. Whose view of black political abilities does it express?
2. What is the significance of the Columbia figure standing at the speaker's platform, and what is she trying to accomplish?
3. To what extent do the stereotypes Nast employed reflect the historical context of race relations during the Reconstruction period?

14-6 | African American Congressman Urges Support of Civil Rights Bill

ROBERT BROWNE ELLIOTT, *Speech to Congress* (1874)

While planters and their former slaves negotiated a new relationship in the wake of slavery's abolition, Congress was abuzz with legislative activity to secure the rights of citizenship freedmen had so recently won. The Civil Rights Act of 1875, which the African American member of Congress Robert Elliott supported in a speech to Congress, guaranteed to African Americans equal treatment in public accommodations. In 1873, the U.S. Supreme Court decided in the *Slaughterhouse Cases* to construe the Fourteenth Amendment protections narrowly, arguing that states properly retained the exercise of power over domestic and civil rights. Here Elliott is attempting to counter anti–civil rights efforts to use these cases to frustrate federal legislative action on behalf of freedmen.

Mr. Speaker: While I am sincerely grateful for this high mark of courtesy that has been accorded to me by this House, it is a matter of regret to me that it is necessary at this day that I should rise in the presence of an American Congress to advocate a bill which simply asserts equal rights and equal public privileges for all classes of American citizens. I regret, sir, that the dark hue of my skin may lend a color to the imputation that I am controlled by motives personal to myself in my advocacy of this great measure of national justice. Sir, the motive that impels me is restricted by no such narrow boundary, but is as broad as your Constitution. I advocate it, sir, because it is right. The bill, however, not only appeals to your justice, but it demands a response from your gratitude. . . .

[S]ir, we are told by the distinguished gentleman from Georgia (Mr. Stephens[3]) that Congress has no power under the Constitution to pass such a law, and that the passage of such an act is in direct contravention of the rights of the states.

Lift Every Voice: African American Oratory, 1787–1900, eds. Philip S. Foner and Robert James Branham (Tuscaloosa and London: The University of Alabama Press, 1998), 521–524, 527–528, 532–533, 535–536.

[3] **Mr. Stephens**: Alexander Stephens, senator from Georgia who was elected vice president of the Confederate States of America during the Civil War.

I cannot assent to any such proposition. The Constitution of a free government ought always to be construed in favor of human rights. Indeed, the thirteenth, fourteenth, and fifteenth amendments, in positive words, invest Congress with the power to protect the citizen in his civil and political rights. Now, sir, what are civil rights? Rights natural, modified by civil society. Mr. Lieber says: "By civil liberty is meant, not only the absence of individual restraint, but liberty within the social system and political organism—a combination of principles and laws which acknowledge, protect and favor the dignity of man . . . civil liberty is the result of man's twofold character as an individual and social being, so soon as both are equally respected." . . .

Are we then, sir, with the amendments to our Constitution staring us in the face; with these grand truths of history before our eyes; with innumerable wrongs daily inflicted upon five million citizens demanding redress, to commit this question to the diversity of legislation? In the words of Hamilton, "Is it the interest of the government to sacrifice individual rights to the preservation of the rights of an artificial being called the states? There can be no truer principle than this, that every individual of the community at large has an equal right to the protection of government. Can this be a free government if partial distinctions are tolerated or maintained?"

The rights contended for in this bill are among "the sacred rights of mankind, which are not to be rummaged for among old parchments or musty records; they are written as with a sunbeam in the whole volume of human nature, by the hand of the divinity itself, and can never be erased or obscured by mortal power."

But the Slaughterhouse cases!—The Slaughterhouse cases!

The honorable gentleman from Kentucky, always swift to sustain the failing and dishonored cause of proscription, rushes forward and flaunts in our faces the decision of the Supreme Court of the United States in the Slaughterhouse cases, and in that act he has been willingly aided by the gentleman from Georgia. Hitherto, in the contests which have marked the progress of the cause of equal civil rights, our opponents have appealed sometimes to custom, sometimes to prejudice, more often to pride of race, but they have never sought to shield themselves behind the Supreme Court. But now, for the first time, we are told that we are barred by a decision of that court, from which there is no appeal. If this be true we must stay our hands. The cause of equal civil rights must pause at the command of a power whose edicts must be obeyed till the fundamental law of our country is changed.

Has the honorable gentleman from Kentucky considered well the claim he now advances? If it were not disrespectful I would ask, has he ever read the decision which he now tells us is an insuperable barrier to the adoption of this great measure of justice?

In the consideration of this subject, has not the judgment of the gentleman from Georgia been warped by the ghost of the dead doctrines of states' rights?

Has he been altogether free from prejudices engendered by long training in that school of politics that well-nigh destroyed this government?

Mr. Speaker, I venture to say here . . . that there is not a line or word, not a thought or dictum even, in the decision of the Supreme Court in the great Slaughterhouse cases, which casts a shadow of doubt on the right of Congress to pass the pending bill, or to adopt such other legislation as it may judge proper and necessary to secure perfect equality before the law to every citizen of the Republic. . . .

These [Civil War] amendments[4] . . . are thus declared to have as their all-pervading design and ends the security of the recently enslaved race, not only their nominal freedom, but their complete protection from those who had formerly exercised unlimited dominion over them. It is in this broad light that all these amendments must be read, the purpose to secure the perfect equality before the law of all citizens of the United States. What you give to one class you must give to all, what you deny to one class you shall deny to all, unless in the exercise of the common and universal police power of the state, you find it needful to confer exclusive privileges on certain citizens, to be held and exercised still for the common good of all. . . .

Sir, it is scarcely twelve years since that gentleman [Senator Stephens] shocked the civilized world by announcing the birth of a government which rested on human slavery as its cornerstone.[5] The progress of events has swept away that pseudo government which rested on greed, pride and tyranny, and the race whom he then ruthlessly spurned and trampled on is here to meet him in debate, and to demand that the rights which are enjoyed by its former oppressors—who vainly sought to overthrow a government which they could not prostitute to the base uses of slavery—shall be accorded to those who even in the darkness of slavery kept their allegiance true to freedom and the Union. Sir, the gentleman from Georgia has learned much since 1861, but he is still a laggard. Let him put away entirely the false and fatal theories which have so greatly marred an otherwise enviable record. Let him accept, in its fullness and beneficence, the great doctrine that American citizenship carries with it every civil and political right which manhood can confer. . . .

Sir, equality before the law is now the broad, universal, glorious rule and mandate of the Republic. No state can violate that. Kentucky and Georgia may crowd their statute books with retrograde and barbarous legislation; they may rejoice in the odious eminence of their consistent hostility to all the great steps of human progress which have marked our national history since slavery

[4] **Amendments**: Elliott is referring to the Thirteenth, Fourteenth, and Fifteenth Amendments, which, respectively, prohibited slavery, guaranteed due process and defined citizenship, and forbade the denial of the vote on the basis of race.

[5] **Gentleman . . . cornerstone**: See Document P5-4.

tore down the Stars and Stripes on Fort Sumter; but, if Congress shall do its duty, if Congress shall enforce the great guarantees which the Supreme Court has declared to be the one pervading purpose of all the recent amendments, then their unwise and unenlightened conduct will fall with the same weight upon the gentlemen from those states who now lend their influence to defeat this bill, as upon the poorest slave who once had no rights which the honorable gentlemen were bound to respect. . . .

The results of the [Civil] war, as seen in reconstruction, have settled forever the political status of my race. The passage of this bill will determine the civil status, not only of the Negro, but of any other class of citizens who may feel themselves discriminated against. It will form the capstone of that temple of liberty, begun on this continent under discouraging circumstances, carried on in spite of the sneers of monarchists and the cavils of pretended friends of freedom, until at last it stands, in all its beautiful symmetry and proportions, a building the grandest which the world has ever seen, realizing the most sanguine expectations and the highest hopes of those who, in the name of equal, impartial and universal liberty, laid the foundation stone.

The Holy Scriptures tell us of an humble handmaiden who long, faithfully and patiently gleaned in the rich fields of her wealthy kinsman, and we are told further that at last, in spite of her humble antecedents she found favor in his sight. For over two centuries our race has "reaped down your fields," the cries and woes which we have uttered have "entered into the ears of the Lord of Sabaoth" and we are at last politically free. The last vestiture only is needed—civil rights. Having gained this, we may, with hearts overflowing with gratitude and thankful that our prayer has been answered, repeat the prayer of Ruth: "Entreat me not to leave thee, or to return from following after thee, for whither thou goest, I will go; and where thou lodgest, I will lodge; thy people shall be my people, and thy God my God; where thou diest I will die, and there will I be buried; the Lord do so to me, and more also, if ought but death part thee and me." [Great applause.]

READING AND DISCUSSION QUESTIONS

1. Summarize and evaluate the argument Elliott makes in support of the civil rights bill. What can you infer about the opposition from his argument?
2. What does it suggest to you about the nature of politics in the Reconstruction-era South that an African American member of Congress from South Carolina was able to speak in support of a civil rights bill on the floor of the House of Representatives in 1874? How does this document help you to understand the historical context of the period?

▪ COMPARATIVE QUESTIONS ▪

1. Explain whether you see the era of Reconstruction as the end or the beginning of a distinctive period in American history. What evidence from the documents in this chapter can you provide to prove your thesis?
2. What challenges did the nation face during the Reconstruction period? Based on the sources provided in this chapter, how were the challenges the North and South faced similar and different?
3. To what extent was the Jeffersonian regard for land as a source of one's independence (Document 7-2) an enduring ideal in the era of Reconstruction?
4. Historians have debated whether Reconstruction was a success, a failure, or an incomplete fulfillment of the American promise. How do the multiple perspectives represented by the sources in this chapter help you develop your own argument about the historical significance of Reconstruction?

Acknowledgments *(continued from page iv)*

13-1 Ambrose Bierce, "What I Saw of Shiloh (1881)" from *Ambrose Bierce's Civil War*, edited by William McCann. Copyright © 1996 by Regnery Publishing. All rights reserved. Used with permission.

1-5 Council of Huejotzingo, "Letter to the King of Spain (1560)," *Beyond the Codices*, trans. and ed. Arthur J. O. Anderson, Frances Berdan, and James Lockhart. Copyright © 1976 by The Regents of the University of California. All rights reserved. Used with permission.

12-1 Stella M. Drumm, ed., excerpt from *Down the Santa Fe Trail and Into Mexico: The Diary of Susan Shelby Magoffin, 1846–1847*. Copyright © 1926 by Yale University Press. All rights reserved. Used with permission.

2-1 From Don Juan de Oñate: *Colonizer of New Mexico, 1595–1628*, ed. by George Hammond and Agapito Rey. Copyright © 1953 University of New Mexico Press, 1953.

2-2 Lisa M. Lauria "Sexual Misconduct in Plymouth Colony," The Plymouth Colony Archive Project, 1998. http://www.histarch.illinois.edu/Plymouth/Lauria2.html#II. Copyright © 1998 by the author. All rights reserved. Used with permission.

Emmeline B. Wells, "Diary (1846)," Emmeline B. Wells diary, vol. 1, 1844–1846. Copyright © 2002 Brigham Young University. All rights reserved. Used with permission.

2-5 Edmund White, "Letter to Joseph Morton (1687)," The South Carolina Historical and Genealogical Magazine, Vol. XXX, January 1929. Copyright © 1929 by The South Carolina Historical Society. All rights reserved. Used with permission.